Philosophical Traditions

ROYAL INSTITUTE OF PHILOSOPHY SUPPLEMENT: 74

EDITED BY

Anthony O'Hear

CAMBRIDGE
UNIVERSITY PRESS

PUBLISHED BY THE PRESS SYNDICATE OF THE UNIVERSITY OF CAMBRIDGE
The Pitt Building, Trumpington Street, Cambridge, CB2 1RP,
United Kingdom

CAMBRIDGE UNIVERSITY PRESS
The Edinburgh Building, Cambridge CB2 8RU, United Kingdom
32 Avenue of the Americas, New York, NY 10013–2473, USA
477 Williamstown Road, Port Melbourne, VIC 3207, Australia
C/Orense, 4, planta 13, 28020 Madrid, Spain
Lower Ground Floor, Nautica Building, The Water Club, Beach Road,
Granger Bay, 8005 Cape Town, South Africa

Printed in the United Kingdom at Bell and Bain Ltd.
Typeset by Techset Composition Ltd, Salisbury, UK

A catalogue record for this book is available from the British Library

ISBN 9781107434486
ISSN 1358-2461

131795

Contents

List of Contributors

Yoko Arisaka – Institut für Philosophie at Universität Hildesheim

Alan Montefiore – London School of Economics

Richard Sorabji – Wolfson College, Oxford

Jonardon Ganeri – University of Sussex

David Cooper – Durham University

Barry Hallen – Morehouse College

Matthew Kapstein – University of Chicago

Tamra Wright – London School of Jewish Studies

Bret Davis – Loyola University, Maryland

Vrinda Dalmiya – University of Hawaii at Manoa

Fraser MacBride – University of Glasgow

Keith Ansell-Pearson – University of Warwick

Ali Paya – University of Westminster

Preface

In one sense all philosophies attempt to analyse a small number of questions central to human life: the self, knowledge, the nature of the cosmos and reality, God or the divine. But while topics may be common, approaches have differed historically, and according to the traditions and times in which particular thinkers have worked. The Royal Institute of Philosophy's London Lecture series for 2012–13 brought together contributions from scholars expert in different traditions in order to explore continuities and discontinuities in world philosophy. In this volume there are papers on Indian thought, including Buddhist and Jain contributions, on Daoism, on Modern Japanese approaches, on Jewish and Islamic thought, on stoicism, and on African philosophy, as well as on modern analytical philosophy, the so-called 'Continental' tradition and on the thought of Nietzsche.

doi:10.1017/S1358246114000162   ©The Royal Institute of Philosophy and the contributors 2014

Royal Institute of Philosophy Supplement **74** 2014

Modern Japanese Philosophy: Historical Contexts and Cultural Implications

YOKO ARISAKA

Abstract

The paper provides an overview of the rise of Japanese philosophy during the period of rapid modernization in Japan after the Meiji Restoration (beginning in the 1860s). It also examines the controversy surrounding Japanese philosophy towards the end of the Pacific War (1945), and its renewal in the contemporary context. The post-Meiji thinkers engaged themselves with the questions of *universality* and *particularity*; the former represented science, medicine, technology, and philosophy (understood as 'Western modernity') and the latter, the Japanese – 'non-Western' – tradition. Within the context, the question arose whether or not Japan, the only non-Western nation to succeed in modernization at the time, could also offer a philosophy that was universal in scope? Could Japanese philosophy offer an alternative form of modernity to the global domination of Western modernity? In this historical context, the philosophies of Kitaro Nishida and Tetsuro Watsuji, two of the tradition's most prominent thinkers, are introduced. Nishida is considered the 'father of modern Japanese philosophy' and his followers came to be known as the 'Kyoto School'. The essay ends with a brief reflection on the influence of philosophy on culture, focusing on the aftermath of the tsunami catastrophe in 2011.

1. Historical Background

Japan has a unique history. From 1639 until the mid-1800s it remained isolated from the rest of the world; in order to control the spread of Christianity, the Tokugawa Shogunate closed all the ports, except the port of Nagasaki in the southernmost island of Kyushu, and only China and Holland were allowed to continue trade (under strictly controlled conditions). By the time the American 'Black Ships' lead by Commodore Perry arrived at the shores of Yokohama in 1853, Japan had missed out on the industrial advancements and revolutions that occurred in Europe and America during the 18th Century. With his modern weaponry and superior military power, Perry demanded the opening of the country, and Japan faced two alternatives: either to become a

doi:10.1017/S1358246114000022

Yoko Arisaka

victim of Western expansionism, or to open itself up to modernization, and thereby protect itself.[1]

So began the period of rapid modernization with the official Meiji
Restoration of 1868. Due to its 250 years of isolation, the contrast
between 'what is Japanese, traditional, always existed' and 'what is
Western, modern, foreign/exotic and new' was clearly perceivable.
Simple choices of clothing (kimono or dress/suit), eating utensils
(chopsticks or silverware), whether to eat beef (a new custom),
where to sit (a mat on the floor or a chair), entertainment (traditional
or Western-style) and other daily practices all became markers of this
cultural transformation. The daunting processes of change reached
all aspects of life – social, political, economic, educational, technological, cultural, aesthetic, and of course, intellectual.[2] It is not an
exaggeration to say that the history of post-Meiji Japan is shaped
by the cultural understanding of a *difference* between 'Japanese vs.
Western', or more commonly, 'East and West', where the East
represented what is traditional, spiritual, indigenous, cultural, backwards, particular (to Japan or Asia), and the West represented its
contrast, namely what is modern, materialistic, foreign, scientific,
advanced, universal (as science and technology, the chief markers
of modernity, were said to be based on the principles of universal
truth). Reactions to 'things Western' were at first mixed; while the
newly elected Meiji government fully endorsed the creation of a
modern nation, the remaining powers from the feudal lords protested
with uprisings and attempts at counter-reforms.[3] As the initial shock
of 'either-or' difference has subsided, the Meiji intellectuals began to
grapple with the idea of advancing a hybrid culture of 'Japanese yet
modern', epitomized in Shozan Sakuma's well-known slogan,

---

[1]   James Heisig notes that by the time the Black Ships arrived, Japan
knew enough about the industrial and technological advancements in the
West that it was ready to end its isolation. James Heisig, *Philosophers of
Nothingness* (Honolulu: University of Hawaii Press, 2001), 10
[2]   Cf. G.B. Samson, *The Western World and Japan* (Tokyo: Charles
Tuttle, 1984) and Marius Jansen (ed.), *Changing Japanese Attitudes
Toward Modernization* (Tokyo: Charles Tuttle, 1965)
[3]   See Bob Tadashi Wakabayashi, *Anti-Foreignism and Western Learning
in Early-Modern Japan: The New Theses of 1825* (Cambridge: Harvard
University Press, 1986), as well as Wakabayashi, *Modern Japanese
Thought* (Cambridge: Cambridge University Press, 1998). The 'ideology
of nation building' in the new Meiji Government is discussed in Carol
Gluck, *Japan's Modern Myths: Ideology in the Late Meiji Period*
(Princeton: Princeton University Press, 1985).

wakon yosai, or 'Eastern spirit, Western science'.[4] The hope was to combine and develop the best elements of both, to form a unique, modern yet non-Western culture of Japan.

Japanese philosophy was born in this milieu, and it too was pre-occupied with the theme of developing a philosophy based on Japanese culture, yet embodying the systematic universality of the Western philosophical tradition.[5] In fact the term 'philosophy' (*tetsu-gaku*) had to be coined in Japanese, as the form of systematized, scientific philosophy did not exist in the traditional neo-Confucian or Buddhist traditions.[6] At first, the Meiji intellectuals such as Amane Nishi and Yukichi Fukuzawa concentrated on exegesis of Western philosophers (Mill's utilitarianism was one of the first philosophies to be introduced to Japan) – but as they became more aware of the differences between Western modes of rational thinking and 'traditional Japanese values', philosophy became a site of intellectual negotiation among rationality, system, logic, on the one hand, and spirituality, holistic thinking, artistic thinking, on the other.

What enormously appealed to the Meiji thinkers at the time was the power of science, especially its universalist implications. During this period, Western philosophy also aspired to be scientific and construct a universal system (such as Hegel's *Logic*) or develop theories of 'truth' about the mind or the nature of human being. Western philosophy was not understood as 'representing the thoughts of Europe' but the 'truth about reality'. It was taken for granted that philosophy should apply to all human beings and the nature of reality as such. Japanese philosophers thought that there are unique elements in their own tradition that must be universal, and that they too could find philosophical expressions. The question is

[4]   Shozan (1811–1864) was educated in the neo-Confucian tradition but he also learned Dutch and modern technology. For discussions on post-Meiji thinkers and developments, see Ryusaku Tsunoda, W.M. Theodore de Bary, Donald Keene (eds), *Sources of Japanese Tradition Volume II, 1600–2000* (New York: Columbia University Press, 1958, 2005).
[5]   For overviews and translated essays by Japanese philosophers from the 7th to the 20th Century, see James Heisig, Thomas Kasulis, and John Maraldo (eds), *Japanese Philosophy: A Sourcebook* (Honolulu: University of Hawaii Press, 2011). This comprehensive 1300-page volume is a *tour-de-force* on the major thinkers of Japan. For a shorter summary and introduction see H. Gene Blocker and Christopher Starling, *Japanese Philosophy* (Albany: State University of New York Press, 2001).
[6]   Amane Nishi (1829–1897), who traveled to Holland and brought back Comte's and Mill's philosophies, coined the term in 1862.

which elements, and how can they be philosophically articulated? By the time of the victory over the Russo-Japanese War (1904–1905), Japan succeeded in becoming the first non-Western nation to become modernized. General cultural confidence increased, such that Japan too was seen to be able to contribute to world civilization in the way Europe and America had done.

In this mood of optimism, some thinkers and cultural leaders (such as the founder of 'Japanese arts' Tenshin Okakura) began to critique the inherent 'Eurocentrism' of Western thought. In the European tradition at the time, it was rather taken for granted that the philosophical 'center of truth' and the most advanced and civilized culture was that of Christian Europe.[7] The metaphysical and historical view still reflected the developmentalism in Aristotelian naturalism (in which entities developed according to their natural endowments and capacities over time, to reach fully developed states), and the newly emerged Darwinism substantiated the developmental 'scheme of things' scientifically. The long-standing Christian ontology that contrasts reason/faith/civilization vs. irrationality/heathen/barbarism became combined with the developmental thinking, so that the heathen non-West, including Japan, was seen simply to fall outside the realm of truth or 'behind and backwards' in the timeline of societal development.

Theoretically, then, philosophical universalism is supposed to apply to all human beings, yet – in practice – the Western thinkers took it for granted that only Euro-American civilization represented the truth. The Meiji intellectuals were dissatisfied with such imperialistic arrogance and aspired to develop a philosophy that is 'Japanese yet universal'; *if* Japan could develop a culturally non-Western yet universal form of philosophy, then that would be a proof that European civilization is not the only center of truth. If such a philosophy could indeed be universal, then it would necessarily mean that European and American minds would be able to understand it as also applicable to the nature of the human mind or reality. If that could be achieved, then Japan could contribute to the creation of a more globally balanced world culture, offering a possibility of a counterbalance and a conception of an 'alternative, non-Western modernity' to the Western-dominated world.

---

[7]   The influence of this development-based metaphysical thinking on colonialism and racism is undeniable. For an excellent discussion see Thomas McCarthy, *Race, Empire, and the Idea of Human Development* (Cambridge: Cambridge University Press, 2009).

In the following I will introduce two of the best-known Japanese philosophers of this turbulent post-Meiji period. The discussions are meant to provide a broad orientation; for detailed discussions some sources are listed the footnotes.

2. Kitaro Nishida (1870–1945)

Known as the 'Father of Modern Japanese Philosophy', Nishida aspired to construct a systematic philosophy (in the Western sense) that expressed non-Western ideas that were not present in European or American philosophies.[8] He was a professor at the Kyoto University from 1914–1929, and his students came to be known as the 'Kyoto School'.[9] Beginning around 1911 (with the publication of his first work, *The Study of Good, Zen no Kenkyu*), Nishida began to develop what might be called an 'experiential ontology', a form of philosophical logic based on 'experience' broadly

[8]   For an intellectual biography of Nishida, see Michiko Yusa, *Zen & Philosophy: An Intellectual Biography of Nishida Kitaro* (Honolulu: University of Hawaii Press, 2002). See also Keiji Nishitani, *Nishida Kitaro* (Berkeley: University of California Press, 1991) for a personal recollection as well as an excellent introduction to the theory of pure experience. Nishitani, a philosopher of his own right, was a student of Nishida's and a leading figure in the Kyoto School. See also Heisig for the discussions on Nishida's key concepts. John Maraldo's entry on Nishida at the online Stanford Encylopedia of Philosophy also offers a good overview (http://plato.stanford.edu/entries/nishida-kitaro/). Nishida's works, as well as lectures, letters, diaries, chronology, and bibliography, have been collected as the *Nishida Kitaro Zenshu* (*NKZ*), from Iwanami Shoten. The latest edition has 24 volumes (2003–2009). The quotes in this essay are from the 1966 edition. Several of his books are translated into English, but the majority of his works remain untraslated. Due to the difficulties of the language in the original texts, 'translating Nishida' is itself a topic of research. See John Maraldo, 'Translating Nishida', *Philosophy East & West* **39**(4) (1989): 465–496.

[9]   On the Kyoto School, as well as on the three of its most characteristic philosophers—Nishida, Tanabe, and Nishitani, see Heisig. A good collection that connects the philosophies of the Kyoto School to the Continental tradition, see Bret Davis, Brian Schroeder, and Jason Wirth (eds), *Japanese and Continental Philosophy: Conversations with the Kyoto School* (Bloomington: Indiana University Press, 2011). Bret Davis also offers a good summary of the Kyoto School in the online Stanford Encyclopedia of Philosophy (http://plato.stanford.edu/entries/kyoto-school/).

conceived.[10] His first attempt was to ground ontology in what he called 'pure experience' (borrowed from William James' 'radical empiricism' as well as influenced by philosophers such as Bergson, Dilthey and Royce). 'Pure experience' was defined as 'prior to subject and object', but containing the principles and contents of both. As Nishida states, 'in the immediate experience, there is not yet the distinction of subject and object'.[11] 'Reality' is this 'field of experience' that is prior to the individuation of 'experiences' belonging to persons; as such, it was not a psychological notion but rather an ontological 'field' or a 'ground' that contained in itself principles that defined what would be subsequently called 'subjective and objective'. Thus according to Nishida, 'it is not that the individual has experience, but in Experience emerges the individual. The individual experience is only a small part of Experience'.[12]

The distinctively Japanese (or East-Asian, in particular 'Chan/Zen Buddhist') element in this theory is the identification of this 'field of experience' with the spatio-temporal immediacy of the 'Here/Now', not as abstractly conceived in space/time but as a 'concrete universal' that is the Here/Now (i.e., as you read this paper right now). Nishida calls it the 'eternal present' and it is a philosophical elaboration of the Buddhist notion of time, although Nishida deliberately avoids making references to Buddhism.

During the 1920s, Nishida tried to account for the principles of division within this 'immediate field' following Fichte's notion of Pure Act (*Tathandlung*), and during the 1930s he developed further the dynamic structure of this 'field/reality' as a metaphysical system, a Logic of 'Place' (*basho*), in an attempt to avoid the subjectivistic or idealistic tendencies in his earlier theories. Reality, in its manifold, is a constant 'expression' of this Place conceived as the absolute, yet this Place itself cannot be a metaphysical object in any sense, such as 'substance' or Hegelian 'Spirit'; rather, the Place is simply a 'that through which' or 'that in which' reality manifests itself, as a pure 'negative' of Being. As such, it must be 'Absolute

---

[10]   See Kitaro Nishida, *An Inquiry Into the Good* (New Haven: Yale University Press, 1992). For the notion of experiential ontology and for the comparions with James, see Andrew Feenberg and Yoko Arisaka, 'Experiential Ontology: The Origins of the Nishida Philosophy in the Doctrine of Pure Experience', *International Philosophical Quarterly* **30**(2) (1990): 173–205.

[11]   *NKZ* 1: 29. All of the translations from the Japanese are by the author.

[12]   *NKZ* 1: 51

Nothingness'. If it is 'something' (including the 'idea' of nothingness), even conceived as an ultimate ontological field or anything similar, then it would still be defined as a 'something' which would require a contrast, a not-something. So this 'not-something' cannot be a conceivable entity in any way; it must simply be referred to as Absolute Nothingness but without the reduction of it into a 'notion' of any sort.[13]

If the ultimate field of reality is Absolute Nothingness, then it would also mean that it is actually identical with all the Being; a mirror reflects all its images, precisely because the surface itself is purely empty. One can never see the surface of the mirror as such but only what is reflected on it. Nishida calls this feature of reality-qua-emptiness 'the identity of the absolutely contradictory opposites'. Again the Buddhist theory of *sunyata*, or emptiness, is evident, although he does not elaborate his theory in terms of it.[14]

From the mid- to late 1930s the abstract Logic of Place as Absolute Nothingness acquired a distinctively historical content, influenced by Hegel and Marx's dialectic. The difference from Hegel, Nishida maintains, is the nature of ultimate reality; Hegel's Absolute Spirit must have a 'background' (otherwise one cannot identify it as such), and such a background must be Absolute Nothingness. Here Nishida adds some metaphysical elements from the Buddhist tradition. The historical development (qua the self-development of Place as Absolute Nothingness) takes place through what Nishida calls 'Action-Intuition' (*Koi-teki-Chokkan*, '*Koi*': Action, '*Chokkan*': Intuition). Historical development is to be understood as the dialectic of the subject making the world (object) which in turn forms the subject. The original insight of the 'experiential field' that is supposed to develop into subject and object is now historicized and concretized through action.

The dialectical structure (as well as all of his earlier theories) was developed as a universal system, which was particularly important as a *philosophical* system (and not just a cultural or religious theory which would merely be a 'particular'), so Nishida avoided references to Buddhist metaphysics even though his thought was much

---

[13]   For recent translations as well as commentaries on Nishida's difficult texts, see William Haver, *Ontology of Production: Three Essays* (Durham: Duke University Press, 2012) and John W.M. Krummel and Shigemori Nagamoto, *Place and Dialectic: Two Essays by Nishida Kitaro* (New York: Oxford University Press, 2011).
[14]   See Heisig for discussions on the notion of nothingness in Nishida's philosophy.

influenced by it. As noted above, the universalism was needed in order to stake a claim that Japanese thought could transcend its marginalized cultural bounds (which they knew to be denigrated in the Euro-American view), as well as to try to establish a place in world culture.

3. Tetsuro Watsuji (1889–1960)

Watsuji was a younger colleague of Nishida's at the Kyoto University, where he served as a professor from 1925–1949. His interests were much wider than philosophy; in addition to his extensive commentaries and analyses of Western philosophers, he is widely known for his cultural theories, aesthetics, ethics, and intellectual history in Japan. While Nishida never studied abroad, Watsuji went to Germany in 1927 and studied under Heidegger. Through his comparative studies, he too was deeply interested in cultural elements that might be theorized as being unique to Japanese or East-Asian traditions.[15] His philosophies combine influences from Nishida, Heidegger, and Kierkegaard.

Two theories that are best known from Watsuji are those of 'climate' (*fudo*) and 'ethics' (*rinri-gaku*). In his theory of *fudo* (literally *fu*: wind, and *do*: earth), developed around 1935, Watsuji argues that human beings are existentially intertwined with the environment, both social and natural.[16] By '*fudo*' Watsuji means 'the climate, characteristics of the soil, landscape, etc.' yet the notion should not be confused with the scientific notion of 'nature' or the 'natural

[15] Robert Carter offers a good overview of Watsuji in the Stanford Encyclopedia of Philosophy (http://plato.stanford.edu/entries/watsuji-tetsuro/).

[16] There is an English translation available, Tetsuro Watsuji, *Climate and Culture: A Philosophical Study* (Westport: Greenwood Press, 1971); however, it is out of print and the translation is not very accurate. There is a better German translation: *Fudo. Wind und Erde. Der Zusammenhang von Klima und Kultur* (Darmstadt: Primus Verlag, 1997). Although it is in French, probably the best translation is by Augustin Berque, a long-time scholar of Watsuji as well as on Japanese culture, geography and spatiality. See his *Fudo: le milieu humain* (Paris: CNRS, 2011). See also Berque's *Thinking Through Landscape* (London and New York: Routledge, 2013) for discussions that extend Watsuji's intuitions. All of Watsuji's writings are collected as *Watsuji Tetsuro Zenshu* (*WTZ*), 25 volumes. The latest edition is from 1989–1992. The translations in this essay are from the 1977 edition.

environment'.[17] The notion of 'nature' or the 'natural environment' is an object that is seen by 'human beings' already conceived as the subject, yet Watsuji argues that in the notion of *fudo* refers to a much broader sense of one's surroundings, a *milieu*. Human beings are existentially formed *through* the place of one's being, i.e., prior to the ontological separation of subject and object. It is with one's interaction with the environment that one 'becomes' the particular subject. The conception of 'who one is' should not be abstract, as in the notion of 'personhood' or the 'individual', but it should reflect ontological connections to the 'existential place' of where one lives and becomes who one is.

Watsuji engages Heidegger's notion of Being-in-the-World yet criticizes Heidegger's emphasis on temporality and individuality; human existence is just as spatial as temporal, and the *place and space* of existence must equally be a fundamentally constitutive part of a human self. Likewise, over time someone growing up in Germany would necessarily be culturally different from someone growing up in Japan (or different places even within one cultural or linguistic group), but this difference is not simply about culture or language; the difference is geographical, involving different environmental factors, weather patterns, soil, landscape, etc. These elements provide contours and qualities for the very being of who that person can be, and when the person moves to another place, new elements absorbed from the environment become mingled with the original elements, creating a new sense of self over time. The self is never an enclosed 'essence' but a dynamic interconnection with and through the environment. Our actions constantly reflect this interconnection and societies are organized through it as well:

> We put on clothes when it is cold or go near a stove, nay, more than that, we put on clothes on the children and urge the old folks to go near the fire. Or we would labor in order to buy coal and clothes. Coal-makers make coal in the mountain and fabric factories produce cloth. Thus in order to protect ourselves from the cold, individually and socially we have complex ways of "dealings" with it.[18]

Our lives and selves are shaped over time and the totality of such 'dealings' express who we are/have become. One can, in this sense, never be cut off from the *place* of one's being. Cultural differences are geographical differences as well, as different groups living in

[17] *WTZ* 8: 7
[18] *WTZ* 8: 11

different climates develop different ways of dealing with the environment.

Extending the human ontology of interconnectedness, during the late 1930s and 40s Watsuji develops an ethic that is based on the notion of 'in-between-ness' or 'Being-between' (*aida-gara*; lietrally aida: in-between, and *gara*: characterstics of), whereby this 'in-between-ness' is both spatial and temporal.[19] In-between-ness constitutes not only our selves-through-*fudo* but also our identities with and through others. Watsuji argues that human beings, in their ontological meaningfulness, are not fundamentally separate 'individuals' but rather their fundamental characteristics are mutually co-determined through the interactions that take place over time.[20] As babies we are dependent on our parents, as children socialized through our family, friends, and school, and as adults these circles get wider and may include extended communities and acquire national/cultural characteristics.[21]

In fact, Watsuji extends the notion of Being-between to claim that it should be read as the fundamental feature of a 'human-being'. The term for 'human being' is '*nin-gen*', which is ordinary Japanese, but Watsuji analyzes it with his notion: '*Nin*' means 'person'and '*gen*' means 'between' (although it is pronounced differently, the Chinese character is the same as '*aida*' in '*aida-gara*' above, the Being-between). Referring to the original meanings of the characters Watsuji claims that 'what is meant by 'human being' (*nin-gen*) is not simply 'man' (*anthropos, homo, man, Mensch*), but it implicitly includes society as the co-existence of a people, as the fundamental

---

[19]   Watsuji's ethics is translated: Tetsuro Watsuji, *Watsuji Tetsuro's Rinrigaku: Ethics in Japan* (Albany: State University of New York Press, 1996).

[20]   For a good introduction to Watsuji in English as well as an interesting comparison to feminist theories, see Erin McCarthy, *Ethics Embodied: Rethinking Selfhood through Continental, Japanese, and Feminist Perspectives* (Lanham: Lexington Books, 2010). See also Yoko Arisaka, 'The Ontological Co-Emergence of "Self and Other" in Japanese Philosophy', *The Journal of Consciousness Studies* **8**(5–7) (2001): 197–208.

[21]   Watsuji's notion of Being-between emerges out of his critique of Heidegger. For example, in the Preface to Fudo he writes: 'The limitation (of Heidegger's approach) is due to the fact that Heidegger's *Dasein* is ultimately an "individual". He grasped human existence as an existence of a self. But this is merely an abstract aspect within the double-structure of our individual-qua-social existence' (*WTZ* 8: 2). Heidegger does discuss a notion of a *Mitsein* (Being-with) but it remains underdeveloped, according to Watsuji.

double-structure'.[22] This structure, moreover, involves negation and emptiness. Here the influence from Nishida's dialectic is evident: An individual negates himself in his identification of himself with the whole (society, community), and simultaneously negates the whole in order to determine itself as the individual. The individual 'empties itself' in the whole, yet the whole gives particular characteristics to the individual.

Perhaps for Watsuji the socially mediated and the 'empty' nature of the self is noticeable also from the fact that in the Japanese language there are several words for the 'I', and one must use the appropriate one depending on one's gender, age, levels of familiarity/formality and social context. For example, whether a man or a woman is speaking with another man or woman (and the degree of familiarity), whether the speaker occupies a lower or a higher social status, and/or is older or younger than the other, and whether it is a public or private occasion, all affect which 'I' one should use. There is no such thing as a neutral 'self' apart from these embedded relations, in the sense that one cannot even form a sentence referring to oneself. (There is a neutral 'I', but this only indicates a 'neutral context' that is consciously chosen, such as for newspaper reporting, which still indicates a socially mediated context. So the 'I' refers to the indexical focal point in the system of reference and not to a substantial subject. There is no such thing as a 'real' self apart from such systems of reference; it is in this sense that the self is said to be 'empty'.)

It is not that Watsuji rejects the notion of the individual. Of course we take ourselves to be individuals in an ordinary sense, physically separate and having 'different thoughts' from others. Watsuji's point is rather that ontologically speaking, the notion is subordinated under or abstracted from the more fundamentally conceived notion of the Being-between. The very notion of an 'individual' is even possible at all because we have relations to others, in that it is only in contrast to others that we form our idea that we are individuals. In this sense Being-between is already *presupposed* in the notion of an individual.

4. Philosophy and the Pacific War

Up to the 1930s, as Japan succeeded in becoming the first Asian nation to modernize, it also began its expansion into the East-Asian

---

[22]   *WTZ* 10: 16

continent. The colonization of Formosa (Taiwan) began as early as in 1895, the colonization of Korea began in 1910, the Manchurian government north of the Korean peninsula was established in 1931, and the invasion of China began in 1937. During this time the intellectual currents that favored the combination of modernity and Japanese culture became more dominant. Let me review, in some detail, 'Nishida's Case' as he was considered the most important Japanese philosopher at the time.

Up until the mid-to-late 1930s, Nishida's theory was metaphysical and apolitical; in fact it was criticized by his Marxist student Jun Tosaka to be a bourgeois idealism, 'merely phenomenological and historically insignificant'.[23] Partly in response to such criticisms and partly also in order to voice his views in the increasingly urgent political situation of Japan's expanding empire in Asia,[24] in the late 1930s and early 1940s Nishida began to lecture as well as write about the political application of his theory. In 1938 at Kyoto University he delivered the lecture series *The Problem of Japanese Culture*, which was published in 1940. In 1943 at the request of the Tojo Government and its Imperial Army which was seeking a theoretical expression for Japan's role in the construction of the 'Greater East Asian Co-Prosperity Sphere' (*Dai toa kyoeiken*) Nishida (who was by then considered to be the most important philosopher in Japan) wrote his controversial essay, *The Principle of New World Order* (*Sekai shinchitsujo no genri*).[25] That Nishida disliked and

---

[23] *Tosaka Jun zenshu* (Collected Works of Tosaka, Tokyo: Keiso-Shobo, 1966) 3, 172–3. At that time, Nishida accepted this criticism; for instance, in his letter to Tosaka written in October, 1932, Nishida writes: 'I appreciated and learned much from your astute criticism – since I have not yet written anything on praxis, I can understand the criticism that my ideas appear phenomenological [...] however, I am not a Marxist, and I do believe there is something *einseitig* [originally written in German] about Marxism [...] but I would of course learn and incorporate Marxist thought when I understand it more fully, so please don't hesitate to send me more of your criticisms'. Letter #749, NKZ I, 18:460.

[24] Nishida was writing some of his most mature philosophical work in the volatile political climate of the mid 1930s to early 1940s. After the take-over of Manchuria in 1931–32, the Sino-Japanese War erupted in 1937; by then the whole country was swept by nationalist sentiments and the military government was becoming increasingly authoritarian.

[25] See Yoko Arisaka, 'The Nishida Enigma: "The Principle of the New World Order"', in: *Monumenta Nipponica* 51:1 1996, 81–99, for an English translation as well as an introduction to the background and the debates surrounding the essay. For a collection of essays on the connection between

even opposed the actions of the Imperial Army was a known fact, but nevertheless the essay could be seen as providing a philosophical justification or at least an articulation for the establishment of the Greater East-Asian Co-Prosperity Sphere.[26]

In *The Principle of the New World Order* the metaphysical-dialectical theory of Nishida's 'Historical World', which posits all entities to be mediated through the process of historical action-creation-mediation, was applied to a theory of the 'Age of the Self-Realization of the World' through nation-building. Every nation, in order to establish itself, would do so through a negation of itself (in the recognition of other/difference) as well as a negation of the other (to establish itself as the other of the other) and through this dialectic each nation affirms itself in relation to others. In this process the particularities of cultures are preserved and the essential interdependence of nations is recognized. Through this process on a global scale, the 'realization of the Global-World' (*sekaiteki sekai no jikaku*) is achieved. In Nishida's words,

> Every nation/people is established on a historical foundation and possesses a world-historical mission, thereby having a historical life of its own. For nations/peoples to form a global world through self-realization and self-transcendence, each must first of all form a particular world *in accordance with its own regional tradition.* These particular worlds, each based on a historical foundation, unite to build a global world. Each nation/people lives its own unique historical life and at the same time joins in a united global world through carrying out a world-historical mission. This is the ultimate Idea [principle] of human historical

---

Japanese philosophy and nationalism, see James Heisig and John Maraldo (eds), *Rude Awakenings: Zen, the Kyoto School, and the Question of Nationalism* (Honolulu: University of Hawaii Press, 1994). For further discussions on the politics of Nishida and the Kyoto School, see also Christopher Goto-Jones, *Political Philosophy in Japan: Nishida, the Kyoto School, and Co-Prosperity* (London and New York: Routledge, 2005), and C. Goto-Jones (ed.), *Re-Politicising the Kyoto School as Philosophy* (London and New York: Routledge, 2008).

[26] Supporters of Nishida today generally point out that he could not have done otherwise – at the time the perceived 'traitors' were incarcerated or forced to resign, and given his public position he could not have refused to participate nor could he have presented something that would openly criticize the Imperial Army without seriously jeopardizing his life or position.

development, and this is the principle of the New World Order which should be sought in the current world war.[27]

The dialectic (as well as the idea that the self-realization of the parts increasingly unfolds and realizes the whole) is rather explicitly borrowed from Hegel's notion of the development of *Weltgeschichte*, but Nishida rejects Hegel's process-oriented dialectic as well as his European provincialism that the world civilization culminates and finds true expression in Europe. To this extent Nishida's theory was ahead of time for today's postcolonial critiques of Eurocentrism as well as the move to include the legitimate participatory capacities of non-Western civilizations in global culture.

At the abstract and universal level of this description (which was not dissimilar to Herder's view that all cultures had a role to play in the creation of world culture), the theory is not politically problematic. What made it problematic was Japan's position in this dialectic at the time of Japanese colonialist expansion in Asia: It so happens that it was Japan that expressed this universally applicable, globally significant world-making dialectic, and as such, it was the 'historical mission of Japan' to bring this insight to the greater world ravaged by Euro-American imperialism (which Nishida criticized to be operating under the principle of the 'egoistic imperialism of the 19th century' that merely dominates and subjugates others for its own purposes). The creation of the Greater East-Asian Co-Prosperity Sphere is a step to consolidate the world-historical expressions of the peoples of East Asia (against the Euro-American domination), and Japan self-appoints itself to be the leader of this mission:

> Up to now, East-Asian peoples [*minzoku*] have been oppressed under European imperialism and viewed as colonies. We were robbed of our world-historical mission. It is time now for the East-Asian peoples to realize our own world-historical mission. Each people [in East Asia] must transcend itself to form a particular world [of East Asia] and thereby carry out the world-historical mission of the East-Asian peoples. *This* is the principle of the formation of the Greater East-Asian Co-prosperity Sphere. We the people of East Asia must together assert our principle of East-Asian culture and assume our stance world-historically. But in order to build a particular world [of East Asia], a central figure that carries the burden of the project is necessary.

---

[27]   NKZ I, 12: 428

In East Asia today, there is no other country but Japan [that can undertake such a role].[28]

Here not only the imperialist wartime program of the Greater East-Asian Co-Prosperity Sphere, but all of the other war-slogans and symbolisms, such as National Polity (*kokutai* – literally 'national body'), the Imperial House (*koshitsu*), Imperial Way (*kodo*), Imperial Spirit (*kodo seishin*) 'Oneness of the Emperor and his people' (*kunmin ittai*) and 'All the people assisting the Emperor' (*banmin yokusan*), were used and given a philosophical re-interpretation within his theory. The Imperial House of Japan embodies the universal principle of 'world-formation', yet since it is an 'empty' subject (referring to his theory of 'Place' as 'Absolute Nothingness', in turn suggesting that the Japanese Polity should be seen as the Place of Absolute Nothingness in which all entities show themselves), metaphysically speaking Japan itself cannot be an oppressive force and a dominating particular, like England or America. As Nishida puts it:

> As this is the essence of our national polity, formative globalism does not lose the subjectivity of our nation. Rather, *this* is precisely the principle of subjectivity unique to our country, that it contains others by emptying itself. To abide by this principle is to demonstrate to the rest of the world the essence of our national polity. It is fair to say that the principle of our national polity can provide the solution to today's world-historical problems. Not only should the Anglo-American world submit to it, but the Axis powers too shall follow it.[29]

The metaphysical placement of Absolute Nothingness in Japan is ingenious and to a certain extent it made sense, given the fact that it was the only nation that succeeded in modernity at the time. However, the problem is that the presumed universality of 'Absolute Nothingness' becomes identified with a historical particular, a Japanese National Polity, the symbol of the atrocious colonial expansion in Asia during the Pacific War, and the formative principles of the dialectic represents Japan's 'logic' for the establishment of the New World Order. At this point, the philosophical universal collapses into a standard wartime imperialist narrative, regardless of its original metaphysical meaning or intent. As John Dower notes,

> [...] the Kyoto School also made it clear that the current conflict represented Japan's ascension as the leading 'world-historical

28 NKZ I, 12: 429
29 NKZ I, 12: 434

17

race.' To them as to all other Japanese patriots, the war in Asia and the Pacific was a 'holy war', and represented an unprecedented struggle for the attainment of a transcendent Great Harmony (*Taiwa*).[30]

Apart from whether it was realistic to do so, theoretically Nishida could have used his world-historical dialectic in order to *oppose* the Imperial House (which cannot be but a historical particular). In fact, that would have been more consistent with his theory. The concretization/self-determination of Absolute Nothingness could occur everywhere (and in fact, it does, given the theory) and there is no logical or metaphysical necessity that *Japan* would have to embody the principle. Every nation is theoretically an individual in the dialectic that affects others, and the particular 'hierarchy' of powers comes from the particular power relations that are at work in the particular situation. Here then, the connection to Japan was made politically, in that it was the leading modern nation most powerful in East Asia at the time, but the idea that the most 'advanced' nation should lead and free the less advanced peoples belongs to the standard European colonial procedure (which Japan adopted). It was not a necessary component of the theory.

In addition, the metaphysical connection which allowed the theory to work perniciously was precisely the notion of 'Absolute Nothingness', the most 'universal' of all notions – in fact it is strictly speaking no 'notion' at all but a metaphysical postulate 'in which' or 'through which' all notions can appear – as such, it can only be negatively 'postulated'. The 'emptiness' allowed Nishida to claim that his theory differs from the European colonialist discourse; if Japanese Polity, in essence, is absolutely empty, then it merely serves as a metaphysical 'placeholder' and cannot be an aggressive force. But here the theory contradicts itself if one tries to make it a theory of historical development, with *one leading nation* as the ultimate Place through which the world realizes itself. Nevertheless, *The Principle of the New World Order* in its insight is a good example of the theory of the dialectic universal at work, especially if we could re-work it today. Nishida died in June, 1945, two months before Japan's ultimate defeat.

Watsuji's case was more straightforward, in that he was involved, albeit in the early stages, in the drafting of the *Fundamental Principles of the National Polity* (*Kokutai no Hongi*), which was

---

[30] John Dower, *War Without Mercy: Race and Power in the Pacific War* (New York: Pantheon Books, 1986), 227

published by the Ministry of Education in 1937. The book endorsed the importance of the Japanese citizens' total support of the Emperor and it was a required reading for the schools. In terms of theory, Watsuji's notion of 'human-being' as fundamentally interconnected not only to others but also to the whole, was used as a support for the National Polity.[31] He openly discussed and defended the role of 'totality' in which a human being would become who she is and, in return, a network of such individuals contribute to the development of the totality. Such totality has power and role to play in the historical context at the time, and he defended Japan's use of its power. For example:

> The essential characteristic of the power of totality...is not simply force but also military force...The source of national power is the authority of the totality. It is not that the totality acquires authority because it is powerful, but rather *its power comes from its authority*' (emphasis by Watsuji).[32]

Watsuji's writings made it clear that the Japanese culture possessed unique characteristics (such as the notion of nothingness and deep aesthetic sensibilities) which were superior to the vulgar and materialistic Euro-American cultures. His cultural nationalism supported the common nationalistic sentiments of the time.

However, the most infamous case from the post-war perspective was the participation of Nishida's students in the Overcoming Modernity (*Kindai no Chokoku*) symposia in 1941–1942, which were published in the major journal *Chuokoron*.[33] Some of the members of the Kyoto School (Keiji Nishitani, Masaaki Kosaka,

---

[31]   For the various analyses of Watsuji's theoretical complicity with nationalism, see Robert N. Bellah, *Imagining Japan: The Japanese Tradition and Its Modern Interpretation* (Berkeley: University of California Press, 2003), Chapter 3; Steve Odin, *The Social Self in Zen and American Pragmatism* (Albany: State University of New York Press, 1996), especially 65–; Christopher Goto-Jones, 'The Way of Revering the Emperor: Imperial Philosophy and Bushido in Modern Japan', Ben-Ami Shillony (ed.), *The Emperors of Modern Japan* (Leiden: Brill, 2008), 23–52. For a well-known reflection on Watsuji, Eurocentrism, and reverse-orientalism, see Naoki Sakai, 'Return to the West/Return to the East: Watsuji Tetsuro's Anthropology and Discussions of Authenticity', H. D. Harootunian and Masao Miyoshi (eds), *Japan in the World* (Durham: Duke University Press, 1993), 237–270.

[32]   Tetsuro Watsuji, *Rinrigaku* (Tokyo: Iwanami Shoten, 1965), 603.

[33]   Translation of the discussions is available in English: Richard Calichman (ed and trans), *Overcoming Modernity: Cultural Identity in*

Shigetaka Suzuki, Toratoro Shimomura, and Iwao Koyama) actively defended the role the Japanese Imperial Army played in the Pacific War, in order to 'overcome' the Euro-American forms of modernity and its domination across the globe. The hitherto dominant version of modernity was criticized as being mired in materialism, rationalism, individualism, selfishness, pursuit of profit, and the like; it lacked spiritual wholeness and ground. They had hoped that the newly emerging 'non-Western' modernity and its emphasis on culture, such as represented by Japan, could provide a positive alternative ('modern yet spiritual'). The ideas reflected the contents of Nishida's Principle of the New World Order essay, although the support of the Imperial Army was much more explicit among his students.

After the war the participants were labeled 'right-wing' and were forced to resign from their academic posts. Watsuji did not participate in the symposia but he also became the target of criticism by the left in the postwar period. Once prominent, the Kyoto School thus acquired the notorious image of an ultranationalist enclave and gradually declined and became isolated after the late 1940s. Nishida never participated in the roundtable discussions, but since his students' ideas were heavily influenced by his philosophy, among the left-circles he is often held 'guilty by association'. During the postwar period, 'Japanese philosophy' was thus forced into oblivion, and just as at the beginning in the Meiji Period, 'Philosophy' in Japan became 'Western Philsosophy' again, and Eurocentrism was even justified in the face of Japan's defeat. It was unfortunate that the particular historical context and the language of the philosophy of East-Asian modernity caused much grief and even a demise of the tradition of Japanese philosophy at the time. Yet it would probably be just as much of a mistake to reject all further forms of philosophical examination, as if the historical contingency of a theory could force it to be invalid, for good.

5. Philosophy and Culture Today

After the recovery period of the 1960s into the 1980s, as postwar Japan again emerged as a global economic success, the national confidence grew again and the leading elites again began to represent

---

Wartime Japan (New York: Columbia University Press, 2008). For analyses see also Heisig and Maraldo, *Rude Awakenings*.

Japan as a unique center of non-Western modernity. This time, the kind of universalism Japan spread to the world was not philosophy or cultural discourse but through consumer technology and pop culture; nevertheless, Japan finally succeeded in having a globally recognized presence and power. In this milieu of optimism, there had been a renewed interest in the themes of the interwar Overcoming Modernity debates. The new interest was not so much to rekindle the old debate, but think anew the possibility of 'overcoming' the West by studying some unique features of the 'Japanese mind and behavior' which purportedly gave the Japanese a special cultural advantage. Without much actual study of the old debate, the phrase 'Overcoming Modernity' was resurrected and popularized again in the renewed atmosphere of cultural nationalism. Growing self-confidence and a renewed sense of identity produced what is known as '*nihonjin-ron*' (Theory of Japanese-ness), engaging numerous scholars (from the natural sciences to sociology, politics, arts and humanities, cultural geography, literature) to speculate on the uniqueness of being Japanese.[34] Interest in Japanese philosophy, including Nishida and Watsuji, was rekindled and a new generation of scholars appeared, who wanted updated theories that reflected elements in Japanese culture. For example, Yujiro Nakamura's 1987 book, *Nishida Tetsugaku no Datsu-kochiku* (Deconstruction in Nishida Philosophy) opened up a new circle of Nishida scholarship, and Bin Kimura's innovative use of Watsuji's theory of Being-between in psychiatry became well-recognized.[35]

This tendency continued to grow particularly after the 1970s, this time with the idea that Japan is the genuine 'post-modern' nation. The underlying reverse-orientalist claim is still that Japan is somehow positively different, the real Other of the West, and that this accounts for Japan's amazing civilizational recovery since

[34] Perhaps the harshest criticism of Nihonjin-ron is found in Peter Dale, *The Myth of Japanese Uniqueness* (London and New York: Routledge, 2011). The book was previously published in 1986 by Croom Helm.
[35] Yujiro Nakamura, *Nishida Tetsugaku no Datsu-kochiku* (Tokyo: Iwanami, 1987). Unfortunately there is no English translation. Bin Kimura's collected writings span 8 volumes (*Kimura Bin Chosaku-shu*, 8 vol., Tokyo: Kobundo, 2001), but the groudbreaking works that reflect Watsuji's theories are *Hito to hito to no Aida: seishinbyourigaku-teki Nihon-ron* (Between Human Beings: Theory on Japan from a Perspective of Psychiatry, Tokyo: Kobundo, 1972), and *Jiko, Aida, Jikan: Gensho-gaku-teki Seishin Byori-gaku* (Self, In-Between, Time: Phenomenological Psychiatry, Tokyo: Kobundo, 1981).

W.W.II, an event unprecedented in world history. According to this reasoning, what makes Japan so special culturally are the supposedly indigenous notions of 'emptiness' and 'harmony'. Because of its emptiness, Japan is able to absorb advanced technologies readily, and it is also perfectly suited for the internationalized 'information society' which is to prevail in the coming century vis-a-vis the material industrial civilization of the past. As the 'post-Western' world arrives in the late-20th Century with its multiple global power-centers, Japan will be able to offer a leading paradigm of world-civilization for the next millennium. Note the contemporary significance of the ideas expressed by Nishida in the New World Order essay in such a rhetoric. This sort of neonationalist discourse was consciously promoted by the Ohira and Nakasone cabinets during the early to mid-1980s, with their optimistic portrayal of Japan as the leader of the internationalization movement. Thus, as cultural critic Akira Asada notes, far from being an embarrassing memory, today the issues raised in the 'Overcoming Modernity' debate are 'ideologized and revived like ghosts' in contemporary Japan's 'groundless self-confidence'.[36]

The cultural-nationalist sentiments continued to grow in the 1990s, and as Japan commemorated the fiftieth anniversary of the end of the Pacific War in 1995, the issue of how to account for its colonial activities in Asia attracted renewed interest in the public sphere. Although the stories of atrocities are no longer a secret, the once-sloganized justification, the 'liberation of Asia from Western imperial powers', still enjoyed (and continues to enjoy) considerable support among the conservative sector of society. Although Prime Minister Murayama finally issued a formal apology on August 15, 1995, the event was shrouded in controversy and resistance; the preferred national discourse is that of being a victim (of the atom-bombings) and 'in humiliation' there is considerable resistance in recognizing Japan as the *perpetrator* of violence. The issue is far from settled. We can detect three currents of thought underlying such resistance: that Japan's *intent* to liberate Asia was noble; that war (and its associated atrocities) is simply a part of history; and that Japan should not be 'singled out' for its violent actions. Retrospectively, one could read all of these ideas already expressed in Nishida's and Watsuji's writings, as well as in the Overcoming of Modernity

---

[36] 'Kindai no Chokoku to Nishida Tetsugaku' ('Overcoming of Modernity' and Nishida Philosophy), a roundtable discussion with Hiromatsu Wataru, Asada Akira, Ichikawa Hiroshi, and Karatani Kojin, *Kikan Shichô* 4, 1989, 10.

debates. Critics on the left continued to be weary of the use of inert historicism to evade responsibilities and worried about the re-affirm-ation of nationalist sentiments that its resurgence implies, yet the once-forgotten giants of Japanese philosophy and the cultural ideas they represented, too, became a focus of attention again.

After nearly 50 years of avoidance, in 1995 the Kyoto University officially re-established 'Japanese Philosophy' in the graduate cur-riculum. After the war, the descendants of the Kyoto School, most notably the students of Nishitani, continued primarily in religious philosophy in an academically isolated environment but they now gained a recognized center again where they continue the tradition. Nishida scholarship boomed again, although the criticism from the left continued. It is still the case that the vague image of the 'right' continues to follow those who study Japanese philosophy today, but it is no longer a shunted field in the academy. There are indeed excellent scholarship emerging from the new generation of the Kyoto School scholars, as well as others in the West who specializes in the Kyoto School philosophies.[37] The renewed focus is on inter-cultural or global modes of philosophizing, which continues the themes of the traditional Kyoto School in today's contexts.[38]

The cultural discourse of emptiness, interconnectedness, and the dialectic which were central themes of Japanese philosophy, are still alive today. In closing, let me reflect on the reactions after the '3.11. Catastrophe' (of the tsunami and the Fukushima nuclear acci-dents) with references to the relevant philosophical ideas.

First, the idea of emptiness or nothingness is not only an important notion in philosophy but also in cultural discourse, having its root in Buddhism. All that happens in reality, is 'in essence' empty; they are mere temporary and colorful reflections arising out of nothingness. As such, life is fleeting, ephemeral, fragile, and *therefore* all the more precious, and we must appreciate every moment of it. Both Nishida's and Watsuji's philosophies express this cultural idea, although articulated in abstract philosophical languages. In our

[37]   The notable modern-day Kyoto School scholars include Shizuteru Ueda, Masakatu Fujita, and Ryosuke Ohashi; there are also productive scho-lars *on* the Kyoto School outside Kyoto today, such as James Heisig, John Maraldo, Rolf Elberfeld, Graham Parkes, Michiko Yusa, and Bret Davis, among others.
[38]   See, for example, Masakatsu Fujita and Bret Davis (ed.), *Sekai no Naka no Nihon no Tetsugaku* (Japanese Philosophy in the World, Kyoto: Showa-do, 2005), and James Heisig (ed.), *Nihon Tetsugaku no Kokusai-sei* (The Global Significance of Japanese Philosophy, Kyoto: Sekai Shiso-sha, 2006).

present context, catastrophes are also part of this occurrence-in-nothingness, in itself neither good nor bad, but simply to be experienced and be dealt with. The appropriate attitude would be acceptance. There is a Japanese expression, '*shouganai*', which was heard over and over after the tsunami: It means 'it cannot be helped' or 'what it must be, must be', but not so much in the spirit of resignation but as a recognition of reality-at-hand. In its positive sense it helped those who lived in the region face the horrendousness of the situation steadfastly without unnecessary drama.

In its negative sense, the idea of emptiness can also lead to nihilism, cynicism, or fatalistic attitudes. If everything that happens is in essence empty in the end, then it does not really matter what one does or does not do. Catastrophes happen and there are good people and bad people, but that is the way it is; why should I act? It is difficult to generate a moral *ought* from nothingness, as the sufferings of the people could also be viewed as fleeting and in essence empty. The understanding of emptiness could also contribute to a lack of orientation or direction: why should a certain goal, and not the other, be chosen? Why should it matter?

Second, and perhaps more notably, the notion of the fundamental interconnectedness among people was also clearly discernible in the reports of the aftermath. The remarkable communal unity and collective efforts in the immediate recovery period were reported in foreign media as evidence of 'Japanese togetherness'; indeed, the consciousness of the 'we' is much stronger than the 'I' generally in Japan, but especially so in such times of emergency. It is simply taken for granted that 'we must help ourselves and others together'.[39] On its negative side, such pressure for solidarity made it difficult for individuals to opt for autonomous decisions, for example, to move out of community. It was not impossible but the one who 'abandons the group' risked being labeled a 'traitor' and could not expect to return and be accepted with open arms.

Philosophy and culture are remarkably intertwined. Philosophers are cultural beings, and philosophizing occurs in a cultural context. Putting aside the anti-essentialist critiques, we still understand the

---

[39]   Having spent most of my adult life in the U.S.A. and witnessed numerous cases of looting in the Los Angeles area during various emergencies such as black-outs and riots, I asked a Japanese friend about such possibilities. The reply was, 'You must be joking. No one dares to act so selfishly, for fear that he or she will be ostracized'. The reason was not so much out of moral considerations but rather out of the fear that one may be banned from the group.

term 'culture' as referring to geopolitical particularities, yet we can also understand the universal elements in our humanity. Tracing the development of Japanese philosophy over 130 years of turbulent history shows first an exercise in the pursuit for universality in cultural particularity, followed by the pursuit for particularity in the particularity, then reflecting on the process on a global setting. Today our philosophical discourse goes beyond such categories, yet our fascination and interest in different philosophical traditions and imaginations, as well as ways of philosophizing, are worth preserving.

Institute of Philosophy at the Universität Hildesheim
yokoarisaka@gmail.com

The 'Continental' Tradition?

ALAN MONTEFIORE

Abstract

There is – of course – no one such thing as *the* continental tradition in philosophy, but rather a whole discordant family of notably distinct traditions. They are, nevertheless, broadly recognisable to each other. For much of the last century, however, most of those engaged in or with philosophy in continental Europe, on the one hand, and in the English-speaking world, on the other hand, had surprisingly little knowledge of, interest in or even respect for what was going on in the other. Happily, the situation today is vastly improved on each side of the philosophical channel. What follows is an attempt to gain some understanding of the background to this long-standing (and still to some diminishing extent persistent) mutual incomprehension from the standpoint of one who came to philosophy as a PPE student in the Oxford of the late 1940s.

My invitation to contribute to this series of lectures on 'Philosophical Traditions' came with the kindly flattering explanation that it was being made in the light of (what was alleged to be) my 'expertise in continental philosophy'. There are, however, two problems with this explanation. In the first place it is by now pretty widely recognised that the term 'continental philosophy' is one of a far from precise art rather than of any sort of geographical, or indeed numerical, accuracy – there is, of course, no such thing as one identifiable school of thought that might be called 'continental philosophy'. And secondly, although there are by now a considerable number of people in the English-speaking philosophical world who do have a genuinely specialist knowledge of the loose group of traditions which came to be more or less recognisably referred to by this term, I cannot in all honesty pretend to belong to their expert company. Moreover, there now exist a respectable number of books designed to explain this ensemble of traditions, many of which include useful bibliographies listing their fellows. Let me here refer simply to two of them that, in their brevity as in their clarity, are most accessible, namely Simon Critchley's *Continental Philosophy – A Very Short Introduction*, published (by Oxford University Press) in 2001 and Simon Glendinning's *The Idea of Continental Philosophy* published (by Edinburgh University Press) in 2006. (Both authors, incidentally, express strong reservations about the key term appearing in the very titles of their books.)

doi:10.1017/S1358246114000101   © The Royal Institute of Philosophy and the contributors 2014

Royal Institute of Philosophy Supplement **74** 2014

Alan Montefiore

The story of how and why I may have acquired a thus doubly misleading reputation has, inevitably, its purely personal side, which as such is of no general interest. However, it does also have aspects that belong to the (still on-going) history of a certain academic culture – one in which the boundaries between it and the not so strictly academic are both uncertain and potentially shifting. In what follows I shall try to reflect on those aspects of this story as I have seen it, and in particular on the factors that made it so difficult for us, students in the middle of the last century, to recognise what presented itself as philosophy coming from across the Channel as belonging to the same subject as that on which we ourselves were embarked. I should make it clear at the outset, however, that my own, in fact relatively quite limited and non-expert, experience of the kinds of philosophy going on in continental Europe grew essentially from an effort to try and make sense of what was being produced, published and debated under the title of philosophy in France – much of which, of course, derived from philosophy which had come to France from Germany).

It is fair to say, then, that when I first came, in the autumn of 1948, to study philosophy as an undergraduate at Oxford reading for the ex-serviceman's shortened version of PPE, it was there quite generally held that whatever might be thought of as falling under the heading of 'continental philosophy' could safely be dismissed as irrelevant to any serious philosophical study or debate. Not that this was an assumption for which anyone seemed to feel a need to present us students with detailed exemplification or argument; most of us, indeed, very largely took it on board as going in effect without saying. It was in any case very effectively embodied in what was and, even more significantly, what was not available to us in the philosophy syllabuses and in the philosophy tutorials, lectures and seminars on offer.

Students taking courses in literature, and more especially in French literature, were, no doubt, less cut off than were we from the writings of, for example, Sartre, Gabriel Marcel, Camus and perhaps even Merleau-Ponty, the first three of them at least being not infrequently lumped together under the broad title of Existentialists. Indeed much of what they produced was regarded as being quite properly to be appreciated as novels, plays or essays of a type belonging to what was recognisable as broadly one and the same, if internally highly discordant, literary (-cum-political-cum-ideological) field rather than to what we were learning to think of as philosophy as such. Of the first three, it was Sartre whose writings, or at least some of them, seemed to make most obvious claim to the status of philosophy, in particular, of course, his massive *L'Etre et le Néant* (1943). But, as I say, no hint of its existence, let alone of any possible significance that it might have had, was to be found on any of the philosophy syllabuses available to us in Oxford or, so far as I know at any rate, on those provided by the philosophy departments of any other British universities of that time.

The article on Sartre in the Stanford Encyclopaedia of Philosophy starts with the assertion that 'Sartre (1905–1980) is arguably the best known philosopher of the twentieth century.' So, even if the argument in question is one that may be impossibly hard to pin down, one may well ask how it could be that as a student embarking on a course of philosophy in the very middle of that century, I should have found myself so much at a loss to know what to make of a work such as *L'Etre et le Néant* – with, moreover, the at least tacit discouragement from the great majority of my philosophical elders and betters from spending (or 'wasting') my time in struggling over it rather than any suggestion that I should do philosophically well to persevere?[1]

There were, it seems to me, two fairly straightforward immediate reasons why we should have found ourselves left in such a state of perplexity. The first was that we were being taught, by explicit precept, by constant encounter with appropriate example and by regular exposure to detailed and probing discussion, that it was fundamentally incumbent on philosophers to tease out and to establish the proper

---

[1]   Things seemed not to have changed very much, indeed, when I returned to Oxford at the beginning of the 60s as a philosophy Fellow and tutor at Balliol. At some point during those years I found myself, together with two very senior and well-known philosophers of the time, as the third (and very junior) member of a Bodleian Library philosophy book selection sub-committee, when among the books presented to us for decision was *La Voix et le Phénomène* by Jacques Derrida, whose name clearly meant nothing to either of my colleagues. As one of them flicked over its pages in order to get an idea of what was inside, he noticed that one of its chapters bore the title 'Le signe et le clin d'oeil' ('The sign and the wink'), saying, as he passed it over to my other senior colleague, something to the effect of 'The Library surely won't want a book containing chapters with a title such as that in its philosophy section'. To this the other senior colleague in question immediately agreed, and if I, who happened to have met Derrida at a conference in France, had not been there to point out (rather meekly) that this book and its author had already acquired a certain importance across the Channel, *La Voix et le Phénomène* would not have been available to would-be readers at the Bodleian for at least some time to come.

Alan Montefiore

working of arguments – that is to say, to check on their validity or invalidity, to determine whatever might count as confirming or falsifying their premises and/or their conclusions and to make explicit their relevance (or irrelevance) to the issues in question. There was, moreover, a general presumption that in looking for the structures of arguments we should seek always to present the concepts crucial to their construction in terms that were as perspicuous as possible. There were, of course, well-known differences of view as to just how such structures should be modelled or re-presented and as to how best to understand the relations between the given terms of the arguments under analysis and those of their analytically clarified versions. (Should one, for example, take some version of formal logic as one's ideal model, or was it more appropriate to think in terms of some kind of informal or so-called 'contextual' logic?) But though it was largely accepted - in the title words of H.H. Price's Inaugural Address to the first post-war meeting of the Aristotelian Society – that 'clarity is not enough', it was generally taken for granted that to seek such conceptual clarity as might be possible was, if not a sufficient, then at least a necessary mark of any serious philosopher. No doubt there might be considerable room for uncertainty as to in what exactly the proper criteria of clarity might consist. But, it is fair to say, it did not seem to us that a concern for clarity or rigour of argument as such had any sort of priority for philosophers of the then contemporary continent.

The second main reason was that the works of the philosophers with and against whom Sartre was primarily arguing – and with their works much of their conceptual vocabulary – were almost entirely absent from the lists of reading prescribed to students of my generation. In particular these absences included the writings of such relatively recent figures as Bergson, Husserl and Heidegger. Virtually every serious student of philosophy in France of the time could be expected to have at least some familiarity with the leading ideas and terms of their philosophies, as well as of those earlier philosophers whose writings, agreements and disagreements would in turn have formed such a major part of their own background – above all, perhaps, the writings of Hegel, mediated as often as not through their differing presentations by such influential commentators as Jean Hyppolite and Alexandre Kojève. One has also to bear very much in mind the historical reasons for which virtually all French intellectuals at the time felt obliged to situate themselves in relation to the different versions of Marxism that were then competing with each other and, in more directly political terms, in relation to the Communist party itself.

So far as I myself was concerned, Hegel himself figured on none of my reading lists in his own right, as it were, but only indirectly in the contexts, on the one hand, of such references to Marxism as were to be found in the otherwise little that there was of political philosophy at that time and, on the other, in the still surviving references on our reading lists to such works of earlier British philosophers as F.H. Bradley's *Ethical Studies*, T.H. Green's *Lectures on Political Obligation*, (which were as much Kantian in inspiration as Hegelian) and Bernard Bosanquet's *The Philosophical Theory of the State* – and, as an accompanying antidote to this latter, L.T. Hobhouse's *The Metaphysical Theory of the State*. Marx, himself, of course, made no appearance at all in our philosophy courses as such other than in those specifically designated as political philosophy. (We may have known or been told virtually nothing of Hegel, but I do still remember the impression made on me when I first came across it in my edition of Hobhouse's book,[2] by the letter to his son, then a lieutenant in the RAF, which served as the book's introductory dedication. In it Hobhouse tells of how he had been working on Hegel's theory of freedom in his garden in the summer of 1917 at the moment of a bombing raid by three German aircraft: 'In the bombing of London', he wrote, 'I had just witnessed the visible and tangible outcome of a false and wicked doctrine, the foundations of which lay, as I believe, in the book before me. To combat this doctrine effectively is to take such part in the fight as the physical disabilities of middle age allow. Hegel himself carried the proof-sheets of his first work to the printer through streets crowded with fugitives from the field of Jena. With that work began the most penetrating and subtle of all the intellectual influences which have sapped the rational humanitarianism of the eighteenth and nineteenth centuries, and in the Hegelian theory of the god-state all that I had witnessed lay implicit.')

Hegel's virtual disappearance from the syllabus as it came down to us is not, of course, to be explained simply as a result of this sort of reading (or mis-reading). Of the many factors involved, one of the most important lay in the fact that while access to Hegel's thought, as to that of the other German idealists and their successors, lies in a certain way of reading and of reacting to the philosophy of Immanuel Kant, only very few of the philosophy students of my time and place actually studied Kant at all – or indeed were

---

[2]   *The Metaphysical Theory of the State* (George Allen and Unwin Ltd., 1918)

encouraged to do so[3]; and for those who did, 'up to date' commentaries on and/or discussions of his great Critiques were still few and far between. As Simon Critchley so rightly says, 'Much of the difference between analytic and Continental philosophy simply turns on *how* one reads Kant and *how much* Kant one reads.'[4] Of the Kantian commentaries that were then available, strikingly few were in tune with the dominant and widely taught 'analytic' philosophy of the time, whether in its so-called ordinary language or its more formally, or quasi-formally, logical versions. (Sir Peter Strawson's widely influential *The Bounds of Sense* and Jonathan Bennett's *Kant's Analytic* were both only published in 1966.[5])

Kant had thought that the only way to deal with the problems inherent in the accounts of consciously reflective experience proposed by his various (but all still essentially Cartesian) rationalist and empiricist predecessors, was to accept that the human subject must somehow belong to, or participate in, two *prima facie* incompatible realms of being at one and the same time – in that of a causally determinate order of nature, on the one hand, and, on the other hand, in an unknowable (and even strictly speaking unconceptualisable) order of self-determining rational autonomy. (Even this use of the expression 'at one and the same time' is, of course, strictly out of place, as time, according to the Kantian account, belongs only to the natural order as an indissociable element of its very structure.) He thus left himself and his successors with the problem of what to make of this transcendentally dual status – transcendental in the sense that the presumption of its existence rests on its claim to be a necessary presupposition of our very capacity for meaningful conceptualisation and thought, i.e. of our capacity to make sense of all of which in practice we find ourselves already making some sort of sense – of our ability to direct our lives as embodied inhabitants of our everyday physical world and of our abilities both to think of what we may there set out to do and to communicate meaningfully with others.

---

[3]   I remember one at the time well-known philosopher saying to me that, given that a central Kantian preoccupation was with the attempt to exhibit the strategic possibilities of synthetic a priori propositions (or, rather, judgments), and that it was now well-known that there could be no such propositions, he could see no point is expending a great deal of effort on the study of Kant.

[4]   *Continental Philosophy: A Very Short Introduction* (Oxford University Press), 17

[5]   *The Bounds of Sense: An Essay on Kant's Critique of Pure Reason* (London, Methuen, 1966). *Kant's Analytic* was published, also in 1966, by Cambridge University Press.

It would, of course, normally be thought to be a likewise necessary condition not only of philosophical argument, but of rational (and practically effective) thought in general that it should be uncompromisingly committed to the resolution of any and all such contradictions as might seem to arise within it. And yet any attempt to explain of what sort of elements the postulated realm of things-in-themselves might really consist or how it might interact – as it allegedly must – with the natural order of space and time would seem to run into ever renewed contradiction.

My own reading of Kant is that, however reluctant he may have been to admit it even to himself, he increasingly came to find himself having to struggle with the higher order contradiction involved in his commitments *both* to the rationally imperative demand to resolve or to eliminate from his philosophy any element of contradiction *and* to the recognition that at one level or another contradiction would nevertheless always recur. Taken together, these may be thought of as amounting to an (however unwilling) commitment to an acknowledgment of paradox as an ultimate limit to rational enquiry, a limit that may be endlessly deferred but never definitively set aside. Acceptance of any such limit would be evidently unacceptable to the great majority of philosophers, above all to those who, like Kant himself, held fast to the values of the great Enlightenment. Broadly speaking, then, his successors reacted to the challenges presented by his Transcendental Idealism in two very different ways, leading – it is fair to say – to the onward development of the mutually estranged traditions of what have come to be known as Continental and Analytic or Anglo-Saxon philosophy. There were those who thought that, if Kant had found himself in such an impasse, this was because he had not gone far enough in showing how all the essential structures of natural experience were to be understood as deriving from those of subjective consciousness as such. Efforts to work out the fuller implications of this view resulted in the movement known as German Idealism; and it was above all in Hegel's version that it became for those following in its wake the model against which to measure the nature and extent of their own reservations and modifications. Others reacted by taking in effect the view that if Kant had dug himself into this sort of hole, it made better sense not to follow him into it, but rather to pick up the threads from where their own ancestors, those would-be hard-headed and common-sensible empiricists, had left them. Broadly speaking still, it was this view that took most lasting hold in the English-speaking world, while across the Channel Hegel, whether in his own terms or in his

Alan Montefiore

Marxist-inverted version, retained his stature as one of the great figures with whom any serious student of philosophy would be expected to be at least reasonably familiar and to come to some sort of terms.

These are, of course very broad generalisations and neither development took place without there being a number of notable exceptions along the way. There was, for instance, the once influential but now largely neglected movement known as British Idealism, composed mainly of philosophers also known as the British Hegelians.[6] I have already cited Hobhouse's startlingly vigorous reaction to what he took to have been the overall influence of Hegel and his philosophy. Wikipedia's article on British Idealism puts the matter almost equally starkly: 'The doctrines of British idealism so provoked the young Cambridge philosophers G.E. Moore and Bertrand Russell that they began a new philosophical tradition, analytic philosophy.' Although this too is an example of very abruptly potted history, it is certainly the case that while both Russell and Moore figured prominently on my reading lists as a budding student, the only fleeting references to be found there to anything remotely Hegelian were, as I have already mentioned, to the political and ethical writings of Bradley, Bosanquet and T.H. Green, none of which would have provided much help to the understanding of such leading 'continental' philosophers of the time as, for example, Husserl, Heidegger, Sartre, Karl Jaspers or Gabriel Marcel. Merleau-Ponty was, in patches at any rate, perhaps a little more accessible.

The reason, however, why we found it so difficult to gain any foothold of understanding of what these 'continental' philosophers were on about – and why, it has to be admitted, the struggle seemed to be so little worth while – was not simply that we lacked the right sort of historical background; the fact is that the philosophy that we were taught

---

[6]   There were also, of course, a few – though, I think it is fair to say, only a few – later exceptions of note. One certainly worth remembering would be that of J.N. Findlay, a distinguished scholar who both taught and wrote not only on Plato and Wittgenstein, but also on Meinong, Kant and (extensively) on Hegel, as well as being both an admirer and translator of Husserl. Findlay retired from his Chair in London in 1966, from where he moved to the States, where he taught at one university or another for the rest of his life. Around the first half of the sixties at any rate I was certainly very aware of Findlay and his philosophical views, which indeed struck me as both stimulating and well worth engaging with; but this was, I have to say, a reaction from a certain distance, and my impression was and is that, for whatever reasons, he remained overall a philosophically very lone wolf.

and encouraged to practise for ourselves carried with it what may now seem to be curiously little concern for its own culturally embedded history. This is not to say that the syllabuses on offer did not provide for – or even to some extent insist on - the study of any of the great philosophers of the past. For Oxford PPE students the so-called General Paper, whose core component consisted of the basic works in the theory of knowledge of Descartes, Locke, Berkeley and Hume, was a compulsory element, and for most of us the given starting-point of our course. We had also the options of taking a special paper on the 'Rationalists' and/or that on Kant (with an over-whelmingly heavy concentration on the *Critique of Pure Reason* and the *Groundwork to the Metaphysic of Morals*); but those availing themselves of either of these options were very much a minority. Those reading for Greats (or Literae Humaniores) were, of course, required to study both Plato and Aristotle. But in all these cases, over and above the requirement to exhibit a good knowledge of the relevant texts, the emphasis was above all on a critical evaluation of the arguments contained therein rather than on any attempt to inter-pret them in the light of the contexts in which they had been pro-duced and to which they belonged. The distinction was well and strikingly brought out by Bernard Williams in the Preface to his Pelican book on Descartes, which, as he made clear in his opening sentence, was explicitly intended as 'a study in the history of philoso-phy rather than in the history of ideas.... [and] is meant to consist, to a considerable extent, of philosophical argument, the direction of it shaped by what I take to be, now, the most interesting philosophical concerns of Descartes.'[7]

'Continental' philosophers, on the other hand, have generally tended to incorporate their awareness of the ways in which their pre-decessors expressed themselves in the development and expression of their own thinking with the result that such philosophically historical references become built into the very texture of their own texts. Given that many, if not indeed most, of the references in question were largely absent from our own syllabuses and curricula, and given that we were anyhow being taught to work out our lines of argument in our own non-historically loaded terms, these differences in relation to the historical background constituted a formidable further barrier to any effective mutual understanding between students on opposite sides of the Channel.

There were undoubtedly many other important (and in many ways interconnected) factors at work, but whose importance is hard to

[7]   *Descartes: The Project of Pure Enquiry* (Pelican Books, 1978), 9/10

measure. I remember, for example, how, when I was still a young and inexperienced lecturer, one of my more senior colleagues explained to me that, however interesting in itself the history of philosophy might be, a knowledge of it was no more relevant to the contemporary production of first-rate philosophy than was a knowledge of the history of physics to the production of first-rate work in, say, contemporary quantum mechanics. Again, it is in general the case – so far at any rate as my experience goes – that in the English-speaking world philosophy has closer institutional links with the natural and social sciences as compared with those that exist between philosophy and letters on the continent of Europe. In France, certainly, philosophy is generally first taught within a context of learning to express oneself effectively and with what I would be inclined to call distinctive literary effect. The result may seem to be, as an unsympathetic critic once put it, that rhetoric (in the modern pejorative sense of the term) tends only too easily to take the place of argument – though it might be that what may strike a typical analytic philosopher as 'mere' rhetoric is better understood as functioning as a different form of argument.

Rhetoric, according to the Wikipedia article on the subject, 'is the art of discourse, an art that aims to improve the facility of speakers or writers who attempt to inform, persuade, or motivate particular audiences in specific situations' – an art that, as Aristotle saw it, can be just as essential to the pursuit of good as to bad or dishonest purposes. Thus a philosopher with a trained sense of his intellectual allegiances within an historical tradition may, in setting out his position to an audience with a similar awareness of history, be able to convey the general context of his thinking 'simply' by use of terms belonging to, say, a recognisably Hegelian, Heideggerian or, one might add, Freudian (or Lacanian) discourse. To those in the know this may function very well as a way of situating, if not exactly proving, one's argument; while those not in the relevant know will be left frustratingly in the dark.

It is thus understandable that where philosophy finds itself institutionally so embedded within the extended family of literary disciplines, it should come to express itself in such historically and traditionally fashioned forms of rhetoric and argumentation – and understandable too that the use of such forms should make for mutual failures of understanding between insiders and outsiders to the relevant traditions. But this is not the only way in which the nature of the institutions within which philosophy is produced and disseminated may impact on the structure and content of what is there produced. In my lifetime, certainly, it would have been (and, no doubt, still is) most unusual for any philosophical work of any importance in the analytic or English-speaking tradition to be published that had not already been tried out in the form of papers given in seminars and/or at meetings of one relatively small and face-to face philosophy society or another, all of these being contexts in which there is opportunity for critically detailed examination of the very nuts and bolts of the arguments deployed. Again, it is quite common in the English-speaking world for books eventually to emerge as a considered reaction to criticisms and comments received in responses to a previously disseminated series of articles. And even in cases where there has in fact been little or no such previous interchange, there is a tendency to think and to write as if in already prepared response to such potentially significant objections as one may anticipate, as an ingrained way of clarifying for all concerned one's own meaning and intent.

While it is true that in more recent times there have been increasing signs of change taking place on the other side of the Channel, during the greater part of my philosophical lifetime philosophical exchange there has tended, at one end of the scale, to take the form of the publication of books and counter-books, and, at the other end, that of more or less openly polemical interventions in the media – with little by way of detailed co-operative discussion in between. Again there are a number of reasons why this should have been so. In France most notably, as to some varying extent no doubt in the other countries of continental Europe, philosophy – and philosophers – belong very much to the public culture. To quote from the blurb on the back cover of Jean-Louis Fabiani's widely informative book on the sociology of what it is to be a French philosopher: 'The philosopher constitutes one of the most remarkable figures of French intellectual life...[French philosophy] is a conceptual construction all of whose readings and impacts are to be taken into account; it is an institution and an ensemble of social practices ranging from those of the classroom to the public media.'[8] (Fabiani also notes[9] the revealing remark by Gilles Deleuze and Félix Guattari in their

---

[8]   *Qu'est-ce qu'un philosophe français? – la vie sociale des concepts (1880 – 1980)*, Edition de l'Ecole des Hautes Etudes en Sciences Sociales, 2010: 'Le philosophe français constitue l'une des figures les plus remarquables de la vie intellectuelle française...[la philosophie française est] une construction conceptuelle, dont toutes les lectures et les receptions sont à prendre en compte, une institution et des pratiques sociales, de la salle de classe à la scène médiatique.'

[9]   Ibid, 23

Alan Montefiore

Qu'est-ce que la philosophie? of 1991 that 'le philosophe ne discute jamais'.) A high proportion of the educated public in France will have studied philosophy to at least some extent in their final year of secondary school, and every lycée will include among its staff at least one qualified teacher of philosophy, which makes for an already significant number of qualified philosophers in the country as a whole. Philosophers are, moreover, very much among those readily recognisable in the traditionally familiar role of 'public intellectual'. There is thus a potential readership for books of philosophy – and an even wider one for the interventions of well-known philosophers on matters of public debate, but in both cases a readership interested for the most part less in the logical nitty-gritty of such arguments as may – hopefully – be found in professional philosophical journals than in the overall positions that may be presented to them for adoption, rejection or support.

Another striking feature of philosophical activity on the continent during the greater part of my philosophical lifetime has been the often open and explicit political significance attached to the different ways in which it might be pursued almost as much as to the particular positions adopted. It has been hard, if not indeed virtually impossible, for philosophers there to carry on their philosophical work in a wholly non-political or politically neutral way, even if that was their own conception of what most philosophy was or should be about; the very claim to political neutrality was quite generally taken on the left to be (whether intentionally or simply in practical effect) a hypocritical posturing typical of the political right. Any philosopher intent on working in areas of the conceptual-cum-logical analysis more typical of 'Anglo-Saxon' and American philosophy would have been automatically regarded by many of their most vocal colleagues and students as belonging to 'the right', and thus as ideological opponents with whom serious discussion, as contrasted with polemical exchange, was hardly to be envisaged. It was not that anyone thought that any great political significance attached to the particular way in which one might, for instance, analyse the logical status of a proposition such as 'Nothing can be both red and green all over'; what *was* held to be politically significant was a readiness to treat such a matter as being of any philosophical interest or importance whatsoever.

It is hardly surprising, then, that when I first came to philosophy – and for some continuing time thereafter – communication between philosophers on either side of the Channel should in general have been so lamentably bad. From here, 'philosophy' from the other side seemed to consist very largely of a kind of intellectual posturing, at once learned, empty and opaque; seen from the other side, our own efforts struck them as both historically and politically naive and superficial. If I nevertheless showed some persistence in trying to make some better sense of our respective situations than this, I have to admit that this was due less to any specifically philosophical motivation than to a set of circumstances through which I came to find myself with a whole range of personal contacts and commitments in France. Whatever the differences in our background experiences – I, for instance, had been safely at school in this country during the whole of the still very recent war, while they had been living the many and varied stresses, traumas and divisions of the German occupation – and whatever the differences in the (largely hidden) assumptions underlying our different ways of thinking, I could not believe that these obviously intelligent and often passionately committed people, most of them much better read than myself, were, when it came to philosophy, all simply engaged in a literary enterprise accountable to no recognisably determinable rules of argumentation. That there was some element of public and/or political display in much of what was produced under the banner of philosophy was certainly one feature of the prevailing culture. But surely this could not have been all that there was to it. (No doubt too that there was an element of pure cussedness in my reaction to the then prevailing 'Anglo-Saxon' tendency to dismiss all that was lumped together under the heading of 'Continental philosophy' as mere literary hot air.)

Be that as it may, my occasional participation in philosophical events in France must have started to attract some degree of notice among my 'Anglo' contemporaries and colleagues – notice of what was no doubt regarded as a certain eccentricity. Certainly, when I came back to Balliol in 1961 as a PPE Fellow (after ten years teaching at the then new University College of North Staffordshire), I was one of the very few philosophers in Oxford to show signs of knowing anything at all about the mysterious world of 'Continental' philosophy. So when it started to become impossible simply to ignore a new and growing, even if still very small, student demand for a paper allowing for the study of such philosophers as Husserl, Heidegger, Sartre and Merleau-Ponty, Patrick Gardiner, Charles Taylor and I were constituted a small sub-committee charged with the responsibility of devising such an option. Taylor, having himself a dual francophone and anglo-phone background, was admirably well equipped for this task; and Patrick Gardiner too in his own way, through his special knowledge of such nineteenth century philosophers as Schopenhauer, Hegel and Nietzsche, who also, and very properly, found their way onto the new syllabus as we then determined it. But, it is worth noting, when this new option was first introduced (under the title of Post-Kantian Philosophy), it was decided that it could not yet be made available to the whole range of courses of which philosophy was a component, the simple fact being that there were still not enough philosophers in Oxford capable of acting, year after year, as examiners in such a subject.

Gradually, then, my interest in current French philosophy and in what lay behind it, came to be seen as an eccentricity of a certain usefulness. It was almost as if there existed an assumption that, since some of my philosophical interests were distinctly odd, graduate students who wished to work on 'odd' subjects of one sort or another, and for whom no other supervisor could be found, might not unreasonably be sent to me – whether I actually knew very much about them or not! (There were indeed times when I found myself with a share of responsibility for students working on topics wholly unfamiliar to the great majority of colleagues from my own Sub-Faculty of Philosophy, topics about which I knew just about enough to find them of genuine interest, but about whose substance I quite certainly learnt more from the graduates working on them than they could possibly have learnt from me.)

By now, happily, things are looking distinctly different on both sides of this strange philosophical Channel. Increasing numbers of French philosophers – especially, but not only, the younger among them – are showing themselves to be not only very well-read, as indeed one would expect of philosophers trained and working in France, but genuinely expert in such typically 'analytic' areas of philosophy as (often, but not only, Wittgensteinian) philosophy of language and moral and political philosophy. Where, for example, the work of John Rawls was once regarded as belonging too indisputably to the 'liberal' right to be worthy of serious attention, there are now few, if any, countries in continental Europe – including France – where there are not young philosophers to be found deeply engaged in detailed Rawlsian studies and debates. Part of the explanation for this transformation undoubtedly lies in the virtual collapse of what for a long time after the war had been the dominating preoccupation of most intellectuals with Marxist related concerns. But there have certainly been other, if not wholly dissociated, factors at play, such, for example, as the fact that increasing numbers of young philosophers from the continent – including very notably from France – have been spending some time working in British or, above all, in American universities.)

The English-speaking world too, has seen a steadily increasing interest in a wide range of what still tends to be called 'continental' philosophy. Many of the philosophers concerned have been trained in and are in some cases very expert in whole areas of the most strictly analytic philosophy. In particular, there has been an almost extraordinary explosion of interest in such philosophers as Derrida, Deleuze, Foucault, Habermas and now Badiou. And if the word 'extraordinary' comes to mind in this context, it is when I think of the contrast between the way things are now and how they were when, for example, I first embarked with Jacques Derrida, on a (very limited) programme of exchange visits between Oxford and the Ecole Normale Supérieure in Paris, where he was then teaching. The (now long ago) arrangement was that once a term one or two of us from Oxford would go to address his group of students in Paris, while he, or later one of his colleagues, would in turn come to Oxford to talk to the then very small *ad hoc* group, mainly of graduate students, interested to try and make out what he was about. But this group included none of my more senior colleagues from the Philosophy Sub-Faculty, while Derrida's students in Paris, preoccupied as they were with the looming competitive examinations on the outcome of which their future career prospects depended, displayed very little interest in whatever we might have to say. Or again I remember how Habermas on an early visit to Oxford was for the most part met with what may not unfairly be described as a mixture of more or less polite disinterest and incomprehension. (As for the reaction to Lacan when he came to talk at the Maison Française in Oxford, that is in itself a whole other story.) Nowadays, of course, experts on all these philosophers are to be found virtually all over the so-called Anglo-Saxon world.

So what lessons may be drawn from this, I fear over-personalised, story? First, that if anyone should have come to think of me as possessing any sort of expertise in continental philosophy, this can best be understood as an illustration of just how wide was the gulf, between philosophers at any rate, of mutual ignorance, mutual misunderstanding and – it is hardly too strong an expression – mutual cultural contempt in the middle of the last century. For a long time I myself only understood much too little of what then counted as philosophy on the other side of the intellectual Channel; but then there were very few philosophers on this side who knew anything about it at all – or if they did, as was certainly the case with a few of the more senior of them, they tended, in philosophical public at least, to pretend that they did not. Secondly, but this should not be of any surprise, that there is not really any such thing as *the* tradition of continental philosophy. There has existed rather a somewhat unruly, but to some extent inter-related, 'continental' family of traditions – Marxist, Thomist, phenomenological, psychoanalytical, existentialist in some broadly contestable sense of the term, traditions which, however much they may have differed among themselves, nevertheless had enough in common to understand what their differences and disagreements were. Thirdly, that what they did have crucially in common, and what we most notably did not share, was a common framework of reference grounded in a thoroughgoing training in the historical philosophical background – and in particular in those of its aspects to which entrance could only be secured through a certain knowledge of Kant and, beyond him, of Hegel and his successors.

Fourthly, that the origins of this gulf of failure of mutual understanding lay not in intellectual differences alone, but also in deep differences of background political, institutional and historical experience. One of those great differences lies, of course, in the dominant importance in the history of so many continental countries, and in particular in that of France, of the political and cultural role played by the Catholic Church and by philosophies both associated with and opposed to it. The prospect of engaging in detailed critical discussion, and the importance of such discussion for the testing and clarification of arguments, must inevitably have presented itself very differently to adherents of such hierarchically authoritarian intellectual structures as the traditional Church or to its in many ways mirror image, the traditional Communist party in as much as such discussion carries always a potential threat to established authority and, by further implication, the counter-threat of authoritative sanctions against any over-persistent critics. Hence a certain pervasive wariness of uninhibited discussion within the membership of such powerful institutions, which, in remoter turn, may have had not a little to do with differences in the practices of working out and presenting arguments in what we have here still been calling the continental and analytic traditions.

And, fifthly, that things are by now significantly different on both sides of the philosophical Channel, across which genuinely informed discussion and working exchange has once again become possible. The how and why of this evolution would involve once again the telling of a number of interconnected stories. On both sides of the Channel there were in the beginning, no doubt, significant elements of anti-establishment reaction involved. But, of course, the prevailing establishments on each side were and are very different, and so to react against them carries very different significance in both intellectual, career and, in the broadest sense, institutional practice. However, the proper telling of these stories would call for far more time and space than we can dispose of here – and, for that matter, a far greater and more confident mastery of their varied circumstances than any I can pretend to possess.

Balliol College, Oxford
alanmontefiore@compuserve.com

Philosophy and Life in Ancient Greek and Roman Philosophy: Three Aspects

RICHARD SORABJI

Abstract

Philosophy, in the ancient Graeco-Roman world, and in various other cultures too, was typically thought of as, among other things, bearing on how to live. Questions of how to live may now be considered by some as merely one optional specialism among others, but Derek Parfit for one, we shall see, rightly treats implications for how to live as flowing naturally from metaphysical theories. In the hope of showing something about the ancient Graeco-Roman tradition as a whole, I shall speak of things that I and others have said before,[1] but I will highlight certain *aspects* of how the various groups or individuals related their philosophy to their lives. I shall start with the ancient Stoics as providing a clear case, then move on more briefly to their rivals, the Epicureans, and finally, more briefly again, to consider their predecessors and successors in other ancient schools and periods. This will not be a survey of the main central doctrines, although that is also something useful to attempt. But it will involve a selection of important ideas to illustrate their application to how to live.

1. Stoics

Stoicism was founded in 300 BCE in Athens by Zeno of Citium, who had first been trained by a Cynic, as well as by a Platonist, and Cynicism was very strikingly a way of life. Its first exponent, Diogenes, lived in a wine jar, rather than accept conventional comforts, and, when visited by Alexander the Great and asked what he would like from the conqueror of the world, he is said to have replied only, 'Stand out of my light'. Although his un-conventionalism was admired, few self-respecting Athenians would copy his lifestyle, and one of the clever things achieved by Zeno was to make some of the Cynic ideals a respectable philosophy that could be widely followed.[2] He used the word 'indifferent' in a new way to express agreement with the Cynic rejection of conventional objectives, but qualified it, by saying that some indifferent things were preferred

---

[1]   To avoid excessive reference to ancient texts, I will sometimes refer to an earlier treatment where references have been given.

[2]   Sorabji, *Gandhi and the Stoics* (henceforth *Gandhi*) (Oxford, 2012), 58–61.

doi:10.1017/S1358246114000125   © The Royal Institute of Philosophy and the contributors 2014
Royal Institute of Philosophy Supplement **74** 2014

by nature, not by convention, and these it was right to prefer for oneself and others, so long as they were available. Their indifference should be acted on only to remind oneself that it would not matter if they were to prove or had proven unavailable. On this view, very little mattered without qualification, only good character and the rational understanding on which character was taken to be based, and these were to be chosen. But still, natural objectives had a 'selective value', that is to say, they were the right thing to 'select' for oneself or others, where 'selection' expressed a more reserved attitude than choice. A typical reservation was 'if God wills'. Zeno thus gave a place after all to widely accepted objectives, and at the same time a central place to good character or virtue. To this he added another reassuring requirement, that people should take part in public life and rear a family, at least in normal circumstances.

Early Stoicism, however, still retained a very discouraging idea that anyone who is not virtuous is vicious, just as a drowning person cannot breathe, whether near the surface or at the bottom.[3] This was still compatible with the idea of moral progress, for a person struggling up towards the surface is progressing, though still not breathing. But since it allowed no degrees of virtue or vice, it moved the emphasis from distance travelled to the virtually unattainable terminus of the perfect Stoic sage, even though such sagehood was admitted to be as rare as the proverbial phoenix. Panaetius by contrast made Stoicism much more directly valuable to ordinary imperfect people. I do not mean that Marcus Aurelius, the Stoic Emperor of the Roman world, was ordinary, but he was neither an ideal sage, nor a wicked sinner, but a human who recognised his own imperfections and made light of his unusual liabilities. What Panaetius said (born c. 185 BCE, head of Stoic school 129–109), if Cicero is reporting Panaetius in his account in Latin, could be applied to Marcus too: since we do not live among perfect people, we should most cultivate those who are *most* adorned with propriety, temperance and justice.[4] The reference to those *most* adorned transforms Stoicism by allowing *degrees* of these virtues after all, and by attending to the achievements of ordinary people with their foibles and weaknesses. Cicero comments again on the greater utility of later Stoicism in his *On Laws*. The old Stoics, he says, before

---

[3] Cicero *On Ends* 3.14.48; Plutarch *On Common Notions* 1063A; *Gandhi* 116–7

[4] Cicero *On Duties* 1.46

Diogenes of Babylon and Panaetius, discussed the State alright, but not as a guide to popular civic utility.[5]

Cicero follows Panaetius' work on duties which considered how to decide on conflicts between moral considerations and between prudential considerations, and he takes up a promise, which he says Panaetius never fulfilled, of considering conflicts between moral and prudential considerations, although Cicero considers the last only *apparent* conflicts.[6] In Book 3 of his *On Duties*, Cicero reports the rival solutions of other Stoics on the last type of case: should the seller of a house warn the prospective buyer of rot? Other examples, such as who should get the only plank offering survival in a shipwreck, had been started by the challenging Platonist Carneades in 155 BCE. The debates give a foretaste of the casuistry of 1550–1650, and they concern dilemmas that people can imagine being real for themselves, although so far they concern special *types* of case, rather than the individuality of the moral agent. But Cicero records Panaetius as addressing *individuality* with his advice on *personae*.

In making decisions in life, one should consider who one is,[7] and not only, like Kant nearly two millennia later, that one is a rational being. That universally shared *persona* is indeed always to be observed, and ethics here appeals to a fact about human nature. But on its own our rationality does not give us enough guidance and is only the first *persona*.[8] Within the constraints of rationality, one must think also of particular duties to which one was born, or which one chose, and of one's particular abilities. In choosing a career, for example, should one follow one's parents' profession? If a parent was a successful lawyer, piety might suggest that one should follow the family precedent. But would you be good as a lawyer, or would you only let your parents down? Sometimes a *persona* is unique and calls for a unique decision. When Julius Caesar in the civil war captured the town of Utica, it was right for the Stoic Cato among the defenders to commit suicide, but not for anyone else in the same situation – the last phrase present only in some manuscripts – apparently because he had always stood for such uncompromising rectitude. No doubt, if there *had* been anyone else exactly like Cato, suicide would have been right for

---

5   Cicero *On Laws* 3.14
6   Cicero *On Duties* 1.9; 3.7
7   Different from 'Who am I?' is the question 'What sort of person do I *want* to be?'. This belongs not so much with Panaetius' subject of making right decisions (*kathêkonta*), as with the further objective of reaching virtue.
8   Cicero *On Duties* 1. 107–121

him too, but that is not mentioned because the morally interesting point is that there *was* no one exactly like Cato. Pierre Hadot, who has made the idea of Philosophy as a way of life so prominent, made the interesting point that Cato was a Stoic, without writing any Stoic texts. It should be added, however, that he *studied* Stoicism – Cicero met him reading in the same library[9] – and he built his life on what he read.[10] Under the Empire that followed the Roman Republic, Roman Senators are credited with resisting the Emperor to carry out their now restricted *persona* as senators, and it has been said that the charges against one of those executed included his being a Stoic.[11]

The Stoics have much advice on getting rid of undesirable emotions (*pathê*), that is, emotions based on false values. To show that they can be got rid of by taking rational thought, they developed the first systematic cognitive therapy. The Stoic Seneca in the first century CE took up the founder's view that emotions involve, and from the third head Chrysippus onwards, that they actually are, value judgements. Except in the case of a short list of good emotions (*eupatheiai*), they are *mistaken* value judgements, and so lead to collision with reality, but since they are *judgements*, not for example sensations, reason should be able to correct them. In a statement which, I think, is nearly true, they said that each emotion involves (or more dubiously is) two value judgements, the judgement that good or bad is at hand, and the judgement that it is appropriate to react accordingly.[12] The two judgements provide us with two targets for demolition, and demolishing either should demolish the emotion. It helps to distinguish the initial *appearance* of good or bad and of appropriate reaction, from the actual *judgement*. The *judgement* is produced by giving the assent of reason to the *appearance* and that assent can be withheld, while you assess the truth of the appearance. But non-Stoics are not trained to notice that there are two stages, and that one can stand back and reconsider the appearance. If it appears that something really bad has happened, as opposed to something merely dis-preferred, it may help to reflect that you are not the

---

[9]   Cicero *On Ends* 3.2.7

[10]   Pierre Hadot, 'Philosophy as a way of life', in his *Philosophy as a Way of Life* (Blackwell, Oxford, 1995), Ch. 11, page 272, translated from the French of *Exercices spirituels et philosophie antique* (Paris, 1981).

[11]   Epictetus *Discourses* 1.2; Miriam Griffin, *Seneca, A philosopher in Politics* (Oxford University Press, paperback 1992), 363, citing Tacitus *Annals* 16.22

[12]   Seneca *On Anger* 2.2–4

only one to have suffered this. If it appears that retaliation is the appropriate reaction, it may help to reflect that you have recently treated someone else the same way. There is another safeguard besides that of distinguishing the two judgements from each other and from the two appearances with a view to demolishing one of the appearances. The appearances may first produce an initial shock, a 'pre-passion' or 'first movement', before they lead on to assent or judgement, which is said to be the real emotion. The shock may be a sensation or a physical reaction of teeth chattering, hair standing on end, growing pale or heated. It helps to distinguish the mere shock from the emotion, so as to avoid what I have called the William James effect. William James said, 'we do not cry because we are sad; we are sad because we cry'. That is a danger: we are inclined to think, 'I am crying; I must have been badly treated'. But that does not follow. You are crying, so you are crying, and you should ignore that as unimportant. The important question is whether you have really been badly treated. For assessing the two appearances the Stoics have a whole host of further questions to ask yourself, many of which I have described elsewhere.[13] Particularly useful is distinguishing the un-expected from the bad, since the unfamiliar often presents itself as harmful, when in fact it may be neutral or even advantageous.

This appeal to the deceptions of the unexpected, of the merely dis-preferred, or of forgetting the similarity of your own past conduct is an appeal to life, rather than to philosophy. But if philosophy is to be applied to your life, it is not surprising that you have to take life into account as well as philosophy. The philosophy here is not, or not exclusively, a piece of ethics. It is a very penetrating analysis of the nature of emotions as involving two value-judgements and two stages, the first of which can give rise to shocks. This would be put in the separate compartment of philosophy of mind, not ethics, in the modern philosophy curriculum. But for the Stoics, the braches of philosophy are a seamless whole. How to tackle your emotional life is an ethical question. But I believe that philosophy of mind and other branches of philosophy are actually needed for the ethical conclusions about what to do. Seneca's *Letter* 95 is about the value of doctrines in ethical life. I believe the doctrines are not necessarily ethical. I imagine they would include doctrines from the philosophy of mind. A view has been put on the other side that philosophy cannot

---

[13]   Richard Sorabji, *Emotion and Peace of Mind: From Stoic Agitation to Christian Temptation* (Oxford University Press, 2000), Chs 15 and 16

Richard Sorabji

help with emotional life; that is the task of psychiatry.[14] Indeed, it is true that only some emotional problems yield to cognitive therapy. The Stoics themselves believed that their therapy would deal with bereavement. I have said elsewhere that in my view that involves a kind of detachment from friends and family that is impoverishing. But there is no price to be paid for using Stoic therapy for the ordinary ups and downs of daily life.

The doctor Galen in the second century CE, though first stabilising emotion and mental capacities by the right diet,[15] used Stoic techniques for eradicating anger and distress in two works, one only recently discovered, *On Avoiding Distress*.[16] Here he explains how he avoided distress after losing much of his highly original work in a fire after storing it in the safest place in Rome with a view to organising back-up copies later in the year.

The Stoics advocated a special kind of freedom, being one's own agent, which did not require freedom in the sense of not being subordinate or not being a slave.[17] An account of it was given by Epictetus in his discourse on freedom.[18] By making sure that your heart is set only on what is within your power, you can be freed from both inner tyrannies and outer, so that you are enslaved to nothing, not to house, farm, horses, clothes, furniture, family. As if writing for academics, he adds books,[19] and, finally your own body. He gives his students a large number of exercises to rehearse setting their hearts only on what is so fully under the control of their will that no tyrant could take it away. They are to engage in the mental exercise of imagining a threatening outer tyrant. You can tell him that he cannot put *you* in chains, only your leg, since you have identified yourself only with a will (an inadequate rendering of *prohairesis*) that cannot be constrained. In other words you have created a self, and a self which is inviolable. Such exercises are to be 'ready to hand (*prokheiron*)'. Philosophers ought to practise them (*meletân*),

---

[14] Bernard Williams, 'Stoic philosophy and the emotions: a reply to Richard Sorabji', in Richard Sorabji, ed., *Aristotle and After*, Bulletin of the Institute of Classical Studies, supplementary volume **68** (1997), 211–13, available from http://events.sas.ac.uk/support-research/publications/596
[15] Galen, *That states of mind follow the chemistry of the body*, 67, 2–16
[16] The other is Galen, *On the diagnosis and therapy of the distinctive passions of the individual's soul*.
[17] Diogenes Laertius, *Lives of Eminent Philosophers*, 7.121
[18] Epictetus, *Discourses* 4.1
[19] Epictetus, *Discourses* 4.4, 1–2

write them down every day, and train themselves (*gumnazein*).[20] He sends his students out at dawn to report what they saw: a consul passing by, a man grieving over his dead child. When they give their reports, he asks if the consulship or life and death are under the control of the will. No? Then they must throw their attachment to such things away.[21] Epictetus finds only two examples of this freedom as inviolability, namely Diogenes the Cynic and Socrates. In a famous lecture, 'Two concepts of liberty',[22] Isaiah Berlin said that this was not freedom, but sour grapes, the attitude that what is unavailable is no good anyhow. But, rare though it is, in adverse circumstances it has supplied more than one person with genuine freedom. This is how Gandhi remained freer than the viceroys when they had him put in prison, since they were afraid of the consequences if he came to harm, while he had abandoned all such attachments.[23]

Seneca's *Letters*, an artistic exercise in correspondence, though written as to his real friend Lucilius, address the anxieties of an ordinary person who is to be introduced gradually to Stoicism. Should he take early retirement from the rat race? Is he too anxious about his health? What physical exercise is appropriate for a philosopher? Not exercise that builds up the body, nothing more than walking. But even better is being carried in a litter, which joggles every muscle in your body, while allowing you to continue dictating your thoughts to the secretary who is hurrying alongside. At the same period, Epictetus' teacher Musonius Rufus addresses equally common anxieties in short essays. Should a young person always obey their parents? What if your father forbids you to study philosophy?

The Stoics argued that it was in accordance with nature and right, which is not to say that it was easy, to extend a feeling of kinship to all humans, recognising them as fellow rational beings, and that this made justice to all humans, even foreigners and slaves, natural and right. Hierocles around the end of the first century CE spoke of circles of fellow-humans surrounding each person and advocated drawing outer circles nearer in to oneself at the centre. He further

[20]   Epictetus, *Discourses* 1.1.23
[21]   Epictetus *Discourses* 3.3.14–19
[22]   1958, first printed in Isaiah Berlin, *Four Essays on Liberty* (Oxford University Press), reprinted in his *Liberty*, ed. Henry Hardy (Oxford University Press, 2002)
[23]   Richard Sorabji, *Gandhi and the Stoics* (Oxford and Chicago University Presses, 2012), Ch. 3

suggested exercises for doing so: we should call cousins 'brothers' and aunts and uncles 'fathers and mothers'.[24] Some cultures indeed do draw family distinctions differently and partially follow this advice.

The Stoic idea of justice being naturally owed to all humans was to have a long history. It would be used in the 16th century Spanish opposition to the conquest of the American Indians in Latin America.[25] It contrasted with the view of their Epicurean rivals of humans as gaining security from each other only by contracts not to harm or be harmed, whether or not Epicurus' successors Hermarchus and (writing in Latin) Lucretius, added modifications.[26] This suggests a very different psychological view of one's fellow-humans as potential threats. Such a view might be needlessly self-fulfilling. But it was to be equally influential. Thomas Hobbes drew on it in the 17th century in his *Leviathan*, to make a case for a contract with a powerful sovereign to guarantee security, a role he would present as fitting equally the king's replacement, Oliver Cromwell, or the restored monarch, Charles II.

I have left to last the most discussed example of the Stoic interconnexion of the nature of the universe with ethics. This was their belief in divine Providence as a backing for ethical conclusions. I have postponed it for two reasons. First, I have been looking for examples, such as the analysis of emotion – whatever analysis may commend itself to the reader – which do not depend on views that many nowadays repudiate. Not everyone now believes in divine Providence. Secondly, the Stoic conception of Providence is different from that of the Christian New Testament, according to which every hair of your head is numbered and not a sparrow falls to the ground without God, or is forgotten before him.[27] Stoic Providence attends to individual humans indeed, but neglects small matters

---

[24] Hierocles *Elements of Ethics*, excerpts preserved in Stobaeus *Florilegia*, ed. Hense, 4.671,7–673,11, partly translated in A.A. Long. D.N. Sedley, *The Hellenistic Philosophers* (Cambridge University Press, 1987), Ch. 57, text G.

[25] Relevant texts are cited in Richard Sorabji, 'Just war from ancient origins to the Conquistadors debate and its modern relevance', in Richard Sorabji, David Rodin, eds, *The Ethics of War: Shared Problems in Different Traditions* (Ashgate, Aldershot, 2006), 18.

[26] Epicurus *Key Doctrines* 31–7; Hermarchus ap. Porphyry *On Abstinence*, 1.7.1–1.12.7, but the reference in 1.7.1 to fellow feeling as one factor may be a comment by Porphyry. Lucretius inserts a stage of monogamy, families, winsome children and friendships as leading to contracts, *On the nature of things*, 5.1011–27

[27] Matthew 10:29; Luke 12:6.

like the destruction of an individual's crops,[28] which are anyhow indifferent. Later the Stoic Emperor Marcus Aurelius in the 2nd century CE went further. He coped with the dangers he faced by stressing that we are *only* parts of a larger whole, which seems to make us less significant as individuals.[29]

In this short recapitulation, I have highlighted three features of Stoicism, and particularly of later Stoicism. One is the use of mental exercises to give the philosophy impact on one's life.[30] A second, prominent in later Stoicism from Panaetius onwards, is the concern with the particular. A third is the need to bring other branches of philosophy to bear, besides ethics, in drawing ethical conclusions, so that ethics is treated as but one part of philosophy as a seamless whole. Although I shall speak of exercises quite frequently, I am not using the term here in as broad a way as has been made famous by Pierre Hadot's talk of spiritual exercises. For Hadot is not merely saying, as I will, that the Socratic dialogues *contain* some exercises useful for life that the reader can re-use, such as Socrates' appeal at one point to his *persona*. Rather, his point is that a Socratic dialogue *is* a spiritual exercise for the reader, because it seeks to convert the reader's soul, so that someone entering into philosophy will be entering into a way of life. I shall later come to a very clear example of this happening in the Neoplatonist Simplicius. But I am not otherwise addressing philosophy as *itself* an exercise, nor, in a phrase that Hadot has also made famous, as a *way* of life, but only as *containing* exercises which are a *help* to life. Hadot also draws attention to what I have called the seamlessness of the branches of philosophy, logic, physics and ethics. But he is not speaking, as I am, of them often entering into a seamless *exposition*. Rather he is willing to concede that for *expository* purposes they are divided into branches by seams. His point is rather that, as a spiritual exercise, philosophy is a 'single act, renewed at every instant, that one can describe, without breaking its unity, as being the exercise of logic as well of physics or of ethics, according to the directions in which it is exercised'.[31]

---

[28] Cicero *On the nature of the gods* 2. 167
[29] Julia Annas, *The Morality of Happiness* (Oxford University Press 1993), Ch. 5, on Marcus especially pages 175–6
[30] On this see Paul Rabbow, *Seelenführung* (Munich, 1954)
[31] I am here following Arnold I. Davidson's quotation from a work of Pierre Hadot's, in the introduction to a set of Hadot's papers, translated by Michael Chase and edited by himself, *Philosophy as a Way of Life* (Blackwell, Oxford, 1995). The collection contains a translation of some of

Richard Sorabji

As regards seamless *exposition*, the situation in Stoicism has been made very clear by others, and my main task will be to consider other groups. At first it was widely thought that Stoic ethics rested on physics as a base. But an influential paper by Jacques Brunschwig showed the situation to be more complex. He cited Plutarch as complaining[32] that the Stoic Chrysippus gave the right order of exposition as logic, ethics, physics, but that he contradicted himself because in three of his texts physics formed a basis for ethics. Brunschwig pointed out, however, that these three texts were texts about *physics*, but that there were other texts which treated ethics on its own. He concluded that ethics would be presented *twice over* to Stoic students, first on its *own*, as Hadot had been willing to concede, but later enriched, when physics was expounded, by being shown to fit in with the larger picture of the physical universe. This finding was developed by others and now has a wide following, but some interrelation between the exposition of ethics and physics was never in doubt among the parties to the discussion.[33] As for Stoic *logic* permeating their ethics, Brunschwig found logic also treated twice over in an ancient catalogue of Chrysippus' works, arranged in his preferred order of logic, ethics, physics. Although works on the *theory* of dialectical argument came in the opening section on logic, the second section on ethics contained logic *all over again* as applied to ethics, with works on dialectical premises for ethical arguments and demonstrative proofs of ethical arguments.

2. Epicureans

Of the three features I have been stressing, particularism is the least common, but the other two features, the seamlessness of philosophy and the value of exercises for guidance, are found in the Epicurean school, founded also in Athens seven years before the Stoics in 307

---

the most relevant articles at chapters 3 and 11, but Davidson is here referring to several other papers by him and quoting one of them.

[32] Plutarch *On Stoic Self-Contradictions*, 1035A ff

[33] Jacques Brunschwig, 'On a book title by Chrysippus, "On the fact that the ancients admitted dialectic along with demonstrations"', *Oxford Studies in Ancient Philosophy*, supplementary vol. (1991) 81–96; developed by Julia Annas, *The Morality of Happiness* (Oxford University Press, 1993), Ch. 4; Gabor Betegh, 'Cosmological ethics in the *Timaeus* and early Stoicism', *Oxford Studies in Ancient Philosophy*, **24** (2003), 273–302, and others.

BCE. A major concern of the Epicureans was avoiding fear of death, which Lucretius describes as acting unconsciously to drive restlessness and ambition.[34] The fear can take many forms, a number of which they discussed. One form is horror, shared only by some people, not others, at the thought that after death, one will never exist again. We will not then know, but we can be harmed by things of which we never know, and in this case we may now know, or expect, the outcome which instils horror. The Epicureans thought that freedom from pain was our primary aim, and we will, admittedly, not then be in pain. But the Stoics held that our primary initial aim was self-preservation, and we will not then be preserved.[35] Epicurus said that we are made of atoms which will be dispersed at death, and so are our souls. So many of the fears are groundless. We will not be there to be punished or to suffer in any other way. This provides another case of the seamlessness of philosophy, because a materialist theory of humans and indeed of the universe, is used to advise us on the right attitudes to life and death. But the answer does not so far address horror at non-existence, as opposed to suffering.

Epicurus' follower Lucretius has been credited with a reply to this, that we feel no horror at our past non-existence before birth, so why should we feel horror at future non-existence, since the two are mirror-images of each other?[36] In my 1983 treatment of this subject, I expressed doubt whether Lucretius was addressing horror at future *non-existence* or fear of future *suffering*, and this doubt is corroborated in a very thorough treatment by James Warren, who also looked to see whether the argument about future non-existence is to be found in non-Epicureans.[37] The author in whom I was inclined to think that there may be such an argument, but concerning the death of *another* person, was the Platonist Plutarch, to whom I shall come later, in his *Consolation to his wife*, 610D concerning the death of their daughter. He said: 'Try in your thought to move and restore yourself repeatedly to the time when the child was not yet born, and we had no complaint against fortune. Then match this present time to that one, seeing that our

---

[34] Lucretius *On the nature of things* 3. 59–97; 1053–70
[35] Epicurus *Key Doctrines* 2; Stoics in Cicero *On Ends* 3.16
[36] Lucretius *On the nature of things* 2.972–7
[37] Richard Sorabji, *Time, Creation and the Continuum* (Duckworth:London, 1983; repr. Chicago University Press, 2006; Bloomsbury London, 2012), 176–9; James Warren, *Facing Death, Epicurus and his Critics* (Cambridge University Press, 2004).

circumstances have become the same again. If we make things before she was born less a cause of complaint, we shall seem to be regretting her birth.'

Whoever did or did not address horror at future non-existence, the argument is a powerful one, and my reaction to it was that the difference of attitude to future and past, though widespread in human attitudes, is shown to be irrational in the case of non-existence, but that that does not help us, because the difference of attitude to past and future non-existence has been made inescapable at least for many people by natural selection. Those little children, if there were any, who felt less anxiety about future non-existence than about past non-existence did not live long enough to pass on their preferences to any offspring. Derek Parfit came up independently with a partly similar conclusion shortly afterwards, that natural selection may have established our various preferences between past and future, but argued with highly thought-provoking examples for a different conclusion, that we might be better off without these preferences in a variety of cases, not only concerning our non-existence.[38] In returning to the subject in 2006, I considered the limitations of philosophy in affecting our attitudes. The argument about past non-existence will not liberate those who feel horror from a feeling caused by natural selection. But by convincing them that the horror is irrational, it can prevent the horror being intensified through the thought, 'how rational it is to be horrified'.[39] Even if Lucretius' appeal to past non-existence does not address horror at future non-existence, but only fear of future *suffering*, it still constitutes a thought exercise, and the Epicurean discussion of how to face death, illustrates not only the value of thought exercises, but also the seamless connexion of a materialistic physics with ethical conclusions. I should say that Parfit does the same. His use of thought exercises to draw conclusions on how to live is as powerful as any of the ancient examples, and he also illustrates the seamlessness of Philosophy, by bringing to bear arguments about personal identity on appropriate attitudes.

The Epicureans also made a contribution to the subject of moral conscience, and this brought in exercises of various kinds. This is despite Cicero and Seneca ascribing to to Epicurus a view of

---

[38] Derek Parfit, *Reasons and Persons* (Oxford University Press, 1984), corrected 1987, 174–7; 186. I discuss his view in *Self: Ancient and Modern Insights about Individuality, Life and Death* (Oxford and Chicago University Presses, 2006), Ch. 15.

[39] Richard Sorabji, *Self: Ancient and Modern Insights about Individuality, Life and Death*, 337–341

conscience as merely *fear* of detection and punishment.[40] Cicero finds this an unsettling form of conscience and complains that Epicurus rejects the steady conscience that he believes in.[41] It is true that the Epicurean Lucretius in the first century BCE, using a standard Latin term for conscience, says that the mind which shares consciousness with itself (*sibi conscia*) of bad deeds torments itself with *fears* about the Furies and punishment after death in Tartarus, even though punishment cannot come from supernatural sources, nor after death, when our atoms will have dispersed.[42] But Cicero ascribes to Epicurus a more fruitful idea, closer to our own idea of conscience: that of being *watched*. People believe (wrongly according to Epicurus) that even if they escape human eyes, they are watched by the gods, and so they are troubled in conscience (*conscientia*).[43] Epicurus held that members of the school should *imagine* that *he* was watching them as a witness to avert wrongdoing.[44] As well as imagining a watcher as *witness*, Epicurus is credited by Seneca with the idea of imagining an admired philosopher as an example (*exemplum*). This moves from one function of conscience, averting wrongdoing, to another, directing towards doing right. Both ideas are credited to Epicurus in a single passage.[45] Epicurus' imagined philosophical watcher was approved by the Stoics, who allowed a choice of imagined watchers, not confined, as by Epicurus, to any one person. I believe that it was from the Stoics, and hence indirectly from Epicurus that Adam Smith in the 18th century acquired his idea of conscience as an imagined impartial spectator.[46]

Still more striking is the connexion made by the Epicurean Philodemus around 100 BCE between conscience and the practice of *confession*. Philodemus' *Rhetoric* describes people who because of a guilty conscience (*syneidêsis*) engage in law suits until they are convicted and ruined.[47] But more striking for our purposes is the treatise *On frank criticism* about the practices in the residential school in Athens two hundred years after Epicurus, which included confession by students and even teachers more than a hundred years before the

---

40 Seneca, *Letters* 97, 15–16; Cicero, *On ends* 2.16.53
41 Cicero, *On ends* 2.22.71
42 Lucretius *On the Nature of Things*, Book 3, lines 1011–1024
43 Cicero, *On Ends* 1.16.51
44 Seneca, *Letters* 25.5
45 Seneca, *Letters* 11.8–10
46 Adam Smith, *Theory of Moral Sentiments*, Part III, Ch. 1
47 Philodemus, *Rhetoric* II, *frg.* 11, lines 1–9 (Sudhaus), 139–40

Richard Sorabji

birth of Christ.[48] One fragment declares: 'Even the servants share his (guilty) knowledge (*synoidasin*)'.[49] Another fragment, on the standard reading, says that if the professor quickly turns away from assisting the student who is slipping up, the student's swelling (*synoidêsis*) will subside.[50] Why should professorial neglect make a *swelling* subside? This makes no sense, and an emendation suggested a long time ago by C. J. Vooys should be accepted. *Syneidêsis* (conscience) differs from *synoidêsis* (swelling) by only the one letter 'e', which, in Greek as in English, looks very like an 'o'. Moreover four short lines later the related verb *syneidenai* appears. It makes perfect sense that the student's conscience will become less intense, if the professor does not attend to criticism and help of the right sort. This gives us a picture of the Epicurean school in Athens at the time of Philodemus' teacher, Zeno of Tarsus, in the second century BCE which Philodemus is describing. Confession is concerned with the past, but the school is concerned with the future-looking functions of conscience and wants to develop the consciences of its students through a process of confession of misdemeanours and carefully tailored, but frank, criticism. Both the confession and the imagining of a witness or an exemplary model are thought exercises designed for guidance. Both involve something highly personal, an imagined witness or model chosen in the Stoic case by the individual and a confessional interchange between student and teacher. Of course the guidance supplied by the imagined model or by the teacher conducting the confession would vary according to the teacher or the model in question. In the case of Epicurus, we can tell from his writings what the guidance would be like and it would follow *general* Epicurean principles even though it was addressed to a *particular* individual about their particular circumstances.

3. Pre-Socratic philosophers

I will now go back to the beginnings of Greek Philosophy, to the Pre-Socratic philosophers of the 6th and 5th centuries BCE, and will proceed in chronological order. The Pre-Socratic philosophers were individuals, Greek-speaking, but starting on the coast of what is now Turkey and quickly spreading to Sicily and the heel of Italy.

---

[48] Philodemus, *On frank criticism, frg.* 41
[49] Philodemus, *On frank criticism,* col. XIIa, line 5
[50] Philodemus, *On frank criticism, frg.* 67. I thank David Sider for showing me the emendation.

58

Some began schools in their areas, but no one school or town was dominant. However, because the Greeks were sea-farers and many towns were by the coast, they could much more quickly hear of developments elsewhere, or even move, as Pythagoras did by 530 BCE from the island of Samos in the East to the Italian town of Croton in the West.

The most discussed case of seamlessness in philosophy concerns Empedocles of Agrigentum in Sicily (c. 495–435 BCE), who accepted some of the views of Pythagoras in his philosophical poetry. Poetry was a common medium for important ideas and we are told of two titles for Empedocles' poetry, *Purifications*, and *On nature*. Because we have only fragmentary excerpts preserved, it was long thought that there were two poems. In *Purifications*, Empedocles laments that, though he is a *daemon*, a divine spirit, he has been punished for eating meat and needs to be purified by being reincarnated in successive different forms which he can remember, currently as a human, but at other times as an animal or even a bush. The fact, earlier accepted by Pythagoras and others, that one can be reincarnated as an animal Empedocles takes as meaning that in sacrificing and eating animals one may be eating one's own family: 'The father lifts up his own son changed in form, great fool, and with a prayer slays him shrieking piteously and beseeching as he sacrifices. But he, heedless of his cries, slays him and has an evil meal prepared in his halls. Likewise son seizing father and children their mother, tear out the life and eat the flesh of their own'.[51] We do not have his explanation of why it is alright to eat plants. Other fragments describe the history of the universe and the periodic evolution of animals and humans, capable of sexual reproduction after natural selection has eliminated unviable combinations of organs. These bodies are made from what Empedocles is the first to identify as the four elements, earth air, fire and water, themselves divine beings that are cyclically combined or separated by the two forces of Love and Strife. It was occasionally suggested that the two themes might belong to one poem, a view argued in detail in 1987,[52] and the editing and publication of new fragments in 1999,[53] confirmed that at least the themes were *connected*, as a

---

[51] Empedocles, Fragment 137, Diels-Kranz

[52] A powerful case was made by Catherine Osborne, now Rowett, in 'Empedocles Recycled', *Classical Quarterly* **37** (1987), 24–50. She saw the ethical theme of purification as dominant.

[53] Alain Martin, Oliver Primavesi, *L'Empédocle de Strasbourg, Introduction, édition et commentaire* (De Gruyter, 1999)

number of ancient sources had claimed, whether or not there was only one poem. For our purposes what matters is that the reconstructions showed various ways in which it would be perfectly possible to inter-connect Empedocles theory of the history of the universe with ethical conclusions about bloodshed, and that Empedocles seems to have done so.

Pythagoras (who had left Samos by 530 BCE) left no written phil-osophy behind. One of the few pieces of contemporary evidence about him comes from Xenophanes (c.570–c.475), that he forebade the beating of a dog, because he heard in its yelping a friend's voice. So we can take it that, like Empedocles after him, he drew con-clusions from his views about our reincarnation as animals concern-ing how we should treat them. Even so, later authors claim that his rules were adapted to circumstances, one might say to *personae*, in that he allowed meat to an athlete.[54] If Pythagoreans lived then, as later, in secluded communities,[55] he might well have made stricter rules for them, but not the same rules for everyone. What he is said to have warned the athlete against was concern with victory. We hear later of many Pythagorean exercises which may have originated in these communities, some that were to be adopted by Stoics, such as nightly self-interrogation on one's day-time conduct, or renouncing a feast at the last moment, avoiding soft beds and warm baths, and cor-recting anger by looking at its effect on your face,[56] while other exer-cises, poverty and silence, are said to have lasted for the first five years of initiation.[57] The practice of self-interrogation at bedtime was learnt from the Pythagoreans by the Christian Origen as well as by the Stoics Seneca and Epictetus, but whereas Origen and Epictetus applied it with the compunction originally intended, Seneca was more self-congratulatory with his different perspective of progressing towards virtue.[58]

There is no contemporary evidence for Pythagoras already having the later Pythagorean interest in numbers in things in the physical

[54] Porphyry, *On Abstinence* 1.26; *Life of Pythagoras* 15; Diogenes Laertius *Lives of eminent philosophers* 8.12, disbelieved by Iamblichus, *On the Pythagorean Life* 5.25
[55] Porphyry, *On Abstinence* 1.36; Iamblichus *On the Pythagorean Life* 21.96
[56] References in my *Emotion and Peace of Mind* (Oxford University Press, 2000), 213–4
[57] Timaeus frag. 13a Jacoby; Schol. on Plato *Phaedrus* 279C; Diogenes Laertius *Lives* 8.10 and 23; 10.11; Iamblichus *On the Pythagorean Life* para-graph 72. 17
[58] Richard Sorabji, *Gandhi and the Stoics*, 147

world. But the Pythagoreans were credited with discovering the mathematical ratios of string lengths in pairs of plucked consonant notes, and with looking for numbers in astronomy and cosmology. Plato was to take over both the interest in reincarnation in his *Meno*, *Phaedo* and *Phaedrus*, including reincarnation as animals in his *Timaeus*, and the interest in numbers, even though he claims to go beyond the Pythagorean concern with using numbers to explain music[59] and perhaps astronomy. Indeed, it has been argued that he makes numbers responsible for the entire orderly structure of the cosmos, going beyond the Pythagoreans in making arithmetic prior to geometry, with numbers defining the triangular shapes of which the three-dimensional universe is physically composed and defining the soul which makes it rotate. The connexion of physical philosophy with mathematics is seamless.[60]

Democritus of Abdera in Northern Greece (fl. After 435 BCE), though most famed as the co-inventor with Leucippus of the theory of atoms, has far more fragments surviving on ethics, many of them conjecturally assigned to his treatise *On Contentment*. Two fragments, 3 and 191 Diels-Kranz, advise moderate pleasures, like the later atomist Epicurus, keeping in mind what you can attain, and recognising those less fortunate than yourself, and keeping in mind the limits to what you can attain. The last has been compared with the later appeal to *personae*.[61] We need not believe the story that he accepted the request of the bereaved King Darius of Persia to bring his wife back to life, but on condition that the king found three members of his great kingdom who had not suffered bereavement too. This circulating story has been attached to more than one philosopher and has an analogue in Indian thought. Did Democritus connect particular kinds of atomic motion in the soul with cheerfulness? Fragment 191 says that souls are not cheerful if big movements are set up which move them out of large intervals (*diastêmata*). If the reference is to physical motions of atoms, are they being moved by large disparities of fortune, or by large movements, or, as James Warren has suggested possible, away from the

---

[59]   Plato *Republic* 531C

[60]   Marwan Rashed, Nellie Wallace lectures (Oxford University, 2013), partly explained in his 'Plato's Five Worlds hypothesis (*Ti* 55cd)', in Riccardo Chiardonna, Gabriele Galluzzo, eds, *Universals in Ancient Philosophy* (Edizioni della Normale, Pisa, 2013), 87–112

[61]   Christopher Gill, 'Peace of mind and being yourself: Panaetius to Plutarch', *Aufstieg und Niedergang der römischen Welt*, 2.36.7, 4599–4640.

wide intervals needed for quick-moving atoms?[62] Unfortunately, it has not proved possible to determine whether Democritus intends such a seamless connexion between his atomism and his ethics.

4. Socrates and Plato

Socrates (469–399 BCE) left no writing, but is represented in the dialogues of Plato (427–348 BCE) as talking to individuals about their beliefs and values. The dialogues are not historical records, but works of art based on Plato's knowledge of Socrates. In the *Euthyphro* Socrates is imagined as starting from a particular action, Euthyphro's proposal to sue his father. He conducts the discussion on the basis of the interlocutor's own beliefs, but he draws it away from the particular to the general, in this case to the question, what is piety? He typically ends in uncertainty. Plato makes Socrates claim in his *Gorgias*, despite his turning people away from current political values, that in trying to make people good, he alone was practising true politics.[63] These dialogues have been judged early on stylometric grounds. Rather different from the other early dialogues was Plato's *Apology*, in which Plato makes Socrates put forward his *own* views in his defence at his trial on capital charges of introducing new gods and corrupting the youth. In Plato's *Crito,* Socrates is made to explain why he should not avoid execution by escaping from prison. He is persuaded among other things by an appeal to his *individual* history, which foreshadows the systematic appeal to individual *personae* later on in Panaetius, the Stoic. Since Socrates has been content never to leave Athens, except on military service, he has thereby shown himself satisfied with Athenian laws which have condemned him and should abide by them.[64] Socrates' claim to be warned off certain particular decisions by an inner guardian spirit, or *daemôn*, is first found in Plato's *Apology*, and was a ground for the charge of introducing new gods. Although the *daemôn* addressed *particular* decisions, it was later equated by Plato in his *Timaeus* with Socrates' intellect,[65] and the principles on which it admonished would in that case have been understood to be *general*. The individual debates in which Plato shows Socrates engaging are not like the

[62] James Warren, *Epicurus and Democritean Ethics* (Cambridge University Press, 2002), 58–72

[63] Plato *Gorgias* 521A-D

[64] Plato *Crito* 52A-D

[65] Plato *Timaeus* 90 A-D

thought exercises we have found in others. But Socrates is credited by Plutarch, and by the Stoic Seneca, with an exercise noticed by his friends not so much in thought as in behaviour. To avoid becoming harsh in his arguments, he would lower his voice, put on a smile, and change his facial expression. Seneca recommends this behavioural exercise, adding slowing one's gait.[66]

Plato was not present on the day of Socrates' execution, which he describes in the *Phaedo*, and it is commonly thought that the theory of Forms he here puts into Socrates' mouth, was not Socrates' but Plato's. He also represents Socrates as telling his grieving companions that philosophy is, in a certain sense, practising death.[67] Practising death here is purification of the soul by separating it from bodily desires; it is emphatically not suicide, a misconception which Socrates corrects. This gave rise in the Neoplatonists to the idea of levels of virtue. Plato went on later in his *Republic* to describe the virtue instilled into his ideal city there as civic (*dêmotikê*) virtue. Justice and other virtues in that ideal city involve the *irrational* parts of the soul, the parts concerned with indignation and *bodily* appetites. But if we could see the soul in its true nature, without parts, not encrusted by barnacles from the *body*, but in its philosophy or love of wisdom, then we would see justice more clearly.[68] From Plotinus and Porphyry onwards, the Neoplatonists distinguished the merely civic (*politikê*) virtue of the *Republic* from the purified (*kathartikê*) virtue of the *Phaedo*, and still higher levels of virtue than these. In Alexandria of the 6th century CE, prolegomena were written to the philosophy curriculum, which offered different definitions of philosophy, including practising death by purification from the body. They also warned against the misinterpretation of one, Cleombrotus, who accepted the definition of philosophy as an invitation to commit suicide, so that discussion was required of when and whether suicide was permissible.[69]

I have already mentioned Plato's interest in reincarnation in the *Meno* and *Phaedo*, and in the later dialogues *Timaeus* and *Phaedrus*, and how it illustrates the seamless connexion of ethics with other branches of philosophy. But the *Phaedrus* gives the most poetic illustration of this. Erotic love is justified through Socrates' mouth by a theory of the universe. It is a divine madness caused when physical

---

[66] Seneca *On Anger* 3.13.3; Plutarch *On freedom from anger* 455A-B
[67] Plato *Phaedo* 64A
[68] Plato *Republic* 500 D; 611A–612A
[69] Richard Sorabji, Introduction to *Aristotle Transformed*, (Duckworth, London, 1990)

beauty reminds one unconsciously of the Form of Beauty glimpsed by the soul to various degrees when it is allowed every 10,000 years, or in the case of philosophers every 3000, to process, disembodied, round the heavens in the train of an appropriate god, before again losing its wings and returning to successive incarnations.[70]

As brought out by Myles Burnyeat and Marwan Rashed,[71] Plato asserts a seamless connexion also between *mathematics* and ethics, as well as aesthetics, in his *Republic*, *Timaeus*, *Philebus*, and perhaps in his lost but legendary mathematical lecture on the Good, identifying it with unity, although no one else understood, according to Aristoxenus.[72] Mathematical ratios are found not only in music and astronomy and the other mathematical sciences, but also in the constitution of the World Soul, which supposedly drives the stars around us and of human souls and in the constitution of cities, and in the virtues of the soul and virtues in cities, where the ratios are harmonious. The reference to virtue expresses a connexion between mathematics and the Good, which is the supreme subject to be understood by the rulers of the ideal State described in Plato's *Republic*. Their training gives their souls harmonious ratios first by music and gymnastics and then by ten years of higher mathematics, culminating in harmonics, the study of ratios. By studying the ratios in the circuits of the stars they make similar the ratios in the circuits of their own rational souls. The virtues they need and the virtues they will need to understand and to inculcate into citizens all involve harmonious ratios in the soul. Mathematical training is not enough on its own for coming to understand the Good, but mathematics gives the first understanding that ordinary justice is a mere shadow, and if the Good has a mathematical character, this will be used in applying true justice in governing the State.

Plato, then, not only ascribes to Socrates a particularist reason for not escaping prison, but also gives expression to the seamless connexion of ethics with other branches of philosophy and with mathematics. We might expect him as one of the most imaginative of all

[70]   Plato *Phaedrus* 243E–257B
[71]   Myles Burnyeat, 'Plato on why mathematics is good for the soul', in Timothy Smiley, ed., *Mathematics and Necessity*, Proceedings of the British Academy vol. 103 (Oxford University Press), 1–81; Marwan Rashed will, 'Plato's five worlds hypothesis (*Tim 55* c-d), mathematics and universals', in R. Chiaradonna, G. Galluzzo, eds, *Universals in Ancient Philosophy*, Pisa 2013, pp. 87–112.
[72]   Aristoxenus, *Elementa Harmonica* II I, 30, 20–31, 2, Meibom

Philosophy and Life in Ancient Greek and Roman Philosophy

Western philosophers to provide the third feature of inquiry, thought exercises for guidance. Certainly he portrays characters being given thought exercises, as when the slave in the Meno is given a geometrical exercise, or he makes Glaucon object to Socrates in the *Republic*, that everyone would be unjust, if they owned the magic ring of Gyges which could make them invisible. This is used as a ground for suggesting, before Epicurus, that justice is not natural but based on contract.[73] But Plato does not use these thought exercises to help the individual reader decide what to do, or how to maintain resolve. Perhaps there is a reason for this. Although Plato came to abandon the argument he gives Socrates against Protagoras that it is not in human nature to be willing (*ethelein*) to go after what one *thinks* (*oiesthai*) bad, instead of good things,[74] he nonetheless held to the view that genuine *knowledge* of what is the better course is effective. So *knowledge* will not need further exercises as aids. Even Aristotle was prepared to say that what is overthrown by temptation is not knowledge (*epistêmê*) from one's deliberations about the best policies for a good life, but the full awareness of the particular fact that you are failing to follow them.[75] What Plato does do in the *Republic* is to offer a discussion that would later be used by others as a helpful thought exercise. He discusses how the philosopher is a lover of the whole of knowledge, just as an erotic lover is a lover of the whole person and may even be found to re-label the sallow as honey-coloured.[76] The Epicurean Lucretius derides such re-labelling, in order to cure us of the disturbances of passion, but the Latin poet Ovid goes one better by *advocating* the re-labelling for purposes of seduction, and reverse-labelling to cure ourselves of love.[77]

Whatever the general tendencies in Plato, he provides guidance for life even in stray examples. In the *Gorgias*, he makes Socrates speak against the insatiability of an unrestrained life, as something that can never satisfy,[78] and he compares a bird, the plover which is forever eating and simultaneously excreting, whence its name (*kharadrion*), which means a running torrent. Past food never satisfies; more is always needed. Are there careers which make this inevitable,

---

[73] Plato *Republic* 357A ff.
[74] Plato *Protagoras* 358 B-E
[75] Aristotle *Nicomachean Ethics* 7.3, 1147b15–17
[76] Plato *Republic* 474D–475A
[77] Lucretius *On the nature of things* 4. 1160–70; Ovid *Art of Love* 2. 657–62; *Remedies of Love* 325–30
[78] Plato, *Gorgias* 494B

Richard Sorabji

trying to be the richest, and lives which avoid it, a simple life of neighbourliness? Plato does not ask the question, but it is in the spirit of what he puts in the mouth of Socrates. The Stoics, characteristically, go uncomfortably further with a hard saying. We should never pin our hopes on the future, but should live each day as if our last, able to say at any moment, 'I have lived'.[79] This implies that, for a life complete at any moment, a philosopher should not set his or her heart on finishing the next book, but be content with the thought, 'I am thinking philosophy'. Teaching might come nearer the mark with the thought, 'I am teaching now'.

5. Aristotle

It is remarkable that so imaginative a philosopher as Plato should have had as his pupil a philosopher so keen as Aristotle to get everything sewn up and secured. Both qualities are needed in philosophy. Aristotle (384–322 BCE) more than anyone except the later Stoics and perhaps the Platonist Plutarch was concerned with the *particular* in ethics. He thought that he could help mature people already brought up in good habits to see what were the important objectives in life, objectives valuable in themselves. He encouraged them to deliberate on policies for securing those objectives, always subject to the disappointments of bad luck. Only some could hope to do philosophy, one of the important objectives. Carlo Natali's biography of Aristotle describes his ideals of philosophy and leisure as aristocratic, which was not the perspective of the Stoics, among whom one of the most influential figures, Epictetus, was an ex-slave. Although *Nicomachean Ethics* 10.7 presents the case for philosophising as the best activity to aim at in life, as Plato had made Socrates suggest in the *Phaedo*, I believe the case is hedged with many qualifying expressions such as 'it is thought' and 'if', and the opposite case that such a life is possible for God, not for humans, seems to be confirmed in the next chapter, 10.8, where the view is only that the more philosophy you can fit in, the happier your life will be. But for Aristotle virtue of *character* was also an objective valuable in itself. Moreover, we could never pass beyond the need for social virtues, because (*Nicomachean Ethics* 10.8), we are social beings dependent on food, and will not survive death to become like the gods, or as Socrates

---

[79]   Seneca, *Letters* 12.9; 101, 10; *On Benefits* 7.2.4–6; Marcus Aurelius *Meditations* 2.5; 7.69

had hoped in Plato's *Phaedo*, pass to the joys of the Blessed (115D) to do philosophy without such bodily needs.

Virtues of character, however, bring in *particularity*, because they require more than recognising their value and adopting the right policies to implement them. You have to spot what the virtues call for in particular situations, because their different requirements have all to be taken into account. This calls for perception, not sensory, but more like intellectual spotting in mathematics, or the spotting of defining characteristics in science. It requires an 'eye of the soul', an expression ascribed earlier to Socrates, which belongs only to the wise (*phronimoi*). In reasoning what to do you have to be able to see what the virtues require of us now in this situation, and this forms the minor premises of moral reasoning, in other words, the premiss concerned with *particulars*.[80] This does not tell us what to do, but I once thought that one could hardly say more. I now think that the Stoic Panaetius' advice on decision-making by reference to individual as well as shared personae does go further in supplying guidance.

Aristotle gives a different answer to a problem about particularity put by Plato into the mouth of the visiting stranger in *Statesman* 294A-C. How are we to deal with the fact that law is too general to be applicable to the details of particular circumstances. The stranger suggests that law is an inevitable second-best, since the wise person cannot sit beside everyone telling them what to do. Aristotle's solution is that judges must be allowed discretion in applying the law, and he compares the carpenters of Lesbos who used a leaden ruler, flexible enough to go round corners, *Nicomachean Ethics* 5.10, 1137b30–1.

Aristotle in *Nicomachean Ethics* 1.6 addresses Plato's view that there is a single Form of the Good. He calls it an uphill discussion because friends had introduced the theory of Forms. But perhaps it is better, he thinks, especially for philosophers, though both are dear, to honour the truth above friends. He does not accept such a *general* idea of good, but insists that different goods are needed for war, medicine and gymnastics.

Friendship is another subject involving particularity, and it occupies two whole books, 8 and 9, of the *Nicomachean Ethics*. It is another of life's objectives valuable in itself, and Aristotle says much about the value of friendship.[81] Plato had said in his *First*

---

[80]   Aristotle *Nicomachean Ethics* Book 6, 1142a23–30; 1143a35-b5; 1144a28–31; 1143b11–14

[81]   Richard Sorabji, *Self*, 233–9

Alcibiades, 132C–133C, that we know ourselves best by seeing our-selves reflected in another as in a mirror. But he had intended this knowledge to be of a general sort, knowledge of human nature as rational. Aristotle as so often moves from the general to the particular and applies the point to friendship. We take pleasure in our friends' good actions as if they were our own. One of the pleasures of friend-ship is that, because the friend is another self, we gain knowledge of ourselves through knowledge of them. Again, friends give us the pleasure of shared attention to things and of recognising that the attention is shared.

As regards the other two features of interest, Aristotle is not a great source of thought *exercises* to help with character, perhaps because the people he is addressing will be mature and already have acquired the right habits.[82] As regards the *seamlessness* of philosophy, the 6th century CE Neoplatonist Simplicius recognised that Aristotle's ethics presupposes his *logic*, and for that reason Simplicius chose instead to discuss Epictetus for his ethical lectures to beginners. For Aristotle's *Nicomachean Ethics* introduces syllogistic arguments, de-monstrations and logical divisions.[83] On the other hand, I am not sure that it presupposes much knowledge of *physics*. At most, Aristotle's *Eudemian Ethics* in its last few lines makes contemplation of God a central objective, 8. 16, 1249b26–31, and the first book of his *Politics* appeals to human nature in order to decide what is right for society.

6. Middle Platonists

Plutarch of Chaeronea (c. 46–120 CE) was a Platonist contemporary of Epictetus. His *Moralia* is a huge collection of essays, and many of them include exercises on foibles of character on which we might not have reflected and on which advice is hard to come by, as a glance at the table of contents shows. *On Garrulousness* tells us of the shortest reply in history: when Philip threatened the Spartans, 'if I invade, I shall turn you out', they replied, 'If'. *On inquisitiveness* advises that you should practise not looking through people's windows or reading graffiti, and that you should never tear open letters with your teeth. In *On fear of giving offence*, you are advised not to stay and listen to a bore, not to consult your local doctor if you need a

---

[82]   Aristotle *Nicomachean Ethics* 1.3, 1095a 1–13
[83]   References in Richard Sorabji, *The Philosophy of the Commentators 200–600 AD*, vol. 1, Ch. 15a

skilled physician, not to use the local innkeeper if you need someone better, not to invite to a wedding anyone who runs up to you.

Some of the more philosophical essays illustrate the *seamlessness* of philosophy. On contentment (*peri euthumias*) carries the same title as a work by Democritus and may also be influenced by Panaetius, and it discusses the deliberate formation of selfhood, a subject also addressed in a very different way in Epictetus' creation of an inviolable self. Plutarch thinks you should *weave* the narrative of your life, so that the past does not slip away, leaving you with so many momentary selves. Perhaps there would still be a human being there, but not one who had adopted any identity. He compares the painting of a man in Hades plaiting a rope, who does not notice that a donkey is eating it up as fast as he throws the plaited bits over his shoulder. But there is more advice on weaving a tapestry. You must weave in the bad parts as well as the good, because a picture needs dark patches as well as bright. On the other hand, you must not *wallow* in the bad parts, like beetles struggling in the place called 'Death to beetles'.

The concern with weaving an individual self out of an individual life shows Plutarch's interest in *particularity*. He was also interested in another way in particularity, because the essays of the *Moralia* sometimes overlap with the paired individual biographies of great Greeks and Romans in the fifty *Lives*.

Plutarch was very well read in philosophy, although he often mixed different viewpoints without distinguishing them. Unfortunately he is sometimes read chiefly as a source for the ideas of others because of the excerpts cited in the essays attacking Stoics and Epicureans. But there he is not interested in reconstructing their thought, but in alleging absurdities in it. Except as a source for others, therefore, I think these are the least interesting of his essays. The essays as a whole deserve to be on the shelves of every reflective couple starting a family.

7. Neoplatonists

'Neoplatonism' is a name given by modern scholarship to Platonists in the tradition of Plotinus (c. 205–260 CE). Plotinus' pupil and editor Porphyry produced a delightful book, which illustrates the seamlessness of philosophy better than almost any. His *On Abstinence from Animals* makes a case against sacrificing and eating animals, after recording in the first Book the arguments on both sides, by studying in the other three books in turn the nature of the gods, of animals and of humans. If you understood the immaterial gods you would see that they do not want material sacrifice. If you understood animals, you would see that they meet the Stoic requirement for being owed justice, since some of them are rational. If you knew about human races, you would realise that many cultures are vegetarian with no harm to themselves. There is also practical advice on what can be taken without harm – fruit, or on what our work entitles us to share – honey, and on what sacrifice is acceptable to God – that of a pure mind.

It has been argued by G. Fay Edwards that Porphyry had his own different reasons for sparing animals, reasons that throw a flood of light on Neoplatonist ethics. He thought that a taste for meat was incompatible with purified virtue, the higher level of virtue, freed from bodily appetites, that Socrates exemplifies in Plato's *Phaedo*. Purification from bodily appetites would endow one with an *ablabia*, a disposition not to harm.[84] In *On Abstinence* 3.26, the conception is expanded. Escape (*phugê*) from animal food is said to be escape from unjust acts concerned with food – one will not kill animals for that motive. Justice consists in not being harmful to those that are harmless. This aspect of *On Abstinence* throws light on how Porphyry would address a puzzle about purified virtue: if one turns away from the life of bodily desires to the purified life of the mind, will one not be neglecting the bodily needs of others, rather than practising justice? Elsewhere in the *Letter to Marcella*,[85] Porphyry writes to his wife instructing her in acquiring purified virtue, and reminding her that he married her not as a woman. He says in *Marcella* 14 and 16 that that if you love the body, you will also love wealth and then you will be unjust. It might be thought that Marcella would need thought exercises to help her free herself from appetites. But reliance may have been placed rather on a *model*, that of Plato's Socrates. Porphyry's *Sentences* 32 is a commentary on Plotinus' distinction in *Enneads* 1.2.3 of purified virtue from ordinary social or civic virtue.[86] The idea is that the purified are no longer motivated by the temptations which fill us with bodily

---

[84]   I owe these points about his own reasons to G. Fay Edwards, *The Puzzle of Porphyry's Rational Animals*, PhD dissertation (King's College, London, 2012); and 'The puzzle of Porphyry's rational animals: a new interpretation of *On Abstinence from Animal Food*', in preparation. Porphyry's book is translated by Gillian Clark, (Duckworth, London, 2000, and Bloomsbury, London, 2011).

[85]   Available in English translation.

[86]   *The Sentences* is available in English translation.

desires. It fits in with this that in Plato's *Phaedo* Socrates, when purified from bodily desires, neither feared death nor was tempted to
break the law by escaping from prison. Nonetheless, Porphyry's
emphasis on *not harming* seems too *negative* a conception of justice
to answer fully the question whether purified people will not
neglect the bodily needs of others. Does not justice require one positively to *look out* for their needs, rather than merely refraining from
violating them? Will one even succeed in not violating them, if one
does not consider them? Yet Porphyry deliberately rejects the more
positive Stoic view of justice, which goes to the opposite extreme,
by making justice to others depend on *oikeiôsis*, an extension to all
humans of a feeling of kinship such as one feels for oneself and
one's nearest. Porphyry complains that that would be philanthropy
(*philanthrôpia*, *On Abstinence* 3.26.9).

Plotinus speaks not only of an ascent through levels of virtue, but of
an ascent to higher *selves*, such as the intellect. But this does not represent any particularism, because the higher selves, such as intellect,
have shed many individual differentiating characteristics. If intellects
were still further freed from bodies made of flesh or from 'vehicles'
made of finer materials, they might be no more distinct than the different theorems in a unitary mathematical system.[87] Michael Griffin
has pointed out that a late Neoplatonist of the 6th century CE,
Olympiodorus, commenting on Plato's *First Alcibiades*, interprets
his reference to 'each self' as requiring attention to a particular self
and its particular acts.[88] Plotinus gave Porphyry his personal attention when he dissuaded him from committing suicide, so we hear
in Porphyry's *Life of Plotinus*, but the only arguments on suicide
that we know from Plotinus are general.

I should not leave the Neoplatonists without mentioning that the
late Neoplatonist Simplicius (writing after 529 CE) who wrote the
most extensive, highly documented and sometimes technical commentaries on Aristotle and of over 800 years of interpretation of
him, as well as a commentary on Epictetus, concluded three of his
commentaries with a prayer. This was because the reading of
Epictetus and then Aristotle was the first part of a curriculum that
moved on to Plato and culminated in two works of Plato interpreted
as revealing the nature of God. The reading of the commentaries was

---

[87] Richard Sorabji, *Self*, 118–126.
[88] Olympiodorus, *Commentary on Plato's First Alcibiades* 204, 3–11,
discussed in Michael Griffin's introduction to his translation, vol. 1,
(Bloomsbury, London, *forthcoming*).

therefore an exercise, a spiritual exercise, in Hadot's sense, though not in the sense that I have been discussing.

8. Christians in the Neoplatonist tradition

I will mention two Christians steeped in the Neoplatonist tradition, both from the 6th century CE. Both of them illustrate the seamlessness of philosophy. I need not say much about John Philoponus, because I have discussed him extensively before.[89] He wrote seven commentaries expounding Aristotle, studying him word by word, starting under the tutelage of the great master of 6th century philosophy in Alexandria, Ammonius. Consequently he had an understanding of pagan philosophy sufficiently penetrating to be able, as Ammonius' tutelage receded, to argue as a Christian against the pagan philosophers on their own terms. Because they all believed since Aristotle that nothing could finish going right through a more than finite number, much less exceed it, they must agree with the distinctively Christian view, that a Creator God could not have created the universe beginninglessly, as they thought, but must have given it a beginning. Or it would have gone through a more than finite number of years and an even larger number of days. Infinity puzzles of this sort had started with the Presocratic Zeno, the Eleatic (born c. 490–485), as problems that we might classify as logical, although they were classified by Aristotle as being about motion. Now Philoponus was applying such puzzles to physics and the nature of the universe, and hence to differences of religious belief, and by implication to differences of ethical viewpoint.

The other major figure was Boethius, whose commentaries on Aristotle's logic written in the manner of Greek ones but for Latin readers, were the main source for the early Latin Middle Ages. But his project to comment on the rest of Aristotle and on Plato was cut

---

[89] In Richard Sorabji, *Time, Creation and the Continuum* (Duckworth, London, 1983, Chicago University Press 2006, Bloomsbury, London 2013), Chs 13–14; (ed.) *Philoponus and the Rejection of Aristotelian Science* (Duckworth, London, 1987) extensively updated 2nd edition, *Bulletin of the Institute of Classical Studies*, supplementary volume **103** (2010) available http://events.sas.ac.uk/support-research/publictions/ 815, and eventually from Wiley-Blackwell; with some new proposals on dating and authorship of works, in (ed.) *Aristotle Transformed* (2nd edition, Bloomsbury, London, 2014).

short by a very dubious charge of treason, and awaiting execution in prison, he wrote his masterpiece, *The Consolation of Philosophy*, which was to be paraphrased in England by King Alfred, Chaucer and Queen Elizabeth I. His question was whether life is governed by God's Providence, by necessity or by chance. The Lady Philosophy is imagined as visiting him in his prison cell and personally addressing each one of his worries as he expresses them in turn. On Providence and chance, the eventual suggestion is that chance as described by Aristotle is a coincidence, and coincidence leaves room for Providence. A danger for Boethius is that this may violate Aristotle's insight is that coincidences are unexplained conjunctions of things, each of which is itself explicable even as to time and place. If God were to engineer a conjunction, it would no longer be an unexplained coincidence. As regards Providence and necessity, the threat is that if God's Providence means that he foreknows all we will do, our actions and fate will have been inevitable all along. Boethius does not diagnose what I believe to be the real threat here, that if God's awareness of the future has already existed in the past, it is irrevocable, and that his knowledge, unlike human knowledge, is considered infallible. If so, it is both too late so to act that he will have foreknown something different, and his infallibility means that it is impossible for him to be mistaken. Although Boethius in Book 5 leaves the problem undiagnosed, he nonetheless gives a powerful answer. God's knowledge is not *fore*-knowledge, but *timeless* knowledge. If timeless knowledge is an intelligible idea, then Boethius is free to offer his solution, one that he might have learnt from a brilliant and much earlier Christian, Origen from the 3rd century CE. Knowledge which is not foreknowledge of your conduct or fate need no more compel you than the knowledge of someone who *sees* what is happening to you. The point (undiagnosed) about *seeing* is that it parallels timeless knowledge in lacking the element of irrevocability. Here Aristotelian reflections on chance, necessity, time and foreknowledge, lead seamlessly to consolation on the tragedies of life.

9. Retrospect

Of the three features selected for attention, the seamless connexion of ethics with other braches of philosophy, or in Plato's case with mathematics, appears in all periods. Thought exercises to guide the reader's life are also common, although possibly less so in Plato and

Richard Sorabji

Aristotle, and increasingly so with Epicureans and the later Stoics from Panaetius onwards. Least common is particularism in the sense which sees the individual's particular situation, or the perceptive individual's insight into the present situation, as crucial to making moral decisions. Outstanding in this regard were Aristotle and the later Stoics, although there were some anticipations, but among Platonists there was some preference for drawing guidance from the general.

Wolfson College, Oxford

Philosophical Modernities: Polycentricity and Early Modernity in India

JONARDON GANERI

Abstract

The much-welcomed recent acknowledgement that there is a plurality of philosophical traditions has an important consequence: that we must acknowledge too that there are many philosophical modernities. Modernity, I will claim, is a polycentric notion, and I will substantiate my claim by examining in some detail one particular non-western philosophical modernity, a remarkable period in 16th to 17th century India where a diversity of philosophical projects fully deserve the label 'modern'.

It used to be a commonplace in studies of modernity, and remains one still in philosophical historiography, that modernity is something that happened first, and uniquely, in Europe; and attempts were made to convert the supposition into a tautology through defnitions of modernity that exclude nonEuropean periodizations and geographies (for example, in terms of capitalist modes of production, the emergence of nation states and nationalist collective identities, the industrial revolution, secularization, and so on).[1] NonEuropean philosophies are traditional, and only European philosophy is modern. Progress of sorts occurred with the acknowledgement of the existence of alternative regional modernities, but the acknowledgement was tied to a centre/periphery model and to an associated ideology of European diffusionism. Eisenstadt, for instance, is willing to acknowledge 'multiple modernities',[2] but only insofar as these new modernities imitate and copy a first modernity centred in Europe. Post-colonial writers such as R. Radhakrishnan have

---

[1] The following quotation is representative: 'Historically, modernization is the process of change towards those types of social, economic and political systems that have developed in Western Europe and North America from the seventeenth century to the nineteenth' (Eisenstadt 'Multiple Modernities': 1). For similarly Eurocentric definitions of modernity, see also Giddens *The Consequences of Modernity* (Stanford, Calif.: Stanford University Press, 1990); Hall and Gieben *Formations of Modernity* (Cambridge, U.K.: Polity Press, 1992), 1–16

[2] Eisenstadlt, Shmuel N. (2000) 'Multiple modernities', *Daedalus* **129**(1): 1–29

doi:10.1017/S1358246114000071   © The Royal Institute of Philosophy and the contributors 2014
Royal Institute of Philosophy Supplement **74** 2014

struggled with what they term 'the curse of derivativeness',[3] and have sought to find in the interplay between colonised and coloniser, between tradition and modernity, a more dialectical pattern of engagement.

What I will argue for in this essay is a more radical rejection of the commonplace picture. I will claim that we should think instead of modernity as a happening potentially indigenous to any culture, irrespective of period or place, that like the famous Indian banyan tree it is 'polycentric', here borrowing Susan Friedman's very useful term. 'The new geography of modernism', Friedman says, 'needs to locate many centres of modernity across the globe, to focus on the cultural traffic linking them, and to interpret the circuits of reciprocal influence and transformation that take place within highly unequal state relations'[4]; it involves a recognition that these modernities are different, not derivative. There is just one way to substantiate such a claim, and that is through the detailed, painstaking, excavation of modernities that have been lost or lost sight of, and I will spend the remainder of this talk doing precisely that, unearthing an incipient early modernity in pre-colonial Indian philosophical theory.

The arrival of modernity at a certain point in the history of philosophy seemingly admits of two non-compossible explanations. One model presents modernity as involving a thorough rejection of the ancient – its texts, its thinkers, its methods – as starting afresh and from the beginning. This was how the two figures who are emblematic of the 'new philosophy' in Europe, Francis Bacon (1561–1626) and René Descartes (1596–1650), chose to present themselves.[5]

---

[3]   Radhakrishnan, R. (2002) 'Derivative discourses and the problem of signification', *The European Legacy* **7**(6): 783–95

[4]   Freidman, Susan (2006) 'Periodizing modernism: postcolonial modernities and the space/time borders of modernist studies', *Modernism/Modernity* 13(3): 429

[5]   Bacon: 'There was but one course left, therefore,—to try the whole thing anew upon a better plan, and to commence a total reconstruction of sciences, arts and all human knowledge, raised upon the proper foundations.' (*Instauratio magma, Preface*; 1857–74, vol. 4: 8 in *The Works of Francis Bacon*, J. Spedding, R. L. Ellis and D. D. Heath (eds)(London: Longmans)). Descartes: 'As soon as I was old enough to emerge from the control of my teachers, I entirely abandoned the study of letters… For it seemed to me that much more truth could be found in the reasonings which a man makes concerning matters that concern him than in those which some scholar makes in his study.' (*Discourse*, AT vi. 9; 1984: 115, in *The Philosophical Writings of Descartes*, John Cottingham (ed.)(Cambridge: Cambridge University Press, 1984)). 'The following

A second model locates modernity not in a rejection of the past but in a profound re-orientation with respect to it. The ancient texts are now not thought of as authorities to which one must defer, but regarded as the source of insight in the company of which one pursues the quest for truth. This new attitude towards the texts does not imply abandonment but a transformation in their place within inquiry, a change in conception of one's duties towards the past. Going forward doesn't mean forgetting where one has been.

The first model has dominated the standard history of philosophy, which speaks of a revolution in philosophy in early seventeenth century Europe, one in which the Aristotelianism of the schools – with its obscure terminology, doctrine of forms and final causes, and schoolmen who 'loved Aristotle more than the truth'[6] – is cast aside in favour of a new mechanical conception of natural explanation. Recently, however, this familiar account has begun to unravel. John Cottingham says, for example, that 'any picture of Descartes as a lone innovator setting out on a new quest for certainty cannot survive serious scrutiny',[7] while Dan Garber, pointing out that Descartes' correspondents did not find his project seriously in conflict with their own progressive Aristotelian ambitions, speaks of 'the revolution that did not happen in 1637',[8] the year of publication of the *Discourse*. One of those correspondents, Libert Froimont, saw in Descartes' self-portrayal in the *Discourse* the renewal of a very ancient spirit:

> I seem to see a Pythagoras or a Democritus, a voluntary exile from his homeland who has traveled to the Egyptians, to the Brahmans, and around the entire globe, to investigate the nature of things and the nature of the universe.[9]

---

text draws from material in Ganeri *The Lost Age of Reason: Philosophy in Early Modern India 1450–1700 C.E.* (Oxford: Clarendon Press, 2012).'

[6] Mercer, Christia (1993) 'The Vitality and Importance of Early Modern Aristotelianism', in Tom Sorell (ed.), *The Rise of Modern Philosophy: The Tension between the New and Traditional Philosophies from Machiavelli to Leibniz* (Oxford: Clarendon Press): 34

[7] Cottingham, John (1993) 'A New Start? Cartesian Metaphysics and the Emergence of Modern Philosophy', in Tom Sorell (ed.) The Rise of Modern Philosophy: The Tension between the New and Traditional Philosophies from Machiavelli to Leibniz (Oxford: Clarendon Press): 150

[8] Garber, Daniel (1988) 'Descartes, the Aristotelians, and the Revolution That Did Not Happen in 1637', The Monist 71(6): 471–486.

[9] Froimont 1637, quoted in Garber 'Descartes, the Aristotelians, and the Revolution That Did Not Happen in 1637': 476

Jonardon Ganeri

New work has revealed a complexity in Descartes' relationship with late scholasticism, including a tension between the self-presentation of the *Discourse* and views expressed in his private correspondence.[10] In another vein, Julian Martin has described Francis Bacon's self-depiction as 'a studied pose', adding that 'when Bacon painted himself and his natural philosophy as modern and novel, he was moved to do so by local concerns and ambitions'.[11]

There can be no doubt but that the new philosophers in seventeenth century Europe were profoundly innovative, but the standard historiography simultaneously distorts two aspects of their relationship with the ancient. First, it misrepresents the dynamism and openness of progressive peripateticism. Many late scholastics, it is now becoming evident, were highly original in interpreting Aristotle and in fact saw no incompatibility between a re-cast Aristotelianism and the new philosophy.[12] The standard picture, furthermore, radically simplifies the complex ways in which the moderns drew upon the ancients. In the work of Leibniz, Spinoza, Basso, and Gassendi, what one finds is a firm conviction that there is truth in the ancient philosophers, truth which might well stand in need of radical rejuvenation and reconfirguration, but truth which provides a gateway to new philosophy and is not a roadblock to it. Leibniz described himself as seeking a 'reformed philosophy', one which put the mechanical philosophy on sound ancient foundations. Spinoza's engagement with ancient Stoicism has also, recently, begun to be more thoroughly explored and acknowledged (eg. Kristeller).[13] Susan James' assessment is that 'much of the substance and structure of the *Ethics* – its central doctrines and the connections between them – constitute a reworking of Stoicism'.[14] Something

[10] Ariew, Roger. *Descartes and the Late Scholastics* (Ithaca: Cornell University Press, 1999); Secada, Jorge. *Cartesian Metaphysics: The Scholastic Origins of Modern Philosophy* (Cambridge: Cambridge University Press, 2000)

[11] Martin, Julian (1993). 'Francis Bacon, Authority, and the Moderns', in Tom Sorell (ed.) *The Rise of Modern Philosophy: The Tension between the New and Traditional Philosophies from Machiavelli to Leibniz* (Oxford: Clarendon Press): 74

[12] Schmitt, Charles. Aristotle and the Renaissance (Cambridge, Mass.: Harvard University Press, 1983); Mercer, 'The Vitality and Importance of Early Modern Aristotelianism' (1993)

[13] Kristeller, P. O. (1984). 'Stoic and Neoplatonic Sources in Spinoza's Ethics', History of European Ideas 5(1): 1–15.

[14] James, Susan (1993). 'Spinoza the Stoic', in Tom Sorell (ed.) *The Rise of Modern Philosophy: The Tension between the New and Traditional Philosophies from Machiavelli to Leibniz* (Oxford: Clarendon Press): 291

similar is true, as Richard Sorabji has recently demonstrated, of John Locke's theory of conscience. The fact is that the early modern philosophers had a far more subtle and interesting understanding of the relationship between their new work and the past than the standard model can accommodate. It is simply not the case that these early modern philosophers were merely residually scholastic; rather, a revival and retrieval of the ancient and a transformation of it into the modern was at the heart of their philosophical method. And that is not so different from those progressive Aristotelians who 'draw from the *springs* of Aristotle and the ancients rather than from the *cisterns* of the Scholastics'.[15]

When we come to look at early modern India it is especially important that we do so with eyes not blurred by the standard historiography of the battle between ancients and moderns in Europe. I am aware of no Indian thinker from the period who makes the sort of audacious self-proclamation that one finds in Bacon or Descartes, a sweeping dismissal of the ancient tradition and of everything associated with it. And yet a modernity there certainly was, one which had its equivalents of Leibniz, Spinoza, Basso, and Gassendi on the one hand, and Morin, Sennert, and Weigel on the other. I believe that in the sixteenth and seventeenth centuries a remarkable project began to take shape in the Sanskritic philosophical world. It is not just that the philosophers are willing to describe themselves as 'new', though that is indeed a striking feature of the period. By the end of the seventeenth century we find in a work by Mahādeva a daunting array of terms denoting the new:

New	(*navya*)	Gaṅgeśa et al.
Newer	(*navyatara*)	Later Mithilā thinkers
Modern	(*navīna*)	Raghunātha
Very modern	(*atinavīna*)	Post-Raghunātha thinkers
Contemporary	(*ādhunika*)	Contemporaries of Mahādeva.[16]

[15]   Loemaker, L. (ed.) *Leibniz: Philosophical Papers and Letters* (Kluwer Academic Publishers, 1956),124

[16]   Mahādeva Puṇatāmakara (1967). Precious Jewel of Reason (Nyāyakaustubha) Anumāna-khaṇḍa. Damodara Lal Gosvami ed. (Varanasi: Vidya Mandir Press, Saraswati Bhavana Texts 33, Part II); Mahādeva Puṇatāmakara (1982). Precious Jewel of Reason (Nyāyakaustubha), Śabda-khaṇḍa. V. Subrahmanya Sastri ed. (Tanjore: T. M. S. S. M. Library). (*Nyāya-kaustubha*)

Jonardon Ganeri

Yet others before them had done the same, and the question is in what this self-attributed newness consists and what the self-affirmation means. Was it only a newness in the ways that the ideas of the ancient authorities are described, a newness of style but not of substance? In asking this question, I have in mind Sheldon Pollock's well-known assessment of the new intellectuals of seventeenth century India, that their work displays a 'paradoxical combination of something very new in style subserving something very old in substance.'[17] That was certainly how a pre-modern, Jayanta, at the end of the first millennium, conceived of his own originality:

> How can we discover a new truth? So one should consider our novelty only in the rephrasing of words.[18]

This characteristically pre-modern attitude of deference to the past changes fundamentally in the work of Raghunātha Śiromaṇi (c.1460–1540). Raghunātha belongs to a tradition of philosophical speculation known as Nyāya, a term more or less synonymous with the appeal to reason and evidence-based critical inquiry – rather than scriptural exegesis – as the proper method of philosophy. Raghunātha concludes his most innovative work, the *Inquiry into the Nature of Things*, with a call to philosophers to think for themselves about the arguments:

> The demonstration of these matters which I have carefully explained is contrary to the conclusions reached by all the other disciplines. These matters spoken of should not be cast aside without reflection just because they are contrary to accepted opinion; scholars should consider them carefully. Bowing to those who know the truth concerning matters of all the sciences, bowing to people like you [the reader], I pray you consider my

[17] Pollock (2001) 'The Death of Sanskrit', Comparative Studies in Society and History 43(2): 407
[18] kuto vā nūtanaṃ vastu vayam utprekṣitum kṣamāḥ | vacovinyāsavaicitrya mātram atra vicāryatām || (Jayanta Bhaṭṭa. *Nyāya-mañjarī*. With the commentary Granthibhaṅ ga by Cakradhara, Gaurinath Shastri (ed.) (Varanasi: Sampurnananda Sanskrit University, 1982): 1, v. 8). Though certainly exaggerated, Jayanta's disclaimer is still less than that of the influential eighth-century Buddhist writer Śāntideva: 'Nothing new will be said here; nor have I any skill in composition. Therefore I do not imagine that I can benefit others. I have done this [simply] to improve my own mind' (na hi kiṃcitapūrvam atra vācyaṃ na ca saṃgrathanakauśalaṃ mamāsti | ata eva ne me parārthacintā svamano vāsayituṃ kṛtaṃ mayedam || (*Bodhicary āvatāra*1.2).

sayings with sympathy. This method, though less honoured, has been employed by wise men of the past; namely that one ask other people of learning to consider one's own words.[19]

The new attitude was summarised at the time by Abū'l Faẓl, in a work – the *Āīn-i-Akbarī* – which relates the intellectual climate during the reign of the Mughal emperor Akbar. Abū'l Faẓl describes the philosophers as those who 'look upon testimony as something filled with the dust of suspicion and handle nothing but proof'.[20] In the writings of those philosophers who follow Raghunātha from about the middle of the sixteenth century until the end of the seventeenth there is a fundamental metamorphosis in epistemology, metaphysics, semantics, and philosophical methodology. The works of these philosophers – some of whom lived in Raghunātha's home-town of Navadvīpa in Bengal, others in the newly invigorated city of Vārāṇasī – are full of phrases that are indicative of a new attitude, phrases like 'this should be considered further (*iti dhyeyam*)', 'this needs to be reflected on (*iti cintyam*)', 'this is the right general direction to go in (*iti dik*)'. Openness to inquiry into the problems themselves, a turn towards the facts, is what drives the new work, not merely a new exegesis of the ancient texts, along with a sense that they are engaged in a radical and on-going project. The spirit which Raghunātha sought to provoke is clearly on display in a passage which asks about the meaning of historical and fictional terms:

> How does it come about that, from hearing the word 'Daśaratha', people now, who never saw Daśaratha [the father of the legendary king Rāma] come to know of him? Likewise how, from the words [for fictional entities like] 'hobgoblin', do others come to know of them? I leave this for attentive scholars to meditate upon. I shall not expand further here.[21]

[19] Raghunātha Śiromaṇi (1915). Inquiry into the Truth about Things (Padārtha-tattva-nirūpaṇa). V. P. Dvivedi (ed.) (Varanasi). Text and trans. Karl H. Potter (Cambridge, Mass.: Harvard University Press, Harvard Yenching Institute Studies, vol. 17, 1957), 89, 90

[20] [1597] 1873: 537 (cited in D. C. Bhattacharya 1937. 'Sanskrit Scholars of Akbar's Time', *Indian Historical Quarterly* **13**: 31–36). Abu'l Fazl does not mention Raghunātha in the list of philosophers he provides to accompany this description, Raghunātha presumably already dead when Akbar came to the throne; but he does name someone with close ties to Raghunātha, Vidyānivāsa, and he also mentions Raghunātha's best-known student.

[21] Raghunātha Śiromaṇi (1915). *Inquiry into the Truth about Things* (Padārtha-tattva-nirūpaṇa). V. P. Dvivedi (ed.) (Varanasi). Text and

Jonardon Ganeri

Other branches of scholarship, including linguistics (*vyākaraṇa*), philosophical theology (*advaita* and *viśiṣṭādvaita vedānta*), ritual exegesis (*mīmāṃsā*), and jurisprudence (*dharmaśāstra*), encountered early modernity in ways that borrow from but do not always agree that of the 'new reason', the later Navya Nyāya. Particularly worthy of notice are the Kerala mathematical astronomers, whose sensational work in the foundations of infinitesimal calculus and spherical geometry is increasingly being appreciated.[22]

The existence of this modernity, I have emphasised, can be seen only when we free ourselves from the idea that modernity involves a complete rejection of the ancient sources. Our philosophers still, for example, write commentaries, and still use concepts and categories that might, if looked at from a distance, seem archaic. What must be recognised is that the mere activity of writing a commentary, though now strongly associated with conservative scholasticism, does not by itself tell one very much about the author's attitude towards the text being commented on. The fundamental role of a commentary was to mediate a conversation between the past and the present. It therefore offers *us* a route into the question that lies at the heart of *our* study of early modernity in the sixteenth and seventeenth century: the question of *their* sense of *their* duties towards, or separation from, the ancient philosophical world. There are different sorts of commentary, and a fundamental

---

trans. Karl H. Potter (Cambridge, Mass.: Harvard University Press, Harvard Yenching Institute Studies, vol. 17, 1957), 76

[22] Nīlakaṇtha (1444–1545) and Jyeṣṭhadeva (c. 1530) are exemplary figures. Jyeṣṭhadeva's Malayalam *Rationales in Mathematical Astronomy*, for example, contains results, using methods closely analogous to the infinitesimal calculus, for computing the equation of centre and latitudinal motion of Mercury and Venus, derivations in spherical astronomy, and proofs of the infinite series for π, the arc-tangent and the sine functions. See Sharma, K.V., Ramasubramanian, K., and Sriniva, M. D. and Sriram, M. S. Ganita-yukti-bhāsāā (*Rationales in Mathematical Astronomy*) of Jyesth adeva (Dordrecht: Springer, 2008); Narasimha, Roddam (2009). 'The Chequered Histories of Epistemology and Science', in Bharati Ray (ed.), *Different Types of History. History of Science, Philosophy and Culture in Indian Civilization*, vol. 14, part 4 (Delhi: Pearson Longman). Raju presents the case for thinking that Keralan mathematics was transmitted to early modern Europe (Raju, C. K. (2007). Cultural Foundations of Mathematics: The Nature of Mathematical Proof and the Transmission of the Calculus from India to Europe in the 16th Century. History of Science, Philosophy and Culture in Indian Civilization, vol. 10, part 4 (Delhi: Centre for Studies in Civilizations).).

distinction is between those whose ambition is to clarify or systematize the 'truths' already in the ancient treatise, and those which are using the treatise in the process of a creative pursuit of an inquiry into the truth itself. Modernity expresses itself as a distinctive way of reading the past, and in our period this also finds a voice in a new genre of commentary, the commentary which digs up the deep or hidden meaning (*gūḍhārtha*) in an ancient text. A mistaken understanding of the ambitions of commentary has also led to a tendency to read new developments back into the original works, with the result that the originality of the later thinkers tends to disappear from view.

Other works structure themselves as auto-commentarial glosses on groups of tersely stated principles (*sūtra*s; *kārikā*s), in a style familiar to historians of early modern European philosophy through texts like Spinoza's *Ethics* and Descartes' *Principles*. Raghunātha is, nevertheless, also striking in his new promotion of the genre of philosophical treatise in which a problem is discussed directly; his *Inquiry into the Nature of Things* is just such a work. In general, however, the discursive style in the works of the early modern Indian philosophers – mostly devoid of boastful self-assertion – can make it easy to overlook the originality of their ambitions. So the relation between style and substance is more complex: innovations in style sometimes served to camouflage innovativeness about content.

Central to later Navya-Nyāya, the 'new reason', the school founded by Raghunātha, were three ideas. The first was that methods of inquiry have to be evidence-based and collaborative, relying on proof-strategies that are open to empirical confirmation or disconfirmation and involving reasoned decision-making mechanisms in multi-agent environments. The second idea was that of a stratified or layered conception of the world, in which atomism at the lowest level is compatible with the reducible or irreducible reality of other categories of entity, including composite bodies, at higher levels. The third was that a new philosophy needs a new language, one in which the underlying logical form of philosophical claims is exposed and transparent, and which can therefore serve the needs of demonstration in a calculus of relations. These key ideas – and the concomitant reworking of the ancient tradition they presumed – were all essentially in place by the middle of the seventeenth century. Indeed, we can read two very remarkable works of Jayarāma, the *Garland of Principles* and the *Garland of Categories*, as constituting a direct intellectual confrontation between the 'new reason' and Cartesian new philosophy. 'Cartesian' ideas are rejected in favour of a philosophy that could have held its own among any of the early modern philosophies of later seventeenth century

Jonardon Ganeri

European thought. Generally speaking, what we can say is that early modern forms of philosophical inquiry in India are governed by data drawn from logical form and linguistic practice rather than the microscopic and distal observation of natural phenomena. Philosophy in early modern India made the discipline rest instead on the sort of linguistic turn that characterised, much later, the origins of analytical philosophy in European thought. Bearing this point in mind, it is no surprise that profound affinities should have been discovered between early modern theory in India and twentieth century analytical philosophy; I have in mind in particular the discoveries made by Bimal Matilal,[23] in whose name the Matilal lectureship at the University of London was created some years ago.

Raghunātha's fundamental criticism of the orthodoxy might be said to consist in the thought that the traditional Vaiśeṣika view of the world is myopic and flat, seeing only a mechanistic space of objects, compounded from atoms, bearing qualities of various sorts, and moving about in various ways. The inclusion into this picture of human inquirers has them fall under an identical descriptive model, located in space and time, displaying a range of qualities, many of which overlap with those of ordinary physical objects. That might seem like an attractively naturalistic picture, and later 'new reason' thinkers are keen to preserve the naturalism, but the very flatness of the model causes serious fault-lines within it. What it fails to see, according to Raghunātha, are the irreducibly normative structures introduced by the presence of thinking beings who represent and reason about the world they inhabit, and have duties and rights with respect to each other.[24] To say that we therefore need new categories is just a way of claiming that the old model can not accommodate these facts; and part of the point is to throw down a challenge to his contemporaries to show how, if at all, a naturalistic reduction is to be achieved. The force of Raghunātha's challenge is to call for an account of just how to achieve an acknowledgement of the reality of features of human life which the orthodox model seems ill-equipped to accommodate without abandoning naturalism as that model conceives of it (a unified explanation of all objects of inquiry including inquirers).

[23]   E.g. Matilal, Bimal Krishna. Perception: *An Essay on Classical Indian Theories of Knowledge* (Oxford: Clarendon Press, 1986).
[24]   The question about whether there are irreducibly normative properties continues to be a live issue of debate. Many agree with Raghunatha that there are; for example, Shafer-Landau. Moral Realism: A Defence (Oxford University Press, 2003).

In the fifteenth, sixteenth, and seventeenth centuries, the town of Navadvīpa, Raghunātha's home town, which is also known by its latinized name Nadia or Nuddea, was one of the great sites of scholarship in South Asia. During his lifetime Navadvīpa was a place of great scholarship under a comparatively peaceful and cosmopolitan Muslim rule, creating the conditions for an Islamic Bengal politically independent of the Northern Indian sultanate, and drawing Bengal into relationship with the *khalifah* of Baghdad and a wider Muslim world. Considerable historical documentation relates to Navadvīpa in the period, in the form of Islamic histories of Bengal, biographies-cum-hagiographies of the Vaiṣṇava saint Caitanya, documentation internal to the scholarly community of Navadvīpa, chronicles of the Mughal court, and, for the final years, the records of the East India Company. One text from the period concludes by saying that it was written in Navadvīpa in 1494, a place full of learning and learned men, under the peaceful governance of Majlisav-arvaka.[25] Raghunātha, of course, would have been among them. In the century to follow, students from all over the subcontinent, indeed from Nepal and possibly even Tibet, were attracted to a strict programme of studies in the 'new reason', a vigorous intellectual community, and the eventual prospect of prestigious certification by title. The programme of studies was provided in ṭols run by a series of celebrated paṇḍits, whose more important works were frequently transcribed and swiftly distributed throughout India.

It is indeed of enormous significance that ours should be a period of strong Persianate influence and Islamicate power. The problem is to square this fact with another: that one finds very few direct traces, if any, of Islamic or Arabic ideas in the work of the Sanskrit philosophers of the time. It is not at all similar to the situation in astronomy, for example, where the confrontation between ancient Hindu cosmological models and the new Arabic sciences is a topic of heated debate. In philosophy, the causality, if it exists at all, is much more indirect. The Persianate context nevertheless created incentives that had not existed before. One fact to note is that the brightest and best Sanskrit intellectuals were actively encouraged, for instance by Akbar's great minister the Hindu Ṭoḍarmal, to learn Persian and join Mughal imperial office. Those who preferred instead to remain within the intellectual world of Sanskrit faced a very clear challenge to demonstrate the

[25]   Mahādevācārya Siṃhā's commentary on Bhāvabhūti's *Malatim-ādhava* (Sāhitya Pariṣat Patrikā, 245; D. C. Bhattacharya Vāṅgālīr Sārasvat Avadān: Baṅge Navya-nyāya Carcā (Calcutta: Sahitya Pariṣat, 1952), 35).

relevance and vitality of that world.[26] They did this by drawing on its resources without burying themselves within its folds. If in Europe power lay with the Aristotelians in the university departments, in India it was located in the Islamicate administration. By not becoming a part of it, the new philosophers were, one could say, in a state of internal exile. Modernity was the alternative to irrelevance. Another possibility is that rather than writing directly about Islamic thought they wrote instead about constructed surrogates within the Sanskrit milieu, with Advaita Vedānta in particular serving as a pretext for the examination of Islamic ideas. In any case what is clear is that the sheer presence of alternative modalities of thought presented motivations and opportunities that could not have existed before.

India in the seventeenth century, the century after Akbar, was in intellectual overdrive. Muslim, Jaina and Hindu intellectuals produced work of tremendous vitality, and ideas circulated around India, through the Persianate and Arabic worlds, and out to Europe and back. For a flavour of the times let us fix our gaze on a single year, the year 1656. In India, this was the year in which a long running process of religious isomorphism, pioneered by Akbar's chronicler Abu'l Fazl and orchestrated around Ibn al'Arabi's idea of unity in being (*wa ḥdat al-wujūd*), reached fulfilment in Dārā Shukoh's grand project to translate fifty-two Upaniṣads into Persian, a project for the sake of which he assembled in Vārāṇasī (Benares; aka. Kāśī) a large team of bilingual scholars. Dārā believed that he could establish that the differences between Hinduism and Islam were largely terminological, and even that the Upaniṣads can be read as a sort of commentary upon the Qur'ān. The fallout from this remarkable project of Dārā, Akbar's great-grandson and heir-apparent to the Mughal throne, would reverberate throughout the period and long afterwards. (And I am happy to see that today is the opening day of a new exhibition on the Mughal Empire at the British Museum).

1656 would also be the year in which the French philosopher and physician François Bernier would leave behind him the France of *les libertins érudits* on a journey that would bring him soon to Mughal India. In Bernier's travel writings we will find a fragment of

---

[26]   An example is Bhārat Candra Raī, a prominent scholar in the court of Kṛṣṇa Candra. According to an early report, 'his fondness for Sanskrit studies displeased his relations, who thought that an acquaintance with Muhammadan literature was a better passport to wealth and distinction than the Vedas and Purāṇas.' (Wilson, W. W. (1877). A *Statistical Account of Bengal*; vol. 2: Districts of Nadiyā and Jessor (London: Trubner & Co. Reprinted 1973, D. K. Publishing House, Delhi): 155–6).

testimony to the aftermath of Dārā Shukoh's translational project. Before embarking on his travels, Bernier had been the protégé of the early modern philosopher, scientist, and mathematician Pierre Gassendi (1592–1655). Indeed it was Bernier who would eventually – on his return to France – devote himself to making Gassendi's work available to French and British audiences. Before doing so, however, he was to spend years as the court physician first of Dārā Shukoh and then of Aurangzeb. In a letter written from Shiraz in 1667, some ten years after the Vārāṇasī project, Bernier describes how he had come to know one of the paṇḍits whom Dārā Shukoh had used, someone fluent in both Sanskrit and Persian, how they had exchanged the latest medical and philosophical knowledge, and, fascinatingly, how he had translated work by Descartes and Gassendi into Persian for the paṇḍit's benefit:

> Do not be surprised if without knowledge of Sanskrit I am going to tell you many things taken from books in that language; you will know that my Agha, Danishmand Khān, paid for the presence of one of the most famous paṇḍits in India, who before had been pensioned by Dārā Shukoh, the oldest son of Shāh Jahān, and that this paṇḍit, apart from attracting the most learned scientists to our circle, was at my side for over three years. When I became weary of explaining to my Agha the latest discoveries of William Harvey and Pequet in anatomy, and to reason with him on the philosophy of Gassendi and Descartes, which I translated into Persian (because that is what I did during five or six years) it was up to our paṇḍit to argue.[27]

It is of considerable interest to those who are interested in the global circulation of ideas to be told here that the work of Descartes, by this time the leading French philosopher and a key figure in the Early Enlightenment, was available to the Vārāṇasī paṇḍits already in the early 1660s, barely ten years after his death. If Bernier's testimony is reliable, the migration of ideas was already remarkably swift. As for the name of Bernier's paṇḍit, and the nature of his reaction to the work of Descartes or Gassendi, that is a story which Bernier

---

[27] 'Letter to Monsieur Chapelain, Despatched from Chiras in Persia, the 4th October 1667', translated in Bernier (1934 [1670–1]). *Histoire de la dernière révolution des États du Gran Mogol*, 4 vols (Paris: Claude Barbin, 1670–1671); edited as Voyage dans les États du Grand Mogol, France Bhattacharya (Paris: Fayard, 1981). Trans. Irvind Brock, Travels in the Mogul Empire AD 1656–1668 (London: W. Pickering 1834; 3rd edn), 323–5.

neglected to tell. He has now been identified[28] as the very influential scholar-poet Kavīndra Sarasvatī, an important mediary between the Sanskrit intelligentsia and the Mughal court, and someone who built up a great library of beautifully transcribed manuscripts.[29] The patron of Bernier and Kavīndra during this period was the Persian nobleman Danishmand Khān, who was the only person to oppose the capital sentence against Dārā[30] and who afterwards offered Kavīndra and Bernier employment. His generosity and openness created the space for a remarkable exchange of French, Persian and Indian philosophical ideas in the three years from 1658/9 to 1661/2. Kavīndra was on good terms with perhaps the most important of the 'new reason' philosophers in Vārāṇasī, Jayarāma Nyāya-pañcānana. It would be during this period that Jayarāma would write two very unusual and significant works, *The Garland of Principles about Reason*, and the *Garland of Categories*.

Some of the most powerful intellects of South Asia were working in Vārāṇasī and Navadvīpa in the sixteenth and seventeenth centuries. Among them were prominent contributors to the revitalised 'new reason', and it seems very probable that some would be among the 'learned scientists' who associated with François Bernier.[31] These philosophers were engaging in a profound and radical dialogue, with each other and with the tradition from which they had

---

[28]   Gode, P. K. (1954). 'Bernier and Kavīndrācārya Sarasvatī at the Moghal Court', in P. K. Gode, Studies in Indian Literary History (Bombay: Bharatiya Vidya Bhavan), vol. 2: 364–379.

[29]   Shastri, Haraprasad (1912). 'Dakshini Paṇḍiṭs at Benares', Indian Antiquary **XLI**: 7–13. Gode, P. K. (1945). 'Some Evidence About the Location of the Manuscript Library of Kavīndracharya Sarasvati at Benares in A.D. 1665', in C. Kunhan Raja (ed.), *Jagadvijayachandas of Kavindracharya* (Bikaner: Anup Sanskrit Library). Shastri tells us that 'he was a great collector of manuscripts. It is not known how many thousands of manuscripts he collected, but all the manuscripts of his library bear in large, bold, and beautiful Devanāgarī character his signature *sarva-vidyā-nidhāna-kavīndra-sarasvatī*. That signature is a guarantee for the correctness and accuracy of the manuscript. It is not known when and how the library was broken up, but the manuscripts of his library can now be procured in Benares, and they are preferred by all Paṇḍits to other manuscripts.'

[30]   Smith, V. A. (ed.) *The Oxford History of India* (Oxford: Oxford University Press, 2nd edn., 1923), 415, 425.

[31]   Jayarāma, for instance, who knew Bernier's discussant, Kavīndra Sarasvatī, might well have been one of them. Bernier reports that he was introduced to 'the six most learned paṇḍits in the town' of Vārāṇasī (Bernier, *Histoire de la dernière révolution des États du Gran Mogol*, 342).

emerged. Educational networks centred on individuals and their families provided the structures needed for the 'new reason' to flourish in Islamicate India, but I would also argue that their very nature, particular the fiscal arrangements surrounding them, hampered as well as nurtured innovation. It is striking that several of the most original 'new reason' philosophers existed on the periphery of these structures, benefiting from them without being too closely implicated in their perpetuation. Others were able to participate in broader networks, such as those existing in Navadvīpa at the time of Raghunātha, or the type of informal umbrella of association created by a patron like Danishmand Khān, which 'brought together a Frenchman of Paris, a Muslim of Persia and a Brahmin of Benares'.[32]

I believe that in a very complex political and intellectual climate the early modern 'new reason' thinkers were developing philosophical ideas of great radicality and originality, initiating a line of philosophical inquiry that did not so much run its course as was brought to a virtual stand-still, in the first instance by the collapse in stable Mughal power and patronage, and in the second by the disruption caused to established patterns for conducting and financing education by the British imposition of new fiscal arrangements and educational policies. Work in the 'new reason' continued into the nineteenth and twentieth century in an educational set-up now sharply bifurcated between low-prestige traditional networks and well-funded colonial colleges and universities.[33] Sheldon Pollock writes that 'when colonialism made the norms of Europe the norms of India the Sanskrit intellectual formation melted like so much snow in the light of a brilliant, pitiless sun'.[34] I don't see in contemporaneous European epistemology ideas so superior to the Indian ideas surveyed by Mahādeva as to have been powerful enough in and of themselves to accomplish this: what caused the dissolution of Sanskrit culture under colonialism was the dismembering of the systems of education and patronage that held that culture together, along with the simultaneous creation of well-funded colonial universities and colleges. More importantly, it was precisely the 'norms of

---

[32] Gode, P. K. 'Bernier and Kavīndrācārya Sarasvatī at the Moghal Court', 376

[33] See Krishna, Daya. *Developments in Indian Philosophy from Eighteenth Century Onwards. History of Science, Philosophy and Culture in Indian Civilization*, vol. 10 part 1 (New Delhi: Centre for Studies in Civilizations, 2001).

[34] Pollock (2001). 'The New Intellectuals in Seventeenth century India', The Indian Economic and Social History Review **38**, 24

Jonardon Ganeri

India', its modern model of engaging the new in a dialogue with the old, of the outsider with the insider, which enabled it to emerge from British colonialism if not unscathed then at least uncrushed.

Early modernity in India consists in the formation of a new philosophical self, one which makes it possible meaningfully to conceive of oneself as engaging the ancient and the alien in conversation. The Sufi Dārā Shukoh, Akbar's great grandson, is an exemplary early modern thinker, his belief that the Upaniṣads could be read as a commentary on the Qu'rān envisaged a relationship that was based neither on deference nor on rejection.[35] For Dārā the Hindu text was not an authority to which Islam must defer but a partner in a single quest for truth – his sectarian contemporaries' inability to make that distinction cost him his life. The Jaina philosopher Yaśovijaya Gaṇi is a quintessential early modern thinker too: in his case this was due to his search of a theory of individuals and community in which liberal political values occupy the centre stage. Yaśovijaya articulates a key feature of the early modern self when he says that public discussion must rest in balance, neutrality and an openness to the reasonable opinions of others.

What distinguishes the modernity of the 'new reason' philosophers is a new sense of one's duties towards the past. They saw themselves as engaging in 'dialogues with the dead',[36] not in deference, but to collaborate in a new search for the truth. I have characterized *early* modernity not as real modernity mixed up in a confused muddle with premodern habits, as many historians of early modern Europe do, but as the embodiment of a distinctive understanding of one's duties towards the past. The texts of 'new reason' philosophers are full of exhortations to the reader to direct their attention to what matters. The *Inquiry*, in particular, is a challenge: deliberately provocative, it led other philosophers to a far-reaching and sophisticated reformation of realism. The new spirit is succinctly captured by Veṇīdatta at the end of his *Embellishment of the Categories*. He appeals to a model of reasoning as 'adaptation' (*ūha*) and claims that an adaptation of the ancient metaphysics is legitimate as long as it done on the basis

[35] Dārā Shukoh (1929 [1655]). *Majma-ul-Barhain, or The Mingling of the Two Oceans by Prince Muhammad Dārā Shikuh*. M. Mahfuzul-Haq (ed.) and trans. (New Delhi: Adam Publishers, 1929; 2006 edn); Dārā Shukoh (1957 [1656]). *Sirr-i Akbar: The Oldest Translation of the Upaniṣads from Sanskrit into Persian*. Tara Chand & S. M. Raza Jalali Nayni (eds) (Tehran: Taban, 1957).
[36] Curley, Edwin (1986). 'Dialogues with the Dead', Synthese 67(1): 2249.

of a proper deliberation.[37] Veṇīdatta here finds a new application for a conception of reason as modification or adaptation (*ūha*) that had already achieved considerable theoretical articulation, especially in the work of Mīmāṃsā ritualists who sought rationally to adapt the ancient ritual prescriptions to suit the circumstances of contemporary ritual performance. This is the *via moderna*, working with the ancients but not hamstrung by them. Raghunātha revealed himself to be at best uncomfortable with the idea that one can be a reductionist and a realist at the same time: for him the way to defend claims about metaphysical autonomy was by the identification of new irreducible categories of being. The position which emerges as the most attractive in the seventeenth century, consists in a new demonstration that realism is not, as the earlier tradition assumes, incompatible with reduction. The ability to see that there is a way to escape the ancient antinomy produced by the false dichotomy between realism and reduction is one of the great 'conceptual breaks' of the period. It enabled the emergence of a new natural philosophy in the early modern thought of late seventeenth century thinkers, most notably Jayarāma, a philosophy of nature the equal of any to appear in the new mechanical philosophy of early modern Europe or in their progressive Aristotelian interlocutors.

The construction in the nineteenth century of what I earlier called the 'standard history' of early modernity fabricated a mythology which served to exaggerate and dramatize the differences between India and Europe.[38] The standard history about the distinctively European origins of modern philosophy in the seventeenth century was shaped, it seems, by distinctly nineteenth century needs. It is actually rather shocking that this history of the birth of modern philosophy continues to be taught uncritically in university philosophy departments still today.

I spoke at the beginning of Susan Friedman's coining of the term 'polycentric modernities' to capture the idea that modernity has a

---

[37] vic āra; Veṇīdatta. *Embellishment of the Categories* (Padārthamaṇḍa na), Gopala Sastri Nene ed. (Benares: Vidya Vilas Press; Princess of Wales Sarasvati Bhavana texts 30, 1930), 36

[38] Edmund Husserl, for example, identifies 'Cartesian freedom from prejudice' as what distinguishes 'European mankind' from India and the Orient (Halbfass, Wilhelm. *India and Europe: An Essay in Understanding* (Albany: State University of New York Press, 1988) 157). Gottlob Frege says that 'in arithmetic, if only because its methods and concepts originated in India, it has been the tradition to reason less strictly than in geometry, which was in the main developed by the Greeks'. Frege. *The Foundations of Arithmetic*. Trans. by J. L. Austin (Oxford: Basil Blackwell, 1950), §1

spatiality and a geography, and should not be thought of simply in terms of periodization. 'Rupture' is the term she prefers to characterise the onset of a new modernity, suggesting that 'modernity involves a powerful vortex of historical conditions that coalesce to produce sharp ruptures from the past that range widely across various sectors of a given society... Across the vast reaches of civilizational history, eruptions of different modernities ofen occur in the context of empires and conquest',[39] and she stresses that a polycentric model 'recognizes the modernities that have formed not only after the rise of the West but also before the West's post-1500 period of rapid change – the earlier modernities of the Tang Dynasty in China, the Abbasid Dynasty of the Muslim empire, and the Mongol Empire, to cite just a few'.[40] Modernity, and this is a point that has been made forcefully by Sanjay Subrahmanyam in his use of the term 'conjuncturality', is also characterised by the 'intensification of intercultural contact zones... heightened hybridizations, jarring juxtapositions, and increasingly porous borders both characterize modernity and help bring it into being.' Subrahmanyam says, perfectly accurately, that 'modernity is a global conjunctural phenomenon, not a virus that spreads from one place to another'.[41] It has its own distinctive phenomenology too, the phenomenology of the new and the now: there is something that it feels like to be in the grip of modernity, incorporating 'a gamut of sensations from displacement, despair, and nostalgia to exhilaration, hope, and embrace of the new...'. 'Modernity', Friedman says, 'invents tradition, suppresses its own continuities with the past, and often produces nostalgia for what has seemingly been lost. Tradition forms at the moment those who perceive it regard themselves as cut off from it.' I have found all these indicators to be present in my study of the early modernity of India. Friedman, I think, only oversteps the mark when she places too great an emphasis on the centrality of rupture, of a 'dislocating break with the past', citing with approval Paul de Man's statement that modernity, 'a ruthless forgetting' of the past, 'exists in the form of a desire to wipe out whatever came earlier.[42] In this essay I have argued instead that it is better to see modernity as

[39]   Freidman, Susan (2006). 'Periodizing modernism: postcolonial modernities and the space/time borders of modernist studies', 433
[40]   Ibid.
[41]   Subrahmanyam, Sanjay (1998). 'Hearing voices: vignettes of early modernity in South Asia, 1400–1750', Daedalus 127(3): 75–104.
[42]   de Man, Paul (1983). 'Literary history and literary modernity', Blindness and Insight (Minneapolis: University of Minnesota Press), 147–8

involving not radical rupture but a shift of allegiance, a new sense of one's duties to the past, and a transition from deference to dialogue.

University of Sussex
j.ganeri@sussex.ac.uk

Appendix: A Chronology

Until 11th Century. Nyāya philosophy develops in dialogue with Buddhism. Udayana and Vallabha are the last important voices.

12th Century. **Śrīharṣa** writes a set of sceptical 'refutations.'

c.1325. **Gaṅgeśa** writes the *Gemstone for Truth*, and a renovated Nyāya takes root in his hometown of Mithilā.

1460–1540. **Raghunātha Śiromaṇi** invents the 'new reason' in Navadvīpa, a town in Bengal. His immediate followers develop and teach his ideas both in Navadvīpa and also in Vārāṇasī.

1486. Birth of **Caitanya** in Navadvīpa.

1493–1519. Reign of the liberal sultan **Husain Shāh** in Bengal. His ministers include Rūpa and Sanātana Gosvāmī, exponents of Caitanya's Vaiṣṇavism.

1556. **Akbar** assumes the Mughal throne; the empire spreads throughout northern India. His ministers include the Hindus Man Singh and Ṭoḍarmal, both of whom encourage 'new reason' philosophers.

1582. Debate between **Vidyānivāsa,** a 'new reason' thinker, and Nārāyaṇa Bhaṭṭa at Ṭoḍarmal's house.

1597. Abu'l Fazl writes the *Āīn-i-Akbarī*, a synopsis of life at the time of Akbar. Several 'new reason' philosophers are mentioned.

1605. Death of Akbar. He is followed by Jahangīr r.1605–1627, Shāh Jahān r.1628–1658, and Aurangzeb r.1658–1707.

1613. **Roberto Nobili** writes the *Informatio*, containing a description of the new 'natural philosophy.'

1615. **Dārā Shukoh**, eldest son of Shāh Jahān, born 20th March.

1620. **Francis Bacon** publishes the *Novum Organum*.

1621. **Sébastien Basso** publishes the *Natural Philosophy Directed Against Aristotle*.

1634. **Viśvanātha**, son of Vidyānivāsa, writes a commentary on the *Nyāya-sūtra*.

1637. **René Descartes** publishes the *Discourse and Essays*.

1638. **Kavīndra Sarasvatī** petitions Shāh Jahān to repeal a tax on Hindu pilgims.

1650. Death of Descartes.

1655. Death of **Pierre Gassendi**. His protegé **François Bernier** is with him.

1656. Dārā Shukoh assembles a team of Vārāṇasī scholars to translate the Upaniṣads into Persian. Bernier arrives in India, and works as physician to Shāh Jahān and Dārā Shukoh.

1657. Leading Vārāṇasī intellectuals publically meet and sign a letter of judgement.

1659. Dārā Shukoh is sentenced for heresy and executed, after a conflict with Aurangzeb. The key 'new reason' philosopher **Jaya rāma**, an acquaintance of Kavīdra, finishes the *Garland of Categories*. He writes the *Garland of Principles about Reason* around this time too. **Raghudeva**, another 'new reason' philosopher, is doing similar work too and moving in the same circles in Vārāṇasī.

1658–61. **Danishmand Khān**, an accultured nobleman who opposes the execution of Dārā, takes on Kavīndra, Bernier and others when they lose their patron. They exchange ideas, Bernier translating Gassendi and Descartes into Persian, Kavīndra bringing Vārāṇasī thinkers and Bernier into discussion.

1660. Foundation of the Royal Society in London.

1670. Bernier, back in France, publishes his *Travels in the Mogul Empire*. Henry Oldenburg, the first secretary of the Royal Society, will arrange for their English publication; John Dryden bases his 1675 play *Aureng-zebe* on them.

1677. Death of **Spinoza**. The *Ethics* is published.

1678. Bernier publishes his *Abr égé* of Gassendi's philosophy.

1688. Death of **Yaśovijaya Gaṇi**, a brilliant Jaina philosopher responds to the 'new reason' and perhaps also to Dārā's project.

1690. **John Locke** publishes his *Essay Concerning Human Understanding*. He seems to have read Bernier's *Abr égé*.

1690s. Several 'new reason' thinkers are active in Vārāṇasī: **Mahā deva** writes the *Precious Jewel of Reason*, and **Mādhavadeva** the *Essence of Reason*.

1707. Death of Aurangzeb.

1757. The Battle of Plassey.

1765. East India Company obtains taxation rights over Bengal.

1769–70. Great Famine, caused by punative taxation and grain stockpiling.

1776. Britain, defeated in the American war for independence, turns its attention to India. Warren Hastings prepares a 'plan for the administration of justice.'

Daoism, Nature and Humanity

DAVID E. COOPER

Abstract

This paper sympathetically explores Daoism's relevance to environmental philosophy and to the aspiration of people to live in a manner convergent with nature. After discussing the Daoist understanding of nature and the *dao* (Way), the focus turns to the implications of these notions for our relationship to nature. The popular idea that Daoism encourages a return to a 'primitive' way of life is rejected. Instead, it is shown that the Daoist proposal is one of living more 'spontaneously' than people generally do in the modern, technological world, and of allowing other beings to do so as well. These themes are clarified in a final section, inspired by some Daoist remarks, devoted to the relationship of human beings with animals.

1. The appeal of Daoism

As befits the title of the lecture series to which this one belongs, 'Philosophical Traditions', my focus is on so-called 'philosophical' Daoism. Not my term, but one that has often been used to distinguish the thoughts articulated in classic texts like the *Daodejing*, during the Period of the Warring States in China (c.475–221 BCE), from an organized Daoist religion that developed several centuries later. 'Early' Daoism might be a better term, for the once popular older view that Daoist philosophy must be 'kept carefully distinguished from Daoist religion' has given way to a more nuanced perception.[1] Later Daoist preoccupations with longevity and cultivation of the body have their precedents in the classics and it is possible to discern a religious sense expressed in these texts.

By 'these texts', I mean primarily the *Daodejing* ('The Classic of the Way and Virtue (or Power)' – once attributed to a sixth-century BCE sage, Laozi, but actually a work compiled about three centuries later – and the book attributed to Zhuangzi (ca. 369–286 BCE). But I shall refer, too, to a slightly earlier work, *Neiye* ('Inner cultivation'), and to a later compilation of writings albeit attributed to a fifth-century BCE figure, Liezi.[2]

---

[1]   Fung Yulan, *A Short History of Chinese Philosophy* (New York: Free Press, 1966), 31

[2]   References within the text use the abbreviations indicated for the following works: *Daodejing* (D), *The Book of Zhuangzi* (Z), and *The Book of*

doi:10.1017/S1358246114000034

David E. Cooper

The three hundred or so translations of the *Daodejing* into European languages testify to the current appeal of Daoism in the West – as, in a different way, do the many books with titles like *The Tao of Pooh* and *The Tao of Meow*. Like Buddhism, Daoism seems to offer the kind of God-free spirituality sought after by many people in the West. To philosophers still in recoil from Cartesian dualism, yet unable to accept a blunt physicalism, Daoism presents an attractive metaphysical vision of a world inseparable from our experience of it, yet emergent from a source that is mysterious and ineffable.

But it is, perhaps, Daoism's 'green' reputation – as an ecologically enlightened dispensation – that most endears it to people in the West. Lin Yutang no doubt exaggerated the divide between Confucians and Daoists when he described the former as 'too decorous' and praised the latter for 'go[ing] about with dishevelled hair and bare feet'.[3] The impression remains, however, that Daoism is distinctive in a proposal for intimacy or convergence with nature that few other spiritual traditions can rival.

There are, of course, philosophers for whom a rhetoric of 'oneness with nature' does nothing to recommend a proposal. Roger Scruton, for example, has recently criticised the 'tortured' ecocentric or biocentric literature that advocates 'identifying the self' with nature. Even if such calls are intelligible, he complains, their 'practical conclusions' are opaque, for no account is offered of how 'oneness with nature' might motivate people to act in any determinate way.[4] It is easy to sympathise with this criticism, and some claims made on behalf of Daoism are surely open to it. The Daoist, proclaimed one

---

Liezi (L). References are to chapters of these works. (Eg. D 25 refers to chapter 25 of the *Daodejing*). I have drawn on various translations of the works, but especially on P.J. Ivanhoe, *The Daodejing of Laozi* (Indianapolis: Hackett, 2002), Wang Keping, *Reading the Dao: A Thematic Inquiry* (London: Continuum, 2010), A.C. Graham, *Chuang-Tzu: The Inner Chapters* (Indianapolis: Hackett, 2001) and *The Book of Lieh-Tzu: A Classic of Tao* (New York, Columbia University Press, 1990), and B. Ziporyn, *Zhuangzi: The Essential Writings, with Selections from Traditional Commentaries* (Indianapolis: Hackett, 2009).

[3] Yutang Lin, *My Country and its People* (London: Heinemann, 1936), 112

[4] Roger Scruton, *Green Philosophy: How to Think Seriously about the Planet* (London: Atlantic, 2012), 195

hyperbolic author, 'plunges into the unknowable … the way of nature', so as 'to merge into nature'.[5]

Such extravagant prose notwithstanding, the possibility remains that Daoism has the philosophical resources not only to provide an intelligible account of convergence with nature, but to explain why this convergence is a dimension of the good life. This is the possibility I explore in this lecture and, in doing so, I touch upon the spiritual and metaphysical attractions of Daoism that I mentioned earlier.

2. Daoist moods and edification

Attention to Daoism is encouraged by the expression in the classic texts of attitudes or moods that also inform contemporary environmental writings in which the idea of convergence is prominent. To begin with, the texts express a *desire* for convergence with nature. Human beings should, it is said, 'follow the way of the earth', just as in turn the earth 'follows the way of heaven' (D25). For Daoists, as for today's 'greens', people's lives should, in some sense, be more 'natural'. Second, the texts express a nostalgia, palpable too in much 'green' literature, for a time, real or imagined, when people did live more naturally: when, for instance, there was 'plainness and simplicity', a minimum of technology and artifice, so that there was less 'selfishness', and men and women could live more 'peacefully in their homes' (D 19, 80).

As the tone of those remarks suggest, the texts also express criticism of, or disillusion with, human beings for creating a complex civilization in which the plain, simple, peaceful life is impossible, and in which people have become estranged from a more natural existence. In the *Zhuangzi*, especially, there are passages that might almost be mistaken for modern diatribes in which it is a frenzied 'busy-ness', a relentless pursuit of goals and purposes, and a subjection to economic imperatives that are blamed for the loss of a more authentic form of human life. More than two thousand years earlier, according to the *Zhuangzi*, the Chinese were already 'scurrying around even when sitting still', always 'uneasy without the busyness of buying and selling', and constantly 'worried' and 'sad' when their ambitions were thwarted. Their life 'rushes on like a galloping horse', a life 'confined by' or 'submerged in' a world of material goods (Z 2, 4, 24).

[5]   L. Cranmer-Byng, Introduction to Yang Chu's *Garden of Pleasure* (Forgotten Books, e-book, 2010), 25

David E. Cooper

Finally, the texts convey a perception – shared by many modern critics of technology – that the unhappy frenzy of these confined and submerged lives is related to the replacement of a sense of the mystery and wonder of things by hubristic overestimation of the scope of human knowledge and control. The famous opening words of the *Daodejing* tell us that 'the *dao* (way) that can be named is not the constant *dao*', and that the relationship between the *dao* and 'the myriad things' – the world – of which it is the source is itself profoundly mysterious (D 1). Throughout the principal classics, there are calls to 'abandon' confidence in learning and in the ability to articulate the truth of things. 'One who knows does not speak. One who speaks does not know' (D 56).

In conveying a yearning for convergence with nature, nostalgia for an age when people led lives that were simpler and closer to nature, disillusion with the course of human history, and a sense of the mystery of the way of things, Daoism expresses attitudes or moods that are consonant with a tendency in modern environmental thought. It is one thing, however, to recognize this consonance of mood, but another to show that Daoism has the resources to justify these moods and to guide our responses to them – the resources, in effect, to fashion a way of convergence.

The bare structure of the Daoist position is clear enough. Human beings, we saw, should 'follow the way of the earth'. This is because the earth follows the way of heaven, which in turn 'follows the *dao*' itself (D 25). By following nature, therefore, human lives achieve harmony or convergence with the *dao* – with *the* Way, that is. And harmony with the Way is the supreme Daoist imperative. Humankind, one might say, has lost the Way; nature has not. So by returning to living naturally, men and women will once again be 'on the Way'.

While this description of the Daoist position does not address the questions of how and why a life convergent with nature is 'on the Way', it does suggest that mindful attention to natural environments will be edifying. To begin with, nature furnishes the attentive observer with instructive metaphors both for the *dao* and the life of the sage. Like Coleridge's 'symbols', these enable the imagination to give force and life to what would otherwise be inert 'ideas'. The favourite Daoist metaphors correspond, in fact, to one of Coleridge's main symbols, water. Rather as, for the poet, the 'leaping up and plunging forward' of a waterfall is an 'awful image and shadow of God and the world',[6] so for the Daoist water furnishes analogies

---

[6]   S.T. Coleridge, *Collected Letters 1801–06*, (ed.) E.L. Griggs (Oxford: Oxford University Press, 2002), 852–3

that give us a sense for the *dao* and the life of virtue.[7] Like water, the *dao* 'preserves and nourishes all things' without making any 'claim to be master over them' (D 34). Moreover, in flowing downwards to the lowest and most 'detestable' places, such as sewers, water teaches the sage a lesson in humility (D 8).

Second, natural environments provide an arena in which, as the *Zhuangzi* puts it, we are able to 'let go of the world' and escape from the frenetic pursuit of 'rank, wealth and prestige' that characterizes life in the city (Z 19, 23). Countless Chinese paintings and poems of the Tang era convey this Daoist message: paintings in which a small, reflective figure sits perched on a mountain far removed from the dust, grime and frenzy of urban existence; and poems that explain how, to get away from 'the affairs of the world', a man repairs to the forest, watches the moon, and listens to 'the wind of the pines' and 'a fisherman's song going into the deep river bank'.[8] It is a message conveyed millennia later by Iris Murdoch, when describing how her absorbed attention to birds and plants in their 'sheer alien pointless independent existence' offers respite from the demands of the 'fat relentless ego'.[9]

In these respects, then, experience of natural environments may be edifying. This does not, however, answer the question of how, exactly, a life convergent with nature is 'on the Way'. Indeed, the question of what convergence with nature *is* remains unaddressed. To make progress with these questions, we must turn to the Daoist understanding of nature and of the *dao* itself.

3. Nature and *dao*

People sceptical of Daoism's relevance to modern environmental concerns will point out that ancient Chinese had no term for nature in, as it were, the David Attenborough sense – nature as what natural historians study, and what TV nature programmes are programmes about. This does not mean, of course, that the Chinese were unable to talk about natural landscapes and wild things, nor that their concepts of nature were without implications for our

---

[7] See Sarah Allen, *The Way of Water and Sprouts of Virtue* (Albany, NY: SUNY University Press, 1997)

[8] Wang Wei (8th century), in P. Harris (trans.) *Three Hundred Tang Poems* (New York: Alfred A. Knopf, 2009), 224

[9] Iris Murdoch, *Existentialists and Mystics* (London: Penguin, 1997), 378

relationship to nature in this sense. It does indicate, though, that the Chinese were not wedded to 'a wilderness ideal' and that they did not emphasize a sharp distinction between the human and natural worlds. Unlike some modern writers, moreover, Daoists were not guilty of confusing wilderness with what is wild. They would have endorsed Roger Deakin's remark that a patch of lawn is a 'jungle in miniature'[10] – a place where, even in Cheltenham or Chelsea, wild creatures and processes are at work.

The environments that the main Daoist texts mention are, to a greater or lesser degree, 'humanised' landscapes – including gardens, parks, farms, and other places with which people actively engage. The landscapes depicted in Chinese paintings are not, typically, devoid of all human presence: there in the distance are boats, huts, temples, carts and so on.

There are several terms in the texts that can, according to context and with suitable caution, be translated by 'nature' – and in various senses of that versatile word. *Tiandi* (heaven-and-earth) is perhaps the nearest term for nature-as-a-whole, nature as the totality of what is subject to the laws of nature – to the patterns and rhythms, especially of Yin and Yang, which Chinese cosmologists discerned in the world. Important, too, are a number of terms that refer to the nature of a particular being – to its 'essence' or its 'original', given nature. *Xing*, for example, has been defined as 'the course in which life completes its development if sufficiently nourished and not obstructed or injured from outside'.[11]

These various senses of 'nature' are, for Daoist thinkers, more obviously connected than they any longer are for us. And what connects them is their relationship to the *dao*. As the source of 'heaven-and-earth' and the 'mother' of 'the myriad things' (D 1), the *dao* imparts to the world its own 'naturalness', 'spontaneity' or, more literally, 'self-so-ness' (*ziran*). The patterns and rhythms of which it is the source enable the world to continue on its course without further intervention, thereby allowing the myriad things to develop and express their 'original' natures, essences (*jing*) or native powers (*de*) that have been 'opened out and arrayed' by the *dao* (Z 23).

The Daoist notion of nature has, unsurprisingly, referred us to the *dao*. Before returning to the matter of convergence with nature, then, let me briefly turn to this pivotal term. Despite some reductivist

---

[10]   Roger Deakin, *Notes from Walnut Tree Farm* (London: Penguin, 2009), 155

[11]   A.C. Graham, *Disputers of the Tao: Philosophical Argument in Ancient China* (La Salle, Ill.: Open Court, 1989), 124

attempts by recent scholars, *dao* cannot be *equated* with nature. While in some contexts, the term is virtually equivalent to 'nature-as-a-whole', the dominant rhetoric in the texts is of the *dao* as the 'source', 'generator' or 'mother' of heaven-and-earth (eg. D 25, Z 6). It would be quite wrong, however, to interpret this rhetoric theistically. This is despite the tendency of early translators to render *dao* as God, with the express intention in one case, at least, of showing that 'the Mysteries of the Most Holy Trinity and of the Incarnate God were anciently known to the Chinese nation'.[12] The *dao* is without the purposes, the substance, and the independence from the world that characterise a creator God. The *Zhuangzi* emphasizes that the *dao* is not 'something that causes' or creates and that, as what 'forms forms' or 'things things', it is not itself a form or a thing (Z 22, 25). The *dao*, explains the *Neiye*, is not 'separated from us' or things, but 'fills the entire world'.[13]

It helps when thinking about the *dao* to remember that the Chinese term has a verbal as well as a nominal form: *dao*, in this sense, is a dynamic notion, for it refers to 'cutting a path or channel', to the *making* of a way, rather as flowing water does. This is why the *Daodejing* can say that the *dao* stands to the world as rivers do to the valleys they both make and flow through (D 32). The imagery encourages a view of the *dao*, not as a divine substance, but as a constant enabling of a world, a constant process of 'giving forth' that makes it possible for things to be present to experience (Z 17).[14] Martin Heidegger, an admirer of Daoism, aptly glossed *dao* as 'the Way that gives all ways'[15] – the well-spring, as it were, for the various ways followed by animals, plants, and 'the ten thousand things'. For Zhuangzi, at least, the existence of things that can be conceptualized and spoken of is inseparable from experience of them: 'Each thing has some place [perspective] from which it can be affirmed as thus and so' (Z 2). This implies that the *dao* is, in effect, the condition for all possible experience, for the perspectives or ways of experience in virtue of which things figure as the things they are.[16]

---

[12]   Cited in Ma Lin, *Heidegger on East-West Dialogue* (London: Routledge, 2008), 120

[13]   H. Roth (trans.), *The Nei-Yeh* (www.stillness.com/tao/neiyeh.txt, 1999), sections 5 and 14

[14]   See Hans-Georg Moeller, *Daoism Explained* (Chicago: Open Court, 2004), 147

[15]   Martin Heidegger, *On the Way to Language* (New York: Harper & Row, 1971), 92

[16]   For a fuller account, see David E. Cooper, *Convergence with Nature: A Daoist Perspective* (Dartington: Green Books, 2012), Chapter 6.

David E. Cooper

Lacking any form or substance, and not itself an object of possible experience, *dao* is ineffable, since anything is describable only from a particular perspective. Aquatic and maternal characterizations of *dao*, and Heidegger's too, are figurative ones that do not, as it were, try to 'eff' the ineffable. Further characterizations of the workings of *dao* are best postponed until after a discussion of how a life, through its convergence with nature, is 'on the Way'. *Dao*, after all, is what it is that a convergent life accords with. This postponement mirrors the strategy followed in the texts, where analogies with the sage's life are exploited in order to illuminate *dao*. (Notice I've dropped the definite article before '*dao*': it's not there in the Chinese and it encourages the rejected construal of *dao* as a substance or God.)

4. Daoism and 'Primitivism'

So let's revisit, in the light of the above remarks on nature and *dao*, the questions raised earlier about convergence with nature. What is it, and why does it accord with *dao*? I begin by considering an approach that has been labelled 'primitivism'. According to the primitivist interpretation of Daoism, if human beings – unlike other beings in nature – are no longer 'on the Way', the remedy is a return to a state of nature, an abandonment of the humanity that distinguishes them from animals. A life convergent with nature is one assimilated to the existence of animals, or of infants, since theirs is, as Hans-Georg Moeller puts it, 'the least "human" phase in our life – and the most natural'.[17]

The primitivist understanding of Daoism is not unfamiliar: it shapes, for example, that popular image of Daoists going about with dishevelled hair and bare feet. It is an understanding, moreover, that would appeal to some modern environmentalists – to those who, like John Fowles, recommend re-immersion in the 'green chaos' enjoyed by our 'wild, green-men' ancestors,[18] or, like Simon Barnes, 'living a wilder life' suited to our 'ancient wild self'.[19]

There are passages in the texts, certainly, to encourage the primitivist reading. (A.C. Graham, in his celebrated translation of the

[17]   Hans-Georg Moeller, *Daodejing (Laozi): A Complete Translation and Commentary* (Chicago: Open Court, 2007), 128
[18]   John Fowles, 'Seeing the whole', in S. Armstrong and R. Botzler (eds), *Environmental Ethics* (New York: McGraw-Hill, 1993), 138–40
[19]   Simon Barnes, *How to be Wild* (London: Short Books, 2007), 58 & 282

Zhuangzi, gives the label 'The Primitivist' to the author of some chapters later added to those supposedly written by Zhuangzi himself). For a start, there are the remarks directed against Confucian confidence in the beneficial role of rituals, social conventions and moral principles in the good life. According to the *Daodejing,* it is only when '*dao* is lost' that a need arises for 'righteousness' and 'ritual propriety' (D 38). Then there are the many remarks that impugn the value of systematic intellectual knowledge (*zhi*). An important chapter in the *Zhuangzi* calls for a 'fasting of the mind' that will 'expel' such knowledge, so as to enhance both a more practical, 'vital' form of understanding and a still, silent receptivity to 'the presence of beings' (Z 4). Finally, several chapters in the classics decry the emergence of complex societies dependent on sophisticated technology. The penultimate chapter of the *Daodejing* is a portrait of an ideal society in which people live in simple, isolated communities and eschew the use of complicated instruments, means of transport, weapons and advanced methods of writing (D 80). The *Zhuangzi,* similarly, inveighs against the use of new-fangled devices for irrigation and ingenious, state of the art traps to catch animals or fish (Z 10, 12).

It is wrong, however, to read such passages as calling for a return to a state of nature prior to civilization. Zhuangzi is not complaining about the use of technology as such, but about the profit-driven 'cunning, deception' and 'trickiness' that a preoccupation with technical advances involves. And the Daoist utopia described in the *Daodejing* is not a primitive form of existence, but a human society in which, simple as it may be, people 'delight in customs', 'beautify their clothing', employ a form of writing, and rear animals.

Nor is there any suggestion that, in returning to a more natural way of living, people are abandoning their distinctive humanity and assimilating their life to that of animals and infants. Far from a desire to 'strip the human subject of all that is quintessentially human', one author explains, the Daoist aim is rather 'to liberate human existence from the false values and views' that have accrued over the centuries.[20] The main reason that the Daoist call cannot be one for regression by human beings to 'wild green-men' is that the Daoist sage possesses *understanding,* specifically an awareness of *dao* and of the consonance with *dao* of his own life. It is because the good Daoist is 'moved by Heaven' (Z 15) and 'esteems the attainment of *dao*' (D 20), that he is able to exercise an intelligent

---

[20] Eske Møllgard, *An Introduction to Daoist Thought: Action, language and ethics in Zhuangzi* (London: Routledge, 2007), 20

David E. Cooper

impartiality and a reflective mastery over his desires (D 46, 49). These are not capacities available to animals or very young children.

It is important to stress, however, that a distinctively human understanding of *dao* is not an intellectual or scholarly feat. Most of the main examples in the *Zhuangzi* of people possessed of this understanding are 'practical' people whose sense of *dao* is manifested in their style of action and comportment. From the butcher whose cleaver is guided by a recognition of 'heaven's structuring' and what is 'inherently so' (Z 3), to the bell-stand maker whose work responds to 'the inborn heavenly nature' of trees, to the swimmer who 'follows the Way of water itself' (Z 19) – these are men whose practice is enabled by their implicit awareness of *dao*.

Reflection on this same cast of characters will also help in understanding the form of convergence with nature that is sought by Daoists, and in so doing reveal another reason why this is very different from regression to a wild state and from an abandonment of the distinctively human.

5. Spontaneity and *wu wei*

A feature common to the performances and practices of the swimmer, the butcher and many other figures in the *Zhuangzi* is their *spontaneity*. The swimmer does not impose a 'course of [his] own' on the water, but adjusts to its flow; the butcher follows no fixed plan, so that when he encounters a difficulty, he pauses, lets his blade move as if by itself, and Hey Presto!, there is the ox, dismembered at his feet. In the wilderness of Dongting, a musician – the legendary Yellow Emperor, no less – plays music that is 'flowing, unforced and uncontrived', constantly 'adjusting to the mandate of [the] things' surrounding him in the natural environment with which, like a jazz player, he is jamming (Z 14).

The spontaneity manifested here is not that of capriciousness, impulse or surrender to the passions: rather, as one of Zhuangzi's translators puts it, it is alert, flexible 'responsiveness in the impersonal calm when vision is most lucid'.[21] Like the swimmer's or the musician's, the mind of the Daoist sage – as an early Chinese editor of the *Zhuangzi* explains – is spontaneous since it 'follows along with the character of each thing', 'unfettered', 'free of dependence' on prejudices, conventions and *idées fixes* that obstruct attentive openness to things.[22]

[21] A.C. Graham, *Chuang-Tzu*, op. cit. note 2, 14
[22] Guo Xiang, cited in Ziporyn, op. cit. note 2, 132

This is the spontaneity sought, two millennia later, by Rousseau's 'solitary walker', whose soul 'rambles and glides through the universe', allowing ideas to 'follow their own bent without constraint'.[23] It is interesting that precisely this metaphor of rambling was used by Zhuangzi in the opening chapter of his work to refer to the spontaneous heart-and-mind of the sage.

It is this spontaneity that the texts identify with convergence with nature. The calls for simplicity, suspicion of technology and scholarship, and the setting aside of artificial conventions are not a summons to return to a state of nature. They eulogise, rather, a form of life hospitable to the spontaneity that is barely discernible in complex urban societies. 'Attuned' to things and spontaneously responding to them, a person 'arrives up beyond them to the source of things' (Z 33). By 'following the way of the earth', the sage 'follows the way of *dao*', because '*dao* [itself] follows the way of spontaneity (*ziran*) (D 25). Or better, because *dao* is itself a spontaneous process, a 'movement' – like the swimmer's – which 'happens without any effort or "driving force" that tries to impose a certain direction'. The sage, nature, and *dao* all 'move "self-so"'.[24]

Spontaneity is closely related to the Daoist ideal of *wu wei*, literally 'non-action' but a virtual synonym in some contexts for *ziran*. An early Chinese commentator on the *Daodejing* defined it as 'following what is spontaneous or natural ... taking no action that is contrary to nature'.[25] Certainly, the sage who 'conducts affairs through no-action' thereby follows the example of *dao*, which itself leaves 'nothing undone' through 'doing nothing' (D 2, 48). In other contexts, however, *wu wei* is understood not as an exercise of spontaneity by someone, but as a person's helping creatures or things to be 'self-so', to themselves be natural and spontaneous. The sage, it is said, 'supports the own course (*ziran*) of the ten thousand things' (D 64). Here, too, the sage is in emulation of the Way, since *dao* itself is understood as 'giving' to each thing its 'self-so' nature, as the Way that 'gives' the way of each thing.

Wu wei in this sense is exercised by several of the Daoist heroes encountered earlier, such as the bell-stand maker and the Yellow Emperor. The former discerns the 'inborn heavenly nature' of a tree, and will cut it down only if it contains within it 'the completed

---

[23] Jean-Jacques Rousseau, *The Reveries of a Solitary Walker* (Indianapolis: Hackett, 1992), 91

[24] Moeller, op. cit., note 17, 82

[25] Wang Bi, cited in Wang Keping, op. cit., n.2, 37

bell-stand' – only when, in effect, he feels that his work will honour and realize the nature of the wood (Z 19). The Yellow Emperor, meanwhile, regards his music-making to be not simply 'adjusting to the unforced mandates of things' but as 'helping to clear the way for things' (Z 6). In spontaneous engagement with things in the surrounding environment, he imposes nothing on them: indeed, his responses to their sounds render their natures or 'mandates' more salient. Craftsman and musician alike are accomplishing what, in the *Zhuangzi*, is described as the distinctively human task of 'nourishing' things, not by 'trying to add anything to them', but by 'following along with the way each thing is of itself' (Z 5, 33). The Daoist ideal of *wu wei* enjoins what Heidegger called the 'letting be' or 'releasement' (*Gelassenheit*) of things.

Wu wei is a 'doing nothing' through which, however, things get done. And it is through reflecting on spontaneity and *wu wei* that implications for attitudes and practices emerge from the Daoist call for convergence with nature. One important set of implications are those drawn in the texts for our relationship to animals, and it is on these that my concluding discussion focuses.

6. 'Living together with birds and beasts'

Relationship with animals is a prominent theme in the *Zhuangzi* and in *The Book of Liezi*, a later compilation of thoughts albeit attributed to a thinker who predates Zhuangzi. The tone in these works is different from that of many modern environmentalist writings on animal ethics. There is no reference, for example, to the notion of animal rights. Nor is the central focus on the conservation of animals in the wild. Indeed, Liezi rather congratulates himself that the animals who roam in his garden soon lose the desire to live 'deep in the mountains and hidden away in the valleys' (L 2).

Nor, crucially, is the case for enlightened and humane treatment of animals grounded in today's popular, 'naturalistic' conviction that human beings are simply one species of animal, no different in essence from other species with which, as we are constantly reminded, we share most of our DNA. The texts remind us, to be sure, that the intelligence of some animals is 'similar to man's', that they, like we, 'wish to preserve their lives' (L 2), and that people once lived closely together with birds and beasts (Z 9). But the aim of such remarks is not to assimilate human lives to those of animals. Indeed, the texts frequently emphasize that enlightened practice require mindfulness of differences between species. The moral of many anecdotes is that animals are harmed by us because we exaggerate their similarity with ourselves. The sad tale is told, for instance, of a ruler who inadvertently kills a captive bird through providing it with a rich diet and pampered environment totally unsuited to a creature at home in 'deep forests and gliding through rivers' (Z 19). Like the sages of old, we must properly identify 'the habits of all the myriad things' and sensibly 'interpret' the sounds and gestures they make (L 2). Otherwise, we fail to recognize them for what they are and are in no position, therefore, to respect their integrity and respond to their wants and needs.

Horses, for example, have a 'true inborn nature' – chomping grass, running over the terrain, and so on – that is ignored by trainers who bridle, fetter, brand and pen them (Z 9). This 'government' or 'management' of creatures is a crass imposition on the animals of an alien way of life, and the opposite therefore of the treatment enjoined by the ideal of *wu wei* – one that honours, indeed nurtures, the 'self-so' nature of beings. While the texts refer to the part that sheer ignorance or lack of mindful attention plays in our treatment of animals, the equine example indicates that typically other distorting factors are also at work. Above all, there is the powerful tendency to view animals not for what *they* are, but only in relation to our own purposes and needs. Animals, like everything else in a busy, frenzied world of 'buying and selling', organized for the satisfaction of human desires, are seen in terms of their functional roles in this world – as meat on legs, say, or as pets or pests.

In a remarkable passage in the *Liezi*, a plucky young boy chides a visiting dignitary at a banquet for thanking heaven for its gift of fish and birds for humans to eat. 'How', asks the boy, 'can it be claimed that heaven bred them for the sake of man?' It would be no less reasonable to suppose, argues this budding philosopher, that heaven bred human beings for the sake of the mosquitoes that feed on us. More importantly, he accuses the dignitary of a failure to recognize that animals are 'born in the same way that we are' and are like us in having a nature and a purpose of their own, not one engineered for our benefit (L 8). This boy would, one guesses, be an opponent of what some scientists these days proudly refer to as the 'genetic sculpting' of animals.

Liezi and Zhuangzi look back with nostalgia to an age when 'people lived together with the birds and beasts' and shared the world with them (L 2, Z 9). It is not a state of nature they are recalling, but a simpler society not yet subject to economic and technological imperatives, in which it was still possible for human beings to relate to other beings spontaneously – to 'let them be' what they are.

David E. Cooper

There are passages in the Daoist texts – not only the classics, but later, 'religious' texts like the third-century CE *One Hundred and Eighty Precepts* of the Celestial Masters – where concern for the integrity of animals is extended to other living things and to the wider natural environment.[26] So an 'environmental ethic' is present in Daoism, but one that is very different from the kinds that prevail in modernity. It is an ethic without a wilderness ideal, without a vocabulary of rights and intrinsic values, and free from any determination to assimilate human existence to that of other forms of life. The convergence with nature that Daoism recommends is not a 'oneness with nature' that obliterates the differences between the human way and the ways of animals, plants and plankton. It is a convergence, rather, that we achieve when our lives are 'on the Way', consonant with the *dao* that holds sway over nature as a whole. We achieve this, however, not by returning to a state of nature, to the condition of our 'wild green-men' ancestors. We do so, rather, through cultivating mindful, spontaneous responsiveness to the world, and by exercising the distinctive human *de* or 'virtue' of appreciating and nurturing the 'self-so-ness', the *dao*-given natures, of the other beings with whom our world is shared.

Durham University
d.e.cooper@durham.ac.uk

---

[26] On the environmental relevance of these 'religious' texts, see N. Girardot, J. Miller and Xiaogan Liu (eds.), *Daoism and Ecology: Ways within a Cosmic Landscape* (Cambridge, Mass.: Harvard University Press, 2001).

Select Issues and Controversies in Contemporary African Philosophy

BARRY HALLEN

Abstract

African philosophy today is a complicated and dynamic discipline. This presentation will concentrate on two topics that are currently of special interest. One concerns the meaning of the term 'communalism' when it is used to express a defining characteristic of Africa's cultures. The other concerns the reactions on the part of African philosophers and scholars to the movement that has come to be known in Western academia and culture as 'feminism'.

Trying to produce a representative portrait of African philosophy today is a daunting task. We are speaking of a continent that now has a population in excess of one billion people, comprised of 57 sovereign states, with populations that speak 700+ indigenous languages. Because of European colonialism, and the possibly related fact that very few people outside of Africa are fluent in any of those 700+ languages, for both national and international reasons, for the most part African philosophers continue to use the European languages introduced by those colonial powers (English, French, Portuguese, Spanish and, some might argue, Arabic, and perhaps Afrikaans).

I am going to focus on academic African philosophy, since there is no denying that in its various forms it draws significantly on Africa's indigenous intellectual heritage. Yet there is also no denying that, even with that narrower focus, the areas I must endeavor to cover with you this evening are still complex.

Precise figures are not easy to come by, especially since some African countries are contending with the 'private' university phenomenon that is also affecting us in the West. My colleagues in Africa estimate there are presently between 2,000 and 3,000 government and private universities on the continent. But for us the more relevant question is how many of those universities contain Departments of Philosophy? Those same colleagues, who are all philosophers, think there are somewhat under a thousand. And, then finally, there is the issue of how many African philosophers are staffing those departments? Their final guesstimate is somewhere between 2,000 and 4,000.

doi:10.1017/S135824611400006X

Barry Hallen

Now that we have shared this more or less factual information, let's proceed to deal with the two principal philosophical topics I've suggested should receive some form of special attention this evening. One concerns the growing interest in what is most often referred to as *communalism* and its role in contemporary African societies. The second concerns the reactions of several African women philosophers and academics to what is variously referred to as feminism here in the West.

1. Communalism and Moral Theory

Much more has been reported related to Africa's cultures by social anthropologists than by philosophers. It may or may not be significant that the major proportion of the former are Westerners, while the overwhelming proportion of the latter are indigenous Africans. In my discussion of communalism I am going to draw primarily on the writings of one of Africa's most distinguished living philosophers, Professor Kwasi Wiredu of Ghana. Although Wiredu will base his discussion of this topic on a mixture of hard data and theory, he will then propose a more comprehensive model for analysis that he believes, in principle, can help to specify the relationship between morality and community in any human society in the world today.

African communalism is often contrasted with (Western) individualism. This nomenclature highlights literally the underlying and central philosophical issue – why is it the case that the community is still privileged in the African context, particularly with regard to social and moral issues? Is the explanation and justification for this primarily historical and cultural – along the lines of: 'This is what we inherited from the forefathers'? Is it social and political – along the lines of: 'In the African context this has proved to be the most efficacious way to manage relations between individuals and their communities'? Or is it moral, along the lines of: 'This form of social organization is believed to best promote the interests and welfare of all'?

I want to begin by outlining a number of defining points to clarify what is meant by African *communalism*:

1.   On the basis of present-day beliefs and practices in Africa and numerous anthropological and sociological studies, on empirical grounds it is a safe generalization to say that Africa's cultures evidenced, and to a significant degree still evidence, a

communalistic character.[1] Wiredu writes that the 'human person is essentially the center of a thick set of concentric circles of obligations and responsibilities [to others] matched by rights and privileges [that principally benefit the individual] revolving round levels of relationships irradiating from the consanguinity of household kith and kin, through the 'blood' ties of lineage and clan [family and ancestry], to the wider circumference of human familihood . . .'[2]

2.   'Community' in the African sense therefore involves much more than the Western notion of a 'body of people living in the same locality'. For Wiredu, 'a person is social not only because he or she lives in a community, . . . but also because, by his [or her] original constitution, a human being is part of a social whole.'[3]

Simply claiming that African societies are communalistic could be a dated and uninformative generalization. One wants specifics as to what this involves. African philosophers are wary of hasty generalizations along these lines, because we are speaking of living cultures that deserve detailed study in their own right. African philosophers are convinced that, in many cases, an overriding communal element is there, but the precise manner in which it is expressed may vary. This should be an important consideration for, too often in the past, a synopsis of moral values in one particular African culture has been used to stereotype (or stigmatize) African morality generally. African communities have sometimes been characterized by Western scholars as 'organic' in character – meaning that individuals are much more closely bound together in many different ways than is the case in the West. And any individual who dared to challenge the

---

[1]   'Hence any group of humans that can be credited with any sense of morals at all – surely, a most minimal species credential – will have some sense of human sociality. But in the consciousness of moral humankind there is a finely graduated continuum of the intensity of this feeling which ranges, in an ascending order, from the austerely delimited social sympathies of rigorous individualism to the pervasive commitment to social involvement characteristic of *communalism*. It is a commonplace of anthropological wisdom that African social organization manifests the last type of outlook. [My own] Akan society is eminently true to this typology.'

[2]   Wiredu, Kwasi and Kwame Gyekye. *Person and Community* (Washington, DC: The Council for Research and Values in Philosophy, 1992), 199

[3]   Wiredu and Gyekye. *Person and Community*, 196.

status quo, the established beliefs and practices, faced the threat of ex-communalization.

Wiredu is, therefore, willing to go into greater detail, as long as it is about his own Akan culture. But before we proceed, one point of clarification is appropriate, both here and for what will follow in our discussion of feminism. Akan society is *matrilineal*. In other words, one traces one's ancestry through the female line – as embodied by one's mother and her own maternal lineage. But that distinction, at least as far as Wiredu is concerned, does not specifically affect the moral values prioritized by Akan society.

Here are some of the more specific things he has to say:

1. The underlying or foundational notion of the Akan community is linked to a particular view of *morality*. Being moral in a communal setting is what transforms a human being into an authentic *person*. And being a person 'means that an individual's image will depend rather crucially upon the extent to which his or her actions benefit others than himself [or herself] . . . by design . . . . an individual who remained content with self-regarding successes would be viewed as so circumscribed in outlook as *not to merit the title of a real person*.'[4] Becoming and being recognized as a *person*, rather than merely human, therefore involves a moral dimension as importantly as a social one.

2. 'Family' is what is sometimes referred to as the 'extended family' in the African context. As defined by the female line, a family may encompass one's grandmother and all her children and grandchildren, as well as the grandmother's brothers and sisters and their children and grandchildren. This is not to say that all these people live in the same household! But these are the people who constitute one's immediate relations and kin.

> For the dissemination of moral education or the reinforcement of the will to virtue . . . . The theater of moral upbringing is the home, at parents' feet and within range of kinsmen's inputs. The mechanism is precept, example and correction. The temporal span of the process is lifelong, for, although upbringing belongs to the beginning of our earthly careers, the need for correction is an unending contingency in the lives of mortals[5].

[4] Wiredu and Gyekye. *Person and Community*, 200 (my italics)
[5] Ibid., 195

3.   Two more specific moral incentives that are critical to achiev-
      ing *personhood* are as follows:

      a.   Morality is not regarded as a purely intellectual under-
            taking. Passions and feelings may be involved in any
            moral conflict and therefore *goodwill* as well as duty
            becomes involved. This is something Wiredu believes
            generally true of African societies. By goodwill he
            means some form of 'human sympathy' or 'sentimental-
            ity'[6] that goes beyond mere duty, or of goodwill as merely
            a function of duty. As he puts it: 'There will always be
            something unlovable about correctness of conduct
            bereft of passion . . . . the ultimate moral inadequacy con-
            sists in that lack of feeling which is the root of
            selfishness.'[7]
      b.   *Personhood* – being recognized as a morally enlightened
            and responsible member of the community – is the ultim-
            ate moral accolade. But this would never be attributed to
            an individual whose motives were primarily selfish and
            self-interested. Relationships with and responsibilities
            to kith and kin are meant to make moral isolation diffi-
            cult. This means that some everyday actions are deliber-
            ately meant to better others rather than oneself. Indeed
            the typical Akan is conscious of and scrupulous to
            protect his or her *personhood* status throughout their
            lifetime.

As noted above in connection with *goodwill*, the African view of
humanity finds the sometimes rigid Western conceptual and philosophical dichotomy between the rational and the emotional in
human beings unacceptable when formulating a systematic basis for
moral values and moral acts. This is because the notion of 'duty' as
expressed by an exclusively or purely *rational* moral sense of responsibility, is regarded as neither a sufficient nor satisfactory basis for
moral principles. This will shortly be elaborated upon by Wiredu's
introduction of a notion of '*sympathetic* impartiality',[8] which he

---

[6]   Wiredu and Gyekye. *Person and Community*, 197
[7]   Ibid., 197–198
[8]   Wiredu, Kwasi. Cultural Universals and Particulars: An African
Perspective (Bloomington and Indianapolis: Indiana University Press,
1996), 29 (my italics)

will maintain should be the moral principle most fundamental to any human society.[9]

This means that Wiredu's more general approach to morality in any society is that it be approached as a *universal* phenomenon manifesting certain structurally foundational principles or rules that every society or community must strive to implement if it is to survive. This means that all of humanity share certain basic moral principles. Appreciation of how those principles are instituted in a particular culture should be assigned the highest priority for those committed to a vision of philosophy that truly crosses cultures.

How is one to reconcile this universality with the claim that African societies are distinctively communal by comparison with, for example, their individualistic Western counterparts? The argument here seems to have three major components:

(1)   There are strictly ethical or moral universals. 'One is therefore entitled to ask if there is a principle of conduct such that without its recognition the survival of human society *in a tolerable condition* would be inconceivable.'[10] This is where Wiredu introduces what he calls '*the principle of sympathetic impartiality.*'[11] This may be expressed by the imperative 'Let your conduct at all times manifest a due concern for others.'[12] It may seem reminiscent of the Golden Rule. But the reasoning used to justify its foundational character is as follows: 'It takes little imagination to foresee that life in any society in which everyone openly avowed the *contrary* of this principle and acted accordingly would inevitably be "solitary, poor, nasty, brutish", and probably short.'[13]

---

[9]   'The basis of the quest for consensus in many Africa systems of moral thought is said to be social rather than religious. Morality in the African communal setting is therefore also regarded as primarily humanistic in character.' This limits the role of religion in many African systems of moral thought. 'One important implication of the founding of value on human interests is the independence of morality from religion in the Akan outlook: What is good in general is what promotes human interests. . . . Thus, the will of God, not to talk of any other extra-human being, is logically incapable of defining the good.' Wiredu and Gyekye. *Person and Community*, 194

[10]   Wiredu, Kwasi. *Cultural Universals and Particulars: An African Perspective*, 29

[11]   Ibid., 29

[12]   Ibid.

[13]   Wiredu, Kwasi. *Cultural Universals and Particulars: An African Perspective*, 29 (my italics, in part)

(2)   If this principle is supposedly '*a human universal transcending cultures*', (1996, 29; my italics)',[14] then how is one to reconcile its universal status with the apparent significant moral differences found in societies that evidence an *individualistic* rather than a communal orientation? To answer this question, let's imagine that we have a moral tool available that amounts to some kind of sliding scale. At one end of this scale let's place communities that are radically communal in nature and, at the other end, those that would be characterized as radically individualistic in character. But, and this is an important 'but', communal societies would still have to make room for a degree of individuality, and societies that are individualistic would also have to make some allowance for a degree of communality. In any case, the mixture of the two in any society could be measured in an approximate manner by sliding the cursor to the appropriate point on the scale.

> [T]he distinction between communalism and individualism is one of degree only; for a considerable value may be attached to communality in individualistic societies just as individuality is not necessarily trivialized within communalism.[15]

This does not mean that two societies that happened to be rated the 'same' in terms of their communal and invidualistic characters would therefore somehow be identical. But the differences that remained, and that often strike the casual observer as remarkable, would now be attributed to relatively superficial things like '*customs*' and '*lifestyles*', and may therefore be of use for highlighting the diversity of ways in which the universal moral principle of sympathetic impartiality is implemented in different cultures. Wiredu insists that: 'The real difference between communalism and individualism has [more] to do with *custom* and *lifestyle* rather than anything else. . . . [and] both [of these] are *distinct from morality in the strict sense.*'[16]

This would mean that people who exaggerate the differences between moral values in different cultures are in fact themselves exaggerating the relatively superficial anomalies generated by their

---

[14]   Ibid., 29 (my italics)
[15]   Ibid.
[16]   Wiredu, Kwasi. *Cultural Universals and Particulars: An African Perspective,* 72 (my italics)

differences in *customs* and *lifestyles* rather than foundational moral principles. For example, he describes customs as 'contingent norms of life'[17] and argues that they might include *'usages, traditions, manners, conventions, grammars, vocabularies, etiquette, fashions, aesthetic standards, observances, taboos, rituals, folkways, [and] mores.'*[18]

I'm not sure I've done Kwasi Wiredu justice with this abbreviated summary. But before I move on to the discussion of feminism, there are three final points that I think should be made:

1. Wiredu certainly does not think he is providing an account of communalistic morality in Africa that has become an anachronism in the present day, that in effect suffered a mortal blow during and after the era of colonialism. In his informed opinion, as well as the anthropological sources to which he makes reference, it may be the case that the matrilineal extended family in Akan culture has been damaged and is less influential today than in the past. But that does not mean it has suffered a mortal blow. In fact, in his efforts to identify those 'traditions' in Akan culture that deserve re-affirmation rather than elimination, this is one that he emphatically supports.

2. He focuses on his native Akan culture because he knows it, intimately. But the fact that it is one of the relatively few matrilineal cultures in Africa is apparently not enough of a distinction to persuade him that its moral values and the foundation from which they arise are unique and therefore disqualify it as generally representative of Africa's indigenous cultures. Matrilineal or patrilineal, the status of the extended family, of family as involving substantive communal responsibilities, and of the paradigm of *personhood* – all are characteristics that he thinks are appropriate to the African context. (As we shall see, some African women philosophers may disagree with this point.)

3. Wiredu wants his approach to the topic of moral philosophy to be of general philosophical significance. He tries to avoid writing a pseudo-ethnographic account only of Akan culture by going on to formulate his principle of sympathetic impartiality and the notion of a sliding scale. These enable him to move beyond Africa and, in effect, to use insights arising from African philosophy to analyze morality in any society.

[17] Ibid., 30
[18] Ibid., 28 (my italics)

2. Feminism

In this section of my presentation I am going to summarize interrelated arguments drawn from the writings of three contemporary African women academics who do not wish to be identified as feminists or with feminism in any sense of the word. The first, Ifi Amadiume, is a social anthropologist with strong epistemological as well as moral leanings. I will introduce her to you via her following brief statement about Western feminists:

> The dilemma and anger for us African women is the contradiction implied in the actions of these Western women, whose cultural and historical legacies we know. Yet they leave their problems at home, and cross vast seas to go and dictate strategies of struggle and paths of development to Africans, as highly paid consultants and well-funded researchers. At the same time, their own imposed systems [of development] are eroding all the positive aspects of our historical gains, leaving us impoverished, naked to abuse, and objects of pity to Western aid rescue missions.'[19]

Some of the implications of her remark are obvious. Under the auspices of various 'development' programs, Amadiume has had first-hand encounters with a number of Western experts who did not demonstrate an in-depth knowledge of the real-life situations of women in African societies. One is reminded of the stereotype of the female symbolically chained to her cooking pot, doomed to produce endless children as only one among endless wives, all totally submissive to a potentially ungrateful husband, with whom she enjoys questionable sexual pleasure as a consequence of female circumcision. This kind of fixation overlooks the fact that countless African women have for decades been fighting their own battles in Africa against multiple forms of feminine social injustice.

Amadiume paints a different picture of African womanhood, writ large to say the least:

1. She begins by critically embracing the speculative historical hypotheses, for which she believes there are still significant patches of empirical evidence, of the Senegalese scholar and father of Afrocentrism, Cheikh Anta Diop. What attracts Amadiume's interest, in particular, is Diop's hypothesis that

---

[19] Amadiume, Ifi. *Reinventing Africa: Matriarchy, Religion & Culture* (London: Zed Books Ltd, 1997), 197

prehistorical and historical African cultures were *matriarchal* (rather than patriarchal) in character.

2.   She argues that matriarchal cultures tend to favor 'pacifist' moral philosophies that prioritize comparatively 'motherly' values such as compassion, love, and peace.[20] [It would be interesting to hear what Wiredu might have to say about this.] But Africa's days as an independent cultural and imperial power came to an end in 95 B.C. with the Persian conquest of Egypt, and since that time in the face of increasing military invasions, climaxing with European colonialism, the cultures of Africa, to combat this violence more effectively, were compelled to turn to ever increasing ideologies of patriarchy.

3.   That the evidence of these matriarchal influences can be found in the precolonial practices of her own Igbo culture,[21] as evidenced by the following:

   a.   Igbo culture was gendered, but *not* on a strictly biological basis.

   b.   In certain contexts men could be addressed as women and women could be addressed as men.

   c.   'As such, roles in the society were not rigidly masculinized or feminized.'[22]

   d.   There were situations in which women were transformed into 'male daughters', and others in which they were transformed into 'female husbands'. In either capacity women could thereby be entitled to act as head of a family.[23]

   e.   For example, in a situation where a man had no son to serve as the inheritor of his land, it was possible for him to appoint a daughter as a 'son' who would thereby be entitled to inherit that part of the estate. To quote Amadiume: 'Women owned land as "male daughters" when they had been *accorded full male status* in the

---

[20]   Amadiume, Ifi. *Reinventing Africa: Matriarchy, Religion & Culture*, 18, 84

[21]   Amadiume, Ifi. *African Matriarchal Foundations: The Igbo Case*. (London: Karnak House, 1987)

[22]   Amadiume, Ifi. *Male Daughters, Female Husbands* (London: Zed Books Ltd., 1987), 185

[23]   Amadiume, Ifi. *Male Daughters, Female Husbands* (London: Zed Books Ltd., 1987), 90

absence of a son in order to safeguard their father's ancestral home or compound.'[24]

f. On the other hand, 'female husbands' were women who demonstrated the potential to be exceptionally successful in business, farming, or some other profession. Such talented individuals had need of others to work for them, since a one-woman enterprise would be severely limited in scope. These additional personnel were obtained in one of two ways: (1) straightforward employment; (2) on the basis of what was referred to as a 'woman-to-woman' marriage. These new wives might even eventually bear children, but they would carry the family name of the original female husband.

g. What is noteworthy about this arrangement is the social avenue it provided for the social and economic development of women who demonstrated a talent for the kinds of professional careers that false stereotypes of Africa still portray as open only to biological men.

h. Regardless of whether we are referring to 'male daughters' or 'female husbands', there could be no more than one head of a family at a time. When necessary, therefore, some women were transformed into the masters of other people, both men and women. Consequently, it was possible for some men to be addressed with the term 'wife', even though they were, in effect, serving a woman.

Nkiru Nzegwu is a Nigerian philosopher who happens to come from the same Igbo ethnic group as Ifi Amadiume. Nzegwu criticizes Amadiume severely for misunderstanding her own culture, particularly where the status of women is concerned. Amadiume's biggest mistake is the exaggerated role she implicitly assigns to *gendering*, to the status involved with being identified as male or female in Igbo culture. If gendering really is not significant in or to the culture, as Amadiume also claims, why is it that so many women have to go through a socially stipulated process that transforms them into men? Why must a woman be transformed into a man so that she may inherit? And why must a man be somehow de-maled in order to work for a woman. Some form of patriarchy is apparently still in force. This also implies that women continue to have second-rate status in the society *generally* rather than that, less importantly, in

---

[24] Ibid., 34 (my italics)

some situations their status may be enhanced by in effect altering their gender so that they become somehow male.

A better understanding of Igbo society would be achieved by acknowledging the absence of the male-female distinction as a basis for social status and/or roles altogether. Nzegwu argues that lineage (family) and seniority are more important to determining the roles women may play. As, for example, is indicated by the fact that if a woman finds herself in a position where it is appropriate for her to inherit her father's estate, she would have no qualms about walking out of whatever other marriage and family she might already have become a part of, in order to assume that position in the family of her birth. For her primary obligation is to ignore gender and protect the lineage that originally produced her.

For Nzegwu Igbo precolonial society is therefore better understood as a dual-*sex* society, in which there were separate lines of development and roles of governance for men and women. Ultimately the two would have to come together to arrive at some form of general agreement before any decision fundamental to the welfare of the entire community could be agreed upon and implemented.

But what has effectively undermined this independence and equality of the sexes are the combined assaults of Western colonialism, Western development, and Western cultural imperialism. Europeans attempted to enforce their own patriarchal norms, which they took for granted as conventional, on African populations – reducing women to housewives, cleaners, and occasionally secretaries. They then appointed men to any positions of consequence in the colony (including university admissions, etc.). As for the additional inroads pursuant to the widespread marketing of Western popular culture, particularly music, in Africa, the continuing controversy over the disrespect explicitly directed at women more than speaks for itself.

I have saved the discussion of 'Ronke Oyewumi's work for last because, on the subject of feminism generally, she tends to be the most uncompromising of the three. Her controversial book, *The Invention of Women*, is a sustained attack on contemporary African Studies generally (philosophy included) with arguably important epistemological and moral consequences.

Although she too will eventually defend a number of generalizations about Africa's cultures that also are controversial, to give her arguments added empirical weight she begins by exploring the status of women in her native Yoruba culture of southwestern Nigeria.

In that culture, at least prior to European colonization, gender was not an organizing principle as far as the society itself was concerned.

In other words, biological sex did not predetermine the roles a person could occupy or play. Male and female were of course acknowledged as differing anatomically and as playing different physical roles in the reproductive process.[25] But these facts of life were not then used as a basis for a socially gendered hierarchy in which human beings who, biologically, were men were privileged more than human beings who, biologically, were women (or the reverse). This applied to rulers as well as to all the professions.

This gender equality is still manifested, more specifically, by the fact that in the Yoruba language nouns, pronouns, and given names (for the most part) are not gendered. Also either males or females may be the head of a household. Marriage is viewed as a union of lineages (families and ancestries) rather than simply that of a biological male and a biological female. Lineage rather than biological sex is the predominant determinant of whether a particular individual is entitled to enter into a particular vocation (medicine, business, etc.). Finally, in social situations, age or seniority (not sex) is the primary index of status.

Oyewumi ventures more deeply into epistemological territory when she denounces the arrogance or ignorance of non-African scholars who undermine African Studies when they: assume that the concepts involved in gendering are somehow cultural universals to be found in any culture; when they assume that the typing of societies as being either patriarchal or matriarchal also must be some sort of cultural universal; when, as these two initial examples indicate, they ignore the possibility that there is an indisputable epistemological foundation to the methodology used for the study of cultures; and that therefore before engaging in groundless cross-cultural conceptual generalizations, it is imperative to first assess the epistemological basis of the cultures potentially involved.

The social sciences, for example, overflow with Western cognitive and conceptual paradigms and prerogatives. And they then impose, rather than empirically test, them upon non-Western cognitive systems and cultures indiscriminately. Western scholars continue to presume to dictate the correct ways to understand non-Western cognition and cultures to members of those same non-Western societies.

I think by now you've spent more than enough time listening to me hopefully giving fair representation to these African colleagues. I hope you can appreciate their concerns that international scholars

---

[25] Oyewumi, Oyeronke. *The Invention of Women: Making an African Sense of Western Gender Discourses* (Minneapolis: The University of Minnesota Press, 1997), 36

must make more of an effort to listen to their African colleagues if some sort of positive dialogues are to ensue. It would not be an over-statement for me to say that my African colleagues are angry and frustrated that more progress has not been made in this regard. Last but far from least, I hope you also have been able to appreciate that these African scholars are doing more than merely 'looking inwards', in the sense that their single-minded concern is to focus solely on Africa's indigenous cultures. Rather, they want to contribute to the international debates on these topics, but from vantage points that are grounded on and draw upon their own intellectual heritage, which they see as something that should be important to us all.

Thank-you.

Morehouse College
bhallen@morehouse.edu

Buddhist Idealists and Their Jain Critics On Our Knowledge of External Objects*

MATTHEW T. KAPSTEIN

Abstract

In accord with the theme of the present volume on 'Philosophical Traditions', it is not so much the aim of this essay to provide a detailed account of particular lines of argument, as it is to suggest something of the manner in which so-called 'Buddhist idealism' unfolded as a tradition not just for Buddhists, but within Indian philosophy more generally. Seen from this perspective, Buddhist idealism remained a current within Indian philosophy long after the demise of Buddhism in India, in about the twelfth century, and endured in some respects at least until the Mughal age, when the last thinker to be examined here, the Jain teacher Yaśovijaya, was active.

1.

As a philosopher involved in the study of religion, I share with many of my colleagues in the latter field an interest in origin myths. One such myth, which I learned in college, concerned the inception of the analytic movement in British philosophy. It went something like this: during the age of primal chaos, when thought was fuzzy and obscure, the evil genie of Idealism wandered free on earth. Then, a hero named George waved his hands, recited the magic words, 'here is one hand, and here another', and, presto! the genie took flight to return forever to the black depths from which he had sprung. Victorious analysis was born!

Like many myths, however, this one proved to be false. By the time he delivered the 1939 lecture containing the famous argument about his hands, our hero, George E. Moore, had grappled with the genie

* A version of this essay was presented to the Numata seminar of the University of Toronto in January 2013. I thank Professors Frances Garrett and Cristoph Emmrich for their kind invitation and organization of the event, and to their colleagues and students as well for insightful discussion contributing to the present revision of this work.

doi:10.1017/S1358246114000083 ©The Royal Institute of Philosophy and the contributors 2014

for some four decades.[1] In 1920 he had received a warm expression of gratitude in perhaps the greatest achievement of British idealism, McTaggart's *The Nature of Existence*, and he would remain sufficiently troubled by the problems posed by idealism to return to them periodically throughout his career. Other analytic philosophers shared his concerns: in 1946, for instance, John Wisdom and J.L. Austin published a symposium on the problem of other minds, and the same topic preoccupied A.J. Ayer soon after.[2] By 1963, when Michael Dummett delivered his celebrated lecture on 'Realism', the direct realism of the early analytic school, and the revived correspondence theory of truth that accompanied it, were beginning to appear sorely frayed.[3] The genie, indeed, had never quite vanished. As he had been wont to do throughout the centuries, he merely morphed, and, while some philosophers, such as Timothy Sprigge, welcomed him back enthusiastically in something resembling one of his old guises, others appealed instead to a range of non- or anti-realisms.[4] Analytic philosophy, born as it had been from the

[1]   G. E. Moore, 'Proof of an External World', *The Proceedings of the British Academy* **25** (London: Humphrey Milford, 1940), 127–50, and often reprinted. On Moore's argument in the history of analytic philosophy, refer to Scott Soames, *Philosophical Analysis in the Twentieth Century: Volume 1, The Dawn of Analysis* (Princeton: Princeton University Press, 2003), 12–23

[2]   J. Wisdom and J. L. Austin, 'Symposium: Other Minds', in *Logic and Reality*, Aristotelian Society Supplementary Volume XX (London: Harrison and Sons, 1946), 122–87; A. J. Ayer, 'One's Knowledge of Other Minds', *Theoria* **19**(1–2) (1953), 1–20. Of course, the problem of other minds is just as much (or little) a problem for the realist as for the idealist, and none of the authors cited here considers the issue as belonging to idealism in particular. But I believe that the problem came into prominence in connection with idealism's doubts regarding what is external to us and remained current even after idealism was thought to have left the scene.

[3]   Michael Dummett, 'Realism', in *Truth and Other Enigmas* (Cambridge, Mass.: Harvard University Press, 1978), 145–165

[4]   Timothy Sprigge, *The Vindication of Absolute Idealism* (Edinburgh: Edinburgh University Press, 1984) advances a defense of panpsychism. Anti-realism is, of course, not to be identified with idealism simpliciter, though as Dummett, *op. cit.*, suggests at several points, the realism-idealism divide may be seen as one variety of the type of opposition embraced by realism and anti-realism. In view of the current characterization of anti-realism as pertaining to metaontology (or 'metametaphysics') – the questions surrounding the status of ontological claims themselves – and not to ontology, it becomes clear that some forms of idealism (e.g., the 'subjective idealism' attributed to Berkeley) are realist in so much as they assert that

puzzles posed by the effort to clarify the relations among language, knowledge, and the world to which they refer, could never wholly renounce the broad legacy of idealism.

But just what *is* 'idealism'? Part of the unsatisfactory nature of Moore's and others' 'refutations' stems from the fact that idealism, like mind itself, is Protean – there is no one philosophical doctrine that corresponds in all cases to 'idealism'.[5] Kant was already quite clear about this, and accordingly he sought to distinguish carefully among what he termed 'skeptical idealism' – which he identified with the *cogito*-argument of Descartes – 'dogmatic idealism'—typified by the formula *esse est percipi* attributed to Bishop Berkeley – and *transcendental idealism*, the doctrine Kant personally embraced, which holds in effect that all that we know, all that we can ever know, we know only in so far as its appears within the field of our knowing.[6] But many other species and subspecies of idealism may also be noted – Platonic idealisms, Leibnizian idealisms, Hegelian idealisms, and more – so that it probably makes better sense to think of idealism as designating a great and fecund philosophical clan than it does a particular doctrine. The distinction that I wish to accentuate at the outset, however, as it may prove useful in beginning to explore the Indian philosophical landscape, divides what we might term *eliminative* from *non-eliminative* idealisms. Eliminative

---

some determinate ontological claims are warranted. But certain philosophical views that have been traditionally considered 'idealist', notably Kant's 'transcendental idealism', are plausibly treated as responding to the problems that have surfaced in recent philosophy in terms of anti-realism, and Kant's interrogation of the grounds of metaphysics clearly form the background for much of the modern and contemporary realist/anti-realist problematic. See now David J. Chalmers, David Manley, and Ryan Wasserman, *Metametaphysics: New Essays on the Foundations of Ontology* (Oxford: Clarendon Press, 2009), and, on Kant in relation to recent anti-realisms, Lucy Allais, 'Kant's transcendental idealism and comtemporary anti-realism', *International Journal of Philosophical Studies* **11**(4) (2003), 369–392

⁵ Jeremy Dunham, Iain Hamilton Grant, and Sean Watson, *Idealism: The History of a Philosophy* (Durham: Acumen, 2011) offers a generous survey covering a broad range of what, at one time or another, has been labelled as 'idealism' in Western philosophical traditions.

⁶ Immanuel Kant, *Critique of Pure Reason*, trans. Norman Kemp Smith (New York: St. Martin's Press, 1965), 244–47, 344–52

idealisms, sometimes also called 'immaterialism',[7] are those that seek to remove all but minds and mental entities from their ontologies, their inventories of what is, while non-eliminative idealisms accept that the universe really does include at least some non-mental things, but insist nevertheless that mind (or spirit, or reason) in some sense takes precedence over those others; the universe is, if not mind through and through, nevertheless mind-dependent, mind-made, or determined by mind. Eliminative and non-eliminative idealisms as I conceive of them are not simple opposites; they cover broad bands along a spectrum of thought, and the boundary between them may blur around the edges of concepts such as 'mind-made'. A second general distinction, complementing this, that may also prove useful to us here is that separating monistic from monadic idealisms, the former affirming reality to be in the final analysis but a single spirit or mind, the latter committed to a plurality of spiritual or mental entities.

2.

These rough parameters allow us to situate some of the problems posed by Indian, and particularly Buddhist, philosophical idealisms. These, like their counterparts in Western thought, have at times reigned supreme, or been challenged and supposedly refuted, but nevertheless, once present in the Indian philosophical landscape, never quite left the scene. Of course, there is no term in Sanskrit, or in any other pre-modern Indian language, so far as I am aware, that offers a neat equivalent to 'idealism', with all the peculiar messiness of that designation. The western term, however, was frequently taken over by early twentieth-century historians of Indian philosophy and applied to a variety of particular traditions therein.[8] Vedāntic thought, above all, was very often characterised as a type of idealism, most notably Śaṅkara's non-dualistic Vedānta, in which some found

---

[7]   Georges Dicker, *Berkeley's Idealism* (New York: Oxford University Press, 2011), 3–4

[8]   Surendranath Dasgupta, *Indian Idealism* (Cambridge: At the University Press, 1962 [1933]), and P. T. Raju, *Idealistic Thought of India* (Cambridge, Mass.: Harvard University Press, 1953) are perhaps the best-known examples. Nalini Bhushan and Jay L. Garfield, eds., *Indian Philosophy in English: From Renaissance to Independence* (New York: Oxford University Press, 2011) provide pertinent selections from the writings of A. C. Mukerji, Ras Bihari Das, and Hiralal Haldar, among others.

neo-Hegelian affinities.[9] Nevertheless, the better writers on the subject always recognised that, just as idealism covered a wide swath in the history of western thought, so it could be taken over only to refer to a similar sprawl in Indian philosophy, and not to a single school or tradition. From such a perspective Buddhism generally seemed to merit consideration as a tradition tending to idealism of what I am calling the 'non-eliminative' variety, for throughout the Buddhist scriptural corpus the primacy of mind was everywhere affirmed. Had not the Founder himself, in the famous opening lines of the Dhammapada, proclaimed that:

> Preceded by thought are the elements of experience,
> For them is thought supreme,
> From thought have they sprung.
> If, with thought polluted, one speaks or acts,
> Thence suffering follows
> As a wheel the draught ox's foot.

> Preceded by thought are the elements of experience,
> For them is thought supreme,
> From thought have they sprung.
> If, with tranquil thought, one speaks or acts,
> Thence ease follows
> As a shadow that never departs.[10]

The Buddha's emphasis on thought as prime mover, moreover, was firmly maintained even among those early Buddhist philosophical schools that are often held to be 'realist' owing to their assertion of the real existence of the material world and of our veridical sensory knowledge of it. In his great synthesis of early Buddhist philosophy, the fifth-century thinker Vasubandhu, for instance, declares, 'the variety of the world is born of karma', that is, action.[11] And, lest we imagine that 'action' might refer here primarily, as it does in Hobbes, to the movements of bodies, karman, in this context, is

---

[9] Chakravarthi Ram-Prasad, *Advaita Epistemology and Metaphysics: An Outline of Indian Non-Realism* (London: RoutledgeCurzon, 2002), however, argues that Śaṅkara is better regarded as a 'non-realist' than an idealist.

[10] John Ross Carter and Mahinda Palihawadana, trans., *The Dhammapada* (New York: Oxford University Press, 1998), 13 and 89–94 for commentary. I have modified somewhat their translation, which reads 'Preceded by perception are mental states'.

[11] Vasubandhu, *Abhidharmakośam*, ed. Svāmī Dvārikādās Śāstrī (Varanasi: Bauddha Bharati, 1970–72), 567 (verse 4.1)

specfically defined as action impelled by *cetana*, forethought, intention or will. Actions may be physical, as is the motion of a chariot, but for early Buddhist thought it was the mind that held the reins.

Non-eliminative idealism of the sort that I am describing characterised not only early Buddhism, but pervaded much of Indian thought, though with many variants in accord with the nuances of the systems concerned. However, the same Vasubandhu to whom I have just referred was also one of the founders of a particular line of Buddhist philosophy, most often called Yogācāra, 'liberative practice', that adopted a type of eliminative idealism, arguing that the world of external, material objects can be erased from our ontology, and that what we perceive and think of as such a world is in reality wholly constituted by the activity of minds. It is Vasubandhu's philosophy, in fact, that is usually intended when one speaks of 'Buddhist idealism'. This is accentuated in Indian philosophical parlance, too, which designates the teaching of Vasubandhu's school as *vijñānavāda*, the 'doctrine of consciousness', or *cittamātra*, 'mind only', Sanskrit terms that come as close as any to our word 'idealism', at least in certain of its significations. Throughout the discussion that follows, 'idealism' will refer in particular to the eliminative idealism attributed to Vasubandhu's tradition.

Within specialised scholarship on Buddhist philosophy it has recently been much discussed, however, as to whether the designation 'idealist' really fits Vasubandhu or not. It will not be necessary to rehearse all of this here, and the debate has been in my judgement sometimes more concerned with semantics than substance. Some of the discomfort with the characterization of Vasubandhu as idealist perhaps stems from the too hasty identifications that have sometimes been proposed between his thought and specific trends in Western idealism. Thus, he has been considered at one time or another as a type of 'subjective idealist', whose doctrine resembles Berkeley's, or as an 'absolute idealist', as is often associated with some streams of Hegelianism. I concur with the critics that neither of these rubrics is quite suitable here, although, as I have tried to make clear above, I do not think that our use of 'idealism' can be narrowed to refer to just these species of idealism alone.

It has been suggested, too, that the characterization of Yogācāra as idealist is primarily an artifact of the prominence of idealism in Western thought during the late nineteenth and early twentieth century, when Yogācāra began to be studied in the West; but, despite the evident fact that the precise term 'idealism' is a Western one, this line of criticism is, I think, flawed. For it is clear that Indian intellectual traditions considered the cardinal, puzzling doctrine of Yogācāra to be – as it was succinctly expressed by the Jain commentator Guṇaratna in the fourteenth century – that 'this world is only consciousness. There are no external objects, for it is the non-duality of cognition that is real. And there are a plurality of continua of cognition'.[12] Of course, the fact that non-Buddhist thinkers such as Guṇaratna attribute a type of idealism to Yogācāra by no means establishes that they were justified to do so, but this does make clear that the pertinent features of an eliminative, metaphysical idealism were well known to Indian thinkers long before they had our term for it. I believe, too, that, though Vasubandhu's final intentions remain open to dispute, the idealism attributed to him does indeed find its basis in his own work. To show this, I shall rapidly signal some of the key features of Vasubandhu's idealistic turn, while indicating in brief a few points about which I think that there has been legitimate contestation.[13]

As I have shown in detail elsewhere,[14] Vasubandhu's reasoning for the elimination of material objects was expressed as a mereological argument to the effect that the logic of part-whole relations entails that no coherent conception of physical matter can be formed. In a nutshell, the argument holds that atomism is both necessary and false. That Vasubandhu held this much is quite certain. It is tempting to draw from the argument, further, the conclusion that Vasubandhu wished to exclude matter altogether, but it is perhaps also possible to read Vasubandhu as suggesting – for he is not quite explicit about this – that there may nevertheless be an external, physical reality whose constitution and nature are inscrutable to us. Personally, I favor the eliminationist over the skeptical interpretation, but both are suggested in the work of Vasubandhu's successors, as will be seen

[12]   Mahendrakumār Jain, ed., *Saḍḍarśanasamuccaya*, Jñānpīth Mūrtidevi Jain Granthamālā 34, 3rd ed. (New Delhi: Bhāratīya Jñānpīth, 1989), 74

[13]   The secondary literature on Vasubandhu has grown quite large in recent years, and it will not be possible to refer to all of the pertinent discussions that have appeared in the space available here. Opposing perspectives on the question of idealism are developed at length in: Dan Lusthaus, *Buddhist Phenomenology: A Philosophical Investigation of Yogācāra Buddhism and the* Ch'eng Wei-shih Lun (London: Routledge, 2002); and Lambert Schmithausen, *On the Problem of the External World in the* Ch'eng wei shih lun, Studia Philologica Buddhica Occasional Paper Series XIII (Tokyo: International Institute for Buddhist Studies, 2005). It may be noted that both of these are concerned primarily with readings of Vasubandhu in the Chinese Yogācāra tradition of Xuanzang (7th c.).

[14]   'Mereological Considerations in Vasubandhu's "Proof of Idealism"', *Idealistic Studies* **XVIII**(1) (1988), 32–54

Matthew T. Kapstein

below. Some of the peculiar features of Vasubandhu's idealism I take
to be the following:

— The elimination of the object does not entail a pure subjectivity; for object and subject are correlatives, such that the
elimination of the one implies the elimination of the other.
Consciousness, for Vasubandhu, is thus a non-dual consciousness, prior to the distinction of subject and object.[15]
— Individuals correspond not just to numerically discrete
consciousnesses, for consciousnesses are without temporal
extension—they are instantaneous events. The individual,
therefore, is a sort of 'time worm'—to borrow an image that
was current in late-twentieth century discussions of personal
identity— each segment corresponding to a unique, unex-
tended moment of consciousness. I will not broach here the
difficult question of what kind of relationship is required to
join these moments so as to constitute discrete temporally extended individuals; what is of importance in our present
context is just that they are constituted solely by consciousness.[16]
— Perhaps even more than in Buddhist thought generally, where
it already occupies a very large place, error (unknowing, ignorance) must be called on to do a great deal of work in
Vasubandhu's philosophy. Whether one adopts the eliminative or skeptical reading of Vasubandhu on material existence,
it is error that explains physical reality as we conceive it to be.
Given that consciousness, in its proper nature, is for
Vasubandhu nondual with respect to subject and object, it is
error that explains this seemingly fundamental duality.[17]

15   It is, in fact, this feature of Vasubandhu's thought that appears to me
to suggest an anti-realist rather than a strictly idealist reading of him. But I
will defer detailed consideration of this point for another occasion.
16   Vasubandhu, drawing on the established terminology of the
Buddhist Abhidharma schools, calls these 'time-worms' *santāna*, usually
translated as 'continuum'. For the earlier Abhidharma, these continua
were psycho-physical, but Vasubandhu comes to use the term for the
psychic continuum alone.
17   Vasubandhu's nondualism is perhaps most clearly articulated in verse
28 of his *Thirty Verse Proof of Idealism* (*Triṃśikā Vijñaptimātratāsiddhiḥ*):
'When knowledge objectifies no referent and stands in consciousness alone,
then, in the absence of apprehended object, there is no subjective apprehension at all'.

— Finally, in view of the ideal constitution of individuals and the world, and the absence, for Vasubandhu, of an individual corresponding to God (and let us recall here the deity's important role in the idealisms of Leibniz and, especially, Berkeley), the problem of solipsism and the difficulties in accounting for intersubjectivity loom particularly large.[18]

It is important to stress, too, as should be evident from all this, that Vasubandhu's idealism was in no way monistic. This was clearly understood by the opponents of Yogācāra thought, such as the Jain Guṇaratna, cited above, or the Buddhist critic Candrakīrti, who in an interesting passage takes pains both to compare and distinguish Yogācāra from theism. He writes:

> Like those who affirm Īśvara [the 'Lord'] and such to be the creator of beings, those who affirm the *ālayavijñāna* ['ground-consciousness'] state that the *ālayavijñāna*, because it is the foundation for the seeds of the objectifications of all things, is the 'bearer of all seeds' (*sarvabījaka*). The difference is just in their saying that, while Īśvara is eternal, the *ālayavijñāna* is impermanent.[19]

As we know from the *Laṅkāvatārasūtra*, a popular Mahāyāna Buddhist scripture, the adherents of Yogācāra were much concerned to distance their teaching from the suggestion that it involved the tacit affirmation of theistic or Upaniṣadic metaphysics in a Buddhist guise.[20] But genuine Indian theists, such as those of the Nyāya school, were also not adverse to affirming the genuine reality of the

---

[18]   The problem of solipsism is taken up at length by Dharmakīrti, who seeks to refute it, and Ratnakīrti (11th c.), who accepts it as an entailment of the idealist position. Refer to 'Establishment of the Existence of Other Minds' in Debiprasad Chattopadhyaya, ed., *Papers of Th. Stcherbatsky*, trans. Harish C. Gupta, Soviet Indology Series 2 (Calcutta: Indian Studies Past and Present, 1969), 55–92; and Yuichi Kajiyama, 'Buddhist Solipsism: A free translation of Ratnakīrti's *Saṃtānāntaradūṣaṇa*', *Journal of Indian and Buddhist Studies* XIII/1 (1965), 435–20

[19]   Translated following the Tibetan text given in Louis de la Vallée Poussin, *Madhyamakāvatāra par Candrakīrti*, Bibliotheca Buddhica 9 (Rprt. Delhi: Motilal Banarsidass, 1992), commentary ad VI.46

[20]   Thus, the *sūtra* is keen always to affirm, in contrast to the essentialism it attributes to the Brahmanical traditions, that 'without beholding the insubstantiality of phenomena, there is no freedom'. *Laṅkāvatārasūtram*, ed. P. L. Vaidya, Buddhist Texts Series 3 (Darbhanga: Mithila Institute, 1963), 27

world that their god had created.[21] Whereas the scandal of Yogācāra, in the view of most other Indian philosophical traditions, Buddhist and non-Buddhist alike, was crucially to be found in its denial of the external world. It is here, too, that the position of Yogācāra in the history of Indian thought resembles that of idealism in the West. Just how, once skepticism about external reality arises, do we regain our philosophical innocence and return to the unchallenged assurance that what appears to us indeed exists?

3.

Among Vasubandhu's leading disciples, Dignāga (active ca. 500) rivals his master for his broad importance in the history of Indian and Buddhist philosophy. The early Yogācāra school had been interested in the practice of debate, and Vasubandhu in several works had already sought to expound the rules of logic that were to be followed. On these foundations, and in critical dialogue with the major non-Buddhist philosophical traditions, Dignāga elaborated a comprehensive system of *pramāṇa*, a word referring to the measure or 'criterion' of knowledge and used to designate the fields of learning that we cover with the terms 'logic' and 'epistemology', i.e. the 'theory of knowledge'.[22]

Dignāga's greatest work was his *Pramāṇasamuccaya* ('Compendium of Logic and Epistemology'), in which he held that there are in fact just two criteria for knowing, veridical perception and sound inference, and that these, in turn, correspond to just two classes of objects: particulars that are characterised by their unique phenomenal characteristics (*sva-lakṣaṇa*), and concepts that are characterised by their universality (*sāmanya-lakṣaṇa*). In later Buddhist tradition, Dignāga's system as presented in the *Compendium* gave rise to both phenomenalistic and idealistic readings, though a number of his other writings suggest that, like his master, he was partial to idealism. While Dignāga held that the objects of our perceptions are particulars

---

[21] Indian theistic philosophies, as exemplified in particular by the Nyāya and Vaiśeṣika schools, were always strongly committed to both ontological and epistemological realism.

[22] Though much valuable scholarship on Dignāga has appeared during the decades since it was published, Masaaki Hattori, *Dignāga, On Perception*, Harvard Oriental Series 47 (Cambridge, Mass.: Harvard University Press, 1968) provides a still useful introduction to this major figure.

bearing unique characteristics, his concept of the particular becomes the point of departure for a number of difficult questions: Is the object that we perceive actually something that exists 'out there' in the world, just as we perceive it? Or is the object something that arises within our sensory field, perhaps corresponding to an external object that served as a stimulus, but not in fact identical to it? Or is the object exclusively an object *of consciousness*, on the basis of which we construct the *idea* of an external world that does not exist in reality? The first of these alternatives, the 'direct realism' that had been current in early Buddhism and several of the non-Buddhist philosophical traditions, Dignāga, like Vasubandhu, rejected decisively. The second, a type of 'indirect realism' (or, on some readings, 'phenomenalism'), had been embraced by Vasubandhu in his realist writings, and was sometimes regarded as Dignāga's true position as well. The last, of course, is 'idealism'.

Dignāga's short treatise, *Ālambanaparīkṣā* ('The Examination of the Objective Referent'), is his foremost contribution to the problem we have just sketched out. Here he seeks to clarify the difficulties in this area by focusing upon the investigation of the *ālambana*, translated here as 'objective referent'.[23] Sanskrit has a number of distinct specialised terms where we use the one English word 'object' (think of the differences involved when we speak of 'an object in the living room', 'the direct object of a verb', 'the object of her journey', 'an object of yearning', etc.). It is often a challenge for translators of philosophical Sanskrit to find just the right way to modify 'object', so as to accord with the precise usage of the authors they translate.

The term *ālambana* had a long history in Buddhist thought before Dignāga. It had been used in the *abhidharma* literature of early Buddhism to refer to that to which any given mental act is directed; indeed, in some works the very having of an *ālambana* (*sālambanatvam*) is what defines a mental act.[24] In this respect, it resembles what some philosophers in the West have called an *intentional object*. With this latter concept it also shares, as Dignāga's discussion makes clear, a peculiar, problematic status, stemming from the phenomenon sometimes called in Western philosophy

---

[23] Susuma Yamaguchi, in collaboration with Henriette Meyer, 'Dignāga: Examen de l'objet de la connaissance (*Ālambanaparīkṣā*)', in *Journal Asiatique* CCXIV (1929): 1–65; Fernando Tola and Carmen Dragonetti, 'Dignāga's Ālambanaparīkṣāvṛtti', *Journal of Indian Philosophy* 10 (1982), 105–134

[24] For instance, Vasubandhu, *Abhidharmakośam*, op. cit., 90 (verse 1.34ab)

'intentional inexistence', the curious feature of mental objects that permits us to refer to them, without implying their real existence at all. I can desire to visit the Happy Land of Cockaigne, whether or not such a place exists or ever existed. The phenomenon of intentional inexistence by itself, of course, does not establish the general truth of idealism, but it does show that some of our minds' objects do not correspond in any clear way to what we suppose to be really so. For Dignāga, however, the problem of intentional inexistence arises not just in respect to the objects of our intentional attitudes such as desires but includes also perceptual objects, which, he holds, do not correspond to realities external to our perceptions of them.[25] For taking, as his point of departure, the mereological puzzles posed by his master Vasubandhu, Dignāga shifts the ground subtly but significantly, by asking how our perceptions might correspond to an external world, particularly if it is an external world composed of atoms. The assumptions either that atoms possess the properties we attribute to the aggregations we perceive, or that they do not, cannot in his view be coherently maintained, and lead Dignāga to conclude that, because our perceptions do not correspond to the atoms that are their putative causes, the atoms need not be posited at all. But if we are warranted in jettisoning the atoms, what then of the atomic aggregations we had posited? We are left with a world of perceived properties that exist nowhere but in the minds that perceive them. And without external, physical objects, he maintains, apparent causal order can only be an attribute of the relations among our cognitive acts themselves. This pertains equally to the causal order lending coherence to our own sensory apparatus, which, being no longer physical, must be reinterpreted in terms of the potentiality of consciousness to experience specific types of apparent sensory phenomena.[26]

[25] It is owing to the inclusion of perceptual objects here that I have decided against translating *ālambana* as 'intentional object', despite the evident affinities of the philosophical problems that arise in connection with both it and the Western concept, and instead have opted for 'objective referent'.

[26] Dignāga summarises this in his commentary on his closing verse: 'Depending upon that potential which is called "the eye" and an inner form, consciousness is born with the appearance of an object, the objective referent being indivisible from it. These two are mutually conditioning and their potential is without beginning. By turns, from the actualization of that potential, there is consciousness occurring with the phenomenal features of an object, and by turns the potential for those phenomenal features. Consciousness and those two, according to context, may be said to be the same or different.' My translation.

Dignāga's significant contribution to the discussion, in my view, was not so much in the details of his argument as it was in a key strategic step. With Dignāga, idealism in Indian philosophy became primarily a problem in epistemology, and the ontological concerns of Vasubandhu, though certainly not forgotten, were now subordinated to the inquiry into our knowledge of the external world.

This epistemological turn becomes fully explicit in the work of his greatest successor, Dharmakīrti, whose major treatise, the *Pramāṇavārttika* ('Commentary on Logic and Epistemology'), presents itself as a commentary on Dignāga's *Compendium*. On the question of external objects – our central problem here – Dharmakīrti shares with his predecessor some measure of ambivalence, sometimes suggesting a robust commitment to idealist thought, while elsewhere appearing to acknowledge the possibility that external objects do exist, but are merely hidden from us. Moreover, in certain contexts Dharmakīrti definitely adopts a realist standpoint, to explore how things appear to us, whether or not, in the final analysis, they are as they appear. Later interpreters, therefore, tended to divide between those who favored a thoroughgoing idealist reading, considering the realist passages to be only the tentative expression of Dharmakīrti's view of conventional reality, and those who argued that Dharmakīrti's true intentions accorded more closely with those of the indirect realists, his idealism being a provisional bracketing of objects in order to better clarify the puzzles of reflexivity. Among the commentators, none was more committed to the defense of idealism than was Prajñākaragupta (ca. 800), and none more influenced later Indian philosophy, Buddhist and non-Buddhist, than he as well. We shall examine, therefore, some of Dharmakīrti's main arguments together with Prajñākaragupta's remarks on them. The latter introduces the problem, writing:

> You may ask, 'Is not the objective for which the world strives the knowledge of a concrete object?' Here we say: The world's striving for a concrete object has no reason so long as there is no awareness of such a concrete object. For there can be no striving in the world for an object that is never seen. (625)
>
> *Question.* But is it not the case that we are aware of blue and other objects? How is it then that there is no awareness of an object?[27]

[27] My translations in this section from Dharmakīrti and Prajñākaragupta follow the Sanskrit text given in Rāhula Sāṅkṛtyāyana, ed., *Pramāṇavārtikabhāṣyam*, Tibetan Sanskrit Works Series 1 (Patna:

Prajñākaragupta restates Dharmakīrti's response (verse 321) as follows:

> If it is only a matter of a specific determination or a specific act of awareness, then what is termed 'awareness of an object' is just cognition possessing phenomenal features. Hence, this is merely a verbal convention and the awareness of an object remains unproven.

It is just here, I think, that it becomes clear that the position emerging among the Buddhist idealists more closely resembles what we would call transcendental idealism than it does subjective idealism. Dharmakīrti, on Prajñākaragupta's reading, is asserting not that objects *exist* just in being known; he is telling us, rather, that there is no way we could finally *know* either this or the opposite, for there is no position outside of our knowing that we can occupy, such as will permit us to judge just how to construe the relationship between awareness and its object. As Prajñākaragupta notes, 'If one attempts to demonstrate an object ostensibly, it is not seen, for there is no "seeing of an object"'. This, I suppose, would be the essence of his answer to Moore.

Dharmakīrti introduces and responds to three principal objections to this line of thought (verses 322–26). The first, while conceding that there is no 'view from nowhere' that will permit us to assess independently the relationship between perceiver and object as such, nevertheless maintains that we might have good reason to suppose there to be a crucial resemblance between what we perceive and what exists in fact 'out there'. But, following the doubts already raised by Dignāga, it may be asked why it is, in this case, that the material world of perception does not resemble that of theory: 'If the atoms were the object, then, when there is the consciousness of a massive appearance, which does not resemble the atoms, in what sense are they the object of consciousness?' And although, as Prajñākaragupta adds, one alternative might be to consider material things as partless, just like the perceptions in which they are given, the suggestion does not seem to have been seriously countenanced.[28]

Kashi Prasad Jayaswal Research Institute, 1953), 349–52. Verses numbers are given where applicable.

[28] That it was not perhaps reflects the enduring impact of Vasubandhu's arguments in regard to partless wholes, on which see my 'Mereological Considerations', op. cit.

The second objection (verse 324) seeks to reinforce the first by proposing that it is the concurrence of resemblance *and* causation that assures us that our perceptions are objectively founded. Prajñākaragupta presents the argument in these terms:

> If a resemblance arises from some X and due to that there is an awareness of that X, then, at that time, it is the immediately precedent and objectively equivalent consciousness that is the object. For when, for example, it is the case that the feature blue is the precedent from which immediately, in succession, there arises [the awareness of the feature blue], then it is due to the similarity of the precedent and its being a cause for the arising [of that awareness] that objectivity is attributed to it [i.e., to the precedent feature blue]. Hence, that from which there arises a feature such as blue, and which itself possesses that feature, is the object. But, with respect to consciousness corresponding to an object, the feature is not engendered other than by the immediate condition; when the immediate condition is of the feature blue, the consciousness of yellow could not be engendered by it. Hence we consider that, though blue and other features may be affirmed to act as the immediate condition, their objectivity does not follow therefrom.

This will be clearer if we define some of the key terms: a 'feature' here is a phenomenon, or, more precisely, the phenomenal character of an act of awareness. The 'immediate condition', and indeed the entire issue of immediacy in this passage, refers to a peculiar view of consciousness that arose in early Buddhism, according to which the apparent unity of consciousness, synthesizing thoughts, feelings, and our various sensory inputs, was to be explained by the action of a subliminal conscious moment called the 'immediate condition' (*samanantarapratyaya*). But, as Prajñākaragupta notes here, the immediate condition, conceived in this way, might just as well be synthesizing only data supplied by prior consciousness in order to fulfill the conditions of resemblance and causation upon which the objection was based.

The third objection (verses 325–26) relates to the feeling of certitude that we so often attribute to our perceptions. Again, following Prajñākaragupta:

> One may argue that the object is determined owing to certitude, and that certitude has no source besides the object.... Certitude flows from experience.
>
> Here, we say that the determination of the object is not due to

experience. What's more, the assertion that it comes from the certitude that flows from that [experience] comes down to a case of dragging in a second blindman when the first has already lost the way! Amazing! When a cognition evidently arisen from an object fails to ascertain that object, it's astonishing [to affirm] that even weaker [evidence will do so]! (626)

Objection. But certainty flows from experience and that is due to the experience of objects, not just of its [the experience's] own nature! This is understood on the basis of certitude itself and not otherwise.

Response. Not at all. So long as you do not know that of which there is an experience, how can you establish that [certitude] has the property of flowing from experience? And if to the question, 'whence certitude?' you answer, 'from habituation', our reply [is that owing to the habituation of a feature given conceptually, a clear appearance may be generated such that it becomes what one considers an object, so that except for the phenomenal feature, there is nothing that abides as an object.] ... Therefore, there is no determination of an object owing to certitude.

The doubts voiced here concerning the evidential value of the sense of certitude are by no means foreign to recent anglophone philosophy; Peter Unger's fine essay, *Ignorance: A Case for Skepticism* offers an excellent example.[29] The assertion of certitude *as evidence* for our claims to knowledge is a protective strategy, often deployed to mask the unsettling possibility that we might be wrong. Though Dharmakīrti and his school by no means embraced skepticism and indeed affirmed that we can achieve a kind of certainty, they restricted its scope to the conclusions of reasoned investigations, once our doubts have been raised and resolved. In itself, however, it does not warrant the conclusions to which it might be ascribed.

Having dispensed with these objections, concerning causality, resemblance and certitude, what does Dharmakīrti propose as a positive account of our experience of apparently external objects? (For, as we have said, he is no skeptic.) His response is unequivocal:

Cognition experiences itself, and nothing else whatsoever.
Even the particular objects of perception, are by nature just consciousness itself. (327)

---

[29] Oxford: Clarendon Press, 1978

4.

In introducing the final section of this essay, concerned with the Jain critics of the Buddhist idealists, I must begin with a modest disclaimer: I am not at all a specialist in the study of Jainism and am indeed a neophyte in this area. My current engagement in Jain Studies is due to ongoing research on Buddhist idealism and the resulting appreciation of the importance of Vasubandhu's legacy for later Indian philosophy generally. In exploring increasingly the works of non-Buddhist thinkers who were influenced by or critical of this tradition, I have become particularly impressed by the rich contributions of Jain philosophers to the debate, but I am still at the beginnings of this research, and so present here only preliminary observations.

In responding to the Buddhist idealists, the Jains, unlike both Buddhist and Brahmanical opponents of Vasubandhu's tradition, were not primarily concerned to elaborate decisive refutations. For the Jain approach to philosophy overall was based on the principle called literally 'non-one-sided-ness' (*anekānta*), or 'non-absolutism' in Satkari Mookerjee's phrase, that precluded by and large the search for philosophical finalities.[30] Reality, for the Jains, cannot be reduced to any single viewpoint and the rich multiplicity of perspectives required to exhaust the reality of any phenomenon can be only within the purview of an omniscient mind. Accordingly, in their approach to idealism, as in their approach to other philosophical doctrines, the aim of Jain criticism was to point out that what they considered to be the inadequacies stemmed from its one-sidedness, or as we might put it, reductiveness.

Nevertheless, for Jain thinkers it was particularly important to resist the idealist challenge. More than for many other traditions in Indian religions, for the Jains the attainment of liberation, *mokṣa*, was not merely regarded as a spiritual problem, but equally as a physical problem. For the purgation effected by the strict asceticism that is characteristic of Jain spiritual disciple was intended not just to discipline body and mind, but to drive out and cleanse the impure karmic matter which subtly prevades the physical bodies of mundane beings. Hence, it appeared to the Jains that, by eliminating the reality of the physical world, Yogācāra was undercutting, despite its name, the very basis for the practice of *yoga* as conducing to salvation. It is not a matter of astonishment, therefore, that the Jains were particularly determined to overturn this problematical teaching.

[30] Satkari Mookerjee, *The Jaina Philosophy of Non-Absolutism: A Critical Study of Anekāntavāda* (Calcutta:Bharati Mahavidyalaya, 1944).

Matthew T. Kapstein

At the same time, it must be stressed that, despite their disaffection with Yogācāra, this was the Buddhist tradition in whose study the Jains were probably most deeply invested. This was owing to the considerable influence of Dignāga and Dharmakīrti, whose advances in the fields of logic and epistemology were very largely taken over by Jains of the late first millennium as the methodological basis for refinements within their own system.[31] A very large proportion of the Jain philosophical literature written from about the seventh century on – that is to say after the age of Dharmakīrti – thus engages Buddhist *pramāṇa* to varying degrees. To date I have identified over a dozen sustained discussions in Jain philosophical works of the particular problem they regarded as central to the project of Yogācāra, concerning the assessment of arguments bearing on the existence of the external world.

For purposes of illustration, I will focus upon two particular Jain treatments of this subject-matter. The first, by the renowned and prolific eighth-century teacher Haribhadra Suri, is his critique of Vijñānavāda – the 'consciousness doctrine' – in his verse treatise, the *Śāstravārtāsamuccaya*, or the 'Science News Digest', as I like to call it, and its autocommentary. The second is the sprawling subcommentary on this, entitled *Syādvādakalpalatā*, the 'Wishing Vine of the Doctrine of Tentatives', by the remarkable philosopher Yaśovijaya Gaṇi (1624–88), who was a contemporary of the Mughal emperor Aurangzeb.[32] While I am of course concerned here with the content of their treatment of Yogācāra, I wish also to illustrate something of philosophical progress in Indian intellectual history, for during the period of almost a millennium separating Haribhadra from Yaśovijaya, great advances were made in logic and philosophical method and these are clearly reflected in Yaśovijaya's work. Indeed, much as Haribhadra represents a period in the history of Jain thought in which the lessons of Dharmakīrti and his early successors were being absorbed, Yaśomitra demonstrates an analogous movement with respect to developments within the Brahmanical Nyāya tradition, which specialised in logic and debate, culminating in the emergence of the 'new logic', or Navya-Nyāya,

---

[31] See, in particular, Nagin J. Shah, *Akalaṅka's Criticism of Dharmakīrti's Philosophy, A Study*, Lalbhai Dalpatbhai Series 11 (Ahmedabad: L. D. Institute of Indology, 1967).

[32] Mid second millennium developments in Indian philosophy are surveyed in Jonardon Ganeri, *The Lost Age of Reason: Philosophy in Easly Modern India 1450-1700* (Oxford: Oxford University Press, 2011). Yaśovijaya's contributions and career are discussed there in chapter three.

that flourished from about the thirteenth century on. It will be seen that the realism that was a fundamental characteristic of Nyāya thought contributed to Yaśomitra's critique of the Buddhist idealists.

Haribhadra begins his examination by raising a long-standing problem for Indian philosophers: just what are the conditions that permit us to affirm the non-being of anything?[33] For what the Buddhist idealist needs to affirm is the non-being of the external world altogether. Adhering to Dignāga's reduction of the criteria of knowing to veridical perception and valid inference, Haribhadra asserts that because non-being is nowhere perceived, we can only have recourse in this case to inference. But what kind of inference will do? Only one that derives at least one of its premises from what Indian philosophers term 'non-apprehension' (*anupalabdhi*).

In order to explain this concept in brief, as well as why it is that it need not be, for Haribhadra, a tacit admission of a perception of non-being, let us consider an elementary example. (This one is in fact derived from Dharmakīrti.) We are worried that there might be a fire in a given place and, arriving there, exclaim, 'there's no smoke here!' Now, some philosophers may wish to hold that we have just affirmed a perception of the non-being of smoke in that place – indeed, there were Indian philosophers who did adopt just this approach – but Dharmakīrti will have none of it: for him, 'there's no smoke here', is the expression of a peculiar sort of inference. On reaching the place in question, we have no perceptions of non-being; we have, rather, perceptions of the place that, it so happens, do not include the characteristic properties we associate with smoke. And it is based on this assessment of the properties of our perceptions that we draw the conclusion that 'there is no smoke here'. In short, we infer from our perceptions' *not having* particular properties that we regard as evidentiary to the *non-being* of the things that those properties are supposed to be evidence of, but non-being as such is never perceived.

Haribhadra, I think, accepts all of this and then asks how it could possibly apply in respect to external reality overall. For, the kind of instance in which an inference from non-apprehension may be supposed to be valid must conform, he says, to this principle:

---

[33]   My translations in this section from Haribhadra and Yaśovijaya follow the Sanskrit text given in Bhuvanabhānusūrīśvarajī Mahārāj and Badrīnāth Śukla, eds., *Śāstavārttāsamuccaya, stabaka 5–6* (Bombay: Divya Darśan Trust, 2039 Vikrama era [= 1982 C.E.]). Verses numbers are given where applicable.

Matthew T. Kapstein

It is when an object that had obtained the characteristic of being
apprehended is not apprehended that its non-existence is ascer-
tained by non-apprehension. (5.3)

Applied to Dharmakīrti's example of the smoke, this of course means
that in such a case we perform the inventory of our perceptions as we
do only because we had formerly perceived smoke, and so can now
check our current perceptual field in relation to our memory of the
experience. But none of this is applicable when the object whose
non-being is asserted is external reality *überhaupt*. For in this case
what could possibly count as the characteristic property, the not-
having of which conduces to the inference of non-being? And, assuming that such an experience were possible, it could only be so if external reality had in fact been formerly perceived and were now recalled,
in which case, the very denial of such reality entails its existence.

This argument, however, can have little force against the Buddhist
idealist, because it does not really address the major strategies deployed by the Buddhists in seeking to demonstrate idealism. These
involved attempting to demonstrate that the available theories of
external reality were incoherent, to propose that the appearances of
external reality could be as well or better explained by an alternative
theory, one without commitment to external objects, and to show that
we cannot in any case step outside of the circle of our own awareness.
Such a strategy had led to Dharmakīrti's conclusion, as we have seen
above, that 'cognition experiences itself, and nothing else whatsoever'. Haribhadra's argument, in relation to these points, can at
most be taken as indicating – and perhaps this is all he really
intends to indicate up to this point – that, whatever the force of the
Buddhists' arguments, they fall short of a *proof* of idealism. In the
remainder of his discussion he then seeks to offer, if not exactly a
proof of his own contra idealism, then at least a number of suggestions
favoring the affirmation of something rather like commonsense
realism. As an example, one of his more forceful arguments is the
following:

That whereby the characteristic of apprehension is obtained is
the aggregation of its several causes. Given that such is their
nature, how can that [existence] be taken to be unproven? (5.4)

His argument is something like this: Objects are not processed by us
in isolation; indeed, their perception presupposes a rich nexus of
background causes and conditions, in virtue of which the apparent
occurrence of the thing in question is engendered. The mere existence
of some such framework is of course not itself what is in question –

even the idealist affirms that perceptions belong to complexes – but what Haribhadra suggests is that it is not plausible to regard the relevant frameworks as stemming wholly from within ourselves, for, if we posit perceptual frameworks at all, we must also posit their externality.

Yaśovijaya's unpacking of the argument provides an excellent illustration of his commentarial project as one of rational reconstruction of Haribhadra's work, something quite distinct from the composition of a mere gloss upon it. He characteristically employs here later advances in Nyāya, in this case reflecting the contributions of the eleventh-century philosopher Udayana in respect to the logic of non-apprehension, the knowledge of absence, and its entailments with respect to the absentee, called *pratiyogin*, which for Nyāya thought must be something real. The intuition here can be made clear if we consider a statement such as 'there are no square circles in this room'. Now, from one point of view, this statement is an absurd bit of nonsense, much like 'the Jabberwock is out to lunch'. For in both of these cases, because there is no referent, there is nothing that these sentences are about; they are just silly. But whereas it is immediately evident that the latter, concerning the Jabberwock, means nothing at all, the former may appear to affirm a true proposition; for it seems to be indeed that case that there are no square circles here or anyplace else. Does this not show that we can, in some cases, speak meaningfully of things that are unreal? The Nyāya philosopher would hold that this impression is due to a mistaken analysis. We have an idea of squares and an idea of circles, and these have real referents. It is our combination of them in the phrase 'square circle' that is an error; for 'square' excludes the idea of 'circle'. The appearance of meaningfulness is due only to the meaningfulness of the terms that we have illicitly joined in composition. Language, if it refers at all, can only refer to realities, even when it speaks of absence.

Consider now Yaśovijaya's reconstruction of Haribhadra's argument. He expresses it thus:

'That whereby the characteristic of apprehension is obtained is the aggregation of its several causes', i.e. the compresence of the conditions for the objectification of the absentee, as many as there are, and which are other than the absentee or what the absentee comprises. 'Their' = 'of those conditions for the object-ification of pots, etc., as are accepted by others' or 'of the other conditions present in that place'. 'Such nature' = 'a nature such as generates the objectification of external objects' which is what is being affirmed. In which case, 'how can it be taken to be unproven', i.e. unproven as external? Because [if it were taken to be unproven] that would contradict the completeness of the causes whose nature is such as to generate the objectification of that [external object]. For you, who impugn the external object's [role in] generating cognition, are unable to establish the alterity of the absentee and what the absentee comprises.

Yaśovijaya's presentation of the argument here deploys the technical usage of late Nyāya discourse, though, in analogy to the technical usages of analytic philosophy in the anglophone world, the peculiar diction of Udayana and his successors was motivated by the desire to 'make our ideas clear'. And, indeed, once one grasps the argument, it does seem clear. Let us consider an everyday example: I open the refrigerator in search of the mustard jar, and I perceive that there is no mustard. Now, some philosophers would hold that what one perceives is an ontologically peculiar type of entity, namely an absence. Adopting this approach, I find that my refrigerator is quite a populous place, for, besides the absence of mustard, it contains infinitely many other absences, including the absence of the Andromeda galaxy and the absence of Tyrannosaurus Rex. But how can it be that my fridge holds all these things and that I can perceive them? And why is it that, when I'm searching for mustard, that is the absence I find, instead of being overwhelmed by gazillions of absences that must be then laboriously sifted until I find the absence that pertains to my search? Some versions of the Nyāya realism, like the realism of Alexius Meinong, seem to entail just such problems in their treatment of absences.

In Yaśovijaya's construction, however, my refrigerator presents me with a nexus of conditions for my objectifying the mustard jar *as* absent, conditions that are not to be identified either with the mustard jar or whatever it comprises. It is indeed the mustard jar that is my object, but the object is in this case qualified by its absence, and it is this qualification that becomes known to me by reference to what I perceive to be present. Thus we are definitely distinguishing presence and absence, discerning their alterity, which seems not plausible if the present conditions and the absent object are thought to be indiscernible insomuch as they exist only as objects of of mind. Moreover, we must ask, just what are the present conditions that would permit me to know the absence of external objects altogether, as the idealist wishes to do? Given the radical realism of Nyāya, because all absentees must correspond to realia, just to entertain the external world as an absentee would seem now to entail its real existence.

For Dharmakīrti, the difficulties of establishing the independent reality of the object, together with the reflexivity, or self-presentation, of consciousness, incline to the conclusion that what we know is all and only what appears to reflexive consciousness. If my seeing is self-presenting for me, and my object of sight is known only insomuch as it appears within that seeing, then it would seem that the object is known only in relation to my self-presentating awareness. Haribhadra does not exactly say that this is wrong, so far as it goes. Rather, he holds (in verse 5.12) that this is in fact just what we mean by being aware of an object. We cannot, indeed, be aware of it any place except within the confines of our own awareness. It is only by taking too seriously an unwarranted skepticism that one would argue on this basis that objects do not exist, or that their existence must be bracketed. And to one who might retort that, given this much, we would have no basis for distinguishing genuine objects from hallucinations, Haribhadra replies:

> Where there is, for instance, the cognition of a pot, and so on, such that from its presentation there follows an engagement with it, and from that acquisition, from that functional use, from that recollection, and, from that, continuing interest—to say that the [initial] cogntion is consciousness with reference to a 'mere awareness' such that there is no engagement, etc., is unknown to either the world or science. (5.13–14)

We can perhaps get at what Haribhadra means here by a 'mere awareness' by considering what we mean when we say that a bit of knowledge is 'merely theoretical'. Haribhadra is calling our attention, I think, to a distinction we commonly make between cognitions with or without practical value, and he is asserting that, in effect, idealism robs us of the force of this distinction but treating all knowledge as being in a crucial sense 'merely theoretical'. Yaśovijaya makes this point by saying that, on this account, there is 'nothing outside of our delimitations'. Our common notion of external reality makes sense to us not owing to a fully rationalised framework for our affirmation of it, but rather in virtue of its coherence with the network of practices in which we situate both ourselves and the objective world as it appears to us.

In concluding his critique of the Buddhist idealists, Haribhadra returns to the properly Jain refusal of one-sidedness and he applies this to his own critique. The idealists, he holds (verses 6.52–53), are wrong, but not one-sidedly so; for their doctrine, although subject to metaphysical rebuttal, is nevertheless one that may have propaedeutic value for those cultivating a spiritual path; for idealism undermines belief in the ultimacy of external and material goods, so that to entertain it may aid those who find it difficult to achieve equanimity and detachment in regard to worldly things. A provisional acceptance of its truth may therefore be, in some circumstances, practically warranted. But it must be rejected before it can corrode the Jain commitment to ascetic rigor. And about this he is quite decisive (verses 5.29–39): the real danger of idealism stems from its potential to undermine the distinction between bondage and liberation. For the Jains, our impoverished spiritual state stems from corruptions that can be purged only through long and painful ascesis. The fault of Buddhist idealism is, in the final analysis, more soteriological than metaphysical, for it seems to treat our spiritual predicament as a matter of illusion, to be removed, as if it were mere morning mist, by the workings of insight alone.

The fundamental Buddhist error, in the Jain view, therefore seems to have been a penchant for an exaggerated intellectualism, weakening the commitment to the unyielding spiritual discipline that Jainism holds to be the essential foundation for the realization of freedom. It goes without saying, of course, that the Buddhists would not concur with such an assessment. Where both parties agreed was in the proposition that epistemology and metaphysics were of importance for their contributions to the grounding of practical soteriological endeavours.[34]

In accord with my understanding of the theme of the present volume on 'Philosophical Traditions', it has been my aim here not so much to provide a detailed account of particular lines of argument, but rather to suggest something of the manner in which so-called Buddhist idealism unfolded as a tradition not just for Buddhists, but within Indian philosophy more generally. Seen from this perspective, Buddhist idealism remained a current within Indian philosophy long after the demise of Buddhism in India, in about the twelfth century, and endured in some respects at least until the Mughal age, when the Jain philosopher Yaśovijaya was active.[35] Of course,

---

[34] In the case of Buddhism, at least, the relationship between philosophy and soteriological practice has been contested in the recent literature. See my '"Spiritual Exercise" and Buddhist Epistemologists in India and Tibet', in Steven Emmanuel, ed., *The Blackwell Companion to Buddhist Philosophy* (Oxford: Blackwell, 2013), 27–89 for a review of the question.

[35] Other traditions within Indian thought also preserved aspects of the Yogācāra legacy. One notable example is Kashmir Śaivism, whose engagements with Buddhist philosophy have been examined in great detail in Isabelle Ratié, *Le Soi et l'Autre: Identité, différence et altérité dans la philosophie de la Pratyabhijñā* (Leiden: Brill, 2011).

Buddhist Idealists and Their Jain Critics

I have omitted altogether from this discussion the considerable legacy of Indian Buddhist idealism in the philosophical traditions of China, Tibet, Korea and Japan, continuing down to our own time. All that, however, is subject-matter for another occasion.

École Pratique des Hautes Études, Paris, and
The University of Chicago
mkapstei@uchicago.edu

Self, Other, God: 20thCentury Jewish Philosophy[1]

TAMRA WRIGHT

Abstract

Martin Buber, Franz Rosenzweig and Emmanuel Levinas are three of the most prominent Jewish philosophers of the 20th century. This paper looks at the different understandings each author offers of intersubjectivity and authentic self-hood and questions the extent to which for each author God plays a role in interpersonal relationships.

I was invited to speak on Jewish philosophy and, as my title suggests, I have chosen to focus on 20th century Jewish thinkers. Rather than attempting a survey of 20th century Jewish philosophy, I will narrow the focus to three of the period's most significant thinkers: Martin Buber, Franz Rosenzweig, and Emmanuel Levinas. These three are part of what Robert Gibbs has called a 'family' of Jewish thinkers which also includes their predecessor, the Neo-Kantian philosopher Hermann Cohen.[2] I will focus on three books – Buber's *I and Thou*, Rosenzweig's *The Star of Redemption*, and Levinas's *Totality and Infinity* – and on one philosophical question – the relationship between self and other, or 'inter-subjectivity'. In other words, I want to ask, with each of these three authors, 'Who is the other?' In exploring this theme, we will also need to consider their different understandings of authentic selfhood and ask what role, if any, God plays in the relationship with the other.

Buber, Rosenzweig, and Levinas were all thinkers who wrote for a general philosophical audience and leading educators in their respective Jewish communities. In each case, there are some parts of their corpus which are specifically concerned with Jewish texts, practices, and questions and which were written primarily for a Jewish audience. Although, for the most part, we will ignore those writings today and focus on the three books I have mentioned, my primary interest is in understanding each thinker's contribution to Jewish thought rather than to philosophy *per se*.

[1]   I am grateful to Professor Anthony O'Hear and Adam Ferner for their willingness to re-schedule my lecture in order to avoid the Jewish Sabbath.

[2]   Robert Gibbs, *Correlations in Rosenzweig and Levinas* (Princeton: Princeton University Press, 1994).

doi:10.1017/S1358246114000137   © The Royal Institute of Philosophy and the contributors 2014

Tamra Wright

One of the key family resemblances that Gibbs identifies in the three thinkers is their development, following Cohen, of an other-centred ethics. Additionally, in Rosenzweig and Levinas there is a sweeping critique of the totalizing and reductive tendencies of western philosophy, and its inability to acknowledge genuine transcendence or otherness. According to Levinas, the dominant approach in western philosophy is to see the relationship between self and other in negative terms. In Levinas's phrase, western philosophy presents the relationship between self and other as an 'allergic relation'.[3] This approach is perhaps best epitomized by Jean-Paul Sartre. Sartre's philosophical works argue that 'social relations are bound to fail' and portray the other person as an ontological thief, someone who steals the world away from me;[4] and his play *No Exit* gave us the memorable exclamation 'L'enfer, c'est les autres', usually translated as 'Hell is other people!'[5]

For the three Jewish thinkers we are looking at today, hell is most certainly not the other(s). On the contrary, for each of them a positive and responsible relationship with the other is indispensable for authentic selfhood, a meaningful life, and a genuine relationship with God.

These three themes are clearly manifested in Buber's famous 1923 work *Ich und Du*,[6] normally translated as *I and Thou*, in which Buber claims that there are two fundamentally different ways of relating to the world, namely the mode of 'I-thou' and the mode of 'I-it'. The opening passage of *I and Thou* sets out Buber's basic premise:

> The world is twofold for man in accordance with his twofold attitude.

---

[3] In *Totality and Infinity*, tr. Alphonse Lingis (Pittsburgh: Duquesne University Press, 1969), 38

[4] 'The appearance of the Other in the world corresponds therefore to a congealed sliding of the whole universe, to a decentralization of the world'. Jean-Paul Sartre, *Being and Nothingness,* trans. Hazel Barnes (New York: Washington Square Press, 1993), 343

[5] Jean-Paul Sartre, *No Exit and Three Other Plays*, trans. Stuart Gilbert (New York: Vintage, 1989), 45

[6] There are two English translations available: *I and Thou*, 2nd edition, tr. Ronald Gregor Smith (Edinburgh: T & T Clark, 1958) and *I and Thou: A New Translation With a Prologue 'I and You' and Notes*, tr. Walter Kaufmann (London: Simon and Schuster, 1996). The Smith and Kaufmann translations were originally published in 1937 and 1970 respectively. All quotations below are taken from the Kaufmann translation, with 'thou' substituted for 'you'.

The attitude of man is twofold in accordance with the two basic words he can speak.

The basic words are not single words but word pairs.

One basic word is the word pair I-Thou.

The other basic word is the word pair I-It; but this basic word is not changed when He or She takes the place of It.

Thus the I of man is also twofold.

For the I of the basic word I-Thou is different from that of the basic word I-It.[7]

Before looking at the distinction between I-it and I-thou in more detail, I should mention that I am quoting from Walter Kauffman's 1970 translation, but with a significant change. Unlike his predecessor Ronald Gregor Smith, who published the first English translation of *Ich und Du* in 1937, Kauffman chose to translate 'du' as 'you' rather than 'thou'; the only exception he made was in the title. He felt that for a contemporary readership 'thou' sounds both archaic and formal. I understand his concern, but disagree with his decision. I think that our inability in modern English to distinguish between the singular and the plural second person pronouns, and especially between the intimate and the formal, is a major weakness of the language. I also suspect that if Buber had been writing in English he might have chosen different terminology altogether, or even have chosen to revive the word 'thou'. More importantly, I perhaps have more faith in the intelligence and flexibility of educated readers than Kaufmann did. A quick reminder of their high school French, and some judicious quoting of Shakespeare, should do the trick. In Shakespearean English, as is well known, 'thou' and 'you were used, respectively, as the singular and plural second person pronouns. 'You' was also used as a formal second person singular. This usage parallels the use of 'tu' and 'vous' in French and 'du' and 'sie' in German. Remember Juliet:

'O Romeo, Romeo, wherefore art thou Romeo?
Deny thy father and refuse thy name;'[8]

By using 'du'/ 'thou', Buber is conveying that the one who is addressed is a) the singular other and b) someone with whom I have a close relationship – if only in the moment of the address. I have therefore altered the translation of 'du' to 'thou' rather than 'you'.

---

[7] *I and Thou*, 53
[8] *Romeo and Juliet*, Act 2, scene 2, ll. 33–34

Tamra Wright

What does Buber mean by 'I-it' and 'I-thou'? I-it refers to our ordinary mode of engaging with things in the world. We treat them as means to our own ends; we engage with them only on a superficial level; and our knowledge of them is mediated by concepts and categories. There is nothing inherently wrong with this way of relating to objects, and even human beings must often be related to in the mode of I-it rather than that of I-thou. Indeed, Buber acknowledges the absolute necessity of I-it. However, it is of paramount importance for Buber that when I relate to an object or person in the mode of I-it, I am not fully engaged in the world. The self that engages in I-it relations is the 'limited I'.

Buber contrasts this mode of being with the I-thou relation, in which I relate to the other with my whole being. In this encounter, I open myself to the other. I relinquish any thought of objectives or desired outcomes; and the limited, indirect knowledge of the I-it mode of experience is replaced with a deeper, unmediated knowledge. Most importantly for Buber, I emerge from the encounter with a sense of confirmation of my being and an affirmation that existence itself is meaningful.

It is important to recognize that for Buber, certainly in the realm of inter-human relationships, the I-thou is a reciprocal relationship; the other whom I address as my thou similarly says 'thou' to me. This may be one of the reasons that he tells us that there is an element of 'grace' involved in the I-thou; although I can try to be open to I-thou encounter, I cannot make it happen by my own efforts. To understand this, it is helpful to consider the contemporary psychological concept of 'flow'. Mihaly Csikszentmihalyi describes flow as a state in which the person is completely focused, experiencing no distracting thoughts or irrelevant feelings. Self-consciousness disappears and one's sense of time is distorted.[9] Csikszentmihalyi gives numerous examples of activities that may produce flow for different people, including various sports, reading, singing, playing a game, or programming a computer. He also points out that the state of flow may occur during a social interaction, such as a conversation between good friends or a mother playing with her baby.[10]

I would suggest that being in such a state of 'flow' is a necessary, but not sufficient, condition of I-thou encounters. To take the example of a conversation, if I am not completely immersed in

[9] Mihaly Csikszentmihalyi, *Finding Flow: The Psychology of Engagement with Everyday Life* (New York: Basic Books, 1998), 31
[10] Ibid., 29

152

conversing with the other, if I have a distracting thought or a moment of self-consciousness when I wonder whether I'm talking too much or boring the other person, then not only am I not experiencing flow at that moment, I am also not in the midst of an I-thou encounter.[11] But even if I am in this flow state throughout, fully engrossed in the moment, if the other person is not similarly fully engaged in the encounter and in the flow state, then, according to Buber's analysis, no genuine I-thou encounter takes place.

The brief summary I have just given is based largely on Part I of *I and Thou*. It has skipped over some of the major difficulties in the text by focusing only on the relationship with the human other. Buber himself, however, presented I-thou encounter as a possibility in three spheres of relation: our life with nature; our engagement with fellow human beings; and our connection with 'forms of spirit',[12] by which Buber means artistic inspiration and other experiences in which 'we hear no Thou but feel addressed; we answer – creating, thinking, acting.'[13]

Buber's explicit aim in writing *I and Thou* was to help overcome the 'sickness of the age',[14] in which I-thou relations are eclipsed by the predominance of the 'it-world', by awakening his readers to the potential for I-thou relation. He believed that the dominance of the I-it mode of being in modern life had nearly destroyed individuals' awareness of, and therefore their capacity for, I-thou encounter. The book is divided into three parts. The first part, with its highly poetic descriptions of I-thou, is designed to invoke the reader's recollection of their own experience of encounter, and to awaken a desire for future I-thou relations. In the third part, Buber introduces a concept which is central to his dialogical philosophy, but only alluded to briefly earlier on – the idea of the Eternal Thou. Part I states simply that in each thou 'we address the eternal Thou'.[15] In Part III Buber makes it clear that this is not an added extra of I-thou relationships, but is constitutive of them. 'The mediatorship

---

[11]   However, the distracting thought does not necessarily mean that no I-thou encounter has taken place, only that I have now stepped outside it. Similarly, if one entertains the thought 'this is an I-thou encounter' that moment of self-consciousness signals that the encounter itself is over.

[12]   Both Kaufman and Gregor Smith (1957 revised edition) render Buber's phrase as 'spiritual beings'. Given the context, 'forms of spirit' seems a better translation. See Donald L. Berry, *Mutuality: The Vision of Martin Buber* (Albany: SUNY Press, 1985), 104 note 3.

[13]   *I and Thou*, 57

[14]   Ibid., 102

[15]   Ibid., 57

of the Thou of all beings accounts for the fullness of our relationships to them.'[16] In other words, to overcome the 'sickness of the age', we need not only to open ourselves to mutually affirming encounters with others; we must also at the same time be prepared to address, and be addressed by, the Eternal Thou.

According to Buber, God cannot be deduced from either nature or history. Rather, God or the Eternal Thou is 'what confronts us immediately and first and always.'[17] As such, even a self-proclaimed atheist can be in relation with the Eternal Thou: 'whoever abhors the name and fancies that he is godless – when he addresses with his whole devoted being the Thou of his life that cannot be restricted by any other, he addresses God.'[18]

In the concluding pages of *I and Thou* Buber elaborates his vision of a fully actualized person and society. The ideal would not be to refrain from I-it relations, which is impossible in any case, but to allow the relation with the Eternal Thou to imbue all of life with meaning. Each person's life should be so permeated with true I-thou relation that moments of encounter are not transient, like 'flashes of lightning in the dark'; rather, they should be like 'a rising moon in a clear starry night.'[19]

For Buber, then, authentic selfhood, the intersubjective relation, and the relationship with God are all intimately connected with one another. It is only when I engage with the other as my thou that my authentic self, or whole being, comes into play; to encounter the other as my thou is at the same time to be in relation with the Eternal Thou; and it is only through I-thou relations that my existence becomes meaningful.

Both Rosenzweig and Levinas had significant reservations about the main thesis of *I and Thou*. Rosenzweig, who was a friend and colleague of Buber, commented on the manuscript before publication. His main criticism was that the binary categorization of all modes of relation as either I-thou or I-it was a vast over-simplification of the complexities of interhuman relations and relations between God and human beings.[20]

---

[16]   Ibid., 123
[17]   Ibid., 129
[18]   Ibid., 124
[19]   Ibid., 163
[20]   See Richard Cohen, *Elevations: The Height of the Good in Rosenzweig and Levinas*, chapter 4, 'Rosenzweig contra Buber: Personal Pronouns' (Chicago: University of Chicago Press, 1994), 90–114

Before we look at Rosenzweig's own *magnum opus*, a warning: *The Star of Redemption* is one of the strangest books of philosophy one is likely to encounter. As Peter Eli Gordon has pointed out, reading it requires great patience:

> The book is mostly written in a declamatory mode – it does not argue, it simply states – and it is written in a grand and self-confident style that does very little to encourage the reader's confidence in Rosenzweig as a philosophical authority. What readers have come to expect as the customary etiquette of modern philosophy – gestures such as statements of purpose, exposition, and proof – are generally absent.[21]

The opening passage illustrates Gordon's observations about the absence of some customary features of philosophical writings. In what is probably the most famous passage of the book, Rosenzweig writes:

> All cognition of the All originates in death, in the fear of death. Philosophy takes it upon itself to throw off the fear of things earthly, to rob death of its poisonous sting, and Hades of its pestilential breath. All that is mortal lives in this fear of death; every new birth augments the fear by one new reason, for it augments what is mortal. Without ceasing, the womb of the indefatigable earth gives birth to what is new, each bound to die, each awaiting the day of its journey into darkness with fear and trembling. But philosophy denies these fears of the earth. It bears us over the grave which yawns at our feet with every step. It lets the body be a prey to the abyss, but the free soul flutters away over it. Why should philosophy be concerned if the fear of death knows nothing of such a dichotomy between body and soul, if it roars Me! Me! Me!, if it wants nothing to do with relegating fear onto a mere 'body'? ... for all this dire necessity philosophy has only its vacuous smile. With index finger outstretched, it directs the creature, whose limbs are quivering with terror for its this-worldly existence, to a Beyond of which it doesn't care to know anything at all. For man does not really want to escape any kind of fetters; he wants to remain, he wants to – live.[22]

---

[21]   Peter Eli Gordon, *Rosenzweig and Heidegger: Between Judaism and German Philosophy* (Berkeley: University of California Press, 2003), 122
[22]   Franz Rosenzweig, *The Star of Redemption*, trans. William W. Hallo (London: University of Notre Dame Press, 1985), 3

Tamra Wright

This focus on the fear of death is, of course, reminiscent of Heidegger's philosophy, and the similarities between the two thinkers have been explored by Gordon and other scholars. On a slightly less highbrow note, Rosenzweig's claim that the self refuses the sham immortality of philosophy and wants, instead, to remain living in the ordinary sense of the word reminds me of Woody Allen's quip that he doesn't want to achieve immortality through his films, he wants to attain it by not dying.

According to Rosenzweig, western philosophy has sold us a bill of goods. It offers us an escape from human finitude via the intellect; a philosophical idea of immortality. But for Rosenzweig, as Gordon explains,

> [...] the old dream of metaphysics is ludicrous, a philosophical hoax. The deceit of metaphysics becomes most obvious when the individual comes face to face with death as a real possibility. In such moments, the human being becomes enveloped by anxiety (*Angst*) for his this-worldly being (*Diesseits*). But philosophy responds by pointing to a 'beyond' for which the human being can have no concern.

As well as criticizing philosophy for this great metaphysical hoax, Rosenzweig critiques western philosophy's reductive approach to reality, its claim to be able to think 'the All'. It should be noted here that Rosenzweig views the history of philosophy through the lens of German Idealism. In a sweeping overview of the history of philosophy, he argues that every philosophy, from the ancient Greeks to Hegel, has tried to 'reduce the manifold into the one, the sensible into the intelligible, in short, the real into the one'.[23]

As Stefan Moses explains, Rosenzweig thinks that:

> [...] the history of western philosophy is made up of successive attempts at bringing the multiplicity of the real into one great unifying principle. According to ancient classical thought, everything can be brought back to the world, and thus this thought is a cosmological one. According to Medieval Scholastics, everything can be related to God, and thus this thought is a theological one. Since Descartes, everything is related to the thinking subject, the 'I', and thus this thought is an anthropological one.[24]

[23] Stéphane Moses, *System and Revelation: The Philosophy of Franz Rosenzweig*, trans. Catherine Tihanyi (Detroit: Wayne State University Press, 1992), 50

[24] Ibid., 51

Rosenzweig's system, on the other hand, refuses unity and insists on plurality. As mentioned earlier, there are three independent 'elements' that are irreducible to one another: namely God, World, and Man.

The *Star* is divided into three parts, each of which Rosenzweig originally wanted to publish as a separate volume. Each part contains an introduction, three books, and a concluding section which also serves as the 'transition' or 'threshold' to the next book, or in the case of Part Three, a concluding 'Gate'. Most famously, the cover of the book and title pages of each Part feature a geometric shape. Part One and Part Two feature equilateral triangles, one pointing upwards and the other downwards. The first represents the 'elements' of Rosenzweig's philosophical system: God, World, and Humanity. The second triangle represents the relationships between the elements: Creation (God to the World), Revelation (God to Humanity), and Redemption (Humanity to the World). The two triangles represent a key theme of his critique of western philosophy: whereas philosophy, 'from Parmenides to Hegel', claims to think of the 'totality of being' (SR 12) and in so doing, unifies the world, divine spirit, and humanity, Rosenzweig insists on the irreducible separation of God, world, and humanity, and this is symbolized by the points of the first triangle. Although God, world, and humanity remain separate, they are in relation to one another, and this is represented by the lines of the second triangle. The title page of Part III presents the six-pointed Star of David (*magen david*) formed by superimposing the second triangle onto the first. The six-pointed star was also embossed upon the cover of the first German edition of the *Star*. At the heart of the star is the eternal fire of revelation, internalized by the eternal people, the Jews. The rays of the star 'go forth only from this fire'[25] and Christianity, which is evangelical at its core, spreads the light of revelation.

Rosenzweig's *magnum opus* weaves together philosophy and theology in an original way and has given rise to a range of different interpretations. Perhaps unsurprisingly, given all of the challenges the *Star* presents, the book did not easily find an audience of careful readers. Rosenzweig himself expressed shock at how little its purported readers knew it – 'everyone', he wrote to his cousin Hans Ehrenberg, 'thinks it is an admonition to kosher eating'.[26]

---

[25]   *The Star of Redemption*, 298
[26]   Rosenzweig's letter, dated March 11, 1925, can be found in Nahum N. Glatzer, *Franz Rosenzweig: His Life and Thought* (Hackett: Cambridge, 1961), 145–46. Rosenzweig writes of the *Star*: 'Precisely the thing I hoped for when I insisted on a Jewish publisher has happened, while the thing that

Although existentialist readings of Rosenzweig have been dominant for several decades, more recent scholars have presented a range of readings, including approaches that emphasize Rosenzweig's own description of the *Star* as a 'system of philosophy', despite his scathing critique of idealist philosophy and particularly Hegel's system.[27]

Part II of the *Star*, which describes how revelation transforms each of the three 'elements' and brings them into contact with the others, will be our main focus, because it is here that Rosenzweig presents the relationship between the self and the human other. Significantly, he discusses this and other themes in Part II via an extended commentary on biblical texts. Although Rosenzweig's approach to these texts has been called 'midrashic', Mara Benjamin has argued that his methodology is more akin to the literary genre of the 're-written Bible'.[28] Rosenzweig employs four significant features of this genre of writing: he produces an interpretive reading of scripture via an indirect commentary; he follows the Bible serially, in proper order, but is highly selective in quoting and otherwise representing texts; he imposes a single interpretation on the original; and, finally, he does not state the exegetical reasoning that guides this interpretation.[29] Rather, as Benjamin explains, 'The biblical texts that occupy the heart of *Star* anchor the text and, at the same time, are reconstituted in a strong misreading that gives them new shape and meaning.' Rosenzweig uses two broadly defined strategies to integrate the biblical text into

---

I feared, and that made me hesitate to publish it during my lifetime, has not happened: it has made me famous among the Jews but has not obstructed my influence with the Jews. And the reason for both is that they haven't read it. Again and again I am amazed at how little its readers know it. Everybody thinks it is an admonition to kosher eating.'

[27]   Benjamin Pollack stresses Rosenzweig's systematic aims in his monograph *Franz Rosenzweig and the Systematic Task of Philosophy* (Cambridge: Cambridge University Press, 2009).

[28]   Mara Benjamin, *Rosenzweig's Bible: Reinventing Scripture for Jewish Modernity* (Cambridge; Cambridge University Press, 2009), 38. Benjamin notes that Geza Vermes introduced the concept of the 're-written Bible' in his *Scripture and Tradition in Judaism: Haggadic Studies*, 2nd, revised ed. (Leiden: Brill, 1973), 67–126, and Philip S. Alexander lists nine characteristics of this genre in his 'Retelling the Old Testament' in *It is Written: Scripture Citing Scripture: Essays in Honour of Barnabas Lindars*, edited by D. A. Carson and H. G. M. Williamson (New York: Cambridge University Press, 1988), 116–18. Rosenzweig's work does not exhibit all nine characteristics of the genre.

[29]   Benjamin, op. cit., 39

the *Star*: 'the explicit use of biblical texts and the subtle weaving of "unmarked" references into his own prose.' This way of working with the biblical text has caused some confusion among readers. However, as Benjamin explains, Rosenzweig's 'citations of, allusions to, and wholesale reworking of scripture attest to [his] vision of scripture as fulfilling a unique and irreplaceable purpose within his own philosophical tome'.[30] Rosenzweig's *Star of Redemption* is, to a large extent, a biblical commentary that needs to be read alongside the biblical text.

For example, in Book 2 of Part II, which has been described as both the literal and spiritual centre of the book,[31] Rosenzweig weaves together a number of biblical texts with his own philosophical thought: we move from Adam after the sin to a composite portrayal of the prophetic response to God's call – *hineini*, 'here I am'.

> 'Where art thou?' [...] Man hides, he does not respond, he remains speechless, he remains the Self as we know it. The responses which God finally elicits from him are not responses. The divine quest for the Thou receives no 'I' for an answer, no 'I am', 'I have done it.' Instead of an I the responding mouth brings forth a He-She-It. [...] The general concept of man can take refuge behind the woman or the serpent. Instead of this the call goes out to what cannot flee, to the utterly particular, [...] to the proper name [...] the name which God himself created for the man [...] To God's 'Where art Thou?' the man had still kept silence as defiant and blocked Self. Now, called by his name, twice, in a supreme definiteness that could not but be heard, now he answers, all unlocked, all spread apart, all ready, all-soul: 'Here I am.'[32]

Bearing in mind Benjamin's observations on the similarity of Rosenzweig's approach to the genre of the 're-written Bible', we can avoid Hilary Putnam's conclusion that Rosenzweig's text is 'playing a trick on the reader' of this passage.[33] The unmarked transitions from the story of Adam after the sin to the story of Abraham being called by God, and the allusions to other prophets who respond '*hineini*, here I am' to God's call, are not an attempt to

---

[30] Ibid., 40–41
[31] Richard Cohen, op. cit., 76
[32] *Star of Redemption*, 175–76
[33] Hilary Putnam, *Jewish Philosophy as a Guide to Life: Rosenzweig, Buber, Levinas, Wittgenstein (The Helen & Martin Schwartz Lectures in Jewish Studies)*, (Bloomington: Indiana University Press, 2008), 44

Tamra Wright

confuse the reader but to articulate Rosenzweig's own thought using biblical language and allusions. In Book Two of Part II, the *Star* presents an understanding of revelation as divine love. According to this account, the human being is transformed from an enclosed self to a soul when it hears God's voice, responds to His call by saying 'here I am', and becomes aware of divine love. This love is not a universal attribute of God, but is radically particular:[34] To receive the revelation is to become aware of God's love for *me*. Rosenzweig uses the figures of Adam and Abraham respectively to represent the generic human being (in Hebrew, 'adam' is both a proper name and the generic noun for 'man' or 'human being')[35] and a specific, named individual who is loved by God qua individual. (Abraham is named by God in Genesis 17:5 and called by his name, twice, in Genesis 22:11).[36] Whereas for Buber, the authentic self or whole being emerges in any I-thou encounter, in Rosenzweig's narrative it is hearing and responding to the particularist divine call that transforms the self into soul.

[34]   *Star of Redemption*, 164

[35]   Benjamin helpfully points out that in Genesis 'Adam' does not become a proper name until 'the sex differentiation of the first, androgynous human being in Genesis 2:21.' Op. cit., 44

[36]   Here I differ slightly from Benjamin's reading of Rosenzweig. Benjamin reads the unmarked transition in Rosenzweig's text from 'Adam' to the soul who answers 'here am I' as a universalizing move within his reading of the biblical text. However, her reading of Rosenzweig's allusions to the biblical characters who are called twice and respond 'here I am' misses the precision of Rosenzweig's focus on Abraham rather than on a composite of Abraham, Moses, and Jacob (who are the only Pentateuchal characters who are called twice and respond '*hineni*'). Of these three, it is only Abraham who is given his name by God (his name is changed by God from Abram to Abraham in Genesis 17:5). Benjamin suggests that Rosenzweig jettisons 'the particularistic element of God's address to the Pentateuchal characters' in order to produce 'a text in which any and every soul responds to the direct invitation of God' (op. cit., 45). I would suggest that far from jettisoning the particularistic elements of the Abraham story, Rosenzweig highlights them through the emphasis on Abraham being named by God, and that he does so to underscore his own insistence that divine love is not an attribute of God, but is always particular, addressed to a unique individual, who must respond in his or her particularity. Benjamin's otherwise perceptive reading of this text also omits to mention that in the Jewish interpretive tradition God's repetition of the name is seen as a specific linguistic form indicating divine love or devotion (see Rashi on Genesis 22:11 and passim).

This love is revealed in the form of an imperative, namely: love me! Continuing in the same 're-written bible' genre, Rosenzweig writes:

> The summons to hear, the address by the given name [...] preface only the one commandment, which is not the highest, which is in truth the only commandment, the sum and substance of all commandments ever to leave God's mouth. [...] 'Thou shalt love the Lord thy God with all thy heart and with all thy soul and with all thy might.' [...] Can love then be commanded? [...] No third party can, but the One can. The commandment to love can only proceed from the mouth of the lover. Only the lover can and does say: love me! – and he really does so. In his mouth the commandment to love is not a strange commandment; it is none other than the voice of love itself.[37]

How is the soul to love God? Rosenzweig insists that simply returning God's love is not what is required. To do so would be to embrace the path of the mystic, seeking seclusion with God. Instead, the appropriate response to God's love is to fulfil the commandment of loving the neighbour, who is in God's image: 'All commandments which derive from that primeval "love me!" ultimately merge in the all-inclusive "love thy neighbour!"'.[38]

Although we have only considered a few aspects of Rosenzweig's thought, we are now in a position to sketch preliminary answers to our three questions: authentic selfhood arises as a response to the call of God; the other is the neighbour whom I am commanded to love; and love for the neighbour is grounded in the prior revelation of God's love for me.

Rosenzweig's thought had a profound influence on a number of Jewish thinkers, including Emmanuel Levinas, who states somewhat paradoxically in the preface to *Totality and Infinity* that the *Star of Redemption* 'is too often present in this book to be cited'.[39] The comment is made in the context of Levinas acknowledging the powerful influence of Rosenzweig's critique of the reductive and totalizing impulses of western philosophy. In what follows I will give a brief introduction to Levinas's account of the self-other relation and then consider how it compares with Rosenzweig's account.

Totality and Infinity appeared in 1961, forty years after Rosenzweig's *magnum opus*. Its opening paragraph consists of one

[37] *Star of Redemption* 176
[38] *Star of Redemption* 205
[39] *Totality and Infinity: An Essay on Exteriority*, tr. Alphonso Lingis (Pittsburgh: Duquesne University Press, 1961), 28

sentence: 'Everyone will readily agree that it is of the highest importance to know whether we are not duped by morality.'[40] In a late interview, referring explicitly to the Holocaust, Levinas again asks
whether morality is still meaningful – but this time he adds the
phrase 'after the failure of morality'.[41] We will explore the significance of the historical context later, but I don't want to keep you in
suspense – from *Totality and Infinity* onwards Levinas will answer
the question about the meaningfulness of morality in the affirmative,
even if his account of ethics becomes increasingly difficult to
understand.

Levinas is able to affirm the meaningfulness of morality through
his account of the relationship between self and other. Although
Levinas's methodology is grounded in the phenomenology he
learnt from Edmund Husserl and Martin Heidegger, *Totality and
Infinity* can also be read as a narrative. Indeed, as Diane Perpich
has pointed out,

> *Totality and Infinity* exudes the air of a drama [...T]here is an
> identifiable plot that might be summarized [...] as follows: an
> ego absorbed in its needs and living in conditions of relative
> domestic security is confronted by a stranger who disrupts and
> calls into question its manner of being at home in the world.
> The result of the face-to-face encounter is that the ego finds
> itself in an ethical relationship in which it is divested of its
> egoism and invited to the serious work of goodness and
> responsibility.[42]

This is, of course, a vast over-simplification; and, as Perpich emphasizes, the narrative structure of the tale is 'importantly at odds with
the most original impulses of the work'. Nevertheless, I will begin
by fleshing out the story, partly to enable a comparison with the accounts offered by Buber and Rosenzweig, and partly because the
question of the ego's responsibility is central to *Totality and
Infinity*; 'it drives the work forward chronologically, logically, and

---

[40]   Ibid., 21

[41]   'The Paradox of Morality: an Interview with Emmanuel Levinas',
conducted by Tamra Wright, Peter Hughes, and Alison Ainley, tr.
Andrew Benjamin and Tamra Wright, in *The Provocation of Levinas:
Rethinking the Other*, edited by R. Bernasconi and D. Wood (London:
Routledge & Kegan Paul, 1988), 176

[42]   Diane Perpich, *The Ethics of Emmanuel Levinas* (Stanford: Stanford
University Press, 2008), 78–79

dramatically, governing in almost every respect the relationship between its component parts.'[43]

Levinas presents a phenomenological analysis of the self's relationship with the natural world. In this analysis, prior to the encounter with another human being, the ego views itself as the centre of existence. Everything in the natural world is subject to the self's powers: through labour, possession, cognition, and so forth, the self is always able to overcome the alterity or otherness of objects.

> It is enough to walk, to do, in order to grasp everything, to take. In a sense, everything is in the site, in the last analysis everything is at my disposal, even the stars if I but reckon them, calculate the intermediaries or the means.[44]

Levinas's account of embodied human existence is different in important ways from the phenomenologies of both Husserl and Heidegger. One of Levinas's critiques of Husserl was that Husserlian phenomenology focused too much on intellectual operations, looking at intentionality primarily in terms of representation. Levinas's intentional analysis of embodiment focuses on a relation of 'living from' the natural world: '"Good soup", air, light, spectacles, work, ideas, sleep, etc. [...] These are not objects of representations. We *live from* them.'[45]

Levinas also distances himself from a Heideggerian focus on implements, the 'ready to hand'. For Levinas, human life equates with 'love of life':

> Life is not the naked will to be [...] Life's relation with the very conditions of its life becomes the nourishment and content of that life. Life is *love of life*, a relation with contents that are not my being but more dear than my being: thinking, eating, sleeping, reading, working, warming oneself in the sun. Distinct from my substance but constituting it, these contents make up the worth [*prix*] of my life.[46]

Levinas acknowledges that the relationship with nature is challenging. The body is needy; it suffers from hunger, thirst, and so forth. Yet, Levinas says, the self is 'happy in its needs'. Rejecting the Platonic interpretation of need as a simple lack, Levinas argues that even meeting the most basic needs of life is experienced as accomplishment:

---

43 Ibid., 79
44 *Totality and Infinity*, 37
45 Ibid., 110
46 Ibid., 112

'enjoyment is made of the memory of its thirst; it is a quenching.' Although the self is dependent on the world to provide the raw materials with which to meet its needs, it is also independent insofar as the subject is able to plan and take action to meet those needs.[47]

When another human being appears in my world, however, my mastery and enjoyment are called into question. Levinas emphasizes the radical alterity of the other: 'The Other escapes my grasp by an essential dimension, even if I have him at my disposal. He is not wholly in my site.'[48]

Levinas employs the image of the 'face' to describe *autrui*, the absolutely other human being. Although the term 'face' evokes a concrete image, Levinas clearly has something much less tangible in mind. He defines 'face' as 'the way in which the other presents himself, 'exceeding *the idea of the other in me*'.[49]

> The face of the Other at each moment destroys and overflows the plastic image it leaves me, the idea existing to my own measure and to the measure of its *ideatum* – the adequate idea. [...] It *expresses itself.*[50]

Unlike the alterity of objects, the otherness of *autrui* cannot be overcome through possession, comprehension, or any of the ego's other powers. It is important to emphasize that 'alterity' here should not be understood as difference. Levinas writes:

> *The alterity of the Other does not depend on any quality that would distinguish him from me*, for a distinction of this nature would precisely imply between us that community of genus which already nullifies alterity.[51]

What happens when the ego meets the absolutely other, the Stranger who cannot be grasped? How does the ego react to this other? Levinas says that there is an 'epiphany' in the face of the other.[52] Using the biblical idiom of commandment, Levinas writes that the 'primordial expression' of the face is '"you shall not commit murder."'[53] The self experiences the Other not as a threat, but as both vulnerable and commanding.

---

[47] Ibid., 116–17
[48] Ibid., 39
[49] Ibid., 50 (emphasis in the original)
[50] Ibid., 50–51 (emphasis in the original)
[51] Ibid., 194 (emphasis in original)
[52] Ibid., 197
[53] Ibid., 199

> The infinite paralyses power by its infinite resistance to murder, which, firm and insurmountable, gleams in the face of the Other, in the total nudity of his defenceless eyes [...] There is here a relation not with a very great resistance, but with something absolute other: the resistance of what has no resistance – ethical resistance.[54]

Levinas is not a naïve altruist – he knows all too well that murder is common. In the same paragraph in which he speaks of the ethical impossibility of murder, he acknowledges that 'the face threatens the eventuality of a struggle'. However, he says: 'War presupposes peace, the antecedent and non-allergic presence of the Other; it does not represent the first event of the encounter.'[55]

In addition to the ethical obligation of refraining from murder, the encounter with the face of the other leads the self to awareness of its responsibility to care for the other. The expression of the face conveys its 'destitution and hunger', and does so in such a way, Levinas says, that I am unable to be 'deaf to its appeal'.[56]

Through the encounter with the face of the other, the self comes to critique and question its own brutal spontaneity and appropriation of the natural world. It learns to judge itself, and in so doing becomes aware of its responsibility, which Levinas describes as 'infinite', not in the numerical sense, but in that it is a responsibility that increases in the measure that it is assumed. 'The better I accomplish my duty the fewer rights I have; the more I am just the more guilty I am.'[57]

Levinas also insists that this sense of the self as infinitely responsible is not generalizable. To be aware of one's own responsibility is not to perceive infinite responsibility as a general rule for everyone. On the contrary, Levinas insists that the relationship with the other is asymmetrical. 'The I is not a contingent formation by which the same and the other, as logical determinations of being, can in addition be reflected within a thought. [...] Alterity is possible only starting from me.'[58] He expresses a similar idea in a slightly more accessible way when he says that the other's responsibilities are 'his affair'.[59]

This brief exposition of Levinas's drama will suffice for beginning to consider how his account of the relation with the other compares

---

[54] Idem.
[55] Idem.
[56] Ibid., 200
[57] Ibid., 244
[58] Ibid., 40–41
[59] In *Ethics and Infinity: Conversations with Philippe Nemo*, tr. Richard A. Cohen, (Pittsburgh: Duquesne University Press, 1985), 98

with those of Buber and Rosenzweig. Levinas published a few essays on Buber and made some critical remarks in *Totality and Infinity* itself. He insisted that in the ethical relationship the other is not 'thou' but 'Vous';[60] he therefore questioned the reciprocity or mutuality that Buber emphasizes, repeating his own insistence that the ethical relationship is asymmetrical. He also charged Buber's philosophy with 'formalism', with failing to distinguish between the I-thou that puts us in relation with human beings and the I-thou that can relate a person to things.[61] Most significantly, in his discussion of the 'third party' in *Totality and Infinity*, Levinas informs us that:

> The third party looks at me in the eyes of the Other – language is justice. It is not that there first would be the face, and then the being it manifests or expresses would concern himself with justice; the epiphany of the face qua face opens humanity.[62]

In this context, Levinas emphasizes the difference between the ethical relation of the face-to-face and the 'self-sufficient "I-Thou"' in which the happy pair tend to forget about the rest of the world. In contrast to a cosy I-thou relationship, Levinas emphasizes that the face to face 'refuses the clandestinity of love, [where the relationship] loses its frankness and meaning and turns into laugher or cooing'.[63]

Apart from these specific differences that Levinas highlights, there is a more general difference between Levinas's face-to-face, on the one hand, and the accounts of both Buber and Rosenzweig on the other. In both of the earlier thinkers, the relationship with the other is ultimately grounded in the relationship with God or, in Buber's phrase, the 'Eternal Thou'. The difference between Rosenzweig and Levinas is particularly striking, given Levinas's acknowledgement of the importance of Rosenzweig's influence.[64] Unlike Rosenzweig's love of the neighbour, Levinas's ethical relation is neither founded on the prior revelation of divine love, nor inscribed within an over-arching narrative of redemption.

As I noted earlier, Rosenzweig's account of divine love is central to *The Star of Redemption*. Samuel Moyn argues that the experience of divine love is 'the core of [Rosenzweig's] thought, the major alternative he offered to the European traditions of philosophy and theology

---

[60] *Totality and Infinity*, 101
[61] Ibid., 69
[62] Ibid., 213
[63] Idem.
[64] Ibid., 28. (see above)

that he inherited, and the element of his "new thinking" that decisively distinguishes it from Heidegger's secular view.'[65] However, as we have seen, the self's experience of divine love does not form part of Levinas's account of ethics in *Totality and Infinity*. On Levinas's account, the self is indeed called upon to 'love' or, in his words, take responsibility for, the neighbour or the other, and to this extent, Levinas's account is similar to Rosenzweig's. However, despite the occasional use of religious language and even of the word 'God' in *Totality and Infinity*, Levinas's account of the ethical relation does not rely either on either the premise of God's existence or on any sort of existential account of an experience of relationship with God. It is possible to give a consistent secular reading of *Totality and Infinity* but the same cannot be said of either *The Star of Redemption* or *I and Thou*. Regarding the comparison with Rosenzweig, Moyn argues that 'Levinas radicalized, secularized, and moralized' Rosenzweig's thought.[66]

One might think that Levinas's intention of writing philosophy rather than theology would suffice as an explanation for why he doesn't borrow Rosenzweig's notion of divine love as the foundation for ethics. However, I think there is more to say. Firstly, Levinas does use the word 'God' and other theological language in *Totality and Infinity* – although, as I have argued elsewhere, most of what he says about God in this book forms part of his critique of 'positive religions'.[67] More significantly, if we look to Levinas's larger corpus of writings, we will see that this refusal of the language of 'divine love' is characteristic of his confessional writings and not just of his strictly philosophical work.

I would like to suggest that this significant difference between Levinas and Rosenzweig can be better understood by considering Levinas's corpus within the broader field of post-Holocaust Jewish thought. Emil Fackenheim, perhaps the most famous thinker in this field, has argued that Judaism, along with Christianity and western philosophy itself, is ruptured by the Holocaust.[68] Yet Fackenheim himself only came to this realization relatively late in his career. As Zachary Braiterman has pointed out, the leading

[65] Samuel Moyn, *Origins of the Other: Emmanuel Levinas between Revelation and Ethics* (Ithaca: Cornell University Press, 2006), 116

[66] Ibid., 116–17

[67] Tamra Wright, *The Twilight of Jewish Philosophy: Emmanuel Levinas's Ethical Hermeneutics* (London: Routledge, 1999), 76

[68] Emil L. Fackenheim, *To Mend the World: Foundations of Post-Holocaust Jewish Thought* (Blommington: Indiana University Press, 1994)

Jewish thinkers who were writing in the 1940s, 50s and early 60s – including Buber – did not seem to acknowledge the radical challenge posed by the Shoah. On the contrary, despite occasional references to the Holocaust, the work of Buber, as well as that of Kaplan, Heschel and Soloveitchik,[69] exhibited a surprising continuity with their pre-war writings. Braiterman also notes that, as a general rule, writers, artists, and film-makers tackle the subject well before the theologians and philosophers, and that when discursive post-Holocaust thought does emerge, from the late 1960s onwards, it is marked by a new emphasis on anti-theodic texts, motifs, and ideas, even in the case of Orthodox thinkers such as Eliezer Berkovits.

Where does Levinas's work fit within this schema? Although there are only a few texts where he explicitly engages with the significance of the Holocaust at any length, it is not difficult to make the case that the Shoah is central to his thought. Indeed, in his autobiographical essay 'Signature', Levinas writes that his intellectual biography has been 'dominated by the presentiment and the memory of the Nazi horror'.[70]

I have argued elsewhere that Levinas's 'confessional writings' show an evolution of his thought that fits well with Braiterman's observations.[71] Essays from the 1950s, such as 'Loving the Torah more than God', which is itself a commentary on a work of fiction, present contemporary Judaism not as 'ruptured' but as continuous with rabbinic Judaism; and while Levinas does not embrace theodicy, neither does he engage in much critique of it. Later writings, including the 1982 essay 'Useless Suffering' and the 1986 interview cited earlier, however, are strongly anti-theodic. Indeed, in 'Useless Suffering' Levinas completely rejects theodicy and its secular analogues as 'morally scandalous'. Like Fackenheim, at this stage he acknowledges not only that theology is ruptured, but that philosophy – at least moral philosophy – also faces a radical challenge. The question that he poses at the beginning of *Totality and Infinity* – 'are we not duped by morality?' – becomes more radical in the context of the

---

[69] Mordechai Kaplan, Abraham Joshua Heschel, and Joseph Soloveitchik were, respectively, the leading theologians in the Reconstructionist, Conservative and Orthodox denominations during this period.

[70] Emmanuel Levinas, *Difficult Freedom; Essays on Judaism*, (tr. S. Hand) (London: Athlone Press, 1990), 291

[71] Tamra Wright, 'Beyond the "Eclipse of God": The Shoah in the Jewish Thought of Buber and Levinas', in *Levinas and Buber: Dialogue and Difference*, edited by Peter Atterton, Matthew Calarco, and Maurice Friedman (Pittsburgh: Duquesne University Press, 2004), 203–25.

Holocaust: 'Is morality meaningful after the failure of morality?' And although he continues to affirm the meaningfulness of morality, through his account of the ethical relation with the other, Levinas tells us that we need new modalities of both religious faith and moral certainties.

Between the publication of *Totality and Infinity* and that of the essays I have just quoted, Levinas published his *magnum opus*, *Otherwise than Being or Beyond Essence*. In this 1974 work, the voice of the moral sceptic is much powerful and persistent than it is in *Totality and Infinity*, where it is largely confined to the preface. Given Braiterman's insights, it is also interesting to note that it was only in 1974 that Levinas dedicated a major work of philosophy to the memory of his parents, siblings, and in-laws who had been murdered by the Nazis. That is the dedication to *Otherwise than Being* which appears in Hebrew, at the bottom of the page. The French dedication at the top of the page reads:

'To the memory of those who were closest among the six million assassinated by the National Socialists, and of the millions on millions of all confessions and all nations, victims of the same hatred of the other man, the same anti-semitism.'[72]

In 1961, when he published *Totality and Infinity*, Levinas was enough of a post-Holocaust thinker to sense the urgency of the question about the meaningfulness of morality and to avoid any hint of a justifying theodicy or talk of 'divine love' – but not yet so radically post-Holocaust a thinker that he couldn't confidently present an affirmative answer to the question.

London School of Jewish Studies
twright@lsjs.ac.uk

---

[72]   Emmanuel Levinas, *Otherwise than Being or Beyond Essence*, (tr. Alphonso Lingis) (The Hague: Martinus Nijhoff, 1981).

Conversing in Emptiness: Rethinking Cross-Cultural Dialogue with the Kyoto School

BRET W. DAVIS

Abstract

As we attempt to engender a dialogue between different philosophical traditions, one of the first – if not indeed the first – of the topics which need to be addressed is that of the very nature of dialogue. In other words, we need to engage in a dialogue about dialogue. Toward that end, this essay attempts to rethink the nature of dialogue from the perspective of two key members of the Kyoto School, namely its founder, Nishida Kitarō (1870–1945), and its current central figure, Ueda Shizuteru (b. 1926). The Kyoto School is the most prominent group of modern Japanese philosophers, whose thought emerges from the encounter between Western and Eastern traditions. This essay seeks to elucidate and further unfold the implications of rethinking of the nature of dialogue from the perspective of Nishida's and Ueda's primarily Zen Buddhist reception of and response to Western philosophy.

1. The Place of Dialogue – A Japanese Perspective on Universality

In order to carry out a philosophical dialogue between cultures and traditions, we need to address the question of the very nature of dialogue. In other words, we need to engage in a dialogue about dialogue. It is inappropriate to delineate the conceptual parameters – the horizon of sense and significance – of this dialogue in advance, only then to invite others into this space to speak with us on our own terms. Rather, from the start we need to dialogically address questions regarding the 'place', so to speak, in which dialogue is or should be taking place.

It seems that we need a neutral 'place', an unbiased universal medium in which various particular cultures could meet, and converse, without one unilaterally playing the role of host while others are compelled to only ever play the role of guest, that is to say, without the purportedly universal meeting place being in fact merely the home ground of one of the particular interlocutors. Yet without immediate access to a transcultural medium, a standpointless standpoint, how are we to conceive of this universal meeting place?

doi:10.1017/S1358246114000058

Bret W. Davis

How could it be defined, delineated, or circumscribed? We have no view from nowhere. Indeed, were we to have one, it could show us nothing, insofar as forms of being can only be perceived from a determinate and determining perspective. Hence, it would seem that 'universality' can only be endlessly approached by way of taking into account as many perspectives or viewpoints as possible. As Nietzsche suggests, given the perspectival nature of perception and knowledge, 'the *more* eyes, different eyes, we can use to observe one thing, the more complete will our "concept" of this thing, our "objectivity", be'.[1] This epistemological principle applies not only to particular things, but also to universal matters, matters such as the question of, and quest for, an unbiased medium or neutral 'place' in which a genuine dialogue between cultures could take place. Every culture, we can presume, has its particular account of what it considers to be universal. And we can presume that every culture potentially involved in cross-cultural dialogue can contribute to the dialogue a vision of the nature of such dialogue.

What vision of cross-cultural dialogue, and of the universality that makes it possible, might be contributed from Japan? In this essay I reflect on the nature of dialogue from the perspective of thinkers associated with the Kyoto School. The Kyoto School is the most prominent group of modern Japanese philosophers, whose philosophies themselves are enactments of dialogue between Western philosophy and East Asian traditions such as Zen Buddhism.[2] I focus here on two key members of the School: its founder, Nishida Kitarō (1870–1945), and the leading representative of its third generation, Ueda Shizuteru (b. 1926).[3] I attempt to show not only how these Japanese philosophers invite us to enter into dialogue with East Asian thought and with their own cross-cultural thinking, but also how they invite us to reconsider the very nature of both interpersonal and intercultural dialogue as such.

Let us begin with some questions. What is dialogue? Who are the individuals who speak and who listen, and how are they related both to the cultural-linguistic spheres of the traditions in which they find

---

[1] *Basic Writings of Nietzsche*, edited and translated by Walter Kaufmann (New York: Random House, 1966), 555

[2] For an introduction to the Kyoto School, see my 'The Kyoto School', in *The Stanford Encyclopedia of Philosophy*, http://plato.stanford.edu/archives/sum2010/entries/kyoto-school/

[3] Japanese names are given in the Japanese order of surname followed by given name. Unless otherwise noted, all translations in this essay are my own.

themselves and to the wider field of intercultural, interlinguistic, and intertraditional encounter? Insofar as dialogue as *dia-legein* is a 'speaking across', how should we understand the space that is traversed here? The Japanese term for 'dialogue' is *taiwa*, which literally implies a 'linguistic encounter' between two or more persons. In line with Nishida's 'logic of place', according to which two terms are always related on the basis of a third term, namely the place in which their relation takes place, we could ask: What is the place in which this linguistic encounter takes place? It would seem that the space between self and other that is bridged in dialogue must paradoxically be one that both separates and connects, a space that allows for both irreducible singularity and shared community. But how are we to understand this iteration of the age-old question – deeply pondered in the East as well as in the West – of the One and the Many? What is the relation between the one world and the many individuals who inhabit it, or between the universally shared world and the diversity of specific cultural worlds in which, or between which, we live? With these questions we discover that an inquiry into the nature of dialogue is hardly a peripheral matter for philosophers, for it quickly leads us, not only back to basic questions of philosophical anthropology, philosophy of language, and ethics, but also back to the most fundamental questions of ontology or, as it may turn out, 'meontology' or 'kenology' – a logos of 'absolute nothingness' or 'emptiness'.[4]

In order to see how Nishida and Ueda rethink the nature of dialogue, we need to look at how they understand the relation between self and other. We also need to look at how they regard the relation between individual selves and specific communities, which ultimately must be understood in terms of a threefold relation between the individual,

---

[4]   It is crucial to bear in mind that what Kyoto School philosophers such as Nishida and Ueda call 'absolute nothingness' (*zettai mu*) is not a mere privation of being or a nihilistic void (which they consider to be forms of 'relative nothingness'); it is rather the self-determining 'place' that encompasses all distinctions, even that between being and relative nothingness. Whereas the Western tradition has tended to understand the ultimate universal or the absolute in terms of 'being', Eastern traditions such as Daoism and East Asian Mahayana Buddhism have tended to understand it in terms of 'nothingness' or 'emptiness'. Rather than thinking of finite beings as privations of absolute being or as independent substances, these traditions have understood finite beings in terms of the self-emptying or self-delimitation of emptiness into form and in terms of interconnected processes. See my 'Forms of Emptiness in Zen', in *A Companion to Buddhist Philosophy*, edited by Steven Emmanuel (West Sussex: Wiley-Blackwell, 2013).

the communal 'species',[5] and the universal 'place' which encompasses both individual and species. They refer to the all-encompassing universal with such locutions as 'the place of absolute nothingness' (*zettai mu no basho*) and the 'empty expanse' (*kokū*). By way of reflecting on the relations between these three terms – individuals, communal species, and the all-encompassing universal place – they develop provocative and possibly compelling new ways of understanding the nature of interpersonal and intercultural dialogue.

Let me state at the outset that in this essay I attempt to elucidate and develop what I find most valuable and still viable in the thought of the Kyoto School. There has been much controversy surrounding the wartime political writings of its first two generations.[6] Regrettably, the debate has too often digressed into excessively polemical attacks and overly defensive responses. In other essays I have tried to steer a middle course that neither whitewashes nor vilifies the political thought of the Kyoto School during the war, often by way of engaging in an 'immanent critique' that turns the light of their own insights back on their blind spots and missteps.[7] The matter is

[5] It was Nishida's junior colleague, Tanabe Hajime (1885–1962), who introduced the term 'species' (*shu*) to refer to ethnic communities as a third term in dialectical relation with individual humans and universal humanity. Although I do not discuss Tanabe in this essay, it should be noted that Nishida developed his understanding of 'species' in response to Tanabe. See Sugimoto Kōichi, 'Tanabe Hajime's Logic of Species and the Philosophy of Nishida Kitarō: A Critical Dialogue within the Kyoto School', in *Japanese and Continental Philosophy: Conversations with the Kyoto School*, edited by Bret W. Davis, Brian Schroeder, and Jason M. Wirth (Bloomington: Indiana University Press, 2010).

[6] For an orientation to the controversy surrounding Nishida and other Kyoto School philosophers' political writings, see section 4 of my article, 'The Kyoto School', op. cit., note 2

[7] See my 'Nishida's Multicultural Worldview: Its Contemporary Significance and Immanent Critique', *Nishida Tetsugakkai Nenpō* [The Journal of the Society for Nishida Philosophy] 10 (2013), 183–203; and my 'Toward a World of Worlds: Nishida, the Kyoto School, and the Place of Cross-Cultural Dialogue', in *Frontiers of Japanese Philosophy*, edited by James W. Heisig (Nagoya: Nanzan Institute for Religion and Culture, 2006). A revised and expanded version of the sections on Nishida in the latter article have been published in Spanish translation as 'El Uno y los múltiples mundos: acerca de la visión alternativa de la globalización en Nishida', in *Alternativas filosóficas: Investigaciones recientes sobre la filosofía de Nishida Kitaro, fundador de la Escuela de Kioto*, edited by Augustín Jacinto Zavala (Morelia, Michoacan, Mexico: Morevallado Editores, 2012). See also my 'Turns to and from Political Philosophy:

complicated by the fact that they were often endeavoring – even if in the end unsuccessfully – to *reform from within* the ultranationalism sweeping over Japan at the time by way engaging in what Ōhashi Ryōsuke calls 'cooperative resistance' or 'oppositional cooperation' (*hantaisei-teki kyōryoku*)[8] and what Ueda calls a 'semantic struggle' (*imi no sōdatsusen*), that is to say, a tug of war over the meaning of the catchwords and phrases being bandied about by far a less judicious and scrupulous ideologues of the regime.[9] To be sure, even once we take this into account, there remain some troubling aspects of the erstwhile political thought of the Kyoto School philosophers. Be that as it may, my concern in the present essay is not with discarding this political bathwater but rather with nurturing the philosophical baby. I attempt here to bring out their cross-cultural best, rather than to catch them at their political worst.[10]

2. Nishida's Dialectical World as Mutual Determination of Individuals and Cultural Species

Nishida saw the 18th century as an age of abstract individualism, the 19th century as an age of nationalism and imperialism, and the 20th

The Case of Nishitani Keiji', in *Re-politicising the Kyoto School as Philosophy*, edited by Chris Goto-Jones (London: Routledge, 2008).

[8]   Ōhashi Ryōsuke, *Kyōtogakuha to Nihon-kaigun* [The Kyoto School and the Japanese Navy] (Kyoto: PHP Shinsho, 2001), 20ff

[9]   Ueda Shizuteru, 'Nishida, Nationalism, and the War in Question', in *Rude Awakenings: Zen, The Kyoto School, and the Question of Nationalism*, edited by James W. Heisig and John C. Maraldo (Honolulu: University of Hawaii Press, 1994), 90–95

[10]   This applies in particular to the following two sections of this essay, in which I attempt to draw out the cosmopolitan implications of Nishida's thought. In a recent article in Japanese, I argue that these cosmopolitan implications are truer to the religious core of his thinking than are his political thoughts on nationalism and the purportedly national moorings of morality. See my 'Nishida to ibunkakan-taiwa: kongen-teki sekaishimin-shugi no kanōsei' [Nishida and Intercultural Dialogue: The Possibility of a Radical Cosmopolitanism], in Fujita Masakatsu (ed.), *Shisōkan no taiwa: Higashi-ajia ni okeru tetsugaku no juyō to tenkai* [Dialogue between Ways of Thinking: The Reception and Development of Philosophy in East Asia], forthcoming. Since Ueda began his academic career after the war, he did not himself become embroiled in wartime politics. For Ueda's major statement on this issue, see his 'Nishida, Nationalism, and the War in Question', op. cit., note 9.

century as the first truly world-historical age of global awareness.[11] The dawning global era that Nishida envisioned would still involve healthy competition, but no longer imperialistic aggression between nations. It would be an age of self-determination through dialogical exchange. Below I argue that, in an important sense, what Nishida calls 'true individuals' (*shin no ko, shin no kobutsu*) are the ultimate agents of intercultural dialogue.

However, we must first take into account Nishida's critique of 'abstract individualism' and 'cosmopolitanism', and his insistence that concretely existing individuals can never be simply abstracted from their native cultural and ethnic species. Indeed, at times he suggests that ethnic nations are themselves agents of historical development engaged in intercultural competition, and that the current age of global awareness should be understood as one of utmost nationalism rather than cosmopolitanism.[12] Yet, more precisely and more compellingly, Nishida argues that it is neither the individual nor the species on its own that is the locus and engine of historical development; it is rather 'the dialectical universal', which means for him nothing other than the dialectical interaction between species and individuals. 'What decides the course of history is neither the individual nor the species but rather that which creatively forms itself. The historical age determines itself'.[13]

According to Nishida, 'the world determines itself in a unique manner [*kosei-teki ni*]' both as individuals and as cultural or ethnic species. When the world becomes creative, 'we ourselves become creative elements of the creative world'; and at the same time, our species 'comes alive as a self-determining particular'. The individual's self-determination is thus not merely a negation of, or separation from, the species; 'that the individual becomes creative as an individual does not entail that he or she becomes an isolated individual, but rather that he or she fulfills the destiny of the species as a particular

---

[11]   *Nishida Kitarō zenshū* (Tokyo: Iwanami, 1987–89), 10:337; see also ibid., 12:426

[12]   Ibid., 8:500, 514, 519–20. As John Maraldo has pointed out, one serious problem with Nishida's social and political philosophy is that he tended to understand nations monoculturally and monoethnically, and thus failed to see the possibility, and the actuality, of multicultural and multiethnic nations ('The Problem of World Culture: Towards an Appropriation of Nishida's Philosophy of Culture', *The Eastern Buddhist* 28/2, 194). In fact, cross-cultural interaction frequently takes place *within* a nation as well as between nations.

[13]   *Nishida Kitarō zenshū*, op. cit., note 11, 8:452

of the universal'.[14] We are born and act as unique individuals within the unique specificity of this or that national culture and ethnicity, not in an abstract global space. Were an individual to simply 'depart from the species and become an abstract individual', it would not gain but rather 'lose its self'.[15] Thus, Nishida claims, 'we become true individuals not as cosmopolitans but rather as members of nations'.[16] The abstract individualism of the 18th century, according to Nishida, fails to account for the extent to which individuals are first of all determined by their specific nations and cultures. He would presumably agree with recent communitarians who argue that the liberal or libertarian idea of the 'atomistic' and culturally 'unencumbered' individual is itself, ironically, the product of a specific, historically developed cultural community.[17]

Nevertheless, Nishida also repeatedly stresses that the true individual is not merely a product or representative of a cultural species or nation, since he or she also 'at times ruptures the species'.[18] 'Although we are born from a species, it must also be the case that we ourselves go on to form the species'.[19] While initially being determined by the specific ethnicity or national culture in which they are born and raised, true individuals can also turn around and 'counter-determine' (*gyaku-gentei suru*) these. Individuals are thus not merely products of, but also agents in the historical development of cultural species. As participants in the dialectical movement 'from what is made to what makes' (*tsukurareta mono kara tsukuru mono e*), individuals are both determined by and in turn counter-determine the cultures in which they live.[20] Whereas in biological life the species determines the individual in a mostly unilateral manner, 'in historical life, it is possible for the individual to diverge from the species; in other words, there is individual freedom'.[21] 'In short', Nishida argues, 'history is something that humans create and that in turn creates humans', or, put the other way around, history is something

---

[14]   *Nishida Kitarō zenshū*, op. cit., note 11, 8:452–53
[15]   Ibid., 8:453
[16]   Ibid., 10:164; see also ibid., 10:327 and 8:519.
[17]   See Charles Taylor, 'Atomism', in *Communitarianism and Individualism*, edited by Shlomo Avineri and Avner de-Shalit (Oxford and New York: Oxford University Press, 1992).
[18]   *Nishida Kitarō zenshū*, op. cit., note 11, 8:450
[19]   Ibid.
[20]   See *Nishida Kitarō zenshū*, op. cit., note 11, 7:305ff.; also ibid., 8:313–14
[21]   *Nishida Kitarō zenshū*, op. cit., note 11, 14:395

Bret W. Davis

that creates humans and that humans in turn create.[22] For instance, Shakespeare was shaped by the English world in which he was raised, just as Dōgen was shaped by the Japanese world of his origin; yet both – in part by way of learning foreign languages and customs – in turn also creatively contributed to the development of their respective languages and cultures.

To sum up these points: according to Nishida, 'while the individual is born and thoroughly determined by the species, it also determines the species'; 'life is found where there is both the fixed form of a species and the possibility of breaking through this form'.[23] 'Species is form, paradigm. Yet while individuals are born from a species, they also go on to form that species'.[24] On the one hand, an individual cannot create *ex nihilo*; he or she must begin with the forms or paradigms into which he or she is – to borrow an expression from Heidegger – 'thrown' (*geworfen*). On the other hand, a species, such as a national or ethnic culture, is only a 'living species' insofar as it grants the individuals it determines the freedom to in turn counter-determine it. Specific social, linguistic, and cultural paradigms initially shape individuals' lives; but these paradigms are themselves kept alive and more or less continually recreated by individuals.

3. Radical Cosmopolitanism: True Individuals as Agents of Cross-Cultural Dialogue

In a dialogue with Miki Kiyoshi in 1936, Nishida proposed the development of a 'new humanism' that would move beyond the one-sidedness of both atomistic individualism and communal holism by seeing the free individual as a 'creative element of the creative world'.[25] Analogously, and also on the basis of implications of some of Nishida's core ideas, I suggest that we can speak of a 'new cosmopolitanism' that moves beyond both the excessively libertarian idea of a culturally 'unencumbered' individual and the excessively communitarian idea of an individual totally determined by his or her native culture. Nishida and the communitarians are right to reject an atomistic individualism that does not recognize the extent

[22] *Nishida Kitarō zenshū*, op. cit., note 11, 14:394
[23] Ibid., 8:451
[24] Ibid., 8:455
[25] *Miki Kiyoshi zenshū* [Complete Works of Miki Kiyoshi] (Tokyo: Iwanami, 1986), **17**: 492–504

to which individuals become who they are in the context of their native cultures. Yet, insofar as true individuals are never exhaustively defined by their native roots, never entirely restricted to their heretofore cultural determinations, they are not just members of this or that group, not just citizens of this or that nation, but also, and in a still deeper sense, 'citizens of the world'. This new, radical understanding of cosmopolitanism would not see such individuals as rootless atoms floating around in an abstract global space (and racking up frequent flyer miles along the way!), but rather as 'creative elements of the creative world' who, in becoming self-aware of their heretofore determination by their native roots, become able to critically evaluate and thereby enrich these roots by way of branching out into dialogical interaction with individuals stemming from other nations and cultures.

Now, I think that an argument can be made on the basis of Nishida's thought that 'true individuals' – as 'creative elements of the creative world',[26] 'focal points of the creative world',[27] 'self-projections of the absolute',[28] and 'self-determinations of absolute nothingness'[29] – are the pivotal agents of cross-cultural dialogue. In order to understand why this is the case, we need to bring back into the discussion 'the place of absolute nothingness' as the ultimate 'universal' in which the mutual determination of species and individuals takes place. Insofar as the individual touches in his or her depths the wellspring of absolute nothingness, as the inherently indeterminate source of self-determination, he or she can exceed his or her determination by the species. This not only means that he or she can rupture and creatively reform the species, but also that he or she can empathize and engage in transformative dialogue with individuals rooted in other species.

In 'I and Thou' (*Watakushi to nanji*, 1932) and subsequent works, Nishida developed his idea of the place of absolute nothingness in dialectical and dialogical terms to account for the co-existence and mutual interaction of 'true individuals'. 'Between true individuals', Nishida writes, 'there cannot be a so-called universal which includes them'.[30] Why would he deny that self and other could be

---

[26] *Nishida Kitarō zenshū*, op. cit., note 11, 8:314, 339; also ibid., 10:307.
[27] Ibid., 10:289.
[28] Ibid., 10:407.
[29] Ibid., 10:321.
[30] Ibid., 7:312; see also ibid., 6:381. On Nishida's conception of the I-Thou relation, see the following essays of mine: 'Das Innerste zuäußerst: Nishida und die Revolution der Ich-Du-Beziehung', trans.

encompassed by the same universal? Because, if self and other were related merely as different particularizations of the same universal, this essential sameness would undermine their individuality and mutual alterity, reducing, in Levinas's language, the Other (*l'Autre*) to the Same (*le Même*). Nishida does in fact initially say that we must try to think the sense in which 'I and Thou are determined by the same universal'.[31] The equivocation is cleared up, however, insofar as he makes a crucial distinction between 'universals of being' (*u no ippansha*) and the 'universal of nothingness' (*mu no ippansha*).[32] Universals of being have specific content, and we can understand what he subsequently (under the influence of Tanabe Hajime) calls a cultural or social 'species' as a kind of universal of being. The universal of nothingness is the inherently indeterminate place of absolute nothingness, which Nishida comes to think of not only as the creative source of self-determination but also as the 'dialectical universal' that enables the interaction between individual and species, as well as between one individual and another.

Nishida writes: 'Even while my concept of a dialectical universal is a universal, it does not oppose individual determination or negate the individual. It signifies rather the medium of the mutual determination of individuals'.[33] Two individuals truly meet when they interact, not merely as particular manifestations of this or that cultural species or 'universal of being', but rather as two 'focal points' of the self-determination of the ultimate place (or universal) of absolute nothingness,[34] that is, as two uniquely 'creative elements of the creative world'.[35] Such individuals are not only determined by, but are also – insofar as they directly 'touch the creative' source of

---

Ruben Pfizenmaier, Eberhard Ortland and Rolf Elberfeld, *Allgemeine Zeitschrift für Philosophie* **36**(3) (2011), 281–312; 'Nijū naru 'zettai no ta e no naizai-teki chōetsu': Nishida no shūkyō tetsugaku ni okeru tasha-ron' [Twofold 'Immanent Transcendence to the Absolute Other': Alterity in Nishida's Philosophy of Religion], *Nihontetsugakushi Kenkyū* 9 (2012), 102–34; and 'Ethical and Religious Alterity: Nishida after Levinas', in *Nishida Kitarō in der Philosophie des 20. Jahrhunderts*, edited by Rolf Elberfeld and Yōko Arisaka (Freiburg/Munich: Alber Verlag, 2014).

[31] *Nishida Kitarō zenshū*, op. cit., note 11, 6:372.

[32] Ibid., 6:386.

[33] Ibid., 7:315.

[34] See *Nishida Kitarō zenshū*, op. cit., note 11, 7:425; also ibid., 10:437, 441, and 11:378.

[35] *Nishida Kitarō zenshū*, op. cit., note 11, 8:314, 339; also ibid., 10:307.

absolute nothingness[36] – able to 'counter-determine' their specific cultural universals (i.e. 'species').

This is a decisive point, because the capacity to counter-determine one's culture is what testifies, not only to the freedom of self-determination, but also to the possibility of cross-cultural dialogue. If individuals were *exhaustively* determined by their respective cultural universals (i.e. 'species'), genuine cross-cultural dialogue would be impossible. If such were the case, even if it were still somehow possible for cultural expressions to be translated and interpretively reflected in the idiom of another culture, these cultures would remain unaffected by this interpretive reflection, and individuals would always only ever see artifacts of other cultures through their own cultural lenses. Granted that this is what largely happens, for example through the media of dubbed television shows and guided travel tours, yet surely it is also the case that cultures are sometimes genuinely transformed though contact with other cultures, and surely individuals are sometimes able translate other idioms into their own by way of letting themselves be translated into those other idioms. Nishida makes room for such possibilities of radical cross-cultural dialogue and exchange with his idea of an unfathomable, all-encompassing universal or place of absolute nothingness, a place which engenders, through self-determination qua dialectical interaction between individuals and species, the myriad cultures of the historical world. Communication can happen between individuals from different cultures insofar as these individuals are not exhaustively determined by their respective cultures – that is to say, insofar as, in their depths, they transcend their cultures and directly touch the creatively self-determining place of absolute nothingness.[37]

Genuine cross-cultural dialogue happens between such 'true individuals' who are capable, not just of serving as cultural ambassadors or representatives, but also of stepping beyond the horizons of their native cultures and of expanding these horizons by bringing them into contact with other horizons. Because the true individual can experience him- or herself as a focal point of the self-determination of the place of absolute nothingness, that is, as a singular instance or expression of the all-encompassing 'universal of nothingness', rather than merely as a particularization of the 'universal of being' of a specific culture, he or she can enter into dialogue with individuals from other cultures. The place of absolute nothingness is thus the dialectically self-determining medium in which

---

[36] *Nishida Kitarō zenshū*, op. cit., note 11, 7:262–63
[37] See *Nishida Kitarō zenshū*, op. cit., note 11, 6:398

cross-cultural interaction and dialogue takes place between singular individuals and, thereby, between communities and nations.

Singular individuals are never, to be sure, free-floating atoms wholly unencumbered by the cultural contexts in which they find themselves; but neither are they ever wholly determined by these contexts. The ultimate place in which individuals abide is the essentially indeterminate place of absolute nothingness, a fecund wellspring of possibilities of self-determination and a nonreductive medium of dialectical interaction; and it is because individuals share this nothingness in common with other individuals who are, for their part, rooted in but never exhaustively determined by their own cultural contexts, that cross-cultural understanding and dialogue are possible. Such dialogue not only enables individuals to enrich and transform their own personal cultural conditioning, it also enables them to counter-determine their respective cultures in ways that enrich and potentially even transform them.

This is the new, dialogically cross-cultural cosmopolitanism that can be developed on the basis of some core elements of Nishida's thought. This new cosmopolitanism would be 'radical' *both* in the sense that it would maintain a recognition of the proximate rootedness of individuals in specific cultures, *and* in the sense that it would entail an awareness that the deepest roots of individuals extend down beneath the topsoil that sustains their specific cultures, down into the unfathomable depths of the earth that tacitly nourish and bond together the entire ecosystem of humanity.

4. Between I and Thou, the Bow: Ueda on Interpersonal Dialogue

Among Kyoto School philosophers, it is Ueda Shizuteru who most clearly and explicitly articulates a Zen Buddhist understanding of the dialogical relation between persons and, by extension, between cultures. And so, in the second half of this essay I turn mainly to his writings on the topic of dialogue.[38]

---

[38] Unfortunately most of Ueda's work has not yet been translated. He has, however, written many articles in German, some of which have been recently republished in Shizuteru Ueda, *Wer und was bin ich: Zur Phänomenologie des Selbst im Zen-Buddhismus* (Freiburg: Verlag Karl Alber, 2011). English translations of about half of the essays included in that volume can be found in the following issues of *The Eastern Buddhist*: **15**(1) (Spring 1982), **22**(1) (Spring 1989), **25**(2) (Autumn 1992), and **16**(1)

Ueda uses the Japanese greeting of the bow (*ojigi*) as a concrete example to illustrate how mutual self-negation – the emptying of ego-centric presumptions and agendas – returns us to the abyssal ground of an originary nothingness that we share in common beneath the culturally determined roots of our personal being. In a passage on bowing from his essay called 'I and Thou' (*Watakushi to nanji*, 2000), Ueda writes:

> In the encounter with one another, rather than directly becoming 'I and Thou' as in the case of a handshake, each person first lowers his or her head and bows. This does not stop at being a mere exchange of formalities. In the depths of 'the between', each person reduces himself or herself to nothing. Going from the bottom of 'the between' into the bottomless depths that envelop self and other, each returns to a profound nothingness. Both persons, by means of bending their egos and lowering their heads..., return for a moment to a place where there is neither self nor other, neither I nor Thou. Then, by raising themselves up, they once again face one another and for the first time become 'I and Thou'. Having each cut off the root of their unilateral egoism, they become an 'I and Thou' wherein each is opened to their mutuality.[39]

Nishida's student and Ueda's teacher, Nishitani Keiji (1900–1990), explains what Ueda calls here 'unilateral egoism' (*'ga' kara no ippōsei*, literally 'from the ego unilaterality') in terms of the 'infinite drive of karma', that is to say, the egoistic will to power that propels and perpetuates the stream of unenlightened existence.[40] Insofar as 'one ceaselessly strives to expand one's volitional power, one's power of control', one remains self-enclosed. 'The manner of being defined by an egoistic will can never go beyond its own self-extension or the expansion of its own power, and thus can never

---

(Spring 1983). In consultation with Professor Ueda, I am presently working on an English anthology of his work.

[39] Ueda Shizuteru, *Watakushi to wa nani ka* [What Am I?] (Tokyo: Iwanami, 2000), 116

[40] See *Nishitani Keiji chosakushū* [Collected Works of Nishitani Keiji] (Tokyo: Sōbunsha, 1986–95), 10:259; *Religion and Nothingness*, translated by Jan Van Bragt (Berkeley: University of California Press, 1982), 236. See also my 'Nishitani after Nietzsche: From the Death of God to the Great Death of the Will', in *Japanese and Continental Philosophy*, op. cit., note 5.

really encounter the other'.[41] Only by way of emptying the self, giving the self to others and upholding their being, can we realize a true interconnectedness with them and thereby attain our own self-standing by being upheld in turn by them. The true self is not the self-enclosed ego driven by its will to self-expansion and power over others, but rather the self that is open to its interconnection with others. This true self is realized by way of a self-emptying of its egocentric will, and this non-egocentric way of being is implied in the central Buddhist teaching of *anatman* (in Japanese, *muga*), a term that is translated in various contexts as no-self, no-soul, non-ego, or egolessness.[42] In Zen, it is no contradiction to say that the true self is no-self, insofar as this is understood to mean that the true being of the self is a non-egocentric and dynamic mode of existence (or ek-sistence) that cannot be reified as an independent substance.

Ueda understands the Buddhist teaching of *anatman* as a radical negation of egocentric manners of being a self as well as reifying interpretations of the being of the self. Yet, for Ueda, the teaching of *anatman* best serves as an antidote to our tendency toward egoistic self-assertion and self-reification, since, taken on its own, the doctrine can lead to the opposite problem of a mere absence or dissolution of our sense of self. The experience of *anatman* should be understood rather as the second moment in the dialectical movement of the true self, that is, of the self who affirms itself only by way of negating itself. The self-identity of such a self can be expressed as 'I, in not being I, am I'.[43] In other words, Ueda understands the Buddhist teaching of *anatman* as calling attention to the crucial moment of 'in not being I' that breaks open the karmically driven closed circuit of the 'I am I' and enables the self to be itself by way of not being itself.

The true self, for Ueda, is realized as the dynamic entirety of this circling movement through self-negation and self-reaffirmation: I, in not being I, am I. Problems with the self arise when this process is short-circuited: *either* by leaving out the moment of self-negation and misunderstanding oneself as a self-sufficient *cogito* that can monologically say to itself 'I am I', *or* by getting stuck in the moment of self-negation, for example by misunderstanding the doctrine of *anatman* to be a total denial of the existence of the self (in this regard we should bear in mind that the Buddha clearly rejected

---

41   *Nishitani Keiji chosakushū*, op. cit., note 40, 17:9–10
42   Ibid., 17:14–15
43   Ueda, *Watakushi to wa nani ka*, op. cit., note 39, 153–154

nihilistic and annihilationistic views of the self and misinterpretations of the *anatman* doctrine). These two pitfalls, of either attachment to, or loss of, self, are related to two heteronomies: in the former one is ruled by internal 'karmic' impulses, and in the latter one is ruled by external forces. The true dynamic of the self, by contrast, entails two kinds of freedom: freedom-*from*-the-self and freedom-*for*-the-self, both of which are realized in and through genuinely dialogical encounters with others. Of these two types of freedom as they are manifested in dialogue, Ueda writes the following:

> Freedom-*for*-the-self entails assuming the role of host and speaking; freedom-*from*-the-self entails deferring the role of host to the other and listening. The true self is a matter of the complementary joining together of freedom-from-the-self and freedom-for-the-self. When that complementary conjunction is undone, freedom-for-the-self mutates into attachment to the self, and freedom-from-the-self mutates into loss of the self. The true self – as the complementary conjunction of freedom-for-the-self and freedom-from-the-self – is found precisely in the dialogue between I and Thou.[44]

Using Huayan Buddhist and Zen master Linji's (d. 866) language of 'host' and 'guest', Ueda remarks: 'The free exchange of the role of host is the very core of dialogue'.[45] In other words, for a genuine dialogue to take place, one must be able to both listen as 'guest' and speak as 'host'. In the proper time and place, the 'host' takes center stage and commands the attention of the audience; but he or she must not fixate on this role so as to monopolize a discussion and turn what should be a dialogue into a monologue. The audience or 'guest', for its part, must be able to silently and attentively listen, yet without abandoning the response-abililty to speak up and assume, in the proper time and place, the role of host. Sometimes it is proper to speak (for example when one is giving a lecture), sometimes to listen (for example when one is attending a lecture), and sometimes to alternate between speaking and listening (for example when one is participating in a discussion after a lecture). The ability to freely and responsibly alternate between these roles of host and guest depends on one's letting go of attachments to both oneself and others, to both activity and passivity, to both sovereignty and servility.

---

[44] *Ueda Shizuteru shū* [Ueda Shizuteru Collection] (Tokyo: Iwanami, 2001–3), 10:281–282
[45] *Ueda Shizuteru shū*, op. cit., note 44, 10:281

Bret W. Davis

5. Conversing through Silence: Ueda on Being Together in a Twofold World

Let us return now to the question of cross-cultural dialogue, which in many ways is a most radical form of encounter between self and other. What would it mean to develop a philosophy of cross-cultural dialogue on the basis of Ueda's account of interpersonal dialogue? Can we bridge the abyss between Eastern and Western forms of cultural being only by first mutually bowing into the ocean of absolute nothingness that lies between us? Can we learn to play in turn both roles of host and guest with others and their other cultures?

Let us recall the importance of 'place' in the encounter between self and other. Dialogue always takes place in some 'place'. That place is typically a horizonal world determined by the specifics of culture, language, and tradition.[46] The question, then, is how a dialogue could take place between such cultural-linguistic worlds, between, in Heidegger's terms, different linguistic 'houses of being'.[47] In what place could a dialogue between such places take place? In other words, what is the *topos* or *chora* that would be crossed in a *diatopical* conversation between different cultural-linguistic *topoi*?[48] What is the 'world of worlds', the 'region of regions', or the limitless 'open-region' that surrounds every one of our horizons of intelligibility? Borrowing a Buddhist term that metaphorically refers to an 'empty space' that envelops all things without getting in their way, Ueda calls this the 'empty expanse' (*kokū*).[49] He suggests that it can

---

[46]   *Ueda Shizuteru shū*, op. cit., note 44, 10:282

[47]   See Martin Heidegger, 'From a Dialogue on Language between a Japanese and an Inquirer', in *On the Way to Language*, translated by Peter Hertz (San Francisco: Harper & Row, 1971); also my 'Heidegger's Orientations: The Step Back on the Way to Dialogue with the East', in *Heidegger-Jahrbuch 7: Heidegger und das ostasiatische Denken*, edited by Alfred Denker et al. (Freiburg and Munich: Alber Verlag, 2013).

[48]   On the challenges of 'diatopical' versus 'diachronic' hermeneutics, see Raimundo Panikkar, 'What is Comparative Philosophy Comparing?' in *Interpreting Across Boundaries*, edited by Gerald James Larson and Eliot Deutsch (Princeton: Princeton University Press, 1988).

[49]   More literally signifying 'hollow void' or 'vacant sky', this term was used to translate the Sanskrit *ākāśa*. 'The symbols in the early *Prajñāpāramitā* texts show that the Mahāyāna notion of *ākāśa* [i.e., 'space' understood as 'a luminous ether, filled with light'] derives from meditation (*dhyāna*) on the sky, which is experienced as vast, luminous and without boundaries' (Nancy McCagney, *Nāgārjuna and the Philosophy of Openness* [Lanham: Roman & Littlefield,1997], xx). In

only be experienced through silence at the edges of language. The passing experience of the empty expanse, like the turn of the breath, is an experience of both the limits and the provenance of linguistic horizons. Ueda speaks of this experience in terms of a bidirectional movement of 'exiting language and then exiting into language' (*kotoba kara dete, kotoba e deru*).

Ueda develops his philosophy of what he calls 'being-in-the-twofold-world' or a 'two-layered being-the-world' (*nijūsekainaisonzai*) in relation to this irreducibly twofold yet ultimately inseparable experience of 'exiting language and then exiting into language'. Since it will take us to the heart of the question of cross-cultural dialogue, let me quote at length here a key passage from his essay, 'Language in a Twofold World'.

What I am calling 'exiting language and then exiting into language' is not a smooth and automatic movement. It is rather a movement consisting of a twofold breaking through: language is torn through into silence and silence is torn through into language. It is precisely this movement that is primordial experience, which altogether I understand as a living wellspring of the death and resuscitation of experience. ... In order to understand this movement, it is necessary to see that our being-in-the-world is in fact a two-layered being-in-the-world. In short, the world as a comprehensive space of meaning is in turn located within the world of a *limitless openness*, a *hollow*-space of *no*-meaning that is without limits. Insofar as we are in the world, we are located within this limitless openness. Yet, since the world of language is layered upon this world of limitless openness, often, indeed usually, we unwittingly remain bound by the delimiting power of language and the framework of relations of meaning. Hence, the world of language alone is taken to be the world of our being-in-the-world, and the limitless openness which transcends and envelops this world remains closed off to us. ... [Where the] visible and linguistically defined world is taken to be the one and only world, the

---

many Mahāyāna texts, including those of Zen, empty space or the open expanse of a clear sky symbolizes the ultimate Dharma realm of non-obstruction which makes room for all, letting everything within it coexist in harmonious interaction (see *Zen no shisō jiten* [Dictionary of Zen Thought], edited by Tagami Taishū and Ishii Shūdō [Tokyo: Tōkyō Shoseki, 2008], 199; also *Zengaku daijiten* [Large Dictionary of Zen Studies], new edition [Tokyo: Daishūkan Shoten 1985], 332).

human subject that inhabits this world – either individually or collectively, and in various manners and levels – attempts to appropriate it as 'my world'; and this is what gives rise to confrontations, conflicts, struggles, and distortions within this closed off world. This kind of being-in-the-world must be broken open by the true countenance of the world, so that the reality of human existence can be realized. ... If we take the original and fundamental structure of human existence – which takes place in this dynamic of 'exiting language and then exiting into language' – to be a twofold being-in-the-world, then the being of the human should be understood as the double movement of going from the world into the limitless openness and then once again into the world.[50]

As long as I remain completely immersed in the cultural-linguistic determinations of 'my world', there is no possibility of entering into a genuine dialogue with others, who for their part may remain immersed in their worlds. If there is 'nothing outside the text' (to borrow a phrase from Derrida), it is only by passing through this nothingness that I can encounter others on their own terms. If they reciprocate, mutual understanding may take place. This need not occur as a complete 'fusion of horizons' (to borrow a phrase from Gadamer); the common ground found or formed through dialogue may serve rather as a bridge between cultural continents, a bridge that connects the horizons of self and other while at the same time holding them apart and preserving their differences. Dialogue, and especially cross-cultural dialogue, could be understood then as a 'linguistic encounter' (*taiwa*) that proceeds by way of speaking across (*dia-legein*) the nothingness or 'empty expanse' between linguistic worlds, a bridging that preserves as well as traverses cultural differences.

As Ueda points out, it not enough to overcome egoism with communalism, to break out of 'my world' only to remain stuck within the closed horizon of a communal 'our world'. Nishida also says that the world truly becomes world-like only when the third person 'he' (*kare*) is recognized, since without regard for the outsider, the I-Thou relation can easily mutate into a communal egoism.[51] This is

---

[50] Ueda Shizuteru, 'Language in a Twofold World', translated by Bret W. Davis, in *Japanese Philosophy: A Sourcebook*, edited by James W. Heisig, Thomas P. Kasulis and John C. Maraldo (Honolulu: University of Hawaii Press, 2011), 769

[51] See *Nishida Kitarō zenshū*, op. cit., note 11, 7:210, 313–314; also ibid., 8:56–69. In a similar sense, for Levinas, although ethics is rooted in the face-to-face relation with the other, justice arises only when attention

the pitfall of nationalism, ethnocentrism, religious fundamentalism, and, we must add, philosophical Ameri-Eurocentrism. Despite, or rather *because* of their all-inclusive aspirations, these remain dangerously parochial universalisms. The true universal cannot be defined in terms of a particular culture, language, or tradition. The true universal is not literally a 'uni-versal'; it is not a One toward which or around which all particulars turn. As Nishitani suggests, it is not a One, but a None;[52] it is not an absolute being, but absolute nothingness. It is a circumferenceless sphere in which the center is permanently and exclusively nowhere and potentially everywhere.[53] Each true individual is a focal point of the self-determination of this place of absolute nothingness, a focal point which is both determined by, and in turn counter-determines, the horizonally delimited sphere of his or her culture, language, and tradition. Yet insofar as each individual can experience, not only the world as it is shaped by the horizon of his or her culture and language, but also – at least in passing moments of silence – the radical openness of the undelimited sphere of absolute nothingness, he or she can also empathize with other individuals and learn to see the world in terms of their otherwise culturally and linguistically delimited horizons.

Communication within a delimited cultural sphere takes place largely by way of a shared language, which easily degenerates into what Heidegger calls 'idle chatter' (*Gerede*). A genuine cross-cultural encounter not only *requires* but also *enables* us to return to the originarily shared silence covered over by such idle chatter. Insofar cross-cultural or 'diatopical' dialogue must bridge the topoi of two or more cultural-linguistic spheres, it must ultimately take place within the encompassing empty expanse of absolute nothingness. And it must proceed by way of an ongoing and mutual experience of 'exiting language and then exiting into language'. That is to say, a genuine cross-cultural dialogue must also involve what we might call a 'diasige', a mutual passing through silence. Indeed diasige necessarily accompanies any genuine dialogue. We must learn to con-verse, to turn

---

is given to the third person. See Emmanuel Levinas, *Totality and Infinity: An Essay on Exteriority*, translated by Alphonso Lingis (Pittsburgh: Duquesne University Press, 1979), 213, 280

[52]   *Nishitani Keiji chosakushū*, op. cit., note 40, 11:243

[53]   Both Nishida and Nishitani employ the notion of an infinite sphere whose circumference is nowhere and center everywhere, which was used by Cusanus and the Hermetic and Christian mystical traditions to characterize God. See *Nishida Kitarō zenshū*, op. cit., note 11, 7:208; also ibid., 11:130, 423; and *Nishitani Keiji chosakushū*, op. cit., note 40, 10:164

toward one another, to reach out to one another, not only through speech but also, on a still deeper level, by passing through the ocean of silence we share beneath our islands of language. For it is on the basis of an implicit mutual understanding of the radical openness that underlies our cultural-linguistic horizons, and on the basis of a trust in our mutual ability to traverse the silent expanse – the 'nothing' that, beneath everything, we share in common – that we can learn to build ever more explicit and reliable dialogical bridges between us.

6. Cross-Cultural Dialogue and Diasige

Genuine dialogue, and especially cross-cultural dialogue, thus happens by way of a mutual and ongoing process of 'exiting language and exiting into language'. If exiting language is a matter of dying into the silent ocean of absolute nothingness, exiting into language is a matter of rebirth out of that absolute nothingness into linguistically articulated delimitations of being. Here again we find a three-part dynamic of affirmation through negation, in this case: the speaker, by way of not speaking, speaks. And the listener, by way of not listening merely in terms of his or her pre-established linguistic horizon, listens. Self and other converse by way of a mutual and ongoing process of bowing down into and rising up out of absolute nothingness.

Here we might understand the place of absolute nothingness or empty expanse as the unfathomable field of cultural and linguistic possibilities which gives rise to – and is as such covered over by – the actualization of this or that particular cultural-linguistic world. It is necessary to radically step back to, and to pass through, this self-concealing origin of cultural possibilities in order to understand other manifestations of language and culture, and to truly communicate with others who inhabit those other languages and cultures.

This process is exemplified by the experience of learning a foreign language. In my mind there are two astonishing things about linguistic diversity. The first is the radicality of the differences between linguistic worlds or 'houses of being', differences that are disguised rather than dissolved by translation. English and Japanese, for example, can seem to be worlds apart, oftentimes precisely when one is confronted with a 'correct' translation. The second astonishing thing about linguistic diversity, however, is that humans do in fact have the capacity to learn a foreign tongue. To be sure, if one insists on remaining within one's own language, the best one can do is rely on ready-made translations, that is to say, the best one can do is to 'shake hands' and trade words and expressions that are understood in terms of their nearest equivalents in one's own tongue. Everything, of course, can in some fashion be translated; but translation is always, more or less, transformation (if not indeed 'betrayal', as the Italian saying '*traduttore, traditore*' [translator, traitor] has it). Yet it is also possible to immerse oneself in another language until one begins to take part in it and it becomes part of oneself. Indeed such translation *of oneself* into a foreign language is necessary for any original translation to be made from that language. To really enter into a foreign language, which means to let it enter and thus alter oneself, one has to let go of one's native language and bow down into what in Zen is called the 'beginner's mind' of a child; one has to become like a child if one is to learn another mother's tongue. In the openness of this childlike beginner's mind, we return to what Daoists call 'the uncarved block', here symbolizing the uncharted and unchanneled wellspring of linguistic potentialities.

Chomsky suggests that humans are born with an innate ability to learn all human languages. Be that as it may, attempts to make explicit the specifics of our so-called innate 'universal grammar' have been criticized for privileging European languages and especially English. Chomsky himself derides Diderot's claim that French is the language most appropriate for the sciences insofar as it is purportedly 'unique among the languages in the degree to which the order of words corresponds to the natural order of thoughts and ideas'.[54] Of course, it is only natural that speakers of any language will find the syntax of their own language to correspond to the natural order of *their* thoughts and ideas.

It seems to me that, while we share a capacity to learn one another's languages, there is no universal grammar, no ur-language, no common *verbum interius*, no divine Logos *that can be revealed as such*. For the Hindu Mimamsa scholars, Sanskrit is the perfect

---

[54]   Noam Chomsky, *The Essential Chomsky*, edited by Anthony Arnove (New York and London: The New Press, 2008), 36. This francophonic ethnocentrism can apparently be traced back to Antoine Arnauld's *Grammaire Générale*. On the history of the debates surrounding linguistic universality and diversity, see John Leavitt, *Linguistic Relativities: Language Diversity and Modern Thought* (Cambridge and New York: Cambridge University Press, 2011). For an examination of the philosophical implications of the grammatical and semantic differences between Chinese, Japanese, and Indo-European languages, see Rolf Elberfeld, *Sprache und Sprachen: Eine philosophische Grundorientierung* (Freiburg and Munich: Karl Alber Verlag, 2012).

language and the mother of all other tongues. According to other religions, the language of their scripture is the privileged language of
God. Some try to argue that English has become the global lingua
franca for linguistic and not merely political and economic reasons.
For Heidegger, English is a hopelessly unphilosophical language
and 'When [the French] begin to think, they speak German'.[55] All
of these claims are subject to the criticism of what we might call 'eth-
nologocentrism'. Hence, rather than speaking of an ur-language,
perhaps we should practice listening to an originary silence, a
fecund emptiness or indeterminacy teeming with potentialities for
learning to understand and speak a multitude of languages. By
loosening ourselves from our attachment to our own culture and
language, perhaps we are able to step back to and through the preg-
nant stillness from out of which an irreducible plurality of cultural-
linguistic worlds is born.

We can relate this to Nishida's thoughts on globalization. If there is
a goal to world history, a direction in which globalization *should*
proceed, it is not, he clearly states, a matter of realizing a universal
global civilization that would cancel out the uniqueness of individual
cultural traditions. A culture that has lost its particularity, he says, is
no longer a culture. Rather, he suggests that 'the various cultures,
while maintaining their own individual standpoints, would develop
themselves through the mediation of the world, whereby a true
world culture would be formed'.[56] This 'true world culture' would
be a place of cross-cultural dialogue, a dialectically interrelated
unity-in-diversity, wherein differently developing cultures would

---

[55] Martin Heidegger, *Gesamtausgabe* (Frankfurt am Main: Vittorio
Klostermann, 1975–), 16:679

[56] *Nishida Kitarō zenshū*, op. cit., note 11, 7:452–53. Later Nishida
adds to this the idea that, between individual nations and the world, multi-
national cooperatives such as the so-called 'East Asian Co-prosperity
Sphere' should be formed. And, even while he struggled to strictly distinguish this from Western imperialism and colonialism, he played into the
hands of the Japanese ultranationalists when he writes: 'Each people [in
East Asia] must transcend itself to form a particular world [of East Asia]
and thereby carry out the world-historical mission of the East Asian
peoples. ... But in order to build [such] a particular world, a central figure
that carries the burden of the project is necessary. In East Asia today there
is no other but Japan' (*Nishida Kitarō zenshū*, 12:429, translated by Yoko
Arisaka in 'Beyond East and West: Nishida's Universalism and
Postcolonial Critique', in *Border Crossings: Toward a Comparative
Political Theory*, edited by Fred Dallmayr [New York: Lexington Books,
1996], 102)

be open to interaction and exchange with one another while maintaining their own authenticity and autonomy.

According to Nishida, even though 'until now Westerners have thought that their own culture is the most superior human culture that exists, and that human culture inevitably develops in the direction of their own culture', in fact the West will subsume the East no more than the East will subsume the West. 'Rather', he goes on to say, 'East and West are like two branches of the same tree. They are divided in two and yet supplement one another at the base and roots'.[57] Even if humanity does share a common root – what Nishida calls, borrowing a manner of expression from Goethe, an 'ur-culture' (*genbunka*) of multiple possibilities – the development of its branches and leaves is a matter of diversification, not homogenization. Globalization should thus be thought of, in Nishida's vision, as many branches of the same tree supplementing one other on the basis of both their deep-rooted commonality *and* their irreducible diversity.[58] But unlike Goethe, who was tempted to diagram and thus give determinate form to the *Urpflanze* from which all plants are produced, Nishida suggests that the roots of this ur-culture remain buried in the ground of an essentially undisclosable absolute nothingness, a formless origin of all cultural forms.

If the manifold of contrasting and complementary cultural differences is united by a common root of humanity, according to the Kyoto School thinkers we have discussed this essentially self-delimiting and thus self-concealing origin is better thought of as an originary indeterminate nothingness rather than a fundamental determinate being. In this sense we are a global community of those who share – in a radical sense – nothing in common, and it is by returning to this formless absolute nothingness that we can begin to truly understand the form and being of others.[59] In dialogue,

---

[57]   *Nishida Kitarō zenshū*, op. cit., note 11, 14:404–6
[58]   *Nishida Kitarō zenshū*, op. cit., note 11, 14:402–6, 417
[59]   This should not be confused with the claim that there is no human nature or that our minds are 'blank slates' subsequently shaped in full by our cultural environments. Surely we can come up with a long list of cultural universals that would include such items as 'facial expressions of fear, happiness, sadness' and so forth (see Donald E. Brown, *Human Universals* [New York: McGraw-Hill, 1991]). And, even though this list would be compiled by someone who was raised in a particular culture and who is thinking and writing in a particular language, surely it could be translated into other languages. But only the most naïve (and most likely monolingual) universalist would think that words used from other languages to translate an English word such as 'happiness' bear identical connotations. Even an

and especially in cross-cultural dialogue, it is only through mutually bowing down into to the silence between us that we can begin to hear what one another has to say. Genuine dialogue must be accompanied by diasige.

Let me give to Ueda the last word about the silences that are essential to dialogue.

> From the start 'speaking together' fundamentally involves, just on the other side of speech, silence. Not only is it necessary to not say this and that about inessential things in order to say what is really essential, but also, indeed first and foremost, it is necessary to often be silent in order to hear what the other person has to say. Without this silence of listening, a dialogue cannot take place. Yet silence does not stop even there; it leads further down into a profound silence that, as it were, reaches an absolute nothingness. When we speak from there ... [the few words we exchange] quietly ring forth within an expanse of emptiness.[60]

Loyola University, Maryland
bwdavis@loyala.edu

---

expression such as 'need to eat' is laden with the cultural-linguistic connotations of 'need' and 'eat'. On the other hand, equally untenable is the thesis of the extreme cultural relativist who would claim that we are forever imprisoned in our respective cultures and languages. For translation is always to some extent possible, and, more significantly, it is always to some extent possible to *let oneself be translated* into other idioms, and thus to empathize, to understand, and to enter into a profound dimension of dialogue with others.

[60] *Ueda Shizuteru shū*, op. cit., note 44, 10:296

From Good Knowers to Just Knowers in the *Mahābhārata* : Towards a Comparative Virtue Epistemology

VRINDA DALMIYA

Abstract
Adopting the framework of Anglo Analytic Virtue Epistemology, I ask of the Sanskrit epic, the *Mahābhārata*, the question: What sort of character or 'intellectual virtues' must a 'good knower' have? Then, inspired by broadly feminist sensibilities, I raise the concern whether dispositions for knowing the world can be associated with motivations to rectify injustices in that world – whether, in other words, a good knower is also a 'just knower.' I go on to explore the structure of humility and shame as 'virtues of truth' in the epic to see whether they can establish a connection between knowing and justice.

Introduction

The *Mahābhārata* narrative (told in over 100,000 verses) about the Great War within the Kuru clan doubles as the story of 'all humankind.' It calls itself an *itihāsa* which is often translated as 'history'. The *Mahābhārata*, however, is not a mere chronological harking back to what happened once upon a time. Rather, we find here a selection of past events and conversations, mixed in with myths and imaginations of what clearly did not happen., 'History', as Sibesh Bhattacharya puts it, 'was not conceived as an account of the entire body of human past... the past that deserves to be included within the fold of *itihāsa* is the one that is capable of imparting instructions ... basically instructions on 'dos' and 'don'ts and the means of achieving the goals of life'.[1] *Itihāsa* thus dramatizes and makes us literally *see* how we should/ought to live. It is 'philosophy by example',[2] enabling a grasp of oughtness through flashes of intuition (*prajñā*) nurtured by narrative (re)tellings. But what kind of normativity is imparted in this manner by the epic?

---

[1]   Sibesh Bhattacharya, *Understanding Itihāsa* (Shimla: Indian Institute for Advanced Study, 2010) 44–45
[2]   Ibid., 44

doi:10.1017/S1358246114000046   ©The Royal Institute of Philosophy and the contributors 2014
Royal Institute of Philosophy Supplement **74** 2014   195

Vrinda Dalmiya

I answer this question by adopting the stance of 'living within' the tradition in J.N. Mohanty's[3] sense of the phrase. This entails challenging the *Mahābhārata* world view as a dialogic partner in the present. The philosophical contemporaniety from which I approach the epic is constituted by analytic virtue epistemology on the one hand, and a modern feminist sensibility, on the other. Such an intersectional vantage point raises questions about the nature of normativity which the epic might not have been interested in and may well stretch its conceptual resources to limits not dreamt of in its own historical times. This open-endedness would not be frowned upon by the epic itself which after all, welcomes multiple 're-tellings' within its own narrative structure.

On one level, my attempt here is to broaden *ethical* normativity in the *Mahābhārata* to include the epistemological. Living well, uncontroversially presupposes knowing well. There is no *dharma* without *satya*: ethical decisions are based on understanding the situations in which choices are made. But the twist lies in asserting that *epistemic* excellence involves moral dispositions. This is the classic move of virtue epistemology. Thus the *Mahābhārata*'s ruminations on the commendable habits of mind needed for a good life are given a new spin when we ask the question: are the character traits discussed by the epic *intellectual virtues* that a 'good knower' needs to acquire? On another level, according to broadly feminist leanings, excellence in knowing/living entails a political sensitivity to oppressions and the goal of doing away with such injustices. So arises a second question: are the dispositional excellences involved in knowing the world according to the *Mahābhārata,* effective in responding to injustices in that world? Can the ethico-epistemic virtues spoken of in the epic be *virtues of justice* that augment social fairness as well? Thus the central question of this chapter, even while trading on the broad conceptual traffic between ethics, epistemology, and politics, is quite specific: What characterological features must a subject have for successful knowing and can these dispositions motivate her to intervene in systemic injustices?

To anticipate, I read a familiar episode in the *Mahābhārata* against the grain in order to focus on the ethical dispositions of humility and shame. Unraveling the complex structure of these two emotions in the epic, shows their constitutive relation with epistemic character on the one hand, and their potential for initiating social change on

---

[3]   J.N. Mohanty, *Reason and Tradition in Indian Thought* (Oxford: Clarendon, 1992), 9

196

the other. Part 1 tries to critically articulate how the ethical can be broadened to include the epistemic in a non-reductive move within the *Mahābhārata* framework. This leads to a discussion of the epistemic goal of truth as envisaged in a virtue theory. Part 2 discusses the particular virtue of humility in the light of some contemporary discussions. It then explores the structural resources of humility in the *Mahābhārata* in an attempt to cast it as a historically grounded and politically robust virtue. Part 3 brings in the virtue of shame to reinforce the political turn of the previous section. The *Mahābhārata*'s construal of shame as implying rectificatory actions, is different both from the pernicious practices of 'shaming' as well as the humiliating experience of 'traumatic shame.' An ethically induced shame in the elite can perhaps complement resistance originating at the margins to initiate systemic change.

1. From Belief to Virtues: From Ethics to Epistemology

Tired of the impasse between warring theories of justification, some epistemologists[4] in the mid 1980s moved attention to *virtues* in a bid to unify the opposing insights of foundationalism and coherentism. The concept of virtue, however, also shifted focus from good *beliefs* to good *knowers*. The evaluation of epistemic agents, turned on the quality of their 'inner nature' – their possession (or lack) of dispositions called 'intellectual virtues'. Of course, exposition of this crucial notion varied widely. While some speak of reliable *faculties* or skills like perception, memory, and deduction as indicators of excellence in a cognitive agent, others foreground her *character traits* like impartiality, honesty, open-mindedness and the like. Our excursion into the *Mahābhārata* will be in search of 'character virtues' and hence, towards what is called a Virtue Responsibilism[5] that traces successful inquiry to entrenched character traits of the knower.

To use Linda Zagzebski's terminology, intellectual virtues are comprised of a distinct *motivation* or desire for 'cognitive contact

---

[4]   See papers in Ernest Sosa, *Knowledge in Perspective: Selected Essays in Epistemology* (New York: Cambridge University Press, 1991).
[5]   Two kinds of virtue theory mapped on to 'faculty virtues' and 'character virtues' respectively – 'virtue reliabilism' and 'virtue responsiblism' – has been distinguished by Guy Axtell, 'Recent Work in Virtue Epistemology' in *American Philosophical Quarterly* **34**(1) (1997): 1–26.

with reality' along with *reliable success* in attaining it.[6] The phrase, 'cognitive contact' is of course, broad enough to accommodate states like understanding and wisdom that aim at much more than picturing reality in propositional content. Yet for a start, the motivational component of intellectual virtue is best taken as a love of *truth*. The relevant point here is that love of truth (like all loves) tends to go awry in strange ways: Sliding into obsession, it can result in dogmatism; becoming overconfident and lazy, it can lead to fanciful generalizations; and tinged by jealousy, it can prevent truth from circulating. We therefore need regulative controls to keep this primary epistemological motivation on track. We need, in other words, to love *in a specific way* in order to succeed in attaining truth. This, according to virtue epistemologists, requires further dispositions that make us a certain way *qua* epistemic agents. Our character traits, thus, orient us to the world in a manner that can lead to intellectual flourishing (or not). They do so by either directing us straightforwardly to epistemic ends or by overcoming psychological obstacles in achieving that goal.

What then are the specific intellectual virtues that sustain successful inquiry? Though this question arises in a particular moment in the history of Anglo American theories of knowledge, can we find a response to it in the *Mahābhārata*? The answer that is forthcoming comes, like most *Mahābhārata* answers, in the form of a story from the past: 'Once upon a time there lived a sage called Kauśika...'

The Story of the Short Tempered Sage[7]

The learned Brahmin scholar, Kauśika, once lost his temper when a hapless bird disturbed his meditation by defecating on his head. Incensed by this rude interruption, Kauśika unleashed his supernatural powers on the unsuspecting bird and caused it to drop dead. But almost immediately he was overcome with compassion

[6] Linda Zagzebski, *Virtues in the Mind: An Inquiry into the Nature of Virtue and the Ethical Foundation of Knowledge* (New York: Cambridge University Press, 1996).

[7] Vana Parvan, 197–216. Though the details of the narrative are important, what I present here is not a translation but a short summary of the story. All references to the *Mahābhārata* are from Ramchandra Shastri Kinjawadekar (ed.) *The Mahābhāratam* with *Bharata Bhawadeepa* Commentary of Nilakaṇṭha (New Delhi: Oriental Books Reprint Corporation, n.d.).

*and regret at such vengeance. Horrified by his own glaring limita-
tions, Kauśika decided to re-educate himself and embarked on a
quest for instructors.*

*His travels led him to the village of a particular housewife. On
arriving at her doorstep, the sage found her busy with household
chores and the business of attending to the needs of her husband.
An impatient Kauśika stormed (once again!) – this time for having
been kept waiting. The housewife, however, held her ground in the
face of this entitled rage and even berated him for not being a true
scholar. Even though she had not been told, she made it clear that
she was aware of Kauśika's infamous history with the bird.
'Nāham balākā' ('I am no bird!') she suggestively and sarcastically
says in order to stem Kauśika's diatribe – but later openly admits
that she knew all along why Kauśika had left his own village and
come to her. Impressed by her clearly superior cognitive powers,
Kauśika accepted her strident criticisms of him. Filled with
shame, he decided to follow her advice and seek out a particular
butcher to help him retrain himself.*

*Kauśika went to the butcher's town and encountered a humble,
low-caste person skinning, chopping and selling animal carcasses.
While practicing his trade, the butcher led a conventional life
caring for his aging parents. But surprisingly, he became
Kauśika's teacher. The unlikely location of his simple and poor
home transformed into a site for transmission of knowledge.*

*The story ends with a long speech in which the 'virtuous butcher'
(dharmavyādha) explained the nature of righteousness, the nature
of reality and the nature of non-violence. His parting advice was
that Kauśika should return to take care of his old parents and
that this would not interfere with his study.*

The (Epistemic) Moral of the Story

On the surface, this is an ethical tale – a story about a brahmin sage,
Kauśika, learning to control his rage and overcome his pride.
According to a historically contextualised reading,[8] the episode
records adjustments made in Brahmanical theory in order to
withstand criticisms being brought against the Vedic practice of
animal sacrifice. Such critiques could have come from the renunciate
precursors of Buddhism and Jainism who espoused absolute

[8]   Sibaji Bandyopadhyay, 'A Critique of Non-Violence', *Seminar* 608
(2010)

non-violence. The butcher's speech at the end of the episode is a skillful mediation between unavoidable violence and non-violence: it drives home for Kauśika the 'true meaning' of non-aggression or *ahimsā*. This is an ethical message.

However, through a different lens, the story can be seen as plotted around the drama of epistemic displacement and epistemic transformations.[9] It is about someone who, in spite of having the social capital of a high caste 'scholar', did not possess the intellectual virtues necessary for effective inquiry. It shows the re-tooling of an erudite but irate sage into a 'good knower' through engagement with individuals at the social margins. The ethical, here, seems to serve a deeper *epistemic* purpose.

But how can a narrative about pride and aggression speak to the problem of knowledge – not just moral knowledge – but of knowledge pertaining to garden-variety plain truths about sticks and stones? In fact, the didactic portions of the *Mahābhārata* often render the very notion of the 'epistemic' nebulous because of the manner in which they speak of *truth* (*satya*) - the designated goal of cognitive activity. The *Mahābhārata* routinely embeds truth in a list of ethical virtues and sometimes openly dismisses truth-speaking in favor of moral virtues like non-cruelty. Let us look more carefully at the worry that a notion of alethic truth might be absent in the *Mahābhārata*. This is important because without an independent notion of 'truth', endeavors and concepts that define themselves in terms of 'cognitive contact with reality' become shaky.

In response to the direct questions: What is truth? How is it obtained?, the Śānti Parvan in chapter 162.1–26 lists and defines thirteen moral virtues, calling them the thirteen 'Ways of truth' or *satya-ācāra*[10] (*satya* meaning 'truth' and *ācāra* meaning 'ways of conduct' or 'practice'.) The list comprises of standard ethical qualities like impartiality, freedom from envy, self-control, patience, and the like. Now, this can easily be made sense of in a virtue-theoretic framework. Cognitive success depends on possessing thirteen character traits which are the *ways/means* to truth. We are often biased, lazy, hasty. We are also prone to fantasy, wishful thinking, and deceit. Such proclivities routinely scramble 'cognitive contact with reality.' Moral virtues (like the thirteen listed) become 'virtues

---

[9]   Vrinda Dalmiya and Linda Alcoff, 'Are "Old Wives" Tales Justified?' in Linda Alcoff and Elizabeth Potter (eds) *Feminist Epsitemologies* (New York: Routledge, 1993), 217–244 gives an epistemological reading of the episode which is different from the one suggested here.
[10]   Verse 6: *ācārāniha satyasya yathāvadanupûrvaśah.*

of truth' since they help overcome common psychological impediments to accessing reality. They are, as Bernard Williams says, 'qualities of people that are displayed in wanting to know the truth, in finding it out, and in telling it to other people'.[11]

However, the text quickly muddies such an easy interpretation by going on to call these thirteen 'Ways' the '*Forms*' of truth or *satya-ākāra*[12] (*ākāra* meaning 'form.') With this reformulation, moral virtues are no longer simple means or ways *to* a cognitive end, but rather truth becomes incarnated or embodied in thirteen 'forms' *as* the moral virtues themselves. A similar blurring of the ethical and the epistemic occurs in crucial verses in the *Bhagavad Gītā* also. Chapter 13: 7–11, in a bid to tell us what *knowledge* is (*etadjñānam iti proktam*) ends up listing a set of moral qualities! The cognitive here thus seems to be articulated in terms of the ethical.

The problem is that such moves loosen our grip on the notion of an *intellectual* virtue. Note that Zagzebski distinguishes epistemic from moral motivation (and hence the two types of virtues, intellectual and moral) in terms of the difference in their goals – the former aiming at truth and the latter at the good life. However, if truth becomes an embodiment of moral good, as when moral properties designated as '*ācāra*'– the means to/practice of truth – turn into its '*ākāra*' or its forms, then a hunt for the epistemic in the epic becomes futile. Or so goes the objection.

Now this worry misconstrues the *Mahābhārata's* deeply virtue-theoretic endeavor of turning away from belief-based accounts to agent-based ones. A shift from truth-practices to truth-forms (from *satya ācāra* to *satya ākāra*) does not necessarily lose the good old alethic target of inquiry. Rather it signifies a change in how we *understand* what truth is in a virtue-theoretic context. Definitions of truth in terms of propositional fit with reality are basically consistent with belief-based accounts. An agent-based perspective, however, suggests looking at how truth is operationalized in conduct. A life of (moral) virtue is an embodiment of a life free from obstacles to attaining truth. Thus pointing to such a life, becomes a way of alluding to what is attained in such a life and hence to showing us *what truth is*. Just as what 'direction' *is* can be indicated by pointing to what parallel lines have in common, a successful epistemic life can become an indicator of what that life aims at. Truth, in other words, can be

[11]   Bernard Williams, *Truth and Truthfulness* (Princeton: Princeton University Press, 2002), 7
[12]   Verse 9 lists the thirteen virtues as *satyākārāstroydaśa* which literally means 'thirteen forms of truth'.

Vrinda Dalmiya

contextually defined through 'characterizations' of the knower. Because of this, describing the Buddha *himself* as *pamāna bhûta*[13] – as someone who had himself *become* knowledge – is a strategic way of conveying what *knowledge* is. The grasp of the nature of knowledge is now mediated through an encounter with a paradigmatically knowledgeable *person*. Theory of knowledge, it seems, must assume the form of a normative theory of knowers.

The Ethical and the Epistemic

The Kauśika story models a couple of different ways of connecting ethical excellence with cognitive excellence without *reducing* one to the other.

(1) First, by single-mindedly focusing on knowledge in a solitary meditative trance under a tree, Kauśika failed. He burned with an exaggerated 'love of truth' which led him to unravel at the slightest, unintended interruption by the bird. We confront something like the paradox of intention here. The story shows how a direct and intense pursuit of truth can be counter-productive, how Kauśika's excessive eagerness to attain knowledge *reduced* his chances of getting it. The general point is that knowledge is power and power can be corrupting. Epistemic success – especially when self-celebrated, easily slips into hubris that ruins the momentum of initial success. The pursuit of epistemic goals is always on the brink of collapsing unto itself: the more we achieve truth, the greater the probability that we will fail in maintaining the fidelity of inquiry. Successful knowing comes with the risk of generating pride and related ethical vices, which in turn, stymie cognitive progress.

The epic solves the conundrum by making Kauśika de-center or even forget about the cognitive and focus on cultivating the *ethical* instead. This is not *giving up* love of truth. In fact, Kauśika's moral fervor and his realization that he needed to embark on an anger management program is motivated by this very desire (for truth.) Just as the desperate insomniac does not *try* to sleep but starts reading a boring novel in order to fall asleep, an effective, albeit *indirect route* to 'cognitive contact with reality' is to immerse oneself in things non-epistemic: ordinary, interactive life requiring cultivation of self-control, equanimity, patience and the other virtues of sociality. Such self-cultivation brings the very epistemic success that eludes us when pursued directly.

[13] Dignaga, *Pramāṇasamuccaya*, 1.1

Of course, this strategy of resorting to an ethical response in the face of an epistemic failure presumes a particular ends-means relation between the two. A necessary condition of moral conduct is cognitive excellence. One cannot alleviate the needs of others, create conditions for their flourishing, not interfere with their interests and the like, without knowing what they are. In order to better perform one's roles in society one *needs to know* oneself and the requirements of those roles. Thus ethical life brings cognitive success in its tow by the 'relation of requirement' as it were. Consequently, concentrating on the ethical can become a means of achieving the epistemic. Learning to be compassionate, in some forms of Buddhism, for example, sets us on the path to cognitive success *because* a clear mind is a prerequisite for being compassionate. But importantly, the practice of compassion is not as easily wrought with ethical pitfalls that come from pursuing 'clear and distinct ideas' directly - after all, successful pursuit of an ethical life means consciously attempting to stay away from ethical vices. In this way, moral life *is* an epistemically successful life, but one that avoids the dangers of a direct pursuit of cognitive goals.

(2) Second, could Kauśika's killing the bird be construed as an *epistemic* defect itself? Note that 'brahmin' comes from '*brāhmaṇa*' which is etymologically a cognitive epithet signifying someone who *knows* the nature of ultimate reality.[14] Note also that in the narrative, the housewife berates Kauśika by saying that as a brahmin/*brāhmaṇa* he was expected to study and to teach, (*yo' dhyāpayedadhīyīta*. Vana Parvan, 206:36). Yet, it was clear to her that he did not know the truth (about *Dharma*) (*na tu tattvena ...dharmam vesti, na jānīṣe dharmam* Vana Parvan, 206.43) What could this scathing epistemic indictment mean when coming in wake of unethical behavior? The embarrassing incident with the bird could well signify that whatever truths Kauśika might have learned, these were not aligned with other culturally accepted intrinsic values, like for example, non-violence. Now this mis-alignment becomes an epistemic shortcoming once the goal of inquiry is designated to be not truth *simpliciter* or bare truth, but truth *as* related to other correlative values. But why should we thicken the epistemic purpose in this way?

The need for a 'reflective understanding' might lead us in this direction. Drawing on some discussions of the nature of *intrinsic* value, it is clear that though the value of truth is not understood instrumentally as leading to something desirable, it still needs to be 'made sense of'

---

[14]   *brahma jānāti iti brāhmaṇa.*

in terms of its relation to other intrinsic values.[15] The 'fit' of truth in this larger normative matrix results in *understanding* of it. Kauśika's instances of unseemly behavior indicate that though he might have truly believed, yet for him truth itself remained isolated from the broad spread of other non-instrumental values which helps us grasp it as having worth at all. Kauśika failed to reflectively understand whatever truth he was pursuing – which is an epistemic failing.

The general distinction made in the tradition between *dharma* 'with a little-d' and *Dharma* 'with a big-D',[16] throws more light on the pursuit of truth *as* related to a plurality of intrinsic values. Speaking the truth (and thereby investigating it) in isolation, is a small-d dharma or a narrow epistemic duty. But this is embedded in a big-D *Dharma* defined as flourishing in harmony with *all* virtues – including harmony with cosmic Law. Now, when the epic extols that truth can be given up if it causes harm, (Droṇa Parvan, 164.99) it speaks on the level of 'small-d' dharma and narrow epistemic goals. But when it says that 'Truth is the Highest *Dharma*' (Śānti Parvan, 199.63–71), it references 'big-D *Dharma*' and truth as a necessary element in that Ultimate eudaemonic state. The latter is flourishing or well being constituted by a harmonization of a plurality of intrinsic goods, including Truth - which harmony has to be affected each time, in a new way, given the particularities of the situation.

What this suggests is that according to the *Mahābhārata*, a small-d pursuit of truth-speaking should not become a fetish. This is because the ultimate cognitive aim is such truth that can be reconciled with the other values in a big-D *Dhārmic* life. Thus the epistemic agent needs to be open to sometimes giving up a small-d truth for a big-D coherence: Highest excellence comes from understanding the

---

[15]   Williams, *Truth and Truthfulness*, 92–93. This discussion is referenced by Jonardon Ganeri, *The Concealed Art of the Soul* (Oxford: Oxford University Press, 2007), 231

[16]   This distinction is mentioned by Joseph Dowd as taken from a March 2009 lecture by Robert Goldman. See Dowd, 'Maximizing Dharma, Krsna's Consequentialism in the Mahabharata', *Praxis* 3.1 (Spring 2011), 33–50, fn 11. However, it seems that Dowd used the terminology to make a distinction between many dharmas or particular contextual duties and a single universal *Dharma*. I am trying to say that the duty of truth-speaking is a 'little-d dharma' and is not absolute. This duty has to be subsumed in a wider normative framework that involves many intrinsic values which is Big-D *Dharma*. There is also no single formula of achieving coherence of the duty of truth with other values – though of course, that it must be so subsumed holds across the board.

inner structural relations between 'cognitive contact with reality' and other intrinsically valuable goals in a 'living well'. Truth is *ultimately* good when it is incorporated into and becomes a constituent of a good life even as its place in and value for flourishing must be contextually negotiated.

Jonardon Ganeri speaks of a new intellectual virtue called 'Receptivity' introduced by the *Mahābhārata* over and above the standard epistemic virtues of Accuracy and Sincerity. As the 'disposition to resist the insulation of belief',[17] Receptivity is more complex than simple Accuracy and enables truth to affect our lives and 'run riot in the soul'.[18] This means that the only truth worth having is one that leads to good agency. When bare truth conflicts with other intrinsically important values, the virtue of Receptivity pushes for harmonizing them – a contextual synthesis and re-arrangement of priorities that affect behavior.

If not anything else, this indicates the depth of difference between the modern 'purely scientific' inquiry and the classical Indian concept of truth, the knowledge of which, liberates us from existential suffering. The latter always embeds ordinary, epistemic truth in a larger normative framework. But what is important for our purposes is that such embedding is not its denial but rather its expansion. Hence, it would be overreaching to claim that the *Mahābhārata* did not work with epistemic truth as 'we' know it. Truth is not made more nebulous in the epic. Rather it is brought closer to our lives. In different ways then, a good knower in the *Mahābhārata*, has to be both 'good' and a 'knower' in the traditional senses – unlike say a 'good executioner' or a 'good thief'. Kauśika's character thus becomes epistemically exemplary at the end of the story *because* he engages with the ethical. And he must do so *in order* to be epistemically good.

Ethico-Epistemic Exemplary Agents

A virtue theoretic framework requires us to model epistemically virtuous agents in order to attain cognitive excellence. From this perspective, the Kausika story throws up the following two questions:

(a)   What is the *character* of the housewife and the butcher who displace Kauśika as an epistemic paradigm within the story.

17   Jonardon Ganeri, *The Concealed Art of the Soul*, 233
18   Ibid., 54

What traits ground their cognitive superiority and make them exemplary for Kauśika?

(b) What is the *nature* of Kauśika himself who begins as deficient but undergoes an 'improvement of the understanding'? What is the basis of his redemption and why is he, at the end of the story, worthy of emulation by us?

Our primary concern is with the struggling Kauśika and hence, with the second question. Yet, let us briefly look at his teachers – the housewife and the butcher first. The characters of these two protagonists are repeatedly marked in the text by 'ordinariness.' And this is parsed as their leading *conventional* moral lives. Disconcertingly, for the feminist, they both seem content with the status quo: the housewife is happy being a *pativratā* (a woman who considers her husband to be God) and the butcher is content to follow his hereditary caste-duties and familial obligations to his parents. Moreover, both characters emphasize their caring activities. The housewife openly ignores the Brahmin so that she can attend to her husband; the butcher makes much of his 'taking care' of his parents. Both hark back to their *care giving* when explaining to a surprised Kauśika, why and how they know as much as they do.

The narrative movement is also a gradual progression inwards – from a description of the city, to the public marketplace where the butcher practices his trade, to a seeming digression into a detailed description of the serenity of his home space and its inner chambers. It is here that the butcher finally imparts his message to Kauśika. What is highlighted both literally and metaphorically, then, is the domestic, *even while* the housewife and butcher function as *cognitive* exemplars. This suggests fascinating connections between domesticity, the labor of care and knowing and is a startling reversal of the public and the private domains in epistemology. Putting that, and its feminist potential aside,[19] let us move to the character of Kauśika.

Now, even though *within* the story, the housewife and the butcher are cognitive exemplars for Kauśika, for us *readers, Kauśika himself,* works as a role model for 'improvement of the understanding'. What does the fallible yet teachable, *Kauśika* model for *us*? We find him struggling with vanity, arrogance, and a sense of privilege. We find him coming to recognize his own epistemological inadequacies.

---

[19] I have developed this more elsewhere. See for example, 'Care Ethics and Epistemic Justice: Some insights from the *Mahābhārata*' in *Mahābhārata Now: Narration, Aesthetics, Ethics* (eds) Sibaji Bandyopadhyay and Arindam Chakrabarti (New Delhi: Routledge, forthcoming).

And we find him conceding that surprisingly, peripheral figures *do know* what *he*, the professional savant, *does not*. In order to be like Kauśika, therefore, we need to inculcate traits that enabled his interaction across entrenched social and epistemic hierarchies. What are these characteristics? Leaving aside the general involvement of the epistemic with the ethical, let us now pan in on the analysis of two specific qualities in Kauśika's character. Why should we, *qua* epistemic agents, be interested in inculcating dispositions of humility and shame which, according to the narrative, are central in Kauśika's character?

2. On Humility in Epistemic Contexts

Acquiring humility is important for Kauśika's characterological transformation into a good knower. But herein lies a looming paradox. Julia Driver[20] famously calls modesty/humility one of the 'virtues of ignorance.' According to her, humility is a disposition to underestimate one's achievements even when presented with evidence to the contrary. Consequently, humility is constituted by the 'epistemic *defect* of not knowing one's own worth' (my emphasis).[21] To speak of it as an epistemic *excellence* or an 'intellectual virtue', therefore, is odd.

Roberts and Wood[22] who are most associated in recent times with analyzing humility in intellectual contexts, avoid this paradox by delinking humility from ignorance. According to them, a humble person only 'appears' to be ignorant of her excellence, but in effect is one who is merely '*unconcerned* about it and therefore *inattentive* to it'.[23] Kauśika's humility, I suggest, is importantly different and occupies a middle ground between these two analyses. It keeps the association of humility with ignorance (unlike Roberts and Wood), on the one hand. But (unlike Driver), construes ignorance to be a mark of epistemic excellence rather than a defect. Of course, this presupposes that the *Mahābhāratā* has an unusual idea of ignorance that re-works the relation between knowledge and not-knowing. In order

---

[20]   Julia Driver, 'The Virtue of Ignorance', *Journal of Philosophy* **86**(7) (1989): 373–384
[21]   Ibid., 374
[22]   Roberts C. Roberts and W. Jay Wood, *Intellectual Virtues: An Essay in Regulative Epistemology* (Oxford: Oxford University Press, 2007)
[23]   Ibid., 239

Vrinda Dalmiya

to explore how Kauśika's character illustrates this, let us first turn to a textual exposition of the virtue of humility in the *Mahābhārata*.

We have already noted that the *Bhagavad Gītā* 13.7–11 equates *knowing* with a set of moral virtues. Among the many qualities (all of which seem equally unrelated to knowledge) it mentions three - *amānitvam, adambhitvam* and *anahamkāra* – each of which hover around the semantic space of the English terms 'humility' and 'modesty'. Furthermore, each of these are negative terms in Sanskrit, referring respectively to the *absence* of three *vices*. These are the flaws of

(1)   being *mānī*,
(2)   having *dambha*, and
(3)   possessing *ahamkāra*.

The commentarial literature enters into subtle analyses of the differences between the vices of *māna, dambha,* and *ahamkāra*. Glossing over the details, the dispositions comprising their negations (the corresponding *virtues*) are

(1')   *absence* of *falsely thinking/believing* oneself to be superior than others (*a-mānitva*),
(2')   not *publicly behaving as if* one is better than others in order to claim celebrity, even when one is truly better (*a-dambhitva*), and
(3')   lack of egoism or self-absorption (*an-ahamkāra*).

My suggestion is that when taken together, the three absences – (1') – (3') – give us a picture of a complex intellectual virtue which is humility. Humility here is understood in terms of what it is not, bringing it close to the analysis of Roberts and Wood who also articulate intellectual humility as the *absence* of certain vices - particularly, vanity and arrogance.

Now notice that each of the *Mahābhārata* negations (1') – (3') constituting humility consist in an *openness to others*. Not considering oneself to be superior makes it possible to consider others equal to or even better than us; not claiming celebrity status for oneself enables one to recede and celebrate others; and a lack of self-absorption paves the way for an interest in others. The epistemological advantages of such a constellation of other-regarding dispositions are many. The tendency not to think/claim oneself as superior (rightly or wrongly) removes the fear of being proven wrong – a fear commonly leading to desperate justifications of mistakes. When freed from guarding a fragile epistemic superiority, we become open to criticism, sympathetic to unfashionable lines of research, and most importantly, we are receptive to unconventional teachers. Not being self absorbed, further enables absorption in the objects to be known. In this way, even a negative characterization of humility, establishes it as an intellectual virtue – it is a complex negative disposition that augments the 'power' and 'portability'[24] of forming true beliefs in multiple domains.

Within this background, Kauśika's character can now be explored as narratively fleshing out the positive content of what humility *is*. Kauśika exemplifies how a person, in the *absence* of the three vices – which in English may be vanity, arrogance and self-absorption – can actively reach out to others in an epistemologically engaged moment. The distinctiveness of Kauśika's humility, I shall argue is this deep relationality. However, the transition from mere humility to what can be called 'relational humility' is mediated by its association with ignorance. Remember that acceptance of failure was the pivotal moment in Kauśika's transformation.

Ignorance and Epistemic Virtuosity

As the scales of the three vices – of *māna, dambha,* and *ahamkāra* – fall away from Kauśika's eyes, he begins to *recognize the limits* of his excellence. This suggests, contra Driver, that a humble person can well be aware of her accomplishments, as long as she does not exaggerate or over-estimate her worth.[25] However, knowing the limits of what one knows is a gesture to the reality of something beyond the limit: it implies some sort of awareness of that which is not known. Humility thus *does* involve ignorance, but not in the sense of false belief.

The contours of a patch lit up by a searchlight always signals the co-related shape of a dark patch too. As the convex lighted space comes into sharp relief, an awareness of the concave area in the darkness beyond is also deepened. Thus, if knowing is a searchlight, then when we know what we do, we also become aware of the darkness/ignorance that lies beyond what we know. Now such ignorance/darkness conveys an *awareness* of a something which we do not know – even though this awareness is not a *knowing* of it. To put it dramatically, we come in 'cognitive contact with reality' through

---

[24]   Christopher Lepock, 'Unifying the Intellectual Virtues', *Philosophy and Phenomenological Research* **83**(1) (2011): 106–128
[25]   Norvin Richards, 'Is Humility a Virtue?' *American Philosophical Quarterly* **25**(3) (1988) 253–259

ignorance states (inchoately grasp the reality lurking in the dark patch) though of course, this awareness is not the kind of making contact involved in knowing states. On this construal then, ignorance is not a mere *lack* of knowledge. Rather, it is a positive entity with an intentional content i.e., the object/reality *as* unknown.[26]

To illustrate with an example: to the extent that I am aware that my knowledge of the table is limited to its top (is *only* of its top), I am *aware* of the table beyond its top. My knowing a cloth-covered table is not, after all, a knowledge of the cloth floating in air. In the same way, grasping something as masked is not grasping a *mere* mask. 'In the empirical cognitive situation', J.N. Mohanty says, we are in a state 'of light and darkness mingled together... Just as there is awareness of light manifesting whatever is manifested, so there is awareness of darkness concealing whatever is concealed'.[27] Ignorance as 'darkness' is an *awareness* of objects *as concealed.* Humility, in involving ignorance, therefore, involves such a grasp of reality 'known as unknown'.[28]

Now, the concept of an object 'known *as* unknown' or an awareness of reality *as* beyond my knowledge, grants the object known a knowledge-transcending 'excess' which makes room for genuine surprises and ensures a robust realism. However, to the extent the object appears to *me* as unknown, it can appear to *others* as known. Thus acknowledging *my* ignorance makes room for the possibility of *their* knowledge: de-authorizing myself by recognizing where my knowledge ends, amounts to epistemically authorizing others. This last point makes Kauśika's humility deeply 'relational'. As a disposition, relational humility is a double move – of de-privileging myself epistemically by realizing our ignorance *while* privileging others. The heart of relational humility consists in such 'other-regard' in spite of and because of a realistic self-regard. The more sharply we realize what we know in the lighted patch, the more we are aware of how much we do not know; and along with this comes an awareness that there are others who can/do what we do not.

---

[26] J.N. Mohanty, 'Knowledge and Ignorance', in *Concepts of Knowledge: East and West* (Papers from a Seminar held in January, 1995) (Golpark, Kolkata, 2000), 213–222

[27] Ibid., 213

[28] The notion of ignorance as a positive state is a take on Advaita metaphysics. See K.C. Bhattacharya, 'Studies in Vedantism' and 'Fact and Thought of Fact' in *Studies in Philosophy* (ed.) Gopinath Bhattacharya (Delhi: Motilal Banarsidass, 1958).

From Good Knowers to Just Knowers in the *Mahābhārata*

Acknowledging the limits of knowledge does not always make space for other knowers. Classical scepticism is a case in point.[29] Also, Lorraine Code[30] shows how James Mill in writing *The History of British India* was ignorant of Indian languages and culture and was *aware* of his ignorance. But this 'conscious, self-congratulatory ignorance',[31] he believed, gave him the objectivity to understand India. In this instance, self-ascription of ignorance was augmenting of Mill's *own* epistemic agency rather than making room for the authority of others. In Mill's political space, colonial subjects did not even exist as viable Others whose archives, records and ways of knowing could be empowered through his self-ascription of ignorance. By contrast, Kauśika's acknowledgement of his lacks led him on a hunt for teachers who, he presumably believed, knew what he did not.

Kauśika's ignorance-infused relational humility therefore, introduces epistemic community. Self-ascription of ignorance becomes the heart of continued cognitive growth not simply by signaling the vast beyond yet to be known, but by introducing necessary interactions with others in order to know it. But what *kind* of a sociality is sustained by relational humility? Does it involve an awareness of the workings of epistemic power? Note that the marginal status of the housewife and butcher has done no conceptual work in our reading so far. Can humility help foreground an understanding and reworking of structural exclusions within a knowledge-community? Could one argue that Kauśika's epistemic 'other regard' involves a commitment to *justice*? These questions arise when feminists – whether virtue epistemologists or not – encounter Kauśika.

'Historicizing' Relational Humility

Kauśika's story clearly overturns entrenched epistemic hierarchies. Now typically knowledge tracks social power. Thus the re-distribution of cognitive power when the housewife and butcher are made superior to a *brāhmaṇa*, could in principle, trickle down to rectifying

---

[29]   See also Rae Langton's notion of *Kantian Humility*. Rae Langton, *Kantian Humility: Our Ignorance of Things in Themselves* (Oxford: Oxford University press, 1998).
[30]   Lorraine Code, 'The Power of Ignorance', in *Race and Epistemologies of Ignorance* (eds) Shannon Sullivan and Nancy Tuana (Albany: State University of New York Press, 2007), 213–229
[31]   Ibid., 215

socio-economic imbalances. But interestingly, the *Mahābhārata* curbs any such radical potential. Its protagonists speak of very conventional moral and social norms – the subservience to husbands, the adulation of *brāhmaṇas*, unwavering filial piety and a satisfaction with the social roles accorded to them. Kauśika's surprise at finding a knowledgeable person like the butcher at the fringes of society, is explained in the story, not through narratives of oppression and resistance, but through the transcendental theories of *karma* and rebirth (Vana Parvan, 215.21–31). But in spite of this, *could* the disposition of relational humility be deployed to 'socialize' knowledge in a thicker sense? Could it articulate an epistemic agency cognizant of power, even if it did not do so in the *Mahābhārata*?

The notion of a 'realistic assessment' at the core of relational humility affords a cue. Kauśika encountered where his knowledge ended. This was not a negation or under-estimation of his cognitive excellence, but rather a realistic 'non-overestimation' of it. This is a move of keeping our successes in perspective. Now, a *realistic* assessment of success signifies a context-sensitive evaluation that invariably has 'a deflationary effect on one's accomplishments'.[32] Social factors always contribute to success and are not *all* our own doings for which we can personally claim credit. Subjects are embedded in history. Their successes, therefore, are determined at least in part, by the privileges and limitations of their location, by their group membership and by the social positioning of these groups.

When a particular fifth-generation *brāhmaṇa* educator's son outshines a group of fifth generation sons and daughters of low cast butchers, how should the upper caste boy view his epistemic success? The advantages and disadvantages of the lad's location feeds his epistemic excellence. But to the extent such contingencies are contributing factors, they do not seem to be all *his* doings. Moreover, besides a sense of 'equity', this awareness introduces a sense of the co-implication of privilege and disadvantage. What privileges the upper caste boy is implicated in the failures of others. Thus understanding of his social luck is also an understanding of the *exclusions* required to maintain it. In this way, 'realistic' self-assessment understood in structural terms, can bring in the relationality of domination and oppression - the larger relational matrix within which individuals like Kauśika and the butcher are situated.

Interestingly, even when humility is materially grounded in this way, the play of ignorance and knowledge remains formally similar

---

[32] A.T. Nuyen, 'Just Modesty', *American Philosophical Quarterly* **35**(1) (1998): 101–109 (106)

to what we found in Kauśika. A relationally humble person now is one who realizes that he *could have been ignorant* had he not had the social advantages that he does. The *brāhmaṇa* boy might not have succeeded had he had only the opportunities available to the lower caste children. But to the extent that he grasps this fact, he also realizes that those others, who are now not accomplished, *could have easily been so* had they not been excluded from certain opportunities. Thus, the failure of the children at the social margins could well be due to their lack of access to epistemic resources. A subjunctive ascription of ignorance to ourselves now goes hand in hand with a subjunctive ascription of knowledge to others.

Ignorance here is not just a defect on the part of the knower but is 'a structural condition',[33] just as epistemic success is not 'individual' success but structurally enabled.

A 'realistic' assessment includes the imagination of a different distribution of socio-intellectual advantages and disadvantages, along with the unremarkableness of one's own achievements.

Note that such analysis of humility is not an 'unconcern' or 'inattention' to our own successes as Roberts and Wood would like to have it. Rather, in being a nuanced engagement with what success presupposes, it unearths inequalities in socio-epistemic space. Humility therefore, is not also motivated by the simple egalitarian evaluation of the equal worth of all humans (as suggested by Ben-Ze'ev).[34] Rather, it is based on realizing how much our achievements are a product of unearned social luck which makes us very unequal. This leads to a humble person behaving and relating to others in a specific manner – a way that de-emphasizes the importance of ones own accomplishments and foregrounds the possible achievements of others. Thus, in the contemporary taxonomy of theories of humility, the *Mahābhārata* seems to be espousing what is called a 'presentation view'[35] of the virtue.

There is a difference even here. On Scott Woodcock's version of the presentation theory, the humble behavior of de-emphasizing one's accomplishments while recognizing the epistemic agency of others, is partly due to 'caring that people not overestimate the magnitude

---

[33] Alcoff, Linda (2007) 'Epistemologies of Ignorance: Three Types', in *Race and Epistemologies of Ignorance* (ed.) Shannon Sullivan and Nancy Tuana (Albany: State University of New York Press, 2007), 56
[34] Aaron Ben-Ze'ev, 'The Virtue of Modesty', *American Philosophical Quarterly* **30**(3) (1993): 235–246.
[35] See Scott Woodcock, 'The Social Dimensions of Modesty', *Canadian Journal of Philosophy* **38**(1) (2008): 1–29.

or the importance of (their) natural talents'[36] and partly due to 'caring more about not jeopardizing the welfare of others'.[37] Woodcock locates the former condition as arising out of commitments to *justice* and the latter in a commitment to *beneficence*. Now relational humility, in not claiming credit for unjust privilege, is a sensitivity to ensuring justice through equity. But unlike Woodcock, the 'relationality' of humility is not simply abstaining from harming others or 'not jeopardizing' their welfare. It is, as we saw, positively empowering them as knowers. This move is not a matter of mere beneficence. A structural reading of relational humility makes clear that ensuring the knowerhood of those who have been hitherto disenfranchised by social luck is also a matter of *justice*. Receding oneself in order to foreground the epistemic status of others is not charity or benevolence but a rectificatory response to historically entrenched structural inequalities.

However, the awareness of power-knowledge in a relationally humble agent is not the *political will* to change an unjust system. There still remains a gap between relational humility (even when parsed in historicized terms) and the actual motivation for social reform. Are there resources in the virtue perspective of the *Mahābhārata* to make this transition? This is where shame may become helpful as an action propeller.

3. On Shame in Epistemic Contexts

Dipping further into Kausika's emotional profile reveals another cluster of emotions – remorse, contrition, self-censure, and guilt – which, following Jennifer Manion,[38] can be provisionally collated under the broad umbrella of *shame*.

Shame, for the most part, has had a bad press in Western moral psychology and rightly so. There is a lot of discussion on the debilitating and paralyzing aspects of shame[39] and on how it is used to

---

[36]   Ibid., 18

[37]   Ibid.

[38]   Manion, Jennifer, 'The Moral Relevance of Shame', *American Philosophical Quarterly* **39**(1) (2002), 73–79

[39]   Locke, Jill, 'Shame and the Future of Feminism', *Hypatia* **22**(4) (2007), 146–162; Christina Tarnopolsky, 'Prudes, Perverts, and Tyrants: Plato and the Contemporary Politics of Shame', *Political Theory* **32**(4) (August 2004), 468–494

violently police the borders of normality.[40] These refer to mechanisms of *shaming* a group (or individual) to make them conform or to break their resolve to resist. A Chinese student making a presentation in an American classroom may be silently made to feel ashamed of her accent in a way that damages her will to go to school. However, very different from this is a spontaneous shame that may arise in those who are in power and serve as an impetus for rectificatory action. In such forms, shame remains with us as 'a sign of our commitment to act, as a mark of the tension between the present and the future, as a touchstone for understanding what we expect to achieve and how'.[41]

I argue that shame in the *Mahābhārata,* can be constructive along similar lines. It emerges as a global disappointment at oneself for not having met an *ideal* – a form of self-censure through which we realize both what we have *not* done and also what our fundamental commitments are. Shame thus brings us in touch with who we are in contrast with who we want to be. In this sense, it is a reminder of the 'promises we keep to ourselves'.[42] And therein lies its motivational force.

Looking at Kauśika's self-censure, we first confront his lament about having killed the bird (the term used is *paryaśocata*[43] literally, 'felt deep remorse'). This is guilt for having violated the prohibition against rash and retaliatory behaviour towards unsuspecting subhumans. Kauśika expressed his personal acceptance of this norm through his self-description of the situation as *akāryam kritavānasmi*[44] meaning 'I have done what should not be done'. Towards the middle of the story, however, Kauśika is portrayed as experiencing a more globalised failure. The text sees him leaving the housewife's village with a *generalized* self-chastisement in the phrase '*vinindan sa svātmānam*' ('he especially berated himself'). The repetition of this phrase at the end of chapter 206 and in the beginning of chapter 207 in the Vana Parvan, hermeneutically indicates the importance of this non-specific, non-rule based self-censure or

[40]   Martha Nussbaum, *Hiding From Humanity: Disgust, Shame and the Law* (Princeton: Princeton University Press, 2004).

[41]   Berenice Fisher, 'Guilt and Shame in the Women's Movement: The Radical Idea of Action and Its Meaning for Feminist Intellectuals', *Feminist Studies* **10**(2) (Summer, 1984), 185–212. 188

[42]   Elspeth Probyn, *Blush: Faces of Shame* (Minneapolis: University of Minnesota Press, 2005), x

[43]   Vana Parvan 206.5

[44]   Ibid.

svātma-vinindā. But what is the intentional content of such self-chastisement arising in spite of our not being guilty of any specific act of wrong doing?

The capaciousness of shame whereby it can be felt in contexts not involving voluntary action (I can be ashamed of a birthmark, for example) makes possible a shame regarding our *history*. We have argued that Kauśika is made aware of the co-implication of privilege and oppression through a materially grounded humility. This easily spawns a sense of complicity in oppression. Such confessed complicity, can I suggest, trigger shame. The shame here is about a *past* that has given one unfair advantages through systemic exclusion of others - and our having allowed that order to exist. This is an embarrassment at having *failed to uphold the ideal* of equality and justice. The self-censure arising from being a beneficiary of injustices (past or current), indicates that we do *not want* to be such persons, that equality *matters* to us. Kauśika's shame could well be of this kind – a reminder of what is important for him and thereby, a source of motivation to work for rectification and change.

Of course, the narrative itself articulates Kauśika's shame in terms of ahistorical *personal* failures – his rage, pride, impatience and wrong-doing. It does not link it to any discomfort with injustice. But still one wonders whether there could be a gap between what the fictional Kauśika feels and what the text *says* he felt. Kauśika could well have *pre-discursively* (and viscerally) grasped the normativity of justice. 'Blushing', after all, as Elspeth Probyn says, 'is the *body* calling out its interest'[45] (my emphasis). A sensitive Kauśika's shame could well be registering his recoil at the unfairnesses around him. Even so, the *Mahābhārata's* authorial voice, in giving language to this emotion would 'domesticate' it, as it did. However, the point is that if shame is allowed to hold more content than what is consciously and linguistically available given the conceptual resources of the times, then it might well be the springs for reform in a conservative society. This, in spite of the fact that our Kauśika was sadly not such a champion of reform.

That said, resources elsewhere in the *Mahābhārata* surprisingly go a long way to support shame both as a possible motivator for social change and its working as an intellectual virtue.

---

[45]   Elspeth Probyn, *Blush*. 28

From Good Knowers to Just Knowers in the *Mahābhārata*

Shame as an Intellectual Virtue

A Sanskrit cognate for 'shame' in the *Mahābhārata* is *hrī*. *Hrī* occurs in the list of the thirteen 'Ways of Truth' discussed earlier, and hence comes clearly marked as an *intellectual virtue*. Elsewhere in the epic, commentators explain it with the more familiar word, *lajjā*.[46] We come across a fascinatingly odd explication of *lajjā*/*hrī*/shame. *Hrī* is 'doing good/ensuring welfare' (*kalyāṇam kurute*) but 'without gloom' (*na glāyate*) (Śānti Parvan 162.15) But given that shame is squarely an intellectual virtue, there must also be a connection between seeking *truth* and doing good/ensuring welfare. Unearthing these links explains how a 'virtue of truth' transitions into a 'virtue of justice'.

First, the *Mahābhārata* is careful to regulate self-censure associated with shame as a *mean* between the hopelessness of 'traumatic shame'[47] on the one hand, and a smug shirking of responsibility to intervene, on the other. Confronting inequality can result in such extreme self-rebuke for failing the ideal of justice, that the very ideal one fell short of is itself jettisoned. This is the paralyzing *glāni* of hopelessness that makes action seem pointless. On the other hand, experience of inequality can lead to a 'it's-not-my-fault' sort of disengagement such that no action on my part is even called for. An intelligent response to injustice – the response of a *dhīmān* (thinking being) – acknowledges our share of responsibility for injustice but warns against a self-indulgent hopelessness (*na glāyate*). Shame, in the *Mahābhārata*, therefore, leads to a *will* to do better at living up to the ideal we have currently failed – a will to 'do good for others' (*kalyāṇam kurute*). If a historicized humility makes us recognize our complicity in injustice, the consequent shame impels us to try and reverse the inequalities.

---

[46] The *BhagvadGītā* in 16.2 lists 'divine excellences' (*daivī sampad*) which includes *hrī*. Samkara's commentary glosses *hrī* as *lajjā*. The commentarial elucidation of the term explains it as a disposition of self-chastisement that helps us desist from repeating bad actions. An alternative exposition claims it to be a mindfulness of the public eye (*lokalajjā*) that stops us in our tracks as it were if we happen to have embarked on the path of something unsavory. Shame is thus a self-disciplinary disposition based on internalization of public norms. In both instances, shame is linked to the possibilities and regulation of action.

[47] Kathleen Woodward, 'Traumatic Shame: Toni Morrison, Television Culture, and the Cultural Politics of the Emotions', *Cultural Critique* **46** (Autumn, 2000), 210–240

Vrinda Dalmiya

However, two questions come to the fore immediately. First, is not the disposition to 'do good for others' a motivation of beneficence after all, and not one of justice? Second, why is shame defined in terms of such a motivation a 'way of *truth*'? Both questions can be answered together if we realize that (i) the disposition to feel shame is consciously intertwined with the desire to *equalize* (called *samatā*) and (ii) *samatā* is explicitly marked as an intellectual virtue occurring in the same list of Ways/Forms of truth that includes *hrī* or shame. Thus, shame in the epic targets both eliminating inequality and achieving epistemic excellence. *How* this can be possible becomes clear from the textual analysis of *samatā* itself.

Samatā, in the *Mahābhārata*, as the *practice* of equality is not re-iterating a metaphysical sameness. In fact, it is the normative constraint of treating *as if equal* those who are *not* naturally on a par. The four categories that one ought to 'equalize' are:

(1)   myself (*ātma*),
(2)   those who please me, in other words my friends and family (*iṣṭa*),
(3)   those who do not please me (*aniṣṭa*), and
(4)   those I hate, like my enemies (*ripu*)

Such a practice thus involves curbing our natural likes and dislikes and treating these four groups impartially. The epistemological potential of this is obvious for it can be a gesture towards controlling bias – both positive and negative. Accordingly, to 'equalize' would amount to withholding doxastic favors for the views of oneself and one's friends, while also extending sympathetic consideration to the views of one's opponents and strangers. Such impartiality is an attempt to position radical others and even those I actively do not like or agree with, as being as important as myself in a knowledge community. The seriousness with which we take ourselves and our own views, is thereby extended to many different groups in an attempt to move beyond the 'we' of same-sayers.

On a general level, this counters a shame-*less*-ness which is making exceptions for oneself, a smugness that feels superciliously *unequal* to (i.e., better than) others. A shame-*less* person has no sense of failing and no need to self-correct or reconsider. Would Socrates' *elenchus*, for example, work if his interlocutors did not have the virtue of *being ready to be ashamed of their own inconsistency* once it was pointed out to them? Shame then, becomes a corrective to self-exceptionalism and the practice of *samatā* operationalizes this in inquiry. As an epistemic virtue, shame is the quiet confidence to 'make' others equal to us so that our views can be tested against theirs.

Thus, it is a way of avoiding dogmatism and a form of epistemic 'doing good'.

It can now be objected that the 'equality' spoken of here is, after all, confined to equal representation in discursive space. *Kalyāṇam* (welfare) associated with a shame emerging from a historicized relational humility should be the activity of trying to redress social injustice. But when intertwined with *samatā* it becomes parsed as the practice of addressing inequalities in epistemic space. Isn't this too narrow a response? Not necessarily. Once we realize that dialogue and debate are necessary conditions for justice, and any rectificatory move can be easily tinged with paternalistic beneficence if the equal right to think, reason and critique is not granted to those for whom we are attempting to secure equal opportunities. Equality in epistemic space is therefore, necessary for robust political change. Because of this, the three dispositions – humility, shame and equalizing – hang together in a startling echo of the feminist philosopher, Naomi Scheman's, slogan: 'If you want truth, fight for justice'.[48] Now we begin to see how the fight for justice brings truth in tow because it involves epistemic virtuosity. Ultimately then, good knowers cannot just be knowers. They must strive for a just community of knowers in order to be *just* knowers.

Conclusion

To conclude, what we find here is a conceptual cartography involving humility, shame, action/practice, knowledge and a richer notion of truth. This map is drawn from conceptual resources of the *Mahābhārata* and used for contemporary purposes, even though the epic itself navigated the terrain differently. I have argued with contemporary theories of knowledge that we must shift the focus of epistemology from knowledge to the knower; but then, I have gone along with the *Mahābhārata*, to require a good knower to be a relationally humble and socially responsible agent. Am I changing the subject of epistemology here by redefining epistemic excellence and its target truth by virtues ranging from equality to shame? I have tried to show that the new *Mahābhārata*-inspired epistemology that is being envisaged here would still remain about the subject (knower) and the object (truth) of knowledge. But unlike the

---

[48] Naomi Scheman, 'Epistemology Resuscitated: Objectivity as Trustworthiness' in Nancy Tuana and Sandra Morgen (eds) *Engendering Rationalities* (Albany: State University of New York Press, 2001), 23–52 (38).

politically oblivious, theoretically sharp, arrogantly self-confident 'Scientist', the ideal knower would be a self-doubting, active seeker of one's own cognitive limitations. Such a paradigmatic knower would also be a caring, concerned seeker of justice. The subject will have to change after all.[49]

University of Hawaii
vrinda@hawaii.edu

[49] Thanks to audiences in London, Singapore and Shimla for comments. Also to Arindam Chakrabarti.

Analytic Philosophy and its Synoptic Commission: Towards the Epistemic End of Days

FRASER MACBRIDE

Abstract

There is no such thing as 'analytic philosophy', conceived as a special discipline with its own distinctive subject matter or peculiar method. But there is an analytic task for philosophy that distinguishes it from other reflective pursuits, a *global* or *synoptic* commission: to establish whether the final outputs of other disciplines and common sense can be fused into a single periscopic vision of the Universe. And there is the hard-won insight that thought and language aren't transparent but stand in need of analysis – a recent variation upon the abiding philosophical theme that we need to get behind appearances to tell the ultimate truth about reality – an insight that threatens to be lost once philosophers appeal to intuitions.

1. Introduction

What is analytic philosophy? It doesn't have a subject matter to call its own. You can get analytic about more or less anything. So there's no circumscribed list of things that analytic philosophy is really about as opposed to things it really isn't. If it's about anything it's about everything. And despite its name, analytic philosophy has no distinctive method either. Not all analytic philosophers commit themselves to a programme of analysis, whether of language or thought, and even if they do what they have in mind to do is often very different. Some analytic philosophers make it their business to analyse words and phrases of the languages we already speak whilst others dedicate themselves to inventing new languages that improve upon the old ones. When we stand back and really look at it, there seems nothing to constrain our enquiries, curb our excesses. Like Kurtz in Joseph Conrad's *Heart of Darkness* – upstream, beyond civilizing influences – analytic philosophy, or so it appears, 'takes place in an impalpable greyness, with nothing underfoot, with nothing around, without spectators, without clamour, without glory, without the great desire of victory, without the great fear of defeat, in a sickly atmosphere of tepid scepticism, without much belief in your own right, and still less in that of your adversary'. As Marlow,

doi:10.1017/S1358246114000095

the narrator of *Heart of Darkness*, reflects 'If such is the form of ultimate wisdom, then life is a greater riddle than some of us think it to be'. No wonder Kurtz cried out before he expired, 'The horror! The horror!'

Analytic philosophers are confronted by a cultural predicament. Society is impatient with them whilst they are impatient with each other. Everybody wants something palpable to reach out and touch, nobody wants to be awash in a sea of grey scepticism, but analytic philosophers have been unable to supply solid, definitive answers. This impatience has its source in a misconception about philosophy itself, about what it can be expected to have achieved at this point in history, an impatience no doubt fuelled by the demands of late capitalism that lead us to expect rapid results.

2. Cutting the Analytic Knot

Lacking a distinctive subject matter or peculiar method to distinguish them, how can analytic philosophers pick one another out in the crowd when philosophers of all different stripes are jumbled together? If analytic philosophy lacks a matter or a method of its own why bother calling a philosopher analytic at all? You'll knock your head out trying to answer that question if what you're after is some strict definition, in terms of some essential, proprietary feature, for being an analytic philosopher. This makes appealing the suggestion that analytic philosophers resemble one another as the members of a family often do, by virtue of different features overlapping and criss-crossing, even if they don't all have the same nose. A related suggestion is that analytic philosophers share a common ancestry or common influences that allow us to establish an especial, albeit indirect relationship between them even if they diverge in other respects.[1] But the fabric of history is too close knit. The overlapping threads of similarity and influence pull in too many directions.

We need to take seriously the possibility that there is no such thing as analytic philosophy or such a thing as being an analytic philosopher. The beginning of the analytic period is usually identified as

[1] See P.M.S. Hacker, *Wittgenstein's Place in Twentieth Century Analytic Philosophy*, (Oxford Blackwell), 4–5, Hans Sluga, 'What Has History to Do with Me: Wittgenstein and Analytic Philosophy', *Inquiry* **41** (1998), 99–121, 107 and, for a more thoroughgoing development of these ideas, Hans-Johann Glock, *What is Analytic Philosophy?* (Cambridge: Cambridge University Press, 2008), 204–30

coinciding with the decline of idealism and the rise of Moore and Russell's realist philosophy at the end of the 19th century and continuing until the present day. And indeed it's true that there are schools and movements, such as logical positivism and ordinary language philosophy, that can be identified as having emerged during this period and for certain purposes it can be enlightening to track their vicissitudes – although even in such favourable cases when we begin to look more closely what we discover is less of a school and more of a shoal. But what unity there is to be found of shared or overlapping presuppositions amongst these different schools is too diffuse to support significant historical speculation or explanation.

Here is a case of overlapping and criss-crossing in point. Even Moore and Russell shared many of their presuppositions with their idealist predecessors. Even though they were realists, Moore and Russell were only following in the footsteps of their idealist archrival, F.H. Bradley, when they set about analysing relational complexes of the form aRb, complexes wherein one thing is related to another, such as the fact that the cat is to the right of the mouse or the fact that this proton is more massive than that electron. Like Moore and Russell, Bradley had presupposed that an analysis of such a complex would reveal it to consist of two things (a, b) and the relation (R) that holds between them. But he could see no way of explaining how these diverse constituents could be put back together to form a unified complex or fact. It's not enough that they exist because that furnishes no guarantee that they actually embrace to form a complex. So it appears that to restore the unity of the complex (aRb) which analysis destroyed, the relation (R) must itself be *related* to the things (a, b) it was supposed to relate. But this would appear to require a *new* connecting relation (R^*) to relate the relation (R) to the things it relates, a new relation about which the same questions can be raised as the old. It is not enough that the new relation exist; it (R^*) must itself be *related* to the old relation (R) and the things (a, b) the old relation was originally supposed to relate. Bradley inferred that if we employ the machinery of things and relations we can't avoid being hurried off 'into the eddy of a hopeless process, since we are forced to go on finding new relations without end.'[2] But Bradley was no less convinced that discursive thought inevitably employs the machinery of things and relations; we cannot avoid carving up the world that comes to us in terms of

---

[2]   See F.H. Bradley, *Appearance and Reality* (Oxford: Clarendon Press, 1897), 28, and 'Relations', in his *Collected Essays: Vol. II*, (Oxford: Clarendon Press, 1935), 630–76, 643

things that are *adjacent* to one another or *inside* one another, or events where one is *before* another, or one *causes* the other, and so on. So Bradley concluded that discursive thought must inevitably mislead us about the true character of reality because the very idea of a relation – the idea of something whose function it is to relate – is 'unintelligible'.

Russell found himself in exactly the same predicament, unable to account for the unity of relational complexes: 'when analysis has destroyed the unity' of a complex, Russell wrote, 'no enumeration of the constituents will restore' it.[3] He saw that the unity of a complex must somehow arise from the distinction between a relation that succeeds in relating the things it relates and a relation that does not; nonetheless, as Russell openly admitted, 'I do not know how to give a clear account of the precise nature of the distinction', of how it was possible for a relation to fulfil its proper function to relate. Where Russell differed from Bradley was with respect to the intelligibility of relational thought. Whilst Bradley denied it, because of where his argument had led him, Russell saw the absurdity of rejecting the intelligibility of all our thoughts about space, time and causation that constitute the larger part of science. So rather than deny the intelligibility of science, Russell preferred to live with the mystery of how relations fulfil their proper function: 'Even if I could see no way of answering the objections to relations raised (for example) by Mr. Bradley, I should still think it more likely than not that some answer was possible, because I should think an error in a very subtle and abstract argument more probable than so fundamental a falsehood in science'.[4] So where Bradley had taken a modus ponens Russell took a modus tollens instead but the analyses they evoked were the same.

Evidently the pre-analytic period didn't give way to the analytic as the Cretaceous to the Jurassic. When *our* history comes to be written it may even turn out that we have more in common with our predecessors than our successors. Whereas philosophers since Russell have conspicuously failed to supply an intellectually robust account of how relations fulfil their proper function, perhaps our successors may succeed.[5] Of course this doesn't preclude our describing

***

[3]   See Bertrand Russell *The Principles of Mathematics* (Cambridge: Cambridge University Press, 1903), §54

[4]   See Bertrand Russell 'Logical Atomism' in J.H. Muirhead (ed.) *Contemporary British Philosophy* (London: George Allen & Unwin, 1924), 359–83, 378

[5]   Witness the failure of recent attempts to use modern truthmaker technology to account for the proper function of relations. See Fraser MacBride

someone as an analytic philosopher in a loose and popular sense, as someone whose ideas and arguments are influenced by the work of one or other of the historical figures that as a matter of common practice it's become routine to describe as analytic.

3. Confessions of an Analytic Philosopher

In the loose and popular sense I am an analytic philosopher. The philosophers that have influenced me include prominent figures from the analytic pantheon: Moore, Russell, Wittgenstein, Quine, Davidson and Sellars. I cannot speak on behalf of other analytic philosophers today because there is no established peace amongst us. But the vision of philosophy that I hold true, which owes most to these great figures, isn't idiosyncratic.

I believe we are embodied creatures, occupants of an extended Universe of space and time that sweeps away before us. We share this Universe with an enormous number of other things, of one kind or another, standing in an extraordinary variety of relationships.[6] I believe that there are better and worse ways for us to be orientated towards this Universe and towards each other – to think rigorously about the Universe and its denizens rather than fallaciously, to be erudite rather than ignorant, to behave well towards our fellow beings rather than badly. I believe it is possible to secure by reflection an understanding of what makes for a better rather than worse orientation. I also believe that it is possible to achieve by this route an understanding of how we may re-orientate ourselves towards the Universe and to each other to improve our situation. The task of acquiring such reflective understanding is one of theory construction. It is by constructing theories of what makes for a better (rather than worse) orientation and evaluating them that we are able to edge closer to understanding, whether theoretical or practical.

We rely perforce upon language to provide a medium within which to frame our theories – because of their subject matter they're too difficult to get into heads and keep there – and to enable us to lay the results of our cogitations before the tribunal of others. I also

'Relations and truthmaking', *Proceedings of the Aristotelian Society* **111** (2011), 161–79

[6] See G.E. Moore's 1910 lecture, 'What is Philosophy?' in his *Some Main Problems of Philosophy* (London: George Allen & Unwin, 1953), 1–27

believe that the practice of analyzing the meanings of the words and phrases we use to construct our theories plays an exigent role in enabling us to achieve an understanding of what our theories are about. If we don't know what our words or phrases mean then we can't know what claim we're making about the world when we use them – we can't trust ourselves to have control over what we're saying. Nor can we have confidence that what one theory says that makes use of these words or phrases is better (or worse) than what another theory says. So don't trust philosophers who insist that they aren't interested in words but only the world (an unfortunate tendency amongst contemporary metaphysicians). If they don't get their words right they'll likely get the world wrong – and lead the rest of us on a merry goose chase.

It is not a consequence of these remarks that the provision of a systematic account of the meanings of our words and phrases need be the foundation for all the rest of philosophy. Nor does it follow that we cannot think discursively about the world without saying so – that language enjoys priority over thought.[7] To achieve world understanding theory construction is the game and theories need to be written down if creatures like us are to appreciate them. But what we mean by our uses of words and phrases when we construct a theory is often no more available for immediate comprehension than what we think is available for transient introspection. Distrust in the doctrine that minds are transparent to themselves has been a recurrent theme of twentieth century philosophy. The suspicion that languages aren't transparent to their speakers either, and stand in need of analysis if we're not to be misled, belongs to the same influential family of *diaporeses*.

The view that the meaning of a natural kind term (say 'tiger') is determined by pointing at worldly specimens provides one reason for being doubtful that the meanings of words are invariably available for immediate comprehension – because if you don't know what the specimens are you won't be able to fathom from the text what

---

[7] Michael Dummett advanced both of these theses. See his 'Can Analytical Philosophy be Systematic and Ought it to Be?' in *Truth & Other Enigmas*, London: Gerald Duckworth & Co, 1978) 437–58, 441–2. Whilst I deny that a systematic theory of meaning need be conceived as a foundation for all the rest of philosophy, Dummett is entirely right that the production of such a theory, *if there is such a thing to be had*, would not only be a formidable intellectual achievement, but the theory itself would furnish an extraordinarily useful resource for enabling future philosophical research (for reasons that will become clear in the succeeding two paragraphs). I'd be straight online to buy one!

the terms mean. But even a word whose meaning isn't determined by invoking worldly specimens has the potential to bear a significance that comes as a surprise even to its inventors.

The meaning of a word is determined by the contribution that it makes to the different contexts in which it occurs. But, as ordinary speakers of a language, we lack reflective oversight of all the different contexts in which a word occurs – all the different ways in which it is capable of combining with other kinds of expressions.[8] As a consequence we are liable to misconceive the significance or function of a word when we venture an opinion off the cuff. This needn't jeopardize the practical use of language for ordinary transactions because our competent deployment of the expression may be otherwise unimpaired. But when we have before us a theory of the Universe and our orientation towards its constituents, it may make a critical difference to the success of the theory what function the word performs in enabling us to say something; whether, for example, the contribution of the word in question is to pick out a constituent of the Universe, or to perform one or another of a heterogeneous range of other functions, for example, to describe what the constituents of the Universe are like or to logically unite different claims into a single complex statement. So when we come to construct theories about what makes for a better (rather than worse) orientation to the Universe we can hardly neglect the task of scrupulously attending to the analyses – that facilitate reflective oversight – of the words and phrases we use to frame and convey what we deem to be our insights.

There is a sense in which the special disciplines (the sciences, humanities and others) can all be characterized as seeking to develop an understanding of what makes for a better rather than worse orientation *but only within their own chosen fields* – continually reflecting upon the aims and criteria proper to a discipline and updating them. Common sense represents the first proto-reflective efforts of the human species to construct a theory whose network of hypotheses, now embedded in ordinary language, would enable us to systematically understand and control the world surrounding us. This means common sense too can be characterized as the output of a (primordial and long-haul) effort to understand what makes for a better rather than worse orientation towards the world and each other. What distinguishes philosophy from these other reflective or

***

[8]   See Ludwig Wittgenstein, *Tractatus Logico-Philosophicus* (translated by C.K. Ogden with an introduction by B. Russell. London: Routledge & Kegan Paul, 1922), 4.002

proto-reflective pursuits is the *global* or *synoptic* character of its commission.[9] To philosophy falls the ultimate question: When does one orientation towards the Universe constitute an improvement upon another? We cannot begin to answer it until we have at least provisional answers to other questions that require us to occupy scarcely less cloud-capt an outlook: What kinds of thing inhabit the Universe? What distinguishes us amongst them? How are these various kinds of thing related to one another? But these questions cannot receive their definitive answers until the other disciplines that investigate the Universe *from all their different points of view* have completed their labours. So whilst it is continuous with common sense and all the other reflective disciplines, an especial eschatological burden is destined to fall to philosophy: to establish whether, or to what extent, the final outputs of physics, mathematics, psychology, political science and all the other special disciplines can be fused with common sense into one single periscopic vision of the Universe.

We cannot tell from our vantage point in history whether such a periscopic vision is possible. There may be no integrating the final outputs of the different disciplines and what common sense says. What can be said truly about the Universe may consist just in their loose assemblage – about such radically different items as numbers, duties, conscious experiences and neural firings. It is possible that what prevents our now seeing how these apparently categorically different items may be significantly assimilated is a combination of scientific ignorance and conceptual prejudices of which we are barely aware. Future scientific developments may not only dispel the factual ignorance that currently blinkers us but also help to bring such conceptual prejudices to light and lead us to abandon them in favour of novel forms of thinking – as for example, 19th century developments in the mathematics of the infinite revealed to be a prejudice the Aristotelian principle that a whole is invariably larger than any of its parts, a principle mathematicians and philosophers subsequently gave up.[10] But Aristotle couldn't have seen that one coming nor can we foresee when such conceptual developments necessitated by the progress of science will overtake us.

---

[9] See Wilfrid Sellars, 'Philosophy and the Scientific Image of Man' in his *Science, Perception and Reality* (London: Routledge & Kegan Paul, 1963), 1–40

[10] See Richard Dedekind, *Essays on the Theory of Numbers* (edited and translated by W.W. Beman, Chicago: Open Court Publishing Company, 1901), sec. v

Of course this does nothing to diminish the contemporary significance of philosophy for serving the progress of human knowledge by endeavouring to hasten the Epistemic End of Days, which means exposing relevant distinctions and connections, making explicit what has hitherto been implicit, elucidating what was previously taken for granted, seeking system and coherence amongst the myriad answers that the different disciplines have provisionally supplied to their proprietary questions.

4. Why is philosophy so difficult?

Kant famously declared in the *Critique of Pure Reason* (1787) that it 'remains a scandal to philosophy and human reason in general that the existence of things outside us must be accepted merely on *faith* [...] and that if anyone thinks good to doubt their existence we are unable to counter his doubts by any satisfactory proof'.[11] Over two centuries later it appears even more of a scandal to philosophy that we can't even be sure that we'd recognize a satisfactory proof of the external world if we saw one!

This is especially embarrassing for analytic philosophy (in the loose and popular sense) since the twentieth century endured more meta-philosophical soul searching than any other era of human history. Even the giants amongst us have been unable to furnish our subject with generally accepted methods of enquiry whereby results may be accepted or rejected according to commonly accepted criteria. It's not for want of trying. Quine tried to resolve philosophical problems by formalizing problematic ordinary language sentences in the language of logic. Strawson tried to resolve them by translating them back again into ordinary language. The successive failures of repeated efforts to set philosophy upon the path to convergence tempted others to a pessimistic induction, to conclude that philosophy keeps failing to achieve concessive results because it isn't about seeking the truth or stating the facts; philosophy bears some other kind of self-expressive significance, a form of conceptual poetry or the expression of obsessional doubts that require quasi-psychoanalytic treatment.[12] But these ideas didn't stick either.

[11] See Immanuel Kant, *The Critique of Pure Reason* (translated by N. Kemp Smith. London: Macmillan, 1929), Bxl.

[12] Compare W.V.O. Quine, *Word & Object* (Cambridge Mass.: MIT Press, 1960), 260–1, P.F. Strawson, 'Carnap's Views on Constructed Systems vs Natural Languages in Analytic Philosophy' in P. Schillp (ed.)

The historical contrast between the development of philosophy and the mature sciences is difficult to ignore. The sciences progress by incorporating the insights of preceding theories into the more expansive theories that succeed them – as, for example, the insights of wave optics were incorporated into electromagnetism. But philosophers have typically preferred a Sisyphean strategy, starting afresh as each generation declared a new dawn, each original philosopher seeing her task to begin again from the beginning. Analytic philosophers often reassure us that it really will be different this time because modern developments in mathematical logic, most conspicuously Frege's resolution of the logic of generality using the quantifier-variable notation, will lend to philosophy some of the exactitude and certainty of mathematics, enabling us to establish results that can be accepted as definitive by subsequent philosophers and used as a basis for further investigation.[13] But even if God was able to create the world *ex nihilo*, we can't prove something from nothing. We always need to assume something else, even if we usually take this something else for granted because it's embedded in the rules of proof of the system we're using or how we apply them. Whether the techniques of mathematical logic will help stop the ball rolling back down the hill tomorrow remains to be seen.

What makes it so difficult to achieve a knowledgeable consensus in philosophy? This sounds like a substantial question but Russell, at one point, suggested that it isn't. He held that the mark of a philosophical problem is simply the fact that it has hitherto resisted solution by established means: 'I believe that the only difference between science and philosophy is, that science is what you more or less know and philosophy is what you do not know. Philosophy is that part of science which at present people choose to have opinions about, but which they have no knowledge about'.[14] By Russell's lights the

---

The Philosophy of Rudolf Carnap, Library of Living Philosophers, Vol. XI (La Salle, Il.: Open Court, 1963), 503–18, 512–3, and Richard Rorty, *Consequences of Pragmatism* (Minneapolis: Minnesota University Press, 1982), xiii–xiv

[13] See Bertrand Russell, 'On Scientific Method in Philosophy' in his *Mysticism and Logic* (New York: Longmans, Green & Co. 1918), 96–120, and, for a more recent call to logico-mathematical arms, see Timothy Williamson, 'Must Do Better' in P. Greenough & M. Lynch *Truth & Realism* (Oxford: Oxford University Press), 177–187.

[14] See B. Russell, 'Lectures on the Philosophy of Logical Atomism (1918–1919)' reprinted in his *Logic and Knowledge: Essays 1901–1950*, edited by R.C. Marsh (London: George Allen & Unwin, 1956), 177–281,

achievement of knowledgeable consensus deprives philosophy of the problems that previously consumed it, bequeathing them to science as soon as they become tractable. But Russell's suggestion about how to demarcate philosophy from science, whatever other attractions or flaws it may have, sheds no light whatsoever upon the deeper and more puzzling issue that remains. What is it about the problems with which philosophers have perennially concerned themselves – about rationality, knowledge, duty and all the rest – that has kept these problems so firmly rooted on the unknown side of the line, kept them philosophical in Russell's sense?

What makes these problems so resilient is the fact that they are general and pluriform. We cannot expect them to receive a definitive resolution until the Epistemic End of Days. There is no saying what makes an orientation towards the Universe rational or knowledgeable or morally commendable without having a grasp of the copious variety of different acts that count as such, an appreciation of the character of the agents that perform them and a digest of the polymorphic objects to which they are directed. But we cannot acquire such pervasive understanding without relying upon our grasp of other concepts that may also turn out to be problematic and drawing upon the results of other disciplines. And we don't know in advance what other questions will be thrown up by future developments within these disciplines or by the efforts of philosophers to integrate them into a unified scheme. But this isn't a scandal to philosophy. It's a consequence of the encompassing and compounding character of the problems with which philosophy deals that their resolution requires of us a synoptic understanding. Because we cannot foresee completely what discoveries the special disciplines will make, what conceptual hurdles we will have to overcome, what hitherto prized intellectual possessions will need to be abandoned along the wayside, what unprecedented questions will need to be answered, we cannot expect to establish a method today that will be guaranteed to work to the satisfaction of everyone tomorrow. We cannot expect progress in philosophy to be linear because until the Epistemic End of Days the problems of philosophy will remain open ended in a manner that surpasses any other discipline - because philosophy is the discipline that's ultimately there for the sake of putting the rest together.

---

281. Originally published in *The Monist* **XXVIII** (1918), 495–527, **XXIX** (1919), 32–63, 190–222, 345–80

Fraser MacBride

5. Why does history matter to analytic philosophy?

Philosophy is an ultra-speculative discipline so it should come as no surprise that the history of philosophy has been a haphazard one. This doesn't mean that the history of philosophy isn't worth reading, that it's just a compendium of errors and confusions. Original philosophers have always made bold and arresting hypotheses that have contributed, one way or another, to the body or to the organization of human knowledge. Russell's theory of descriptions was especially significant for the development of analytic philosophy because it showed how the logical significance of a sentence might be belied by its superficial grammatical appearance; hence the praise that Russell won from Wittgenstein, 'Russell's merit is to have shown that the apparent logical form of the proposition need not be its real form'.[15] Analytic philosophers and theoretical linguists have subsequently built upon this insight.

Of course there are errors and confusions to be found in the works of historical philosophers too; but more what we discover are thinkers that have expanded or elaborated upon their systems until they have pushed against the intelligible boundaries of speculation, to a point where we can no longer comfortably follow them. This is exactly what we should expect of the great figures of such an ultra-speculative discipline. And it's what makes them worthwhile for us to study. Because philosophy is so speculative – because we lack the established methodology of a mature science to ensure cumulative progression – we cannot expect to have superseded the contributions of our predecessors. For all we know their views may lie closer to the truth in important respects than our own. Our business as philosophers remains to speculate because that is how philosophy contributes to the development of human knowledge. By studying the philosophers of the past we enable and refine and inspire speculations of our own. It may even be the case that because their world-views were less cluttered and confused by the hyperbolic development of other disciplines, philosophers of the past came closer than we have done to attaining the synoptic perspective that constitutes the End of philosophy. Similarly Shakespeare belonged to a time simpler than our own but so far from this rendering his works obsolete their uncluttered character contributes to the especial lucidity of his insights into human nature.

Recognizing that philosophy is ultra-speculative so the works of the great philosophers don't have a definite use-by date doesn't

---

[15]   Op. cit., note 5, 4.0031

232

require us to have confidence in what has been called the 'analytic history of philosophy' – the view which Williams characterized as 'encouraging us to read something written by Plato as though it had come out in *Mind* last month'.[16] Williams is rightly wary of a Whig view of history whereby philosophy has now progressed out of darkness into the light to acquire what is now a definitive list of questions for philosophers to answer and techniques for answering them. He's right that there is no such list available to us. But once we recognize that the articles that appeared in *Mind* last month are just further contributions to a form of ultra-speculative enquiry for which there is no established scientific methodology there should be no objection to reading one of Plato's dialogues alongside them. Williams recounts with approval a passage from Collingwood's autobiography in which Collingwood casts scorn upon the ridiculous view that because 'δει' in Greek is translated by 'ought' in English, Greek ethics and Kantian theories of moral obligation must be about the same thing: 'It was like having a nightmare about a man who had got it into his head that τριηρης was the Greek for "steamer", and when it was pointed out to him that descriptions of triremes in Greek writes were at any rate not very good descriptions of steamers, replied triumphantly, "That's just what I say. These Greek philosophers ... were terribly muddle-headed and their theory of steamers is all wrong"'.[17] But it doesn't follow from the fact that ancient philosophers differed from us with respect to some normative projects that they didn't share *at a deep level* some of our concerns. Otherwise we would be unable to interpret the corpus of ancient writings as featuring philosophical arguments in the first place. It is this shared background that makes it still possible for Plato to share his extraordinarily fruitful speculations with us.

Understanding that philosophy is ultra-speculative not only helps guard us against the 'analytic history of philosophy' Williams dismisses. If philosophical progress cannot be expected to be linear then even present day philosophers cannot be expected to be the generation that succeeded where earlier generations failed. Knowledge of the history of philosophy can often perform a useful role in enabling us to recognize when the maneuvers undertaken by present-day philosophers are regressive. This is possible because it is sometimes the case that our predecessors were ahead of us.

[16]   See Bernard Williams, 'Philosophy as a Humanistic Discipline', *Philosophy* **75**, 477–96, 478

[17]   See R.G. Collingwood, *An Autobiography* (Oxford: Oxford University Press, 1939), 64

It has been an abiding insight of analytic philosophy that thought and language aren't transparent, don't wear their significance upon their sleeves, but stand in need of analysis – a recent variation upon the recurrent philosophical theme that we need to get behind appearances to tell the ultimate truth about reality. But Kripke's celebrated remarks about essentialism rely for their effectiveness upon our relinquishing this hard-won insight. In his lectures on naming and necessity, Kripke invited us to consider whether a given table, composed of molecules, could be this very table without being composed of molecules. Kripke didn't offer an argument one way or another. Instead he introspected before reporting back to us: 'Certainly there is some feeling that the answer to that must be 'no'. At any rate, it's hard to imagine under what circumstances you would have this very object and find that it is not composed of molecules'.[18] Later in his lectures, Kripke invited us to consider whether a given person could have originated from a different sperm and egg. Again it was the results of introspective psychology that supplied Kripke with his answer: 'It seems to me that anything coming from a different origin would not be this object'.[19] On this basis Kripke concluded that material objects must have their origins essentially. But it cannot be assumed that the beliefs made available for immediate introspection, or the linguistic embodiments that we use to express them, wear their significance on their sleeves.

Our intuitions may come easily to us - we may be able to blurt them out without having to think too hard. But it hardly follows that such beliefs enjoy some privileged epistemological status that entitles us to derive from them substantial conclusions about the antics of material objects outside of us. Whatever these judgments *mean* – and that remains to be established – any number of contributory factors may be responsible for holding them psychologically in place, factors that have no especial connection to their veracity. It is only when we have investigated the sustaining factors that surround these beliefs that we will be entitled to draw conclusions about essentialism from their occurrence. Because Kripke willfully refrained from such an investigation his approach was regressive.

Of course there are cases in which it is reasonable to suppose that there is a reliable connection between the intuitions of an ordinary subject and the subject matter at hand. The clearest example of this concerns the grammar of natural language. People's intuitions about what combinations of words are grammatical are partially

[18] See Saul Kripke, *Naming and Necessity* (Oxford: Blackwell, 1980), 47
[19] Op. cit., note 13, 113

constitutive of the very language they speak. Their spontaneous reactions to combinations of words tells us something about the structure of the practical ability speakers of a given language share. Ultimately if we do not share the grammatical intuitions of other speakers we recognize that they speak a different dialect from us. It is for this reason that linguists take the intuitions of ordinary speakers with maximal seriousness. But things that exist outside of us don't have this kind of constitutive connection to our assured beliefs about them. So there is no especial reason to think that the intuitions that are readily elicited from ordinary subjects about the essences of material objects are reliable indicators concerning whether material objects have their constitutions or origins essentially.

Russell and Quine already understood that even our most assured and unreflective beliefs cannot be taken for granted. They recognized that thought and language aren't transparent so even here there is a pressing question of appearance and reality; but a significant minority of subsequent philosophers following Kripke have evidently forgotten. Russell and Quine knew that our most keenly felt common sense convictions about the ordinary things that we encounter in our immediate environment are shot through with theory. Quine recognized that 'Even our primordial objects, bodies, are already theoretical'; whilst Russell credited commonsense to 'prehistoric metaphysicians'. C.D. Broad made a related point concerning our capacity to be positively misled by reflections that come readily to us when they are couched in the idiom of natural language: 'The language in which we... talk about material things and events were formed unwittingly in prehistoric times to deal in a practical way with a kind of normalized extract from our total perceptual experience. It was formed in utter ignorance of a whole range of relevant physical, physiological and psychological facts. It would surely be nothing short of a miracle if it were theoretically adequate, and if it were not positively misleading in some of its implications'. Indeed even Russell's idealist predecessors, including Bradley himself, appreciated that we only think about the world through a network of judgments we make about it: 'In every case that which is called the fact is in reality a theory'.[20] This is another notable point of continuity between them.

---

[20] See W.V.O. Quine, 'Things and Their Place in Theories' in his *Theories and Things* (Cambridge, Mass.: Harvard University Press, 1981), 1–23, 20, B. Russell, 'The Relation of Sense-Data to Physics' in his *Mysticism and Logic* (New York: Longmans, Green & Co, 1918), 140–72, 149, C.D. Broad, 'Philosophy and "Common Sense"', in *G.E. Moore:*

Fraser MacBride

To return to the present, the intuitions to which Kripke *et al* appeal aren't sources of theoretically untainted, pristine evidence of what the Universe and its denizens are like. To switch metaphors, each intuition is just the visible tip of an iceberg, an iceberg whose massive substructure, concealed from view beneath the waves, isn't only theoretical but also perceptual, practical and physiological. Recent Kripke-inspired moves to elicit 'intuitions' as an oracular source of philosophical knowledge represents a abandonment of this hard-won insight, a loss which a more than passing acquaintance with the history of philosophy ought to have prevented.[21]

Glasgow University
fraser.macbride@glasgow.ac.uk

Essays in Retrospect (London: George Allen & Unwin, 1970), 203 and F.H. Bradley, 'The Presuppositions of Critical History', *Collected Essays: Volume I* (Oxford: Clarendon Press, 1935), 1–70, 17.

[21] I am grateful to audiences at the Royal Institute of Philosophy in London, a meeting of SEFA in Madrid and a Graduate Reading Party held by the University of Glasgow at the Burn. I would also like to thank Helen Beebee, Renée Bleau, Tyler Burge, Jane Heal, Ken Gemes, Sacha Golob, Frédérique Janssen-Lauret, Mike Martin, Kevin Mulligan, Chris Pincock and Alan Weir for subsequent discussion.

Heroic-Idyllic Philosophizing: Nietzsche and the Epicurean Tradition

KEITH ANSELL-PEARSON

Abstract

This essay looks at Nietzsche in relation to the Epicurean tradition. It focuses on his middle period writings of 1878–82 – texts such as *Human, all too Human*, *Dawn*, and *The Gay Science* – and seeks to show that an ethos of Epicurean enlightenment pervades these texts, with Epicurus celebrated for his teaching of modest pleasures and cultivation of philosophical serenity. For Nietzsche, Epicurus is one of the greatest human beings to have ever graced the earth and the inventor of 'heroic-idyllic philosophizing'. At the same time, Nietzsche claims to understand Epicurus differently to everybody else. The essay explores the main figurations of Epicurus we find in his middle period and concludes by taking a critical look at his later and more ambivalent reception of Epicurus.

Introduction

Some significant appropriations of Epicurus's philosophy take place in nineteenth century European thought. For Marx, writing in the 1840s, and in defiance of Hegel's negative assessment, Epicurus is the 'greatest representative of the Greek enlightenment',[1] whilst for Jean-Marie Guyau, writing in the 1870s, Epicurus is the original free spirit, 'Still today it is the spirit of old Epicurus who, combined with new doctrines, works away at and undermines Christianity.'[2] For Nietzsche, Epicurus is one of the greatest human beings to have graced the earth and the inventor of 'heroic-idyllic philosophizing'.[3] In this essay my focus is on the figuration of Epicurus we encounter in Nietzsche's middle period writings (1878–82). Nietzsche's interest in Epicurus, which is most prominent in these middle period writings, is, on the face of it, curious: what interest

---

[1]   Karl Marx, 'Difference Between the Democritean and Epicurean Philosophy of Nature' in K. Marx & F. Engels, *Collected Works: Volume One 183–43* (London: Lawrence & Wishart, 1975), 73

[2]   Jean-Marie Guyau, *La Morale D'Epicure* (Paris: Librairie Gemer Baillière, 1878), 280

[3]   F. Nietzsche, *The Wanderer and His Shadow*, trans. Gary Handwerk (Stanford: Stanford University Press, 2013), section 295

doi:10.1017/S1358246114000010

does Nietzsche have in a philosopher of antiquity who was an egalitarian, offered what Cicero called a 'plebeian' philosophy, and that espoused a simple-minded hedonic theory of value? These are all positions we would expect Nietzsche to have no truck with. And yet, in the middle period he is full of praise for the figure of Epicurus. However, as we shall see, Nietzsche's interpretation of Epicurus in his middle period texts, such as *Dawn* and *The Gay Science*, is wide-ranging and, on occasion, enigmatic. Sometimes Epicurus is portrayed as a significant figure on account of him being the teacher of modest pleasures; on another occasion he is viewed by Nietzsche as having a voluptuous appreciation of, and relation to, existence. But even here it is a *modest* voluptuousness that is at play! In Epicurus's teaching Nietzsche locates an appreciation of the moment and a sublimity of existence in which the art of living or existing consists in an attention to the closest and smallest things, and even an enjoyment of simple things: here, in this simplicity, Nietzsche will identify something 'heroic'.

Like the other nineteenth century interpreters I have referred to, Nietzsche is acutely aware that Epicurean doctrine has been greatly maligned and misunderstood in the history of thought. One commentator on Epicurus's philosophy speaks of the 'slanders and fallacies of a long and unfriendly tradition' and invites us to reflect on Epicurus as at one and the same time the most revered and most reviled of all founders of philosophy in the Greco-Roman world.[4] Since the time of the negative assessment by Cicero and the early Church Fathers, 'Epicureanism has been used as a smear word – a rather general label indicating atheism, selfishness, and debauchery'.[5] As Nietzsche observes in *The Wanderer and His Shadow*:

> Epicurus has been alive in all ages and lives now, unknown to those who have called and call themselves Epicureans, and enjoying no reputation among philosophers. He has, moreover, himself forgotten his own name: it was the heaviest burden he ever cast off.[6]

Two aphorisms from *Assorted Opinions and Maxims* reveal the importance Epicurus holds for Nietzsche in his middle period. In the first Nietzsche confesses to having dwelled like Odysseus in the

---

[4]   Norman Wentworth De Witt, *Epicurus and His Philosophy* (Minneapolis: University of Minnesota Press, 1954), 3
[5]   Neven Leddy & Avi S. Lifschitz (eds), *Epicurus in the Enlightenment* (Oxford: Voltaire Foundation, 2009), 4
[6]   Nietzsche, *The Wanderer and His Shadow*, section 227

underworld and says that he will often be found there again. As someone who sacrifices so as to talk to the dead he states that there are four pairs of thinkers from whom he will accept judgement, and Epicurus and Montaigne make up the first pair he mentions.[7] In the second aphorism Epicurus, along with the Stoic Epictetus, is revered as a thinker in whom wisdom assumes bodily form.[8]

In this essay I propose to build up a portrait of Nietzsche's figuration of Epicurus in his middle period writings by providing exegeses of the key aphorisms in which he appears. My contention is that an ethos of Epicurean enlightenment pervades Nietzsche's middle period texts with Epicurus celebrated for his teachings on mortality and the cultivation of modest pleasures. For Nietzsche, Epicurus's teaching can show us how to quieten our being and so help to temper a human mind that is prone to neurosis. The aim of philosophy for Nietzsche is to temper emotional and mental excess, and here Epicurean teaching has a key role to play. In addition, Nietzsche is attracted to the Epicurean emphasis on the modesty of a human existence. Nietzsche admires Epicurus for cultivating a modest existence and in two respects: first, in having 'spiritual and emotional joyfulness (*Freudigkeit*) in place of frequent individual pleasures',[9] and, second, in withdrawing from social ambition and living in a garden as opposed to living publicly in the market-place.[10] As Nietzsche stresses, 'A little garden, figs, little cheeses and in addition three or four good friends – these were the sensual pleasures of Epicurus'.[11] Nietzsche is appreciative of what one commentator has called the 'refined asceticism' we find in Epicurus, which consists in the

---

[7]   Nietzsche, *Assorted Opinions and Maxims*, trans. Gary Handwerk (Stanford: Stanford University Press, 2013), section 408. The other three pairs are: Goethe and Spinoza, Plato and Rousseau, and Pascal and Schopenhauer. On Montaigne's relation to Epicurean doctrine see Howard Jones, *The Epicurean Tradition* (London: Routledge, 1992), 159–62.

[8]   Nietzsche, *Assorted Opinions and Maxims*, section 224

[9]   Nietzsche, *Human, all too Human*, trans. Gary Handwerk (Stanford: Stanford University Press, 2013), vol. II, 400.

[10]   See Julian Young, *Friedrich Nietzsche. A Philosophical Biography* (Cambridge: Cambridge University Press, 2010), 279

[11]   Nietzsche, *The Wanderer and His Shadow*, section 192. Young describes the asceticism advocated by Epicurus as a 'eudaemonic asceticism', which is clearly very different to ascetic practices of world denial and self-denial. Young, *Nietzsche. A Philosophical Biography*, 279

enjoyment of the smallest pleasures and the disposal of a diverse and delicate range of sensations.[12]

We can note at the outset something of the character of Nietzsche's particular appreciation of Epicurus: it is not Epicurus the atomist that he focuses attention on, but Epicurus the ethicist, that is, the philosopher who teaches a new way of life by remaining true to the earth, embracing the fact of human mortality and denying any cosmic exceptionalism on the part of the human. For Epicurus philosophy proves vital to achieving health of one's soul. As he writes in the letter to Menoeceus:

> Let no one delay the study of philosophy while young nor weary of it when old. For no one is either too young or too old for the health of the soul. He who says either that the time for philosophy has not yet come or that it has passed is like someone who says that the time for happiness has not yet come or that it has passed.[13]

It is the strength of the Epicurean attachment to the world that Nietzsche will capture in his conception of 'heroic-idyllic philosophizing', and it is also encapsulated well by the young Marx when he writes that 'Epicurus is *satisfied* and *blissful in philosophy*';[14] that 'embodied in him are the serenity of thought satisfied in itself'.[15]

Although the extent of the influence of Epicurus's philosophy on Nietzsche, especially evident in the middle period texts, has been neglected in recent appreciation of Nietzsche it was fully recognized by A. H. J. Knight in, of all dates, 1933. At a time when Nietzsche was being enlisted by National Socialism as a crude philosopher of war, Knight had the foresight to see in Nietzsche something quite different and sought to reveal to his English-speaking audience the extent of Nietzsche's commitment to a philosophy of peace, goodwill, and serenity. Indeed, one of Nietzsche's texts from this time, *The Wanderer and His Shadow*, closes with the idyllic motto, 'Peace all around me and goodwill to all things closest to me'.[16] Knight recognizes that for Epicurus and Nietzsche philosophy is what today, in the

---

[12]   Richard Roos, 'Nietzsche et Épicure: l'idylle héroïque', in Jean-François Balaudé and Patrick Wotling (eds), *Lectures de Nietzsche* (Paris: Librairie Générale Française, 2000), 283–350, 298

[13]   Epicurus, 'Letter to Menoeceus' in Brad Inwood & L. P. Gerson (eds), *The Epicurus Reader* (Indianapolis: Hackett, 1994), 28

[14]   Marx, 'Difference', 41

[15]   Ibid. 45

[16]   Nietzsche, *The Wanderer and His Shadow*, section 350

wake of the pioneering work of Pierre Hadot, we would call 'a way of life'.[17] As he notes, Epicurean philosophy and Nietzsche's philosophy share many of the same principles. He refers to the definition of Epicurus, in which philosophy is said to be 'daily occupation of discourse and thought in order to attain a blissful life', that is, philosophy is essentially a practical affair with its chief concern being with the health of the soul.[18] Both are 'educators' and despise the mere erudition of the scholar. Epicurus and Nietzsche are both liberators of human life from religious superstition and mystification, and both place ethics at the centre of philosophy (even physics, or the study of nature and natural causes, is to be placed in the service of ethics). If philosophical therapeutics is centred on a concern with the healing of our own lives so as to return us to the joy of existing,[19] then in the texts of his middle period, including *Dawn*, Nietzsche can be seen to be an heir to this ancient tradition. The difference is that he is developing a therapy for the sicknesses of the soul under modern conditions of social control and discipline. Nevertheless, it is the case that Nietzsche at this time is seeking to revive an ancient conception of philosophy. In a note from 1881 he states that he considers the various moral schools of antiquity to be 'experimental laboratories' containing a number of recipes for the art of living (*Kunstgriffen der Lebensklughheit*: literally 'artifices for worldly wisdom') and holds that these experiments now belong to us as our legitimate property: 'we shall not hesitate to adopt a Stoic recipe just because we have profited in the past from Epicurean recipes'.[20]

Let me now begin to examine how Nietzsche interprets and positions Epicurus in his middle period writings.

1. How the teaching of Epicurus helps to temper the human mind

An overriding aim Nietzsche has in his middle period texts is to employ philosophy to temper mental and emotional excess. The

---

[17]   Pierre Hadot, *Philosophy as a Way of Life*, trans. Michael Chase (Oxford: Basil Blackwell, 1995)

[18]   A. H. J. Knight, 'Nietzsche and Epicurean Philosophy', *Philosophy*, 8, 1933, 431–445, 437

[19]   Hadot, *Philosophy as a Way of Life*, 87

[20]   Nietzsche, *Kritische Studienausgabe*, 9, 15 [59])

task, as he sees it, is to help cool down the human mind. He writes in 1878:

> ... shouldn't we, the *more spiritual* human beings of an age that is visibly catching fire in more and more places, have to grasp all available means for quenching and cooling, so that we will remain at least as steady, harmless, and moderate as we are now, and will thus perhaps become useful at some point in serving this age as mirror and self-regulation? —[21]

Epicurean philosophy can play a key role here. Along with science in general, it serves to make us 'colder and more sceptical', helping to cool down 'the fiery stream of belief in ultimate definitive truths', a stream that has grown so turbulent through Christianity.[22] For Lucretius 'there's no good life, no blessedness, without a mind made clear ...'[23] As Lucretius further writes in *De Rerum Natura*:

> Our terrors and our darknesses of mind
> Must be dispelled, then, not by sunshine's rays,
> Not by those shining arrows of light,
> But by insight into nature, and a scheme
> Of systematic contemplation.[24]

In interpreting Epicureanism as a form of knowledge and wisdom that tempers emotional and mental excess, Nietzsche is following a tradition well-established in nineteenth century thought that appreciates this point. Marx, for example, notes that the method of explanation 'aims only at the ataraxy of self-consciousness, not at knowledge of nature in and for itself'.[25] As Lange notes in his *History of Materialism* (1866), a text that deeply impressed the young Nietzsche: 'The mere historical knowledge of natural events, without a knowledge of causes, is valueless; for it does not free us from fear nor lift us upon superstition. The more causes of change we have discovered, the more we shall attain the calmness of contemplation; and it cannot be supposed that this inquiry can be without

---

[21] Nietzsche, *Human, all too Human: volume one*, trans. Gary Handwerk (Stanford: Stanford University Press, 1995), section 38
[22] Ibid. section 244
[23] Lucretius, *The Way Things Are*, trans. Rolfe Humphries (Bloomington: Indiana University Press, 1968), 158
[24] Ibid. 53.
[25] Marx, 'Difference', 45

result upon our happiness'.[26] If we can come to regard change in things as necessarily inherent in their existence we free ourselves from our natural terror at this order of change and evolution. If we believe in the old myths we live in fear of the eternal torments to come; if we are too sensible to believe in these torments we may still apprehend the loss of all feeling which comes with death as an evil, as if the soul could continue to feel this deprivation. As every student of philosophy knows death for Epicurus is an affair of indifference and precisely because it deprives us of all feeling. As Lange glosses Epicurus, 'So long as we are, there is as yet no death; but as soon as death comes, then we exist no more'.[27] If events can be explained in accordance with universal laws, with effects attributable to natural causes, an important goal of philosophy can be attained and secured, chiefly liberation from fear and anxiety.

In *The Wanderer and his Shadow* Nietzsche describes Epicurus as 'the soul-soother (*Seelen-Beschwichtiger*) of later antiquity' who had the 'wonderful insight' that to quieten our being it is not necessary to have resolved the ultimate and outermost theoretical questions.[28] To those who are tormented by the fear of the gods, one points out that if the gods exist they do not concern themselves with us and that it is unnecessary to engage in 'fruitless disputation' over the ultimate question as to whether they exist or not. Furthermore, in response to the consideration of a hypothesis, half belonging to physics and half to ethics, and that may cast gloom over our spirits, it is wise to refrain from refuting the hypothesis and instead offer a rival hypothesis, even a multiplicity of hypotheses. To someone who wishes to offer consolation – for example, to the unfortunate, to ill-doers, to hypochondriacs, and so on – one can call to mind two pacifying formulae of Epicurus that are capable of being applied to many questions: 'firstly, if that is how things are they do not concern us; secondly, things may be thus but they may also be otherwise'.[29]

Nietzsche's middle period writings are marked, then, by an Epicurean enlightenment. What appeals to Nietzsche about Epicurus is the emphasis on a refined egoism, the teaching on mortality, and the general attempt to liberate the mind from unjustified fears and anxieties. The Epicureanism we can find in Nietzsche in his middle

---

[26] Friedrich Albert Lange, *The History of Materialism* (London: Kegan Paul, 1925), First Book, 102
[27] Ibid.
[28] *The Wanderer and His Shadow*, section 7
[29] Ibid.

Keith Ansell-Pearson

period indicates his preference for individual therapy and self-cultivation over large-scale social transformation and political revolution. In *Dawn* (1881) Nietzsche explicitly writes against impatient political invalids and argues instead in favour of 'small doses' as a way of bringing about change.[30] It seems certain that at this time he sought to found a philosophical school modelled on Epicurus's garden. In a letter of 26 March 1879 he asks his amanuensis Peter Gast: '*Where are we going to renew the garden of Epicurus?*' In addition he writes that Epicurus 'is the best negative argument in favour of my challenge to all rare spirits to isolate themselves from the mass of their fellows'.[31] In 306 BC Epicurus founds his school in Athens, and this remains a presence in the city until the second century A.D. In contrast to the Stoics who philosophised in the agora of Athens, never far from the public eye, Epicurus and his followers did philosophy in a garden which bore the injunction 'live unnoticed'. Another injunction was 'do not get involved in political life'.[32] The school took the form of a community of friends who lived within the walls of the garden and worked together, studying under Epicurus, writing philosophical works, and growing their own food: going against the mores of the time it was open to both slaves and women. So, the school was a community based on friendship and friendship was considered by the Epicureans to be the most important thing of all. As one commentator has written:

> Members of the school were actively engaged in self-improvement and the improvement of others by mutual admonition and correction. The aim was to inculcate goodwill, gratitude, respect for wisdom, self-control, frankness, openness and moderation in all things. Arrogance, greed, jealousy, boastfulness, and anger were faults to be removed by gentle correction rather than by coercion or punishment.[33]

Epicureanism was an apolitical or even anti-political philosophy. The ideal mental state to attain for the Epicurean is *ataraxia* (freedom

[30] Nietzsche, *Dawn*, trans. Brittain Smith (Stanford: Stanford University Press, 2012), section 534
[31] *Nietzsche Briefwechsel: Kritische Gesamtausgabe*, ed. G. Colli and M. Montinari (Berlin and New York: Walter de Gruyter, 1981), III, 1, 418
[32] See Diskin Clay, 'The Athenian Garden', in James Warren (ed.), *The Cambridge Companion to Epicureanism* (Cambridge: Cambridge University Press, 2009), 9–29, 16
[33] Gordon Campbell, 'Epicurus, The Garden, and the Golden Age', in D. O'Brien (ed.), *Gardening: Philosophy for Everyone* (Oxford: Wiley Blackwell), 220–232, 222

from disturbance, or imperturbability), and to achieve this the philosopher had to withdraw from the disturbances of everyday life as much as possible, including public affairs which were seen as a particular cause of mental disquiet and disturbance (this is a key difference with Stoicism which advocated involvement in public life). This apolitical, even anti-political stance, is reflected in the ethos Nietzsche adopts in his middle period texts. He writes at one point:

> Live in seclusion so that you *can* live for yourself. Live in *ignorance* about what seems most important to your age … the clamor of today, the noise of wars and revolutions should be a mere murmur for you. You will also wish to help – but only those whose distress you *understand* entirely because they share with you one suffering and one hope – your friends – and only in the manner in which you help yourself. I want to make them bolder, more persevering, simpler, gayer.[34]

'Our age', Nietzsche writes at one point in *Dawn*, 'no matter how much it talks and talks about economy, is a squanderer: it squanders what is most precious, spirit'.[35] Nietzsche succinctly articulates his concern in the following manner: 'Political and economic affairs are not worthy of being the enforced concern of society's most gifted spirits: such a wasteful use of the spirit is at bottom worse than having none at all'.[36] Today, he goes on to note, everyone feels obliged to know what is going on every day to the point of neglecting their own work or therapy and in order to feel part of things, and 'the whole arrangement has become a great and ludicrous piece of insanity'.[37] The therapy Nietzsche is proposing in *Dawn* is, then, directed at those free spirits who exist on the margin or fringes of society and seek to cultivate or fashion new ways of thinking and feeling, attempting to do this by taking the time necessary to work through their experiences.

The view that Epicureanism advocates an apolitical posture is in need of some refinement. It might be suggested that the philosophy of Epicurus offers an alternative way of organising communities, promoting practices – such as justice, friendship, and economic co-operation – that are genuinely useful to people's needs and eliminating all that promotes false conceptions of values and places our happiness in

---

[34] Nietzsche, *The Gay Science*, trans. Walter Kaufmann (New York: Random House, 1974), section 338
[35] Nietzsche, *Dawn*, section 179
[36] Ibid.
[37] Ibid.

danger.[38] It is the case, however, that Nietzsche appropriates Epicureanism for the ends of an ethical reformation Although he anticipates 'numerous novel experiments' taking place in 'ways of life and modes of society'[39], his model at this time for the practice of self-cultivation is Epicurus's garden.

2. The Inventor of Heroic-Idyllic Philosophizing

In each of the different main stages of his intellectual development Nietzsche comes up with a striking conception of philosophy. In his early period he urges philosophy to hold onto to the sublime since it is the sublime, he thinks, that enables us to distinguish between what is great and what is small, and so to appreciate what is rare, extraordinary, and stupendous. Here the philosopher is seen as an abnormality and outsider in search of a new people. In the late period, and as is well-known, philosophy is defined as legislation and creative positing, and the philosopher is a lawgiver who declares 'thus it shall be!' In the middle period Nietzsche offers a conception of 'heroic-idyllic philosophizing' with the philosopher conceived as a figure of great sobriety and extraordinary serenity.

The reality of the 'heroic-idyllic' struck Nietzsche with the force of a revelation. In a note from July-August 1879 he writes, for example:

> The day before yesterday, toward evening, I was completely submerged in Claude Lorrainian delights and finally broke into lengthy, intense crying. That I had still been permitted to experience this! I had not known that the earth could display this and believed that good painters had invented it. The heroic-idyllic is now the discovery of my soul; and everything bucolic of the ancients was all at once unveiled before me and became manifest – up to now, I comprehended nothing of this.[40]

In *The Wanderer and his Shadow* Nietzsche depicts an idyllic scene entitled '*Et in Arcadia ego*', involving looking down 'over waves of hills, through fir-trees and spruce trees grave with age, towards a milky green lake'.[41] Whilst cattle graze on their own and gather in groups, the narrator of the aphorism experiences 'everything at peace in the

---

[38] See A. A. Long & D. N. Sedley, *The Hellenistic Philosophers: volume one* (Cambridge: Cambridge University Press, 1987), 137

[39] Nietzsche, *Dawn*, section 164

[40] Nietzsche, *Kritische Studienausgabe*, 8, 43 [3]

[41] Nietzsche, *The Wanderer and His Shadow*, section 295

contentment of evening.' Whilst looking upon the herders in the field, he witnesses mountain slopes and snowfields to the left and, high above him, to the right two gigantic ice-covered peaks that seem to float in a veil of sunlit vapour: 'everything big, still and bright'.[42] The beauty of the whole scene induces in him an experience of the sublime, 'a sense of awe and of adoration of the moment of its revelation'; involuntarily, as if completely natural, he inserts 'into this pure, clear world of light', free of desire and expectation, with no looking before or behind, Hellenic heroes, and he compares the feeling to that of Poussin and his pupil (probably Claude Lorrain), at one and the same time heroic and idyllic, noting to himself that some human beings have actually *lived* in accordance with this experience, having 'enduringly *felt* they existed in the world and the world existed in them'.[43] Epicurus is singled out for special mention.

The title of this aphorism is borrowed from two paintings of Poussin and was also adopted by Goethe as the motto of his Italian journey (1829). In fact, Poussin's paintings were inspired by Guercino (Giovanni Francesco Barbieri) and his painting of around 1618–22 entitled 'Et in Arcadia ego'. This painting depicts the discovery of death in Arcady, a region of Greece thought to be an earthly paradise: we see two shepherds gazing out of a wood at a skull that has been placed on a masonry plinth, and underneath the skull the inscription 'Et in Arcadia ego' can be read. Such words seem to be intended as a message spoken by death itself, 'I, Death, am also in Arcady'.[44] Poussin's first painting, bearing the same title, dates from 1627–8, and the second painting, with the same title, from 1638–9. In the first painting, which features a skull and two shepherds (but also flanked by a young shepherdess and a river

---

[42] Ibid.

[43] Ibid. One might even see in this contemplation of nature, where all is peace and calm and where we have moved beyond 'desire and expectation', something of Schopenhauer's ideas on art, including the release from the subjectivity of the will. Schopenhauer, in fact, depicted such a state in Epicurean terms: 'Then all at once the peace, always sought but always escaping us on that first path of willing, comes to us of its own accord, and all is well with us. It is the painless state, prized by Epicurus as the highest good and as the state of the gods; for that moment we are delivered from the miserable pressure of the will.' Schopenhauer, *The World as Will and Representation*, in two volumes, trans. E. F. J. Payne (New York: Dover Press, 1966), volume one, section 38, 196. See also Schopenhauer on the 'aesthetic delight' to be had from the experience of light: 'Light is most pleasant and delightful; it has become the symbol of all that is good and salutary', 199.

[44] Henry Keazor, *Poussin* (Köln: Taschen, 2007), 57

god), the main motif is, once again, the recognition of human mortality. In the second version of the painting, from a decade later, a sarcophagus now lies in the centre of the picture and the scene depicted is much more allegorical. Although still a painting about the discovery of death in Arcadia, the foreground depiction of details such as the skull is omitted and instead we are presented 'with subtle allusions that do not disturb the atmosphere of contemplative but cheerful relaxation'.[45] In the second painting the words 'Et in Arcadia ego' are no longer uttered by death itself but might be the lament of a girl who has died young and who is buried in the sarcophagus: 'I, too, was once in Arcady.' This is how the Abbé Dubos interpreted the painting in the early eighteenth century and this interpretation then exerted an influence on writers and poets such as Schiller and Novalis, where the words are employed as a stock-phrase, being adopted in verses that sing longingly of the possibility of a better world and of resignation to the fact of having missed it.[46]

There are several striking things about Nietzsche's turn to, and portrait of, the idyllic. First, we can note the contrast with his earlier critique of the idyll in *The Birth of Tragedy* where it is equated with the superficial and the optimistic.[47] Second, in his depiction of the heroic-idyllic scene the reality of death is completely absent from it. What might be informing Nietzsche's decision to leave death out of the picture is the Epicurean inspiration that the fear of death has been conquered and death is nothing to us.[48]

---

[45]   Ibid., 58

[46]   Ibid. Schopenhauer refers to Schiller's belief that 'we are all born in Arcadia' in chapter five of his 'Aphorisms on the Wisdom of Life', (1974) in *Parerga and Paralipomena*, trans. E. F. J. Payne (Oxford: Clarendon Press, 1974), volume one, 408. Schopenhauer interprets this as the view that we come into the world with claims to happiness and pleasure; he insists though that 'fate' soon enters the picture of life and seizes us harshly and roughly, teaching us that nothing belongs to us but everything to it. In short, our yearning after happiness and pleasure is a fanciful if noble ideal that we have to learn to modify and moderate: 'We then recognize that the best the world has to offer is a painless, quiet, and tolerable existence to which we restrict our claims in order to be the more certain of making them good. For the surest way not to become very unhappy is for us not to expect to be very happy' (ibid.).

[47]   Nietzsche, *The Birth of Tragedy*, trans. Ronald Speirs (Cambridge: Cambridge University Press, 1999), section 19.

[48]   Richard Bett, 'Nietzsche, the Greeks, and Happiness (with special reference to Aristotle and Epicurus)', *Philosophical Topics* 33(2) 2005: 45–70, 65

Thus, Nietzsche does not wish the image of the tombstone to cast a shadow over the idyll he is focusing our attention on: for this reason it is both heroic and idyllic. And third, for Nietzsche the idyll is not in any inaccessible celestial heavens but belongs in this world and is within our reach, and what takes place after death does not concern us anymore.[49] Nietzsche writes in *Dawn*: '...the after-death no longer concerns us! An unspeakable blessing ... and once again, Epicurus triumphs!'[50]

The 'heroic-idyllic' is heroic, then, at least in part, because conquering the fear of death is involved and the human being has the potential to walk on the earth as a god, living a blessed life, and idyllic because Epicurus philosophised, calmly and serenely, and away from the crowd, in a garden. In *Human, all too Human* Nietzsche writes of a 'refined heroism' 'which disdains to offer itself to the veneration of the great masses ... and goes silently through the world and out of the world'.[51] This is deeply Epicurean in inspiration: Epicurus taught that one should die as if one had never lived. As I have already noted, there is a modesty of human existence in Epicurean teaching that greatly appeals to the middle period Nietzsche.

3. Overcoming the Fear of Death

In her *Therapy of Desire* Martha Nussbaum explains well the nature of Epicurus's intervention in a society 'that values money and luxury above the health of the soul', and in which 'every enterprise is poisoned by the fear of death, a fear that will not let any of its members taste any stable joy, but turns them into the grovelling slaves of corrupt religious teachers'.[52] As Lucretius has it:

> ... fear of death
> Induces hate of life and light, and men
> Are so depressed that they destroy themselves
> Having forgotten that this very fear
> Was the first cause and source of all their woe.[53]

[49] Roos, 'Nietzsche et Épicure', 322
[50] Nietzsche, *Dawn*, section 72
[51] Nietzsche, *Human, all too Human*, section 291
[52] In *The Therapy of Desire: Theory and Practice in Hellenistic Ethics* (Princeton: Princeton University Press), 103
[53] Lucretius, *The Way Things Are*, 88

In his middle period Nietzsche picks up the Epicurean doctrine on death and puts it to critical effect. For Nietzsche our religions and moralities do not wed us to the earth as a site of dwelling and thinking; rather, we consider ourselves 'too good and too significant for the earth', as if we were paying it only a passing visit.[54] Several aphorisms in *Dawn* consider humanity's misguided dream of an immortal existence. *Dawn* 211 is an especially witty aphorism in which Nietzsche considers the impertinence of the dream. He notes that the actual existence of a single immortal human being would be enough to drive everyone else on earth into a rampage of death and suicide out of being sick and tired of it! He adds:

> And you earth inhabitants with your mini-notions of a few thousand mini-minutes of time want to be an eternal nuisance to eternal, universal existence! Is there anything more impertinent![55]

Nietzsche champions Epicurus as a figure who has sought to show mankind how it can conquer its fears of death. Identifying the goal of a good life with the removal of mental and physical pain Epicureans place, 'the eradication of the fears of death at the very heart of their ethical project'.[56] As a 'therapy of anguish' Epicureanism is a philosophy that aims to procure peace of mind, and an essential task here is to liberate the mind from its irrational fear of death. It seeks to do this by showing that the soul does not survive the body and that death is not and cannot be an event within life.

In the letter to Menoeceus, Epicurus seeks to identify what the study of philosophy can do for the health of the soul and on the premise that, 'pleasure is the starting-point and goal of living blessedly'.[57] Epicurus stresses that he does not mean the pleasures of the profligate or of consumption; rather, the task, is to become accustomed to simple, non-extravagant ways of living. Although Epicurus regards *voluptas* as the highest good, in which we can take delight in all that nature has provided to stimulate pleasure, it is an error to suppose that for him happiness is to be found 'simply in

---

[54] Nietzsche, *Dawn*, section 425

[55] Ibid. section 211

[56] James Warren, *Facing Death: Epicurus and His Critics* (Oxford: Oxford University Press, 2004), 6

[57] *The Epicurus Reader*, page 30. As Kant notes, the pleasure of the Epicurean is the pleasure of the sage and on this point Epicurus has 'been poorly understood'. See I. Kant, *Lectures on Ethics*, trans. Peter Heath (Cambridge: Cambridge University Press, 1997), 46.

eating, drinking, gambling, wenching, and other such pastimes.'[58] Nietzsche seems to have fully appreciated this point. The key goal for Epicurus is to liberate the body from pain and remove disturbances from the soul. Central to his counsel is the thought that we need to accustom ourselves to believing that death is nothing to us; our longing for immortality needs to be removed: '... there is nothing fearful in life for one who has grasped that there is nothing fearful in the absence of life.'[59] What appears to be the most frightening of bad things should be nothing to us, 'since when we exist, death is not yet present, and when death is present, then we do not exist.'[60] The wise human being 'neither rejects life nor fears death. For living does not offend him, nor does he believe not living to be something bad.'[61] If, as Epicurus supposes, everything good and bad consists in sense-experience, then death is simply the privation of sense-experience. The goal of philosophical training, then, is freedom from disturbance and anxiety in which we reach a state of *ataraxia* or psychic tranquillity: the body is free from pain and the soul is liberated from distress.

According to Martha Nussbaum, Epicurus's teaching amounts to an inversion of Plato because for him truth is in the body and in contrast to Plato for whom the body is the main source of delusion and bewitchment and where the task is to purify ourselves of our bodily attachments through proper mathematical and dialectical training.[62] This inversion was well understood by Nietzsche and appreciated by him. In the texts of the middle period, including and perhaps especially *Dawn*, Nietzsche highlights the dangers of a teaching of pure spirituality. By definition such a teaching is excessive and in the process destroys much nervous energy: 'it taught one to despise, ignore, or torment the body and, on account of all one's drives, to torment and despise oneself'. The teaching succeeds in producing human beings who feel melancholy and oppressed and conclude that the cause of their distress and anxiety must reside in the body, which continues to flourish. As Nietzsche points out, in such cases it is in fact the body that registers a protest against such derision. He draws attention to the irrational mode of existence that spiritual

---

[58]   Howard Jones, *The Epicurean Tradition* (London: Routledge, 1989), 152

[59]   *The Epicurus Reader*, 29

[60]   Ibid.

[61]   Ibid.

[62]   Nussbaum, *The Therapy of Desire*, 110. Nussbaum also offers an imaginative insight into Epicurus's Garden, (119ff)

excess results in: 'A pervasive, chronic hyper-excitability was eventually the lot of these virtuous pure spirits' since 'the only pleasure they could muster was in the form of ecstasy and other harbingers of madness'.[63] Their mode of being thus reaches an apogee when ecstasy is accepted as the highest goal in life and the as the standard.[64]

In Dawn Epicurus is portrayed as the enemy of the idea of punishments in Hell after death, which was developed by numerous secret cults of in the Roman Empire and was taken up by Christianity. For Nietzsche the triumph of Epicurus's teaching resounds most beautifully in the mouth of the sombre Roman Lucretius but comes too early. Christianity takes the belief in 'subterranean terrors' under its special protection and this foray into heathendom enables it to carry the day over the popularity of the Mithras and Isis cults, winning to its side the rank of the timorous as the most zealous adherents of the new faith (Nietzsche notes that because of the extent of the Jews' attachment to life such an idea fell on barren ground). However, the teaching of Epicurus triumphs anew in the guise of modern science which has rejected 'any other representation of death and any life beyond it'.[65] Nietzsche, then, is keen to encourage human beings to cultivate an attitude towards existence in which they accept their mortality and attain a new serenity about their dwelling on the earth, to conquer unjustified fears, and to reinstitute the role played by chance and chance events in the world and in human existence.[66] As Hadot notes, for the Epicurean sage the world is the product of chance, not divine intervention, and this brings with it pleasure and peace of mind, freeing him from an unreasonable fear of the gods and allowing him to consider each moment as an unexpected miracle. Each moment of existence can be greeted with immense gratitude.[67]

Nietzsche finds in Epicurus a victory over pessimism in which death becomes the last celebration of a life which is constantly embellished.[68] This last of the Greek philosophers teaches the joy of living in the midst of a world in decay and where all moral doctrines preach suffering. As Richard Roos puts it, 'The example of Epicurus teaches that a life filled with pain and renunciation prepares one to savour the little joys of the everyday better. Relinquishing Dionysian

---

[63] Nietzsche, *Dawn*, section 39

[64] See also Nietzsche, *Dawn*, section 50

[65] Nietzsche, *Dawn*, section 72

[66] See Nietzsche, *Dawn*, sections 13, 33, 36. On Epicurus on fear and chance see Hadot, *Philosophy as a Way of Life*, 87, 223, and 252

[67] Hadot, *Philosophy as a Way of Life*, 252

[68] Roos, 'Nietzsche et Épicure', 299

intoxication, Nietzsche becomes a student of this master of moderate pleasures and careful dosages'.[69] In Epicurus Nietzsche discovers what Roos calls aptly an 'irresistible power' and a rare strength of spirit, and quotes Nietzsche from 1880: 'I found strength in the very places one does not look for it, in simple, gentle and helpful men ... powerful natures dominate, that is a necessity, even if those men do not move one finger. And they bury themselves, in their life-time, in a pavilion in their garden' (KSA 9, 6 [206]).[70]

There are gaps, potentially significant ones, in Nietzsche's appreciation of the Epicurean teaching with regards to death. For example, he never subjects to critical analysis the effectiveness of Epicurus's arguments but simply assumes that the rediscovery of the certainty of death within modern science, along with the demise of the Christian afterlife, is sufficient to eliminate mortality as a source of anguish. But the triumph of the Epicurean view that we are mortal and need not live in fear of an after-life is not necessarily a triumph for the Epicurean view that we should not fear death: one can eliminate fear of the after-life by exposing it as a myth, but this does not liberate us from the fear of extinction. Nietzsche does not make it clear whether he thinks the Epicurean arguments suffice to console us for the fact of our mortality, though there are places in his corpus where he appears to be offering new post-religious consolations, such as the consolation we can gain from the recognition that as experimental free spirits the sacrifices we make of our lives to knowledge may lead to a more enlightened humanity in the future (others may prosper where we have not been able to).

4. A Gate of Hospitality

Taken as a whole, *Dawn* of 1881 perhaps represents Nietzsche's most avowedly Epicurean moment. It is an attempt to revitalise for a modern age ancient philosophical concerns, notably a teaching for mortal souls who wish to be liberated from the fear and anguish of existence, as well as from God, the metaphysical need, and are able to affirm their mortal conditions of existence. Here one might adopt Hadot's insight into the therapeutic ambitions of ancient philosophy which was, he claims, 'intended to cure mankind's anguish' (for example, anguish over our mortality).[71] This is evident in the

---

[69]   Ibid. 309
[70]   Ibid. 300
[71]   Hadot, *Philosophy as a Way of Life*, 265–6

teaching of Epicurus which sought to demonstrate the mortality of the soul and whose aim was, in the words of a recent commentator, 'to free humans from "the fears of the mind" '.[72] Similarly, Nietzsche's teaching in *Dawn* is for mortal souls.[73]

Dawn occupies a special place in Nietzsche's development because it's with this work, he stresses in *Ecce Homo*, that there begins in earnest his 'campaign against morality', although he adds that here – and this is important – we should not detect the whiff of gunpowder but smell something quite different and much sweeter. Although at this time Nietzsche is in favour of free-minded and progressive social transformation, he is no advocate of revolution: the process of change should be a slow and gradual one, and in *Dawn* we find Nietzsche outlining a therapy made up of 'slow cures' and 'small doses'. If Nietzsche wants his readers to achieve a free-mindedness with respect to religion, the same is also the case with morality, for example, relinquishing the idea that there is a simple definition of morality and embracing the idea that there is no single moral-making morality.

Nietzsche's Epicureanism in *Dawn* is perhaps most evident in the way he polemicizes against morality. The 'campaign' centres largely on a critique of what Nietzsche sees as the modern tendency, the tendency of his own century, to identify morality with the sympathetic affects, especially *Mitleid*, so as to give us a definition of morality. Nietzsche has specific arguments against the value accorded to these affects, but he also wants to advocate the view that there are several ways of living morally or ethically and the morality he wants to defend is what we can call an ethics of self-cultivation. In place of what he sees as the ruling ethic of sympathy, which he thinks can assume the form of a 'tyrannical encroachment', Nietzsche invites individuals to engage in self-fashioning, cultivating a self that others can look at with pleasure and that still gives vent to the expression, albeit in a subtle and delicate manner, of an altruistic drive. We find the allusion to Epicurus and his mode of living is made explicit:

> *Moral fashion of a commercial society* – Behind the fundamental principle of the contemporary moral fashion: 'moral actions are generated by sympathy (*Sympathie*) for others', I see the work of a collective drive toward timidity masquerading behind an

---

[72]   Catherine Wilson, *Epicureanism at the Origins of Modernity* (Oxford: New York, Oxford University Press, 2008), 7

[73]   Nietzsche, *Dawn*, section 501

intellectual front: this drive desires ... that life be rid of *all the dangers* it once held and that *each and every person* should help toward this end with all one's might: therefore only actions aimed at the common security and at society's sense of security may be accorded the rating 'good!' – How little pleasure people take in themselves these days, however, when such a tyranny of timidity dictates to them the uppermost moral law (*Sittengesetz*), when, without so much as a protest, they let themselves be commanded to ignore and look beyond themselves and yet have eagle-eyes for every distress and every suffering existing elsewhere! Are we not, with this prodigious intent to grate off all the rough and sharp edges from life, well on the way to turning humanity into *sand*? ... In the meantime, the question itself remains open as to whether one is *more useful* to another by immediately and constantly leaping to his side and *helping* him – which can, in any case, only transpire very superficially, provided the help doesn't turn into a tyrannical encroachment and transformation – or by *fashioning* out of oneself something the other will behold with pleasure, a lovely, peaceful, self-enclosed garden, for instance, with high walls to protect against the dangers and dust of the roadway, but with a hospitable gate as well.[74]

Nietzsche's ethical commitment is clear from this aphorism: a pleasure and care of self that strives for independence and self-sufficiency. One does not isolate oneself from others, but neither does one seek to effect a tyrannical encroachment on them. Instead, one offers a 'hospitable gate' through which others can freely enter and leave, and through self-cultivation one fashions a style of existing that others will behold with pleasure. As Michael Ure has helpfully shown, in opposition to the desert of undifferentiated atoms offered by modern commercial culture Nietzsche provides the image of an oasis and one that depicts neither the past glories of Homeric agonism nor the resplendent isolation of the noble individual.[75] The image Nietzsche comes up with of a self-enclosed garden clearly draws on ideas of paradise in the Western tradition (our word 'paradise' etymologically derives from the Persian for 'walled garden', *paradeiza*), and he provocatively counters the Christian idea of a locked gate or *porta clausa* with that of a hospitable one:

[74] *Dawn*, section 174
[75] Michael Ure, 'The Irony of Pity: Nietzsche contra Schopenhauer and Rousseau', *Journal of Nietzsche Studies* 32: 68–92, 84

'To cultivate oneself ... is to create oneself as a paradise garden for the other'.[76]

5. The Happiness of the Afternoon of Antiquity[77]

Nietzsche writes in 1882 that he is proud of the fact that he experiences the character of Epicurus differently from perhaps everybody else: 'Whatever I hear or read of him, I enjoy the happiness of the afternoon of antiquity'. In this aphorism, entitled 'Epicurus', Nietzsche writes:

> I see his eyes gaze upon a wide, white sea, across rocks at the shore that are bathed in sunlight, while large and small animals are playing in this light, as secure and calm as the light and his eyes. Such happiness could be invented only by a man who was suffering continually. It is the happiness of eyes that have seen the sea of existence become calm, and now they can never weary of the surface and of the many hues of this tender, shuddering skin of the sea. Never before has voluptuousness (*Wollust*) been so modest.[78]

As Monika Langer has recently noted in her interpretation of this aphorism, although clearly a paean of sorts to Epicurus, Nietzsche does not elaborate on the origin or nature of his happiness and suffering, but rather tacitly encourages the reader to consider various possibilities. In the end she argues that Nietzsche is reading Epicurus as a figure who whilst standing securely on firm ground, gazes at the sea and is able to enjoy the possibility of uncertainty it offers. She writes, 'Literally and figuratively he can float on the sea.'[79] Epicurus is depicted as the antithesis of modernity's shipwrecked man since such is his liberation and serenity he can 'chart his course or simply set sail and let the wind determine his way'.[80]

---

[76]   Ibid., 85
[77]   My appreciation of this aphorism from *The Gay Science* has been greatly enriched by the MA seminar I taught on Nietzsche at Warwick University in the spring term of 2013. I benefitted from the contributions of Kamaran Abdulla, Christopher Howlett, Robert Kron, Luis Mulhall, Andrew Paull, and especially Jeffrey Pickernell. I am also deeply indebted to thoughts suggested to me by Beatrice Han-Pile and Rainer Hanshe.
[78]   *The Gay Science*, section 45
[79]   Monika M. Langer, *Nietzsche's Gay Science: Dancing Coherence* (Basingstoke: Palgrave Macmillan, 2010), 67
[80]   Ibid.

Although he might suffer shipwreck and drown or survive he does not live in fear of dangers and hazards: 'In taking to the sea he might lose his bearings and even his mind.' In contrast to modern man who is keen to leave behind the insecurity of the sea for the safety of dry land, 'Epicurus delights in the ever present possibility of leaving that secure land for the perils of the sea.'[81]

This interpretation misses the essential insight Nietzsche is developing into Epicurus in the aphorism. Rather than suggesting that the sea calls for further and continued exploration, hiding seductive dangers that Epicurus would not be afraid of, Nietzsche seems to hold to the view that Epicurus is the seasoned traveller of the soul who has no desire to travel anymore and for whom the meaning of the sea has changed. Rather than serving as a means of transportation or something that beckons us towards other shores, the sea has become an object of contemplation in the here and now. It is something to be looked at for its own sake and in a way that discloses its infinite nuances and colours. The scene Nietzsche depicts is one of Epicurean illumination or enlightenment: Epicurus is not estranged from nature and recognizes his kinship with animals and the elements of nature. Rather than deploying his contemplation of the sea to bolster his own ego (thinking of his own safety or taking pride in fearlessness), Epicurus abandons his sense of self altogether so that he can open himself up to the sea of existence, and perhaps here we find an alternative to Dionysian ecstasy, entailing a more peaceful and less grandiose loss of the self into the *Ur-Eine*. Unlike Christ, Epicurus does not walk on the water but floats serenely on the sea, buoyed up by it and even cradled by it, happy with the gifts life has to offer, and existing beyond fear and anxiety even though he is opening himself up to troubling realities, such as the approach of death and his personal extinction: 'We are born once and cannot be born twice, but we must be no more for all time.'[82]

As Langer rightly notes, the imagery deployed in the aphorism is striking since far from evoking boredom the serenity of Epicurus signals a kind of ecstatic bliss.[83] And yet there is much in this aphorism that merits careful exegesis and that, in the end, remains elusive. Why is the sea 'white'? What is the role being played by the animals depicted at the heart of the scene? What does Epicurus suffer from and why does he suffer continually? Let's note that the 'afternoon of antiquity' refers to the specific cultural horizon that characterizes

---

[81] Langer, *Nietzsche's Gay Science*, 67
[82] Epicurus, 'Vatican Sayings', number 14
[83] Langer, *Nietzsche's Gay Science*, 67

the moment of Epicurus within the history of philosophy: it is not the 'dawn' of the emergence of philosophy with the pre-Socratics, and neither is it the dark period that philosophy is plunged into with the rise of Christian morality. It would seem that the sea is white because it characterizes the tumultuous nature of human experience: the white colour of the sea comes from the froth of waves crashing against one another and serves as a metaphor for human existence in which life is fraught with difficulties and beset by fears, most notably the fear of death and anxieties about the future. The mention of sunlight is significant since it makes the entire scene clearly visible to anyone who looks upon it; the roll of the waves is obvious to anyone who cares to look and who is not suffering from myopia or a similar affliction, and so it is up to individuals to gaze on the world and attain a standpoint on existence beyond fear and anxiety. We are to learn from animals since they are tethered to the present moment and do not live in anticipation of death and the anxiety this anticipation generates for human beings. Epicurus might be suffering from physical ailments – we know these were acute at the end of his life – but he is also surely suffering from the anxiety of existence. However, Nietzsche sees the philosophical task as essentially a practical one, namely, that of conquering such anxiety, becoming serene in the process and, like a child playing with a kaleidoscope, appreciating, even being enchanted by, the many shades of colour that characterize existence.

At stake in the Epicurean way of life are those things which threaten human happiness, such as disturbances that arise from our irrational fear of death and the idea that divine decisions impact on the world and on the next life. Therefore, at the heart of Epicurean teaching is freedom from the fear of death and freedom from fear of the gods. An important distinction is made between kinetic pleasure and katastematic pleasure and that works as follows: 'kinetic' pleasure is basic instinctive pleasure produced by action to satisfy a need, such as the ingestion of food or the ejaculation of sperm; this is an unstable kind of pleasure since it is temporary and involves pain – the pleasure of eating will soon be followed by the pain of hunger, etc.; 'katastematic' pleasure is 'stable' in that it endures and involves no pain: it is the pleasure of contentment and serenity, involving the absence of need and desire, and psychic equilibrium. It is superior to the animal pursuits of food and sex and for the Epicureans is to be elevated into the highest goal of life, attaining the state of 'ataraxia'. As Gisela Striker puts it, Epicurus was perhaps the first philosopher who sought to bring this mental state into the framework of a eudaemonist theory and by arguing that it is a special sort of pleasure.[84] It is to be reached by true insight and reasoning. James Porter describes it as the 'basal experience of pleasure' on account of it being the criterion of all pleasure'. In this sense, then, it is more than a condition of simple or mere happiness since 'it seems to operate as life's internal formal principle, as that which gives moral sense and shape to a life that is lived ...'[85]

In *The Gay Science* 45 Nietzsche makes a specific contribution to our understanding of Epicurean happiness. According to the portrait of Epicurus he provides this happiness is hard-won and has a precarious character: the sea of existence has become calm but, as one commentator has put it, 'its continued calmness cannot be guaranteed, and the "shuddering skin of the sea" is a constant reminder of the turmoil that may return.'[86] The aphorism, however, is opaque and it has to be acknowledged that Nietzsche maintains in it the distance between his portrait of Epicurus and the existence of Epicurus himself: it's far from clear if he is, in fact, offering Epicurus as some kind of philosophical ideal or whether in fact he is suggesting that the Epicurean mode of living is not available to us mere human beings. There is something god-like, even superhuman, about the Epicurean mode of living, and whilst Nietzsche may on occasion be in awe of it, it's not necessarily the case that he is recommending it to us. The critical concerns he has about it manifest themselves only in his late writings, to which I now turn in conclusion.

6. Conclusion

It is clear that Epicurus is a significant and inspiring philosophical figure for Nietzsche at the time of his free spirit writings. By the time of the late writings (1886–8) he is a more ambivalent figure for him, still celebrated for waging war against Christianity in its pre-existent form but also a said to be a 'typical decadent'.[87] With the return of the Dionysian in his thinking, which disappears in his

---

[84] G. Striker, '*Ataraxia*: Happiness as Tranquillity', in *Essays on Hellenistic Epistemology and Ethics* (Cambridge: Cambridge University Press, 1996), 183–196, 185.

[85] James I. Porter, 'James I. Porter, 'Epicurean Attachments: Life, Pleasure, Beauty, Friendship, and Piety', *Cronache Ercolanesi* **33** (2003): 205–227, 218

[86] Richard Bett, 'Nietzsche, the Greeks, and Happiness', 63

[87] See Nietzsche, *The Anti-Christ*, trans. Judith Norman (Cambridge: Cambridge University Press, 2005), section 30

middle period writings, we get the fundamental contrast between Epicurean delight (*Vergnügen*) and Dionysian joy (*Lust*): 'I have presented such terrible images to knowledge that any "Epicurean delight" is out of the question, Only Dionysian joy is sufficient: *I have been the first to discover the tragic*'.[88] One commentator has suggested that for Nietzsche Epicurus is 'a point of intense equivocation', neither Dionysus nor the Crucified and yet curiously part of both of them. On the one hand, Epicurus affirms life and the moment 'against the melancholy prison of sin, the after-life and punishment'.[89] On the other hand, however, Epicurus is seen to be a romantic figure who, like Christ, offers consolation to those who suffer from the impoverishment of life, seeking a god for the sick, both a healer and saviour. On account of its fear of pain and the need for a religion of love, Epicureanism is a romanticism that 'flows smoothly into Christianity.'[90] Indeed, the late Nietzsche is suspicious of all attempts to attain philosophical beatitude through contemplative states since he thinks they represent a nihilistic flight from existence into a pure realm of being free of pain and free of appreciating the rich ambiguity of existence. The 'tragic' is for him essentially what allows for a greater attachment to life and signifies the affirmation of life beyond good and evil: it affirms and wants the total economy of life. What lies behind the change in Nietzsche's estimation of Epicurus is the fact that he has become again in his late writings a thinker of the tragic, in which suffering and happiness are intimately entwined. For Nietzsche for 'vital thinkers, still thirsty for life',[91] 'a life that is free from problems to solve, riddles to guess, or new worlds to discover, could not possibly be worth living, since it would be a life devoid of challenges for the seekers of knowledge'.[92] Thus, to prefer 'a handful of "certainty" to a whole wagonload of beautiful possibilities … a certain Nothing than … an uncertain Something … this is nihilism, and the sign of a despairing, mortally weary soul'.[93]

---

[88] Nietzsche, *Kritische Studienausgabe*, 11, 25 [95]

[89] Howard Caygill, 'The Consolation of Philosophy; or neither Dionysus nor the Crucified', *Journal of Nietzsche Studies* **7** (1994): 131–51, 145

[90] Ibid., 146

[91] Nietzsche, *Beyond Good and Evil*, trans. Marion Faber (Oxford: Oxford University Press, 1995), section 10

[92] Bernard Reginster, *The Affirmation of Life: Nietzsche on Overcoming Nihilism* (Cambridge, Mass.: Harvard University Press, 2006), 240

[93] Nietzsche, *Beyond Good and Evil*, section 10

We might see, as Schopenhauer did, the Epicurean quest for *ataraxia* as akin to the Buddhist attainment of Nirvana.[94] This is how one commentator has seen the Epicurean philosophy, entailing the attainment of the highest enjoyment in the removal of all vivid sensations, including pain, desire, and activity.[95] However, the garden of Epicurus is not an idyll that seeks escape from being or that refuses to acknowledge the terrible character of existence. As another commentator on Nietzsche's reception of Epicurus has put it, Epicurus's denial of immortality, 'affirms the most terrible character of existence as one of the first principles of the good life'.[96] It is even suggested that we find in Epicurus a conception of human existence and the world that is more finite and hence more terrible than Nietzsche's (Epicurus lives without the consolation – if that is what it is – of eternal recurrence). Moreover, Epicurus's remaining true to the earth 'was not pathologically conditioned by his desire to put an end to suffering and pain'; rather, it is the case that his 'insight into the unity of truth and appearances arose out of a profound recognition of human finitude'.[97] In Epicurean *ataraxia* we encounter the calm of strength and nothing of the calm of weakness. Far from being the repose of the deepest sleep, such *ataraxia* is 'an awakening of the active forces of life, an affirmation of the world as an aesthetic outpouring'.[98] This is to say that for the Epicurean *ataraxia* 'is a direct experience of the intrinsic pleasure of life itself, of the active forces of a life form freed from the reactive force of desire'.[99] We now directly participate in the blessed life of the gods, 'dwelling in the divine state of forbearance from reaction'.[100] There is no rancour towards life in Epicurus, only profound gratitude. The task, with the aid of philosophy, is precisely to go beyond the rancour in our hearts, to not resent mortal fate, and to display towards life a sense of gratitude.

[94]   For further insight into Nietzsche's 'Epicurus' as mediated by Schopenhauer see Fritz Bornmann, 'Nietzsches Epikur', *Nietzsche-Studien*, 13 (1984), 177–89; and Andrea Christian Bertino, 'Nietzsche und die hellenistische Philosophie: Der Übermensch und der Weise', *Nietzsche-Studien* 36 (2007), 95–131. See also Roos, 2000: 293. Roos also notes the influence of Montaigne and Jacob Burckhardt on Nietzsche's appreciation of Epicurus.

[95]   See Knight, 'Nietzsche and Epicurean Philosophy', 439

[96]   Joseph P. Vincenzo, 'Nietzsche and Epicurus', *Man and World*, 27 (1994), 383–97, 387.

[97]   Vincenzo, 'Nietzsche and Epicurus', 390

[98]   Ibid. 392

[99]   Ibid.

[100]   Ibid.

Nietzsche shares in this attitude of gratitude towards life. In addition, though, he has a rich appreciation of the complex character of the turbulent nature of existence. This is why he insists, I think, on the eternal recurrence of 'war and peace'.[101] For Nietzsche it is 'decadent' to suppose that we can attain a life of permanent delight and free of the need to grow through the pain of existence and the stimulus to life such pain gives rise to. As Nietzsche recognizes as early as the first edition of *The Gay Science* if one desires to diminish and lower the level of human pain, one has at the same time to want to diminish and lower the level of our capacity for joy. Nietzsche is of the view that 'new galaxies' of joy are available to us.[102] At the same time, there are weaknesses in his later appreciation. We can note two critical points in conclusion. First, it can be observed that Nietzsche too readily associates Epicurean doctrine with a simple-minded hedonism when in his middle period he is keen to dissociate it from such an easy identification. Second, the overly general character of his Dionysian conception and affirmation of life can be noted. Nietzsche rarely specifies the ends to which he is placing this affirmation and his tragic appreciation of life does not provide sufficient information as to the concrete application of destruction and negation. Rather, it seems that the late Nietzsche is espousing a philosophy of life and of life-affirmation that is designed to work against the fundamentally decadent tendencies of modern society, at least as Nietzsche sees the situation. The problem I have always had with this philosophy of life is, as I have already remarked, with its overly general character. Affirm life, including its eternal recurrence? Yes, but under what conditions of existence? Wage war and practise creation through destruction? Yes, but which wars should I wage, against which enemies and for what ends?

It is odd that Nietzsche should accuse Epicurus of decadence and nihilism, of pursuing nothingness, when it is clear, I think, that much of his thinking was directed at what one might call an incipient nihilism of his time, as when in the letter to Menoeceus he takes to task the wisdom that declares it is good not to be born and once born to then pass through the gates of death as quickly as possible. The kind of intense appreciation of life Epicurus sought to cultivate in his disciples is one that most of us experience rarely and indeed some only experience at the end of life, when life is about to vanish or disappear. In his middle period writings Nietzsche has these insights into the Epicurean appreciation of life and is awe-struck by

[101]   Nietzsche, *The Gay Science,* section 295.
[102]   Ibid., section 12.

the fact that, as he puts it, some human beings, such as Epicurus, have 'enduringly felt they existed in the world and the world existed in them'.[103] In *The Gay Science* Nietzsche has developed what I think is the key insight into Epicurus: in spite of the pain and suffering that characterize existence it remains worthy of our attachment and affirmation and there is no other world for us to seek meaning and value than in this world of mortal delights and pleasures. Here, as Nietzsche so eloquently puts it, we feel that we exist in the world and that the world exists in us; in such a condition our estrangement from life is overcome. Although the Epicurean appreciation of life may be one that is difficult to maintain, and although it may be impractical to practise it as a permanent way of life, it can inspire us in potent ways in our efforts to be equal to the event of our brief, precarious, and ephemeral existence. This seems to be the essential message of Nietzsche about the Epicurean tradition in his middle period.

University of Warwick
K.J.Ansell-Pearson@warwick.ac.uk

---

[103]   Nietzsche, *The Wanderer and His Shadow*, section 295.

Islamic Philosophy: Past, Present and Future

ALI PAYA

Abstract

The aim of this paper is to critically assess the present state of Islamic philosophy in its main home, namely, Iran. However, since such a study requires some knowledge of the past developments of philosophical thought among Muslims, the paper briefly, though critically, deals with the emergence and subsequent phases of change in the views of Muslim philosophers from ninth century onward. In this historical survey I also touch upon the role played by other Muslim scholars such as theologians, mystics and jurists, in shaping Islamic philosophy. The last section of the paper, deals, not in great details, with one or two possible scenarios for the future of Islamic philosophy.

1. Introduction

In his discussion of the 'Myth of the Framework', Karl Popper argues that while the views of the proponents of the 'myth', 'contains a kernel of truth' in that 'discussion among participants who do not share a common framework may be *difficult*'[1], it is, as Popper emphasizes, by no means impossible. He then goes on to make the following important claim which is directly related to the topic of this paper. Popper rejects the views of those who maintain that discussion between adherents to different intellectual frameworks will never be fruitful:

> Against this I shall defend the directly opposite thesis: that a discussion between people who share many views is unlikely to be fruitful, even though it may be pleasant; while a discussion between vastly different frameworks can be extremely fruitful... I think that we may say of a discussion that it was the more fruitful the more the participants were able to learn from it. And this means: the more interesting questions and difficult questions they were asked, the more new answers they were introduced to think of, the more they were shaken in their opinions, and the

---

[1]   Karl Popper, *The Myth of the Framework: in Defence of Science and Rationality* (Routledge, 1994), 35 (italics in original).

doi:10.1017/S1358246114000113

more they could see things differently after the discussion – in short, the more their intellectual horizons were extended.[2]

In this paper I am going to apply Popper's conjecture to the case of Islamic philosophy which emerged, partly as a response to the possibilities latent in the Quran and in the elaborations made by the Prophet and some great Muslim personalities such as the Prophet's son-in-law, Ali, of the Divine message; and partly as the result of an encounter between Islam, and a variety of non-religious cultures or cultures inspired by other religious doctrines different from Islam.

I will begin by discussing the role which was played by early *Kalam* (theology) in introducing substantive food for thought for the earliest Muslim philosophers. Next, I will focus on the influence of the Greek rational culture on the fate of the nascent Islamic philosophy. I will then continue my exploration concerning further evolutions of Islamic philosophy within the ecosystem of wider Islamic culture and with respect to the challenges posed to it by rival intellectual frameworks developed by theologians (*mutakllimun*), jurists (*fuqaha*), and mystics (*'urafa*).

This exploration takes us on a journey from the classic period in the Islamic civilisation (9th to 13th centuries CE) when earlier generations of Muslim philosophers were trying to develop a distinct philosophical framework fit for a religious culture. In this period Muslim philosophers entered into a virtual dialogue with their Greek and Hellenic counterparts whose views they had studied through translations made mostly by Christian priests and Jewish and Zoroastrian scholars.[3]

The next stop in our intellectual journey will be in Isfahan and Shiraz in 15th to 17th centuries where two philosophical schools, named after the two cities, elevated philosophical investigations within Islamic civilisation to a new height. In view of many commentators, these two schools represent purely indigenous philosophical developments in the land of Islam. The founding fathers of these schools and their followers and exegetes, contrary to the

[2] Popper, op. cit., 35–36
[3] Cf. Majid Fakhry, *A history of Islamic philosophy*, Columbia University Press, 2004; M. M. Sharif (ed.), *A History of Muslim Philosophy*, (two volumes) (Weisbaden: Otto Harrassowitz, 1963); Richard Walzer, 'The Rise of Islamic Philosophy', *Oriens*, **3**(1) (1950), 1–19; S. H. Nasr, & Oliver Leaman (eds), *History of Islamic Philosophy* (Routledge, 1996)

earlier generations of Muslim philosophers, were not much interested in philosophical dialogue with their non-Muslim counterparts, past or present. Their dialogue was mostly with their fellow Muslims.[4]

In the last leg of our journey, I follow philosophical developments in Iran since 19th century and in the wake of an eventful encounter between a powerful West and an Islamic civilisation which had its heydays behind it. I shall discuss some of the more influential philosophical approaches introduced by Muslim philosophers in response to challenges posed by modernity.

The conclusion of my exploration is a resounding corroboration of Popper's thesis. Islamic philosophy, and on a larger scale, Islamic culture, both greatly benefitted from their 'discussions' and 'dialogues' with other cultures and other frameworks especially the more rational ones. Consonant with Popper's conjecture, I argue that, in all those periods when Muslim scholars were deprived of intellectual challenges of ideas and views which belonged to other cultures, their dialogue amongst themselves turned more and more introverted and became less and less engaged with issues outside a strictly religious and theosophical framework.

Two last explanatory notes before I begin my exploration.

First: I use the term 'Islamic philosophy' in a neutral way, meaning philosophical doctrines produced by thinkers who happen to be either Muslim or living in Muslim countries or both. This term can be used interchangeably with a similar term, Muslim philosophy, throughout this paper.

Secondly: To encapsulate a 1300 year history in the space of a short paper necessarily involves radical selections and a great deal of omission. For the purpose of the present paper, in view of the fact that the history of the earlier developments of Islamic philosophy is well documented, I have shifted the focus of my attention on more recent developments especially developments in the twentieth century and the first decade of the twenty-first century. However, even here I have had no choice but to be, at once, very brief and extremely selective in my treatment of various philosophers and their achievements.

---

[4]   Seyyed Hossein Nasr, 'Persia and the Destiny of Islamic Philosophy', *Studies in Comparative Religion*, **6**(1) (1972); Henry Corbin, *History of Islamic Philosophy* (Kegan Paul International, 1962)

Ali Paya

2. Islamic Philosophy: A Brief, though Critical, Historical Survey

I. The Beginning: Coming out of the Shadow of Theology (Kalam)

Popper, whose conjecture concerning the fruitfulness of dialogue among diverse frameworks I use as a yardstick in this paper, discusses, in a yet another influential paper entitled, 'The Rationality of Scientific Revolutions',[5] a very important thesis concerning the growth of knowledge. According to Popper, all organisms learn through the mechanism of adaptation which in turn consists of a dual mechanism of instruction and selection, and constitutes a method of trial and error.[6]

The crucial point about this evolutionary/adaptive model is that instructions always come from within organisms. But selections and error elimination always come from without, from the environment. The environment also, by means of posing various challenges to the organism in question, introduces 'problems' for it. It is the organism's proposed 'solutions' (i.e. its responses to the challenges introduced by the environment) which will be assessed by the environment. If the 'solutions' are on the right track, organism's adaptive ability gets enhanced. If they are not, the proposed solutions will be rejected. This means that the organism has not been successful in its bid to adapt to the environment. Such an outcome could be costly for the organism.

'The organism' in question, to which the above evolutionary model is applied, can be a biological or a culturally and socially constructed entity such as a scientific theory or an intellectual tradition[7]. While, for biological organisms the environment will be their natural surroundings, for intellectual traditions other traditions and cultures play, at least to some extent, the role of the 'environment'.

Applying Popper's insight to the case of the emergence of philosophical traditions in Islamic civilisation, it is not difficult to see that instructions concerning the importance of rational thinking and making use of the power of the intellect are something which can be found in the main sources of Islamic civilisation, namely the

---

[5]   Karl Popper, 'The rationality of Scientific Revolutions', in *The Myth of the Framework: in Defence of Science and Rationality* (Routledge, 1994), 1–32

[6]   Ibid., 3

[7]   Ibid.

Quran and the tradition of the Prophet and, (in the case of the Shi'i Islam), also the traditions of Shi'i Imams.

There are many verses in the Quran in which Muslims are instructed to use their reason as their guide in exploring reality, studying natural phenomena, understanding various aspects of reality, and enriching their knowledge of God. The Quran has also reserved some of its harshest admonitions for those who do not use their intellects:

> Have they not pondered upon themselves? Allah created not the heavens and the earth, and that which is between them, save with truth and for a destined end. But truly many of mankind are disbelievers in the meeting with their Lord. (30:8)
>
> Have they not seen how We lead the water to the barren land and therewith bring forth crops whereof their cattle eat, and they themselves? Will they not then see? (32:27)
>
> ...and He lays abomination upon those who have no understanding [do not use their faculty of reasoning]. (10:100)

Similarly, plenty of the sayings quoted from the Prophet and Imams (in the case of the Shi'i Islam) are about the importance of reason and intellect and knowledge for living according to the Islamic standards. In this sense it can be argued that with respect to the question concerning the origin of rational approaches (in the extended sense of the term, 'rational') in Islamic civilisation, as against purely faith-based attitude of blind acceptance, one needs not to look further than the Quran itself and the main Islamic teachings.[8] These internal resources, however, as we shall see later, were further enriched, when Muslims embarked on a mission of digesting and incorporating into their own internal resources, wisdoms of other cultures.

As for the challenges, perhaps, the first intellectual challenges presented themselves to the early Muslims in the shape of political disputes concerning the issue of the succession of the Prophet who died in 632. The question which demanded a satisfactory answer was how Allah would want the believers to go about the task of choosing the political authority. In their efforts to respond to this question, early

---

[8]   Morteza Motahari, *Ashnaei ba 'ulum-e Eslami* (An Introduction to the [classic] 'Islamic Sciences'), (Tehran: Sadra Publications, 1358/1979); Seyyed Hossein Nasr, 'The *Qur'an* and *Hadith* as source and inspiration of Islamic philosophy', *in History of Islamic Philosophy*, edited by Seyyed Hossein Nasr and Oliver Leaman (Routledge, 1996), 27–39; M. M. Sharif, 'Philosophical Teachings of the Quran', in M. M. Sharif (ed.), *A History of Muslim Philosophy*, Vol. 1, 136–154; Massimo Campanini, *An Introduction to Islamic Philosophy* (SEPS, 2009)

Muslims were divided along different doctrinal lines; Sunnis, Shi'as, Kharijites, and Murji'ites were among the first sects which appeared in the newly established Muslim society[9].

The above political question soon gave rise to troubling theological questions concerning the standards which would demarcate a true believer and would determine the after-life station of those who would fall short of (some of) those standards. Out of these disputes and in the second half of the first century Hijri (Islamic calendar, 7th century Christian calendar) the first abstract problem, which was a bridge between theological issues and genuine philosophical problems, emerged. The problem in question was the dilemma of the free will and pre-destination (*qadar*) which, naturally in the context of a religious culture, was related to the issues of Divine justice and Divine power.[10]

Two rival schools of Kalam (theology) namely the Ash'arites and the Mu'tazilites were developed in response to the above problem. The Ash'arites maintained that God's omnipotence means that He directly intervenes in all aspects of the whole realm of being including what is related to human beings in their life in this world and in the hereafter. A direct corollary of this position was that man had no free will. The Mu'tazilites, on the other hand, argued for man's free will. They maintained that God has endowed human beings with the

---

[9] The first two sects gradually turned into the two largest sects in Islam which exist today and each are divided into a number of sub-sects. The latter two sects did not last long, though their ideas are still present in the intellectual ecosystem of Islamic doctrines. Kharijites were advocating a very strict adherence to their own literal reading of *shari'a* law and were intolerant and inflexible in imposing their desired order. Murji'ah, on the other hand, were of the view that, one should not condemn even the most corrupt and cruel individuals who regard themselves as Muslim; only God can pass judgement on their fate. Cf. Khalid Blankinship, 'The early creed', in *The Cambridge companion to classical Islamic theology*, edited by Tim Winter (Cambridge University Press, 2008), 33–54; Fakhry, *A history of Islamic philosophy*, op. cit.; Ignaz Goldziher, 'The Growth and Development of Dogmatic Theology', in *Introduction to Islamic Theology and Law* (Princeton University Press, 1981), 67–115

[10] Morteza Motahri, *'Adl-e Elahi* (Divine Justice) (Tehran: Sadra Publications, 1352/1973); Harry Wolfson, *The Philosophy of Kalam* (Harvard University Press, 1976); M. M. Sharif (ed.), *A History of Muslim Philosophy*, op. cit. (Book Three, Part 1, X & XI), 199–243; Josef van Ess, *The Flowering of Muslim Theology* (Harvard University Press, 1998/2006).

power of intellect, which they regarded as man's inner prophet. Man, according to the Mu'tazilites, is free to choose his path and station in life. Of course, in the hereafter he will be judged according to the choices he has made in this life. It is for this reason that man should use his power of intellect as wisely and as extensively as possible. For the Mu'tazilites justice was an objective value; even God's deeds could and should be judged against such an objective criterion. The Ash'arites would not accept such a thesis. In their view this would mean limiting God's power. To preserve God's omnipotence they developed an alternative theory of justice and argued that justice is tantamount to whatever God does.[11]

For almost two centuries and before the emergence of systematic philosophical approaches amongst Muslims in the ninth century CE, it was the *Mutakallimun* (theologians) who were dealing with issues which were philosophical in nature. Early Muslim theologians however, were not in favour of imported philosophical ideas. In particular they were against Greek's philosophical thoughts. They even rejected Aristotelian logic since they regarded it to be like Aristotelian philosophy an anti-religious knowledge. In place of Aristotelian logic they developed a rudimentary, and to some extent, faulty system of logic. The following quotation from Ibn Khaldun's *Muqadimah* (Introduction) (written in 1377) provides an informative account concerning the Mukallimun's attitude towards logic. We should bear in mind that Ibn Khaldun was writing at a time when the Ash'arites had established themselves as the official theological doctrine in the world of Sunni Islam:

> Thus, (al-Ash'ari's) approach was perfected and became one of the best speculative disciplines and religious sciences. However, the forms of its arguments are, at times, not technically perfect, because the scholars (of al-Ash'ari's time) were simple and the science of logic which probes arguments and examines syllogisms had not yet made its appearance in Islam. Even if some of it had existed, the theologians would not have used it, because it was so closely related to the philosophical sciences, which are altogether different from the beliefs of the religious law and were, therefore, avoided by them.[12]

---

[11]   Motahari, *'Adl-e Elahi*, op.cit., 24; Motahari, *Ashnaei ba 'ulum-e Eslami*, op. cit. chapter on *Kalam*. Goldziher, op. cit., ch. 3; Majid Khadduri, *The Islamic Conception of Justice* (John Hopkins University Press, 1984), ch. 3.

[12]   Abd Al Rahman bin Muhammed ibn Khaldun, *The Muqaddimah*, Translated by Franz Rosenthal, Princeton University Press, 1967

But later generations of theologians (*Mutkallimun*) realised that without logic they will not be able to avoid committing mistakes such as the fallacy of affirming the consequent which Abu Bakr al-Baqillani, one of the most prominent Asha'ri theologians, had committed. They adopted Aristotelian logic and applied it to theological as well as philosophical arguments. This approach gradually paved the way for a closer relationship between *Kalam* and philosophy.[13] As Ibn Khaldun reports [in his *Muqadimah* (Introduction) (written in 1377)]:

> After that, the science of logic spread in Islam. People studied it. They made a distinction between it and the philosophical sciences, in that (they stated that) logic was merely a norm and yardstick for arguments and served to probe the arguments of the (philosophical sciences) as well as (those of) all other (disciplines).
>
> (Scholars,) then, studied the basic premises the earlier theologians had established. They refuted most of them with the help of arguments leading them to (a different opinion). ... This approach differed in its technical terminology from the older one. It was called "the school of recent scholars". Their approach often included refutation of the philosophers where the (opinions of the) latter differed from the articles of faith. The first (scholar) to write in accordance with the (new) theological approach was al-Ghazzali. He was followed by the imam Ibn al-Khatib [Fakhr Razi]. A large number of scholars followed in their steps and adhered to their tradition. The later scholars [however], were very intent upon meddling with philosophical works. The subjects of the two disciplines (theology and philosophy) were thus confused by them. They thought that there was one and the same (subject) in both disciplines, because the problems of each discipline were similar.[14]

(available on the internet at: http://thequranblog.files.wordpress.com/2008/07/al-muqadimmah-for-ibn-khaldoon1.pdf (accessed 10, Jan, 2013) footnotes suppressed; quoted in, Hussein Masumi Hamedani, 'Mian-e Falsafeh va Kalam: Bahthi dar Araa-e Tabi'ee-ye Fakhr Razi' (Between Philosophy and Kalam: A Discussion Concerning Fakhr Razi's Naturalistic Views), *Ma'aref* **3**(1) (1365/1988), 198–199.

[13]   Masumi Hamedani, op.cit. 204; Motahari, *Ashnaei ba 'ulum-e Eslami*, op. cit. chapter on *Kalam*.

[14]   Ibn Khaldun, *The Muqaddimah,* op. cit.

Islamic Philosophy: Past, Present and Future

What Ibn Khaldun is suggesting, as some scholars have pointed out, is that Islamic *Kalam* after a period of remaining alien to Islamic philosophy gradually came closer to it until it somewhat merged with it. From the time of Ghazzali (Algazel d. 1111), who first wrote a masterpiece in explaining the intentions of the philosophers[15] and tried to expose their incoherence by writing yet another epoch making work[16], and Fakhr Razi (d.1209), who obtained the nickname, the leader of sceptics (*Imam al-Moshakkekin*), onward, *Kalam* came very close to resemble philosophy and Islamic philosophy, which emerged in an intellectually hostile environment in which the theologians (*mutakallimun*), the mystics (*'urafa*), and the jurists (*fuqha*) were against it, also tend to pay more and more attention to theological and mystical issues and took a cautious approach towards the *fiqh*.[17]

II. Emergence of Islamic Philosophy— The Era of Philosopher-Scientist/ Philosopher-Technologist

Translation of scientific, mathematical, technological, cultural and philosophical achievements of ancient civilisations like the Greeks, the Indians and the Persians into Arabic, provided the educated Muslims of the classic period of Islam (3rd–7th centuries AH/9th–13th CE) with a rich intellectual heritage[18]. They soon managed

[15]   Ghazzali, *Maqasid al falasifa* (The Intentions of the Philosophers 1094), (Arabic Text), ed. S. Dunya (Cairo: Dar al-Ma'arif, 1961). Available on line at: http://Ghazzali.org/books/maqasid-dun.pdf. A more recent edition has been prepared by Mahmood Biju (Damascus: Maktabat al-Sabah, 2000), Available at: http://Ghazzali.org/books/maqasid-bejou.pdf.
   For other Arabic editions of the book which are available on line visit: http://www.maktabah.org/component/content/article/75-misc/931-maqasid-al-falasifah-aims-of-the-philosophers---by-imam-Ghazzali.html?directory=143
[16]   Ghazzali, *Tahafut al falasifa* (The Incoherence of the Philosophers 1095). There are two English translations of this book, one by Michael E. Marmura, Brigham Young University, 2002, another, earlier, and somewhat abridged version by Sabih Ahmad Kamali (Pakistan Philosophical Congress, 1963)
[17]   Masumi Hamedani (1998), op.cit.; Montgomery Watt, *Islamic Theology and* Philosophy, Edinburgh University Press, 1985; Ayman Shihadeh, 'From Al-Ghazali to Al-Razi: 6th/12th Century Development in Muslim Philosophical Theology', *Arabic Sciences and Philosophy* **15** (2005) 141–179.
[18]   Lacy O'Leary, *How Greek Science Passed to the Arab* (Routledge and Kegan Paul, 1949); F. E. Peters, *Aristotle and the Arabs: The Aristotelian Tradition in Islam* (New York University Press, 1968); Joel L. Kraemer,

to digest and internalise what they had learnt through these sources and embarked on developing new synthetic systems which were novel innovations informed by their newly gained knowledge through translated materials and in tune with the teachings of their religion.[19]

All great Muslim philosophers of the classic period were not only first rate thinkers with regard to abstract philosophical topics they were also excellent natural scientists or master technologists (usually in fields such as medicine or chemistry or logic & linguistics). This trend was so prevalent that the Quranic term, *Hakim*, which means 'wise or endowed with wisdom', and is one of God's names, soon came to refer to philosophers who were being regarded as wise individuals who were capable of curing people from their intellectual/spiritual ills as well as illnesses in their bodies.[20]

Even a quick glance at the fields of expertise of Muslim philosophers of the classic period, reveals the extent to which these scholars had combined philosophical thinking with other disciplines. For example, Al-Kindi (d. 873), the first Muslim philosopher, was also an astronomer, a physicist, a mathematician and a cryptographer; Farabi (Alpharabius d. 951) who was known as *Mu'alim al-thani* (the second teacher after Aristotle who was regarded as the first

---

Humanism in the Renaissance of Islam: The Cultural Revival During the Buyid Age (Brill, 1992); Richard Walzer, *Greek into Arabic. Essays on Islamic Philosophy* (Oxford, Bruno Cassirer, 1962); Dimitri Gutas, *Greek Thought, Arabic Culture: The Graeco-Arabic Translation Movement in Baghdad and Early 'Abbasaid Society (2nd–4th 5th–10th c.)* (Routledge, 1998)

[19] S. H. Nasr, *Science and Civilization in Islam* (Harvard University Press, 1968); S. H. Nasr, *Islamic Science: An Illustrated History*, Kazi Publications, 1976; A. I. Sabra, 'The Appropriation and Subsequent Naturalization of Greek Science in Medieval Islam: A Preliminary Statement', *History of Science* **25**(3) (1987), 223–243; A. I. Sabra, 'Situating Arabic Science: Locality versus Essence', *Isis* **87**(4) (1996), 654–670; David Reisman, Felicitas Opwis (eds), *Islamic Philosophy, Science, Culture, and Religion: Studies in Honor of Dimitri Gustas* (Brill, 2006)

[20] Nasr, 'The Meaning and Concept of Philosophy in Islam', op. cit.; Morteza Motahari, *Ashnaei ba 'Ulum-e Eslami*, op. cit; Anisa Barkhah, 'Hikamt dar Falsafa Eslami' (Hikmat in the Islamic Philosophy), *Encyclopaedia of the World of Islam*, **13**, 752–760. Many of the entries of this Encyclopaedia are available online at: www.encylopaediaislamica.com.

teacher) was logician, philosopher, chemist, psychologist, physicist, political philosopher, and musicologist; Abu Rayhan Biruni (Alberonius d. 1048) was astronomer, historian, botanist, pharmacologist, geologist, philosopher, mathematician, and geographer; Ibn Sina (Avicenna, d. 1037) was logician, philosopher, physician, chemist, geologist, psychologist, astronomer and philosopher of science; Ibn Rushd (Averroës, d. 1198) was philosopher, physician, physicist, astronomer, and psychologist; Nasir al-Din Tusi (d. 1274) was astronomer, physicist, chemist, mathematician, and logician. Other great figures in Islamic civilisation during its classic period were similarly polymaths and experts in a variety of disciplines.[21]

Scientific exchanges between Muslim philosophers and thinkers in this period testify to the extent and diversity of the areas of their expertise.[22] A case in point is the correspondence between Abu Rayhan Biruni and Ibn Sina over a number of philosophical, physical and cosmological issues. Abu Rayhan put eighteen questions to ibn Sina, ten of which were related to various issues in Aristotle's *De Caelo* (*al-Sama' wa'l-'Alam*).[23] This correspondence, which in the words of a contemporary Muslim philosopher 'marks one of the highlights of Islamic intellectual history and in fact medieval

---

[21]   M. M. Sharif, *A History of Muslim Philosophy*, op. cit.; Nasr & Leaman, *A History of Islamic Philosophy*, op. cit.; Nasr, *Science and Civilization in Islam*, op. cit.; Nasr, *Islamic Science: An Illustrated History*, op. cit.; *Charles* Coulston Gillispie (ed.), *Dictionary of Scientific Biography* (Scribner, 1980); J. P. Hogendijk, A. I. Sabra (eds), *The Enterprise of Science in Islam: New Perspectives* (MIT, 2003)

[22]   See H. Daiber, 'Masa'il wa-Adjwiba' in *Encyclopaedia of Islam*, new edition) (Brill, 1991, Vol. VI), 636–9

[23]   Ibn Sina – Al-Biruni Correspondence, Translated by Rafik Berjak and Muzaffar Iqbal, available at: http://www.cis-ca.org/jol/vol1-no1/ibnsina-al-beruni-fp.pdf; *Al-As'ilah wa'l Ajwibah* (Questions and Answers): Al-Biruni and Ibn Sina, Arabic edited text with English and Persian introductions by Seyyed Hossein Nasr and Mehdi Mohaghegh (International Institute of Islamic Thought and Civilization, Kuala Lumpur, 1995); Also see, Mohsen Jahangiri, 'Khordeh Giran-e Ibn Sina' (Ibn Sina's Critics), in *Proceedings of Ibn Sina's Millennium Conference* (Publications of UNESCO's National Commission in Iran, 1979), 225–272. Prof. Jahangiri, besides the case of Ibn Sina–Abu Rayhan Biruni's correspondence, discusses other examples of intellectual correspondence/critical exchanges between Ibn Sina and his peers and responds to some of the well-known critiques of Sinaeian system.

natural philosophy and science in general'[24] could be compared with Newton-Clark and Leibniz correspondence.[25]

In his letters, Abu Rayhan criticizes reasons given by Aristotle for denying levity or gravity to the celestial spheres and the Aristotelian notion of circular motion being an innate property of the heavenly bodies. Biruni also rejects Aristotle's reasoning for his assertion that if the heavens were to be elliptical rather than spherical, a vacuum would be created, and that the motion of the heavens begins from the right side and from the east. He also asks how is it that Aristotle considered the element fire to be spherical. He further asks about the transformation of elements into each other, the natural tendency of the four elements in their upward and downward movements. In his other questions he discusses theories of vision, the habitation on different quarters of earth, and how two opposite squares in a square divided into four can be tangential. There are further questions about vacuum, nature of heat and the burning of bodies by radiation reflecting off a flask filled with water. In this context he also asks if things expand upon heating and contract upon cooling, why does a flask filled with water break when water freezes in it? And that why does ice float on water?[26]

Ibn Sina in his replies tries to defend Aristotle's position. Both masters demonstrate that they are well familiar with not only the philosophy of their time but also the physics of the day. A point worth mentioning here is that they both make use of empirical and logical arguments, including the two important arguments of *reductio ad absurdum* and *modus tollens*.

Being at home with respect to both philosophy and sciences of the day had enabled Muslim philosophers to apply their power of intellect to a wide variety of real problems in different intellectual and practical fields. The achievements of Muslim philosophers and scholars were so impressive that some commentators have rightly termed the classic period of Islamic philosophy as the 'Renaissance of Islam'.[27]

[24] S. H. Nasr, 'Introduction', in *Al-As'ilah wa'l Ajwibah* (Questions and Answers), op. cit., quoted in Berjak and Iqbal, op. cit.

[25] *The Leibniz-Clarke Correspondence*, edited by, H. G. Alexander (Manchester University Press, 1956)

[26] Op. cit., Ibn Sina – Al-Biruni Correspondence, Trans. by Berjak and Iqbal.

[27] Adam Mez, *Die Renaissance des Islams* (Hildesheim, 1968; reprint of 1922 edition); English translation by S. K. Bakhsh and D. S. Margoliouth, *The Renaissance of Islam* (London, 1927), quoted in Joel L. Kraemer, 'Humanism in the Renaissance of Islam: A Preliminary Study', *Journal of*

Islamic Philosophy: Past, Present and Future

Muslim philosophers in this period welcomed acquiring knowledge from all sources. Al-Kindi for example, in his *Fi al-Falsafa al-Ula* (On First Philosophy), writes:

> We ought not to be ashamed of appreciating the truth and of acquiring it wherever it comes from, even if it comes from races distant and nations different from us. For the seeker of truth nothing takes precedence over the truth, and there is no disparagement of the truth, nor belittling either of him who speaks it or of him who conveys it. (The status of) no one is diminished by the truth; rather does the truth ennoble all.[28]

This was, of course in complete agreement with famous saying attributed to the Prophet emphasising the importance of seeking knowledge, such as, 'seek knowledge even if it is in China', or 'seeking knowledge is an ordinance obligatory upon every Muslim'. Muslim philosophers developed an approach to learning which can be dubbed 'religious humanism'. It was based on the idea of cultivating individuals through teaching them various sciences and good habits so that they acquire a personal quality which is called *adab*, a concept very close to the Greek notion of *paideia*.[29] According to philosophers the path to true education (*adab haqiai*) was only through philosophy (i.e. rational deliberation). Ibn Miskawayh (932–1030) a philosopher from Rey and a chancery official at the Buwayhid court, in his *Tahdhib al-akhlaq* (the Refinement of Character) and *Jawidan khirad* (Perennial Philosophy) places *Adab haqiai* higher than *adab shar'i* (religious education). According to him and other philosophers, it was only through the former path, which would include the latter, that salvation could be achieved.[30]

The outcome of the intellectual efforts of Muslim philosophers and scholars in the Golden age of Islam (9th–12th CE) was not only

---

the American Oriental Society **104**(1) (1984) 135–164, (135). See also Kraemer's introduction to the second edition of his book, *Humanism in the Renaissance of Islam: The cultural Revival During the Buyid Age* (Brill, 1992).

[28] Al-Kindi, *Fi al-Falsafa al-Ula* (On First Philosophy), trans. by A. Ivry, Al-Kindi's Metaphysics (Albany, 1974), 58, quoted in Joel L. Kraemer, 'Humanism in the Renaissance of Islam: A Preliminary Study', op. cit., 149

[29] Ibrahim Moosa, 'Muslim Ethics?' in *The Blackwell Companion To Religious Ethics*, edited by William Schweiker (Blackwell, 2005), 237–243.

[30] Kraemer, op. cit. p. 151; Lenn Goodman, *Islamic Humanism* (Oxford University Press, 2003), 108–109

greatly beneficial to the flourishing of Islamic civilisation but also provided European scholars with a rich reservoir of fresh ideas.[31] These ideas played a significant role in bringing about the European Renaissance. In the words of one Western scholar:

> Although there is not a single aspect of European growth in which the decisive influence of Islamic culture is not traceable, nowhere is it so clear and momentous as in the genesis of that power which constitutes the paramount distinctive force of the modern world, and the supreme source of its victory – natural sciences and scientific spirit. ... The debt of our science to that of the Muslims does not consist in startling discoveries of revolutionary theories; science owes a great deal more to Muslim culture, it owes its existence. The ancient world was ... pre-scientific. The astronomy and mathematics of the Greeks were a foreign importation never thoroughly acclimatized in Greek culture. The Greeks systematized, generalized, and theorized, but the patient ways of investigation, the accumulation of positive knowledge, the minute methods of science, detailed and prolonged observation and experimental inquiry were altogether alien to the Greek temperament. Only in Hellenistic Alexandria was any approach to scientific work conducted in the ancient world. What we call science arose in Europe as a result of new spirit of inquiry, of new methods of investigation, of the method of experiment, observation, and measurement, of the development of mathematics in a form unknown to the Greeks. That spirit and those methods were introduced into the European world by Muslims.[32]

Many of the works of Muslim scholars, philosophers, scientists, and theologians, were translated into Latin. Their counterparts in Europe greatly benefitted from the fruits of the intellectual labour of their colleagues in the Muslim world. The works of philosophers such as of al-Kindi, Farabi, Ibn Sina, and Ibn Rushd were eagerly studied by European scholars and their ideas were incorporated in the theses produced by these scholars. In the assimilation of Islamic

[31] George Saliba, *Islamic Sciences and the Making of European Renaissance* (Massachusetts Institute of Technology, 2007); J. P. Hogendijk, A. I. Sabra (eds), *The Enterprise of Science in Islam: New Perspectives*, op. cit.; Nasr, *Science and Civilization in Islam*, op. cit.

[32] Robert Briffault in *The Making of Humanity* (London: George Allen and Unwin Ltd., 1928), 190–1, quoted in M. M. Sharif, *A History of Islamic Philosophy*, vol. 22, 1355–56

thought, as Charles Burnett has observed, several stages can be observed:

> First, there was an interest in Neoplatonic cosmology and psychology in the latter half of the twelfth century, which fostered the translation of texts by al-Kindi, al-Farabi, the Ikhwan al-Safa' and, especially, Avicenna (Ibn Sina). Second, the desire to understand Aristotle's philosophy resulted in the translation of the commentaries and epitomes of Averroes (Ibn Rushd) in the second quarter of the thirteenth century. ...[Third] in the late fifteenth century, a renewed interest in the ancient texts led scholars to search out the most accurate interpretations of these texts, ... they turned for new translations or retranslations of Avicenna and, in particular, Averroes. From the early sixteenth century, Arabic philosophical texts were again translated directly into Latin, Arabic speakers began to collaborate with Christian scholars and the foundations for the teaching of Arabic were being laid.[33]

But while the Latin west was benefiting from the views of Muslim thinkers and foundations for the Renaissance were gradually being laid, a dynamism of a different type was at work in the land of Islam.[34] I deal with this development in the next part of this paper.

---

[33] Charles Burnett, 'Islamic Philosophy- Transmission into Western Europe', *Routledge Encyclopaedia of Philosophy*, Version 1.0 (London: Routledge, 1998)

[34] George Saliba, *Islamic Sciences and the Making of European Renaissance,* op. cit.; A. I. Sabra (eds), *The Enterprise of Science in Islam: New Perspectives,* op. cit., Nasr, *Science and Civilization in Islam,* op. cit.; Dag Nikolaus Hasse, 'Influence of Arabic and Islamic Philosophy on the Latin West', *Stanford Encyclopaedia of Philosophy*, http://plato.stanford.edu/entries/arabic-islamic-influence/; Nayef Al-Rodhan, *The Role of the Arab-Islamic World in the Rise of the West* (Palgrave-Macmillan, 2012); Jonathan Lyons, *The House of Wisdom: How the Arabs Transformed Western Civilization* (Bloomsbury Publishing, 2010); Slaim Hassan (ed.), *1001 Inventions: The Enduring Legacy of Muslim Civilization* (National Geographic Society, 2012); Deborah Howard, *Venice and the East: The Impact of the Islamic World on Venetian Architecture* (Yale University Press, 2000); Jim Khalil, *Pathfinders: The Golden Age of Arabic Science*, Penguin, 2012; Michael Morgan, *Lost History: The Enduring Legacy of Muslim Scientists, Thinkers and Artists* (National Geographic Society, 2008).

III. Decline of Scientific Spirit in Islamic Civilisation

Despite all the emphasis in the Quran and the sunna of the Prophet and Imams (in the case of Shi'i Islam) on the importance of acquiring and developing knowledge, scientific and philosophical spirit in Islamic civilisation took a nose dive and experienced a gradual decline from the twelfth century onward. However, the seeds for this decline had already been sowed in the soil of Islamic intellectual life when in the middle of the ninth century al-Mutawkkil (d. 861) became caliph. He put in motion a programme of purging the rational theologians, the Mu'tazalites, and supporting their literalist rivals, the Ash'arites. Philosophers like Kindi, who were at the receiving end of Mutawakkil's anti-rationality campaign and his policy of repression, also suffered a reversal of their personal fortune[35]. Given Mutawkkil's role in promotion of the orthodoxy and dogmatic approaches to theology, it is somewhat amusing to read the following entry in Wikipedia:

> **Al-Mutawakkil 'Alā Allāh Ja'far ibn al-Mu'tasim** (*Arabic* المتوكل على الله جعفر بن المعتصم) (March 822 – 11 December 861) was an Abbasid *caliph* who reigned in *Samarra* from 847 until 861. He succeeded his brother *al-Wāthiq* and is known for putting an end to the Mihna "ordeal", the Inquisition-like attempt by his predecessors to impose a single *Mu'tazili* version of *Islam.*[36]

The dominance of the Ash'ari thought provided grist for the mills of those who maintained that Islam is a self-sufficient system in every respect, including knowledge production. The gradual but consistent and continuous ascendency of *fuqha* (jurists), *'urafa* (mystics), and *mutikallimun* (theologians) of Ash'ari persuasion, helped to create an intellectual environment in which rational thinking and scientific pursuits were regarded as either non-Islamic or not suitable for the believers and alien to the spirit of Islam. The following story about Abu Rayhan Biruni nicely shows the attitude of the clerics and theologians towards science and scientists. Abu Rayhan, as the story goes, 'was accused by a contemporary divine of heresy when he used the Byzantine (solar) calendar for an instrument he had invented for determining the times of the prayers. Al-Biruni retorted by saying,

---

[35] Majid Fakhry, *History of Islamic Philosophy* (Routledge, 1993), 68.
[36] http://en.wikipedia.org/wiki/Al-Mutawakkil, accessed: 31/1/13.

"the Byzantines also partake of bread. Will you now promulgate a religious sanction against bread?"[37]

By the time of the great Persian Ash'ari jurist, sufi-saint, and *mutikallim*, Abu Hamed Mohammad Ghazzali (d. 1111), the orthodoxy was firmly in place in all parts of Muslim lands in which one of the four Sunni schools of *fiqh* (jurisprudence) was being practiced. Ghazzali, who was for some years the head of the largest university (Niẓamiyeh) in Baghdad, in his capacity as a defender and promoter of the orthodoxy produced a number of extremely influential books which were hugely influential in the intellectual eco-system of both the Sunni and the Shi'a worlds. Although, his influence on the latter's views was indirect. In his *Tahafut al-Falasifa* he argued against many of the main doctrines of the mashsha'i (Peripatetic) philosophers in their own terms. At the end of this long, important and carefully argued book, Ghazzali, in the very last page of the book which was titled, 'Conclusion', suddenly put on his other hat as a *faqih* and in the space of just one page, issued a fateful fatwa (religious edict) against philosophers and philosophy. He wrote:

> If someone says: "You have explained the doctrines of these [philosophers]; do you then say conclusively that they are infidels and that the killing of those who uphold their beliefs is obligatory?" we say: Pronouncing them infidels is necessary in three questions. One of them is the question of the world's pre-eternity and their statement that all substances are pre-eternal. The second is their statement that God's knowledge does not encompass the temporal particulars among individual [existents]. The third is their denial of the resurrection of bodies and their assembly at the day of judgment.[38]

He went on to suggest that there are seventeen other doctrines, including 'Their argument against God's attributes, Their argument that it is impossible that something should share a genus with God, Their argument that God is pure existence with no quiddity' which makes philosopher guilty of the lesser charge of heresy (*bid'ah*).[39]

Having declared philosophy as an unsuitable subject for study in the eco-system of Islamic culture, Ghazzali, in his *magnum opus*, *Ihya*

---

[37]   Abdus-Salam has noted in his *Ideals and Realities* (World Scientific Publishing Co Pte Ltd, 1990), 197

[38]   Ghazzali, *The Incoherence of Philosophers*, trans. by Michael Marmura, op.cit., 226

[39]   Cf. Marmura (2002), op. cit. and Kamali (1963), op. cit.

al-'Ulum al-Din (the Revival of Islamic Sciences) which is a forty-volume encyclopaedia of Islamic sciences of his day, introduced a new classification of sciences.[40] He divided sciences into two general groups, religious and non-religious. And made it clear that only the first group has intrinsic value. Religious sciences are those which 'have been acquired from the prophets and are not arrived at either by reason, like arithmetic, or by experimentation, like medicine, or by hearing, like language.'[41] Non-religious sciences 'are divided into praiseworthy (*Mahmoud*), blameworthy (*madhmum*), and permissible (*mubah*). Using another set of *fiqhi* (juristic) terminology, Ghazzali suggested that sciences, from another point of view, are further divided into two categories. One, whose study is compulsory for all Muslims (*Frad 'ayn* or *wajib 'ayni*). The other, which is *fard kifayah* or *wajib kifa'i*, which covers all those sciences whose study become compulsory if no one in the Islamic society study them. But if at least one individual studies them, then religious obligation will be lifted from others.[42] Ghazzali, then went on to explain that among the non-religious praiseworthy sciences there are some whose acquisition is *fard kifayah* (conditionally obligato) and he singled out medicine and arithmetic as two prime examples of those type of sciences which are indispensable for the welfare of this world.[43]

After defining *fiqh* (jurisprudence) as another type of science whose acquisition is conditionally obligatory, he raised the following question in the form of a dialogue with his reader:

> If you should say, "why have you regarded medicine and jurisprudence in the same way when medicine pertains to the affairs of this world, namely the welfare of the body, while upon jurisprudence depends the welfare of religion ...?" then know that ...

[40]   Ghazzali, *Ihya' 'Ulum ad-Din* (Revival of Religious Sciences), edited by Hafiz Iraqi and Abd al-Rahim bin Hussain, Dar al-Nashr al-Arabi (n.d.p, n.p.p). There are many editions of Ghazzali's *magnum opus* in Arabic. English translations of the volumes of the *Ihya* are done by various translators. Many of these translations can be accessed on-line at http://www.ghazali.org/site/ihya.htm. Also see, The Revival of Religious Sciences, trans. by Bankey Behari, [No place of publication]: Sufi Publ. Co., 1964/1972

[41]   Ghazzali, *Ihya' 'Ulum ad-Din* (the Revival of Islamic Sciences), Book 1, *The Book of Knowledge*, translated by Nabih Amin Faris, Islamic Book Service, 30. This text is available on line at: http://www.ghazali.org/site/ihya.htm

[42]   Ghazazli, *Ihay'*, Ibid, book 1, 30–38

[43]   Ibid.

in fact the two sciences differ. Jurisprudence is superior to medicine on three counts; first because it is religious knowledge and unlike medicine, which is not religious knowledge, jurisprudence is derived from prophecy; second, it is superior to medicine because no one of those who are treading the road to the hereafter can do without it, neither the healthy nor ailing; while on the other hand only the sick, who are a minority, need medicine; thirdly, because jurisprudence is akin to the science of the road of hereafter, ...[44]

Immediately after the above he makes it clear to the reader that: 'whenever the science of the road to the hereafter is compared with jurisprudence the superiority of the former is evident'.[45]

Ghazzali's classification of sciences was whole-heartedly accepted by both the Sunni and the Shi'a Muslims. The latter produced a Shi'atized version of Ghazzali's book under the title of *Mahajja al-Bida fi Tahdhib al-Ihya* (the clear path in refining ihya).[46]

The tendency of placing religious sciences on a higher plane than non-religious sciences was further amplified in the works of Muslim mystics ('urfa) and Sufis. In their teachings, non-religious sciences were regarded as tools and instruments whose purpose was to help Muslims in this life to dedicate themselves to the study of truly worthwhile sciences. The story of an alleged meeting between Ibn Sina and Abu Sa'id Abu al-Khayr (d. 1049), the great Persian mystic is very illuminating in this context. According to one version of the story whose authenticity cannot be corroborated, the two great scholars upon their first encounter remained in private conversation for three consecutive days, only took breaks for performing their daily prayers and having some sustenance. After the meeting, disciples of Ibn Sina asked him how he had found the mystic. Ibn Sina, reportedly, had replied that whatever he knew the mystic also knew not through philosophical arguments but by means of his mystical visions. Devotees of Abu Sa'id asked their master how he had found the philosopher. Abu Sa'id had replied, wherever he had gone in his mystical journeys he had seen the philosopher, in the shape of blind man, who was trying to find his way by means of his stick of reason.[47]

---

[44]   Ibid., 39
[45]   Ibid.
[46]   Mulla Muhsin Faid Kashani, *Mahajja al-Bida fi Tahdhib al-Ihya*, edited by Ali Akbar Ghaffari, Qom, Intesharat-e Jame'a Modarresin Qom, n.d.p.
[47]   Mirza Abu'l Fazl Zanjani, et al. *Nameh Daneshvaran* (Intellectual Biographies of Scholars, 1296/1878), Vol. 1, 613

To better appreciate the intellectual changes that took place between the 10th and 12th centuries from Farabi to Ghazzali, it would be useful to briefly compare Farabi's classification of sciences with that of Ghazzali's. In his *Ihsa al-'Ulum* (The Enumeration of Sciences), Farabi classified all known branches of knowledge of his time under five headings:

I. Science of language (syntax, grammar, pronunciation and speech, poetry); **II. Logic** (including oratory [rhetoric] and study of poetry); **III. The preliminary sciences** (1. Arithmetic: practical and theoretical, 2. Geometry: practical and theoretical, 3. Optics, 4. Science of the heavens: Astrology; Astronomy, 5. Music: practical and theoretical, 6. Science of weights, 7. Science of tool-making); **IV. Physics** (sciences of nature) **and Metaphysics** (science concerned with the Divine and the principles of things); **V. Sciences of Society** (1. Politics, 2. Jurisprudence (law or *fiqh*), 3. Theology (dialectics or *Kalam* [apology])[48]

In the above table there is no mention of *irfan* (mysticism). For Farabi the most important sciences are metaphysics and physics. Philosophers, and not mystics or jurists or theologians, are held in the highest esteem and compared with the prophets. *Fiqh* and *Kalam* are regarded as practical sciences.

Another factor which was instrumental in the eclipse of rational trends in Muslim countries was closing of the door of *ijtihad* among the Sunni Muslims dealt another severe blow to the spirit of critical thinking in Islam. As Joseph Schacht has observed:

By the beginning of the fourth century of the *hijra* (about 900 CE), ... the point had been reached when the scholars of all schools [of *fiqh*] felt that all essential questions had been thoroughly discussed and finally settled, and a consensus gradually established itself to the effect that from that time onward no one might be deemed to have the necessary qualifications for independent reasoning in law, and that all future activity would have to be confined to the explanation, application, and, at the most, interpretation of the doctrine as it had been laid down

---

[48] Farabi, *Ihsa al-'Ulum* (Beirut: Dar wa Maktabata al-Hilah, 1375/ 1996), 15–16; I have used S. H. Nasr, *Science and Civilization in Islam*, 60–62, with some revision based on the original Arabic text. See also Majid Fakhry, *A History of Islamic Philosophy*, op. cit. Fakhry, somewhat misleadingly suggests that Fabari 'classifies them [sciences of his day] under eight headings'. (page 115)

once and for all. This 'closing of the door of *ijtihad*', as it was called, amounted to the demand for *taklid* [emulation], a term which had originally denoted the kind of reference to Companions of the Prophet that had been customary in the ancient schools of law, and which now, came to mean the unquestioning acceptance of the doctrines of established schools and authorities.[49]

To the above intellectual trends, social and political upheavals in Muslim countries should be added. The decline of the Buyid dynasty (934–1055) which was the prime-mover behind what Kraemer has dubbed 'the Renaissance of Islam' and the restoration of the orthodoxy by the Saljuqs (1016–1307), the animosity between the Abbasid dynasty (750–1258) in Baghdad and the Fatimid dynasty (909–1171) in Egypt, the Crusades (1095 and 1291), the invasion of the Moghuls, Hulago Khan (1218–1265) and later Taymour (Tamerlane, 1336–1405) all helped the creation of an environment which was not amenable to free and critical thinking.

The collective result of all the above factors was that philosophy as a discipline and a tradition died a sudden death among the Sunni Muslims in the Eastern flank of Islamic civilisation. Philosophical thinking, however, did not die away among Muslims. It followed two different paths in the eastern and western parts of Muslim lands. In Spain, Muslim philosophers such as Ibn Bajjah (Avempass, 1095–1143), Ibn Tufayl (1105–1185) and Ibn Rushd (Averroës, 1126–1198) continued the *Mashsha'i* (peripatetic) tradition.[50]

Ibn Rushd achieved fame among European scholars as master commentator of Aristotle works. He also established himself as a first rank philosopher by producing a philosophical defence of his fellow-philosophers against Ghazzali's devastating criticisms,[51] and

[49] Joseph Schacht, *In Introduction to Philosophy of Law in Islam* (Oxford University Press, 1984), 71–72, quoted in Wael B. Hallaq, 'Was the Gate of Ijtihad Closed?' *International Journal of Middle East Studies*, **16**(1) (1984), 3–41 (page 5). Hallaq tries to reject the view that the gate of *ijtihad* was closed among the Sunni Muslims. However, his arguments actually corroborate a sad historical fact.

[50] Cf. M. M. Sharif (1963), op. cit.; Nasr & Leamn (1996) op. cit; Fakhry (2003), op. cit.

[51] Ibn Rushd, *Tahafut al-Tahafut* (The Incoherence of the *Incoherence*), edited by Soleiman Donia (Cairo: Dar al-Ma'ariff, 1964); *Averroës' Tahafut al-Tahafut*, translated by Simon van der Bergh (The Trustees of the Gibb Memorial, 1954). See also, Majid Fakhry, *Averroës*

further developing earlier theories of intellect, by suggesting a new model in which individuals' acquired knowledge after unification with the active intellect would lose their identities and instead would collaborate in creating a collective pool of knowledge and ideas. This view somewhat resembles Popper's notion of World 3.[52] However, with the collapse of Muslim dynasties in Spain in the late fifteen century, development of Islamic philosophy in the Sunni Islam came to an end and philosophical spirit vanished from its eco-system.

Even the heroic efforts of Ibn Rushd to show the compatibility between reason and religion[53] could not save philosophy and rational thinking from its fate. The orthodoxy would only endorse the application of reason strictly within the limits of religion alone. And even here, only a literal interpretation of religion was allowed. The victory of *Ahl Hadith* (the literalist transmitters of the tradition of the Prophet) meant that even the Quran could only be studied in the light of a literal or at most analogical understanding of the sayings and deeds of the Prophet.

Philosophy however, survived in the Shiʻi Islam. It is to this development that we now turn.

(Ibn Rushd): His Life, Works, and Influence (One World, 2008). The efficacy and cogency of Ibn Rushd's Arguments against Ghazzali is disputed by some scholars. See for example, Josef Puig Muntada, 'Ibn Rushd vs. Ghazali: Reconsideration of a Polemic', *The Muslim World* **LXXXII**(1–2) (1992), 113–131

[52] Derek Gatherer, 'Meme Pools, World 3 and Averroës' Vision of Immortality' *Zygon* **33**(2) (1998), 203–219. Resemblance between Ibn Rushd's Active Mind and Popper's World 3 (third world) however, should not be exaggerated. With regard to W3 Popper points out that: 'Although man-made, the third world (as I understand the term) is superhuman in that its contents are virtual rather than actual objects of thought, and in the sense that only a finite number of the infinity of virtual objects can ever become actual objects of thought. We must beware, however, of interpreting these objects as thoughts of a superhuman consciousness as did, for example, Aristotle, Plotinus, and Hegel.' (Popper, *Objective Knowledge* (Oxford University Press, 1972), n8, 199)

[53] Ibn Rushd (Averroës), 'On the Harmony of Religion and Philosophy' in *The Philosophy and Theology of Averroes*, trans. Mohammed Jamil-al-Rehman, Baroda: A.G. Widgery, 1921; Majid Fakhry, 'Al-Farabi and the Reconciliation of Plato and Aristotle', *Journal of the History of Ideas* **26**(4) (1965), 469–478

Islamic Philosophy: Past, Present and Future

IV. From a predominantly rational mode of philosophising to developing novel systems of theosophy

A Closer look at the development of philosophical thought in Islam from its early stages onward reveals that the relationship between Philosophy, *Kalam* (theology) and *Irfan* (mysticism) has not been unambiguous and their boundaries have not been clear-cut. Such a study makes it clear that *Kalam* and *Irfan* have always had some sort of influence on rational approaches to philosophising and philosophers have always been acutely aware of the need for addressing the concerns of not only *Mutikallimun* and *'Urafa*, but also *Fuqha*. Exceptions to this rule have remained in a small minority.

Almost all of the first rank thinkers who contributed to development of intellectual heritage of Islamic civilisation were devout Muslims. This trait, amongst other things and as far as Muslim philosophers were concerned, meant that although they were bolder in their intellectual investigations than their theologian counterparts, nevertheless, they did not seem to be willing to go as far as to reject Islamic doctrines. Even someone like Muhammad ibn Zakariya Razi (Rhazes d. 925) who had critical views about prophets and prophecy was a God-fearing Muslim and a respected personality amongst his contemporaries and subsequent generation of Muslims. Some contemporary scholars in the West have appreciated this point and have noted that al-Razi 'far from being a heretic; ... was simply an individualistic thinker, merely anti-establishment or anti-orthodox'.[54]

Religious outlook of these philosophers and thinkers had impacted upon their views. Many of these philosophers had developed ideas which were compatible with their religious beliefs. For example, al-Kindi, the first proper Muslim philosopher, using neo-Platonic ideas, had argued for a creator God and had rejected Aristotelian notion of the Prime Mover. He had also developed arguments against creation *ex nihilo* and also in defence of the possibility of the occurrence of miracles[55].

---

[54]   Martin Plessner 'Heresy and Rationalism in the First Centuries of Islam', quoted in Joel L. Kraemer, 'Humanism in the Renaissance of Islam', op. cit., 160

[55]   M. M. Sharif, *A History of Philosophy*, op. cit; Seyyed Hossein Nasr and Oliver Leaman (eds), *History of Islamic Philosophy*, op. cit.; Reza Akbarian, *Seyre-e Falsafa dar Iran-e Eslami* (Development of Philosophy in Iran) (Tehran: Entesharat-e Mu'asseseh Tahghighat va Tuse'ah 'Ulum-e Ensani, 2008)

Ali Paya

Likewise Farabi, while placing philosophers on the highest rung of the intellectual ladder equating them with prophets, developed an argument for the existence of God based on a difference between a necessary being that is self-subsistent and contingent beings which are dependent upon the necessary being. This is the third form of cosmological argument. The earlier two forms, as formulated by Aristotle, were based on the ideas of motion and potentiality.[56]

Ibn Sina, who is undoubtedly the greatest peripatetic philosopher in Islamic philosophy and more than any other Muslim philosopher has emphasised the importance of intellectual exploration of reality, was proud that for the first time he had been able to develop a completely novel argument for the existence of God. He dubbed this argument, 'Burhan-e Siddiqin = the argument of the righteous'. The novelty of this argument lies in the fact that contrary to other arguments for the existence of God, like the cosmological argument or the argument from design whose starting points are existence of contingent beings and from there they argue for the need for positing a necessary or wise being, it concentrates on the notion of existence itself and demonstrates that this very notion, without any need for making use of the notion of contingent beings, suffices to prove the existence of God as a necessary being.[57] Ibn Sina goes even further than this in taking care of the religious sensitivities of his time; in his discussion of the vexed issue of resurrection he states that rationally he can only establish the resurrection of humankind souls but not their bodies; but then he goes on to emphasise that the bodily resurrection is warranted by *shar'* (religion) and 'there is no way to

---

[56]   M. M. Sharif, *A History of Philosophy*, op. cit., 1371; Akbarian, *Seyre-e Falsafa dar Iran-e Eslami*, op. cit.

[57]   Ibn Sina, *al-Isharat wa al-Tanbihat* (Remarks and Admonitions), ed. Sulayman Dunya (Cairo: Dar al-Ma'arif, 1957, 4 vols. Vol. 3), 66. See also, Toby Meyer, 'Ibn Sina's Burhan al-Siddiqin', *Journal of Islamic Studies* **12**(1) (2001), 18–39; Akbarian, op. cit. 2008. *Burhan-e Siddiqin* is perhaps the most famous and most important argument for the existence of God developed by Muslim philosophers. Since Ibn Sina's introduction of this argument, many of the great Muslim philosophers have tried to develop more complete versions of this same argument. These new versions, in view of their produces, were free from the shortcomings of the previous versions. A twentieth century Iranian philosopher, Mirza Mehdi Ashtiyani, in his commentary on a major philosophy text of nineteenth century, the *Manzumeh* of Haji Sabzevari (Tehran University Press in collaboration with McGill University Press, 1352/1973), has listed nineteen versions of this argument in the works of various Muslim philosophers.

demonstrate bodily resurrection save through the way of *shari'a* [religious (Quranic) teachings] and assent to Prophetic sayings'.[58]

The last great Muslim polymath philosopher of the Golden age of Islam, namely, Khwaja Muhammad ibn Muhammad ibn Hasan Tusi, better known as Nasir al-Din Tusi (1201–1274), while producing scientific and philosophical doctrines, also assumed the mantle of a proper theologian and penned a number of important theological books. In fact, his *Tajrid al-I'tiqad* (Simplifying the Articles of Faith) has been regarded as one of the most important Shi'a theological books, on which both Shi'i and Sunni theologians have written commentaries.[59]

Mystical and Sufi tendencies were also discernible in the works of almost all Muslim philosophers of the classic period of Islam. In this respect it is worth noting in passing that Pythagoras and his mystical school were received more warmly than Thales and his school by Muslim scholars of the classic period and in particular *Ikhwan al-Safa* (the Brethren of Purity) who were one of the major forces behind the Renaissance of Islam in ninth-tenth centuries.[60] Muslim scholars were familiar with the pre-Socratic thinkers like Thales, Anaxagoras, Empedocles, Pythagoras, and Democritus, Heraclitus and Parmenides. However, Empedocles and Pythagoras received more attention. Muslims believed that Empedocles had

---

[58]   Ibn Sina, *Kitab al-Najat* [The Book of Salvation], edited by Majid Fakhry (Beirut: Manshrat Dar al-Jadida al-Afaq, 1986), 326. See also Majid Fakhry, 'Islam' in Routledge Encyclopaedia of Philosophy of Religion, edited by Chad Meister and Paul Copan (Routledge, 2013), 76–86

[59]   Nasir al-Din al-Tusi, Tajrid al-I'tiqad, Mashhad: Ja'fari, n.d.; Norman Calder, Jawid Mojaddedi, and Andrew Rippin provide a translation of al-Tusi's *Tajrid al-i'tiqad: Classical Islam: A Sourcebook of Religious Literature* (London: Routledge, 2003), Section 7.1.

[60]   Popper compares and contrasts the impact of Pythagorean (mystical) and Ionian (Thales) rational schools and their attitude towards open, critical discussion on the subsequent development of knowledge. See his 'Back to Presocratics' in *Conjectures and Refutations* (Routledge, 1963/2002) 183–205. For Ikhwan al-Safa and their School see Joel Kraemer, *Philosophy in the Renaissance of Islam: Abu Sulayman al-Sijistani and his Circle* (Brill, 1986); Godefroid de Callataÿ, *Ikhwan al-Safa'A Brotherhood of Idealists on the Fringe of Orthodox Islam* (Oxford: One World, 2005); Nade el-Bizi, *Epistles of the Brethren of Purity: the Ikhwān al-Ṣafā' and their Rasā'il: an introduction* (Oxford University Press, 2008); Ian Richard Netton, *Muslim Neoplatonists: An Introduction to the Thought of the Brethren of Purity* (Routledge Curzon, 2002)

'received instruction in wisdom from Luqman, the legendary sage mentioned in the Quran'[61] while the latter had been taught by Solomon. As Fakhry has observed, 'many of Pythagoras' moral aphorisms are given in the Arabic anthologies'.[62] Osman Baker has noted that in the classic period of the Islamic civilisation:

> In contrast to Peripatetic philosopher-scientists who emphasize logic and demonstration, the Hermetic-Pythagorean scientists and philosophers, who also played an important role in Islamic science, adopted from methodological approach that is based primarily upon a metaphysical and symbolic interpretation of things. This is the kind of approach used for example by Jabir ibn Hayyan in alchemy and by the Ikhwan al-Safa in the various mathematical sciences.[63]

Immediately after the above observation, Osman adds another remark which, though he does not develop it further, is directly relevant to the topic under discussion in this paper. He says, 'Certain elements of this method [metaphysical and symbolic interpretation of things] are also to be found in the scientific methodology of those scientists whom are usually identify with Peripatetic school such as Ibn Sina'.[64]

The case of Ibn Sina is of particular importance. Ibn Sina, the Persian philosopher is, as pointed out before, undoubtedly the greatest peripatetic philosopher in Islamic philosophy and his encyclopaedic philosophical work, *al-Shifa* is a paragon of rational thinking. Yet despite all his penchants for rational approaches later in his life and in his later works, he laid down the foundations of an intellectual legacy whose hallmark was an emphasis on mystical methods of acquiring wisdom in contrast to rational methods of acquiring knowledge.[65] Ibn Sina's later philosophy, known as *al-Hikmat al-Mashreqiyah* (The Eastern Philosophy) turned into the dominant trend of thought among subsequent generations of Muslim philosophers.[66]

[61] Majid Fakhry, *A History of Islamic Philosophy*, op. cit.
[62] Ibid.
[63] Osman Baker, 'Science', in S. H. Nasr and Oliver Leaman (eds), *A History of Islamic Philosophy*, op. cit., 942–3
[64] Ibid., 943
[65] Muslim philosophers make a distinction between wisdom, which they regard to be of Divine nature, and knowledge, which is produced by man's cognitive faculty. For a detailed discussion see S. H. Nasr, *Knowledge and the Sacred* (SUNY Press, 1989)
[66] The text of *al-Hikmat al-Mashreqiyah* is mostly lost. In what has remained, assuming its authenticity, Ibn Sina completely renounces his

Islamic Philosophy: Past, Present and Future

In turning away from his peripatetic phase towards his new philosophy, Ibn Sina made a move, which though mostly symbolic and formalistic, proved to be very influential: in his *Danishnama-yi 'ala'i*, which was the first encyclopaedia of philosophy written in Persian in the Islamic era he, for the first time in the history of Muslim intellectual thought, began his discussion with the section on metaphysics (*ilahiyat*) and from there proceeded to natural philosophy (*tabi'iyat*). This was in sharp contrast to the way Aristotle and many Muslim authors, including Ibn Sina in his other works on philosophy, would organise the chapters of their books; they would all start with a chapter on natural philosophy (physics) and then move on the metaphysics. Ibn Sina's innovation was emulated by the subsequent generations of Muslim philosophers who came to the scene few centuries after Ibn Sina. As Nasr has observed, 'Later Safavid and Qajar authors, among them Sadr al-Din Shirazi, Mulla Muhsin Faid [Kashani], and Hajji Mulla Hadi Sabzivari, have followed the precedent of the *Danishnamah*'.[67]

The unwanted consequence of this seemingly innocent change was an unfortuante influence on the further development of philosophy: later generations of philosophers and theologians, by and large, paid less and less attention to the study of natural philosophy. Instead, as we shall see below, most of them chanelled their energies into developing theosophical doctrines and systems of theosophy. The section on natural sciences and physics (*tabi'iyat*) in subsequent books on philosophy remained almost the same as it was at the time of Ibn Sina or thereabout. Few centuries after renunciation of peripatetic

---

peripatetic phase: 'We have been inspired to bring together writings upon the subject matter which has been the source of difference among people disposed to argumentation and not to study it with the eyes of fanaticism, desire, habit, or attachment. We have no fear if we find differences with what the people instructed in Greek books have become familiar with through their own negligence and shortness of understanding. And we have no fear if we reveal to the philosophers something other than what we have written for the common people – the common people who have become enamoured of the Peripatetic philosophers and who think that God has not guided anyone but them or that no one has reached Divine Mercy except them.' From *Mantiq al-Mashriqiyyīn* (The Logic of the Orientals) translated by S. H. Nasr, in *An Anthology of Philosophy in Persia*, volume 1, From *Zoroaster to 'Umar Khayyām*, edited by S. H. Nasr and Mehdi Aminrazavi (London: I. B. Tauris, 2008), 321

[67] S. H. Nasr, *An Introduction to Islamic Cosmological Doctrines*, 187, n. 26.

philosophy by Ibn Sina, many of philosophers and theologians had no competence in further developing in natural sciences. Apart from few exceptions, most of the rest, at best, could only explicate the achievements of their predecessors to their students, and at worse, did not have a good grasp of the issues discussed in the sections on *tabi'iytat*. Nevertheless, out of reverence for the past masters, they would dutifully reproduce these sections, now regarded as relics, in their own books on philosophy and *Kalam*.[68]

The main charctristic of Ibn Sina's new school, *al-Hikmat al-Mashreqiyah*, was its emphasis on the power of intuition and mystical experiences, as against rational thinking, as the most effective tool for exploring reality and acquiring knowledge about it.[69]

Al-Hikmat al-Mashreqiyah was further developed into a comprehensive philosophical system by another great Persian philosopher, Shahab/Shihab al-Din Suhrawardi (1158–1191), the founder of *Maktab-i Ishraq* (the School of Illumination) who was killed at the tender age of 38 by the *fatwa* (edict) of the orthodox jurists in Syria.[70] Suhrawardi's system was a novel synthesis of various trends of thought, including Platonic and neo-Platonic ideas, doctrines from the wisdom of ancient Persian sages (*Hukamaye-Pahlavi*), doctrines extracted from the Quran and the teachings of the Prophet. Suhrawardi also, introduced a whole set of new vocabularies into the discourse of Islamic philosophy. The central theme in his philosophy was the notion of light which, to some extent, represented the concept of *wujud* (being) in the earlier philosophies. God for example, was *Nur al-Anwar* (Light of Lights).[71]

[68] Masumi Hamadni, op. cit., 262

[69] It is interesting to note in passing that Ibn Sina's great detractor, namely Ghazzali, in his later life, just like Ibn Sina, developed a mystical approach in his books like *Mishkat al-Anwar* (Nich of Lights) in line with Ibn Sina's *al-Hikmat al-Mashreqiyah*.

[70] For Suhrawadri's life and work see S. H. Nasr, *Three Muslim Sages, Avicenna, Suhrawardi, Ibn 'Arabi* (Harvard University Press, Cambridge). For a comparison between Suhrawardi and Ibn Sina's philosophies see, Mehdi Aminrazavi, How Ibn Sinian Is Suhrawardi's Theory of Knowledge?, *Philosophy East and West* **53**(2) (2003), 203–214. Aminrazavi argues that the two philosophers adhered to the following hierarchy of knowledge: 1. Knowledge by definition; 2. Knowledge by sense perception; 3. Knowledge through *a priori* concepts; 4. Knowledge by presence; 5. Knowledge through direct experience: mysticism.

[71] Suhrawardi, *Himkmat al-Ishraq* (Philosophy of Illumination), translated by John Walbridge & Hossein Ziai (Brigham Young University Press,

Islamic Philosophy: Past, Present and Future

In his captivating works both in Persian and Arabic, Suhrawardi narrated an epic story on a metaphysical plane whose main hero was man who had fallen from the realm of light into the realm of darkness and was longing to get back to his origin. Suhrawardi's philosophical system was, in a sense, a somewhat rational reconstruction of various stages of this existential journey and an explanation of its cosmic scale and stages. The grand metaphysical plot of the story is an augmented neo-Platonic system: The whole realm of being is divided into three or four sub-relams which are sandwiched between the extereme poles of the Light of Lights, whose place in the geographical plane of this cosmic map is above and top, and darkeness, which represents *hyle* (matter) or mere potentiality and therefore nothingness, at the bottom or down. Suhrawardi writes:

> The Essence of the First Absolute Light [i.e. the Light of Lights], God, gives constant illumination, whereby it is manifested and it brings all things into existence, giving life to them by its rays. Everything in the world is derived from the Light of His essence ... .[72]
>
> Know that the number of worlds according to people of wisdom is three. One is called the world of intellect (*'alam-i 'aqal*)... and one is called the world of soul ((*'alam-i nafs*) ... and the other is called the world of body (*'alam-i jism*).[73]

And he writes elsewhere:

> I have correct experiences [which inform me that] the number of worlds is four. The world of dominant lights (*'alam-i anwar-i qahirha*) (i.e. intellects), the world of regent lights (*'alam-i anwar-i mudabbirha*) (i.e. souls), the world of purgatories (*'alam-i barazikh*) (i.e. the spheres and the elements), the world of darkened suspended images (*'alam-i suwar-i mo'alaq-i zulmani*).[74]

1999); Shahabuddin Suhrawardi, *Hayakal al-Nur* (The Shape of Light), trans. by Shaykh al-Halveti (Fons Vitae, 1986)

[72] Suhrawardi, Hikmat al-Ishraq, English translation of M. Smith, *Readings from the Mystics of Islam* (London, 1950), 79, quoted in S. H. Nasr, *Three Muslim Sages*, op. cit., 69

[73] Sheikh Shabuddin Suhrawardi, *Majmu'a Mossanafat* (Complete Works), ed. by S. H. Nasr (Tehran, Mu'assese Motaleat va Tahqiqat Farhangi (1372/1993), Vol. 2), 96, 65, quoted in, Parviz Abbasi Dakaei, 'Qorbat-e Sharqi va Ghorbat-e Gharbi', *Nameh Falsafa* **4** (1377/1998), 112

[74] Suhrawardi, *Hikmat al-Ishraq*, 232, 254, quoted in Dakaei, ibid.

Ali Paya

Man can obtain salvation by God's grace and through the assistance of the active intellect, which is identified as the archangel Gabriel, and also the spritual masters (*pirs* or *ulia*) which earth is never without them.

Suhrawardi had a profound influence on almost all the subsequent generations of Muslim philosophers. From Suhrawardi onward, Islamic philosophy, in a systematic fashion dedicated all its attention to theosophical issues, i.e. issues related to understanding God and His manifestations by means of rational argumentation, intuition and mystical experiences. It took as its main sources of exploration and investigation, the holy Quran and the teachings of the Prophet and the Shi'i Imams.

The result of a full-fledged promotion of a religious outlook in this new econiche in which the notions of *Vali* (friend, Guardian .pl. *Ulia'*) and *Vilayat* (friendship, guardianship) had prominent places was, as far as philosphy was concrened, the emrgence of two exteremly sophisticated intellectual schools, which introduced some of the finest systems of theosophy. These two schools are known as the School of Isfahan and the School of Shiraz. However, before discussing some of the main achievements of these schools, I need to say a few words about the views of a highly influential mystic whose ideas played some important role in the subsequent development of Islamic theosophy. The personality in question is Muhi al-Din al-Arabi, better known as Ibn Arabi.

Ibn Arabi (1165–1240), born in Moorish Spain, is one of the greatest Muslim Sufi masters and mystics.[75] In fact the only other mystic whose standing, fame and influence is equal to, if not slightly greater than, that of Ibn Arabi, is Jalal al-Din Muhammad Balkhi (1207–1273), known in the West as Rumi. While many common themes can be found in the ideas of the two grand Sufi masters, many significant differences could also be discerned in their views and approaches.[76]

Generally speaking, Sufis and mystics played two important roles in the intellectual life of Muslims. On the one hand, they introduced a badly needed element of tolerance and open-mindedness towards other cultures, religions, doctrines, traditions, and practices; and

[75] For Ibn Arabi's life and work see William Chittic, *Ibn 'Arabi: Heir to the Prophets* (One World, 2005)

[76] See William Chittick, *In Search of the Lost Heart: Explorations in Islamic Thought* (State University of New York Press, 2011); William C. Chittic, *The Sufi Doctrine of Rumi* (World Wisdom, 2005)

that in an environment which was dominated by a literalist and ortho-dox approach to religious creed. On the other hand however, they, in a fashion not dissimilar to present day post-modern writers, opened up the floodgate to all sorts of unbounded interpretations and unbridled flights of fancy. The end result was further weakening of rational approaches which were caught between the rock of the dogmatism of the orthodoxy and the hard place of relativism of Sufism.

Ibn Arabi was a master story teller and a prolific writer. His *magnum opus, al-Futuhat al-Makkiyah* (The Mekkiyan Revelations) runs into many volumes.[77] Through his powerful writings he gave further credence to a cultural tradition which became prevalent in almost all fields of scholarly investigations in Islamic lands. The trad-ition in question was confirming one's knowledge claims not by re-sorting to rational argumentation but by citing one's visions and personal experiences. Ibn Arabi was very adept in this art of confirm-ation of knowledge claims. He begins both of his masterpieces, *al-Futuhat* and *Fusus al-Hikam* (the Gems of Wisdom) by narrating two dreams which he confirms as genuine and truthful visions (*al-roya al-sadiqa*). According to Ibn Arabi, in the course of these two visions, the Prophet revealed to him the contents of the two books. With this ingenious stratagem, Ibn Arabi outwitted all of his would-be detractors not only during his own time but throughout the centuries afterwards. With few exceptions, almost all subsequent scholars, whether Sunni or Shi'a, did their best to justify even the most exaggerated claims of Ibn Arabi, since apparently whatever is stated in Ibn Arabi's books, is the Prophet's wisdom and has got nothing to do with Ibn Arabi. It seems one of the important factors which made Ibn Arabi's views, despite his Sunni background, ap-pealing to his Shi'i followers was his great emphasis on the significant role of the *ulia'* (Spiritual Guardians, Sufi Saints) in the great schemes of things. In his writings he placed *ulia'* on a higher plane than even the prophets, claiming that the former are concerned about unveiling truth whereas the latter concentrate on promoting the message and are not much concerned about disclosing truth.[78] Ayatollah Khomeini's theory of *vilayat al-faqih* (the

---

[77]   Ibn Arabi, *Al-Futuhat al-Makkiyah fi Asrar al-Mulkiyah wa-l-Malikiyah*, edited by O. Yahia, 14 Vols (Cairo, 1972–91)

[78]   Ibn Arabi, *Fusus al-Hikam*, translated, and annotated by *Mohammad* Ali Movahid & Samd Movahid (Tehran, Nashr-e Karnameh, 1385 Solar), 78

Guardianship of jurists) is among many Shi'i doctrines influenced by Ibn Arabi.[79]

The intellectual trend towards combining mystical, gnostic, and illuminationist insights with the Quranic and Prophetic teachings, and rational thinking reached its zenith, as was stated above, in two influential philosophical Schools with distinct Shi'i flavour, namely the School of Isfahan and the School of Shiraz. The emergence of both of these Schools was greatly facilitated, if not became possible in the first place, because of the coming to power of the Safavids dynasty in Persia (1501–1736). The fact that Safavids belonged to a Sufi order which traced its lineage as well as its name to the great Sufi-saint, Sheikh Safi al-Din Ardibili[80], provides some explanation for their support of the two philosophical Schools which flourished during their reign, and for the general theosophical orientation of these schools.[81]

V. Schools of Isfahan and Shiraz

The founder of the School of Isfahan was Muhammad Baqir Damad (d. 1631), better known as Mir Damad. His difficult style of writing and his novel neologisms earned him a reputation not dissimilar to what is ascribed to Hegel in the West. He became known as the Third Teacher (*Mu'allim al-thalith*) after Aristotle and Farabi. Many popular anecdotes about his complex philosophical system were in circulation even during his own lifetime. According to one such story after his death the two angels, *nakir* and *monkar* who, according to popular Muslim beliefs, are in charge of interrogating deceased souls to ascertain whether they should be handed over to the angels of mercy or the angles of punishment, went to him and asked him about his deeds and his beliefs. Mir Damad's philosophical replies were so baffling that the poor angels could not make head or tail of them. In desperation they went to God and asked Him about this strange individual. God told them they better leave him alone

[79]   See, Alexander Knysh, 'Irfan Revisited: Khomeini and the Legacy of Islamic Mystical Philosophy', in *Middle East Journal* **46**(4) (1992), 631–653
[80]   S. H. Nasr, 'The School of Ispahan', in M. M. Sharif (ed.), *A History of Islamic Philosophy*, op. cit., 905
[81]   For an informative account of the socio-political, economic and cultural situation in Iran during the Safavid period see *The Cambridge History of Iran,* edited by Peter Jackson (Cambridge University Press, 1986), Vol, 6.

since the philosopher during his lifetime had said things which even God could have not comprehended![82]

Mir Damad's main project was to develop a system of philosophy based on the wisdom revealed by God to the prophets, known as the Yamani wisdom (*Hikmat-i Yamani*) in contrast to the rationalistic philosophy of the Greeks.[83] The name of Mir Damad's system was apparently inspired by a Prophetic *hadith* (tradition), namely, '*al-Imanu al-Yamani va al-Hikmatu al*-Yamaniyatu' (The true faith is the Yamani faith and the true wisdom is the Yamani wisdom).[84] Moreover, Yaman (Yemen) also has mystical connotations in gnostic literature in that it symbolizes the *mashriqi* (i.e. the oriental as well as the illuminated) side of the world and is therefore the source of divine illumination in contrast to the Occident, which is the source of Peripatetic [rationalistic] philosophy'.[85]

Following the precedent set by Ibn Sina in his *al-Hikmat al-Mashreqiyah*, Mir Damad, in his major philosophical writings such as *Qabasat* and *Jadhawat* relegated discussions of logic and themes in natural philosophy to the last chapters and began his discussions with issues concerning the notion of Being and its attributes following by chapters on the appeal to the Quran and the tradition of the Prophet and the Shi'i Imams to shed light on the intricacies of philosophical issues.

In the dispute among Muslim philosophers concerning the status of existence (*wujud*) and quiddity (*mahiyyat*) in the grand scheme of things, Mir Damad argued against Ibn Sina (in his Peripatetic phase) by endorsing the principality of quiddity (*mahiyyat*) and the accidental nature of existence (*wujud*). Among his philosophical innovations the notion of *huduth-i dahri* (a temporal createdness/coming into being/origination/emergence) which he contrasts with two other notions, namely, *huduth-i zamani* (temporal createdness or

[82]   For Mir Damad life and work see, Hamid Dabashi, '*Mir Damad and the Founding of the School of Isfahan*', in S.H. Nasr and O. Leaman (eds) *History of Islamic Philosophy*, op. cit. ch. 34, 597–634; Oliver Leaman, *An Introduction to Medieval Islamic Philosophy* (Cambridge: Cambridge University Press, 1985); Seyyed Ali Mousavi Behbahani, 'Mir Damad: Falsafa, Sharh Hal va Naqd Asar uo' (Mir Damad: Philosophy, life and works), *Maqalat va Barrasiha,* Nos. 3–4, Autumn-Winter (1349/1970), 18–59).

[83]   Nasr, 'The School of Ispahan', op.cit., 915

[84]   Zahra Mostafavi, 'The Implications of the Theory of Dahr and *huduth-i dahri* in Mir Damad's *Hikmat-i Yamani*', *Journal of Religious Thought* (University of Shiraz, 2007), 22.

[85]   Nasr. op. cit., 'the School of Ispahan', 915

coming into being) and *huduth-i dhati* (essential createdness or origi-natation) deserves to be mentioned.[86] He maintained that all entities, apart from God, i.e., all contingent beings, have an unchanging exist-ence in a realm which is called *dahr* (aeon). God is outside of this realm, his existence is *sarmadi* (without beginning and end). According to Mir Damad, all temporal beings, in any moment of their existence have a *dahri* counterpart. *Dahr* acts as a cosmic memory in which whatever is in God's mind has a copy.[87]

Mir Damad rational behind postulating this realm was his view that the notion of emanation, which had been devised in order to solve the problem of the existence of eternal yet contingent entities, could not do justice to God's unique position in the whole realm of being by placing Him over and above all other entities which were totally dependent upon Him. According to Mir Damad, in the theory of essential contingency, each contingent being before coming into being and in respect to its essence alone, is neither exist-ent nor non-existent. This indifference of contingent entities towards non-existence, in Mir Damad's view, means that they are not abso-lutely non-existent and this is enough to imply that they enjoy some sort of existence, even before coming into the realm of being. By contrasting absolute non-existence with the *dahri* existence, Mir Damad, tried to argue that nothing but God deserves to be regarded as existent.[88]

Mir Damad's theory of *huduth-i dahri* was not further developed by his successors, despite the fact Mir Damad was able to provide so-lutions for a number of philosophical as well as theological issues including the problem of 'createdness of time', 'rejection of the Platonic realm of Ideas', the issue of God's foreknowledge, and the changes He effects in the grand design of things (*naskh va bada'*).[89]

The trend of emphasising on the significance of *ishraqi*, illumina-tionist and esoteric approaches to philosophy in contrast to more rational approaches, and giving priority to religious sciences in con-trast to natural philosophy was further emphasised by another prom-inent member of the school of Isfahan, Sheikh Bahaei', who was

[86]   See, Fazlur Rahman, 'Mīr Dāmād's Concept of Ḥudūth Dahrī: A Contribution to the Study of God-World relationship Theories in Safavid Iran', *Journal of Near Eastern Studies* **39**(2) (1980), 139–151
[87]   Fazlur Rahman, op. cit., 139–142; Zahra Mostafavi, op. cit., Nasr, 'The School of Ispahan', op. cit., 916–917
[88]   Fazlur Rahman, op. cit.; Zahra Mostafavi, op. cit., 25; Seyyed Ali Mousavi Behbahani, op. cit., 49–55
[89]   Mostafavi, op. cit.; Seyyed Ali Mousavi Behbahani, op. cit., 55–58

among the clerics migrated from Lebanon to Iran.[90] Sheikh Bahaei',
a close friend and colleague of Mir Damad, was a true polymath in the
tradition of philosophers of the Golden age of Islam; he was the foremost theologian and jurist of his time, an accomplished mathematician and astronomer who had published a widely read treatise on
algebra, *Khulasah fi al-Hisab*, and several treatises on astronomy, a
knowledgeable physicist, a skilful poet, an adept Quranic commentator, and a capable architect.[91] And yet, despite being well-versed in
natural sciences and also maths and technology, in his poems which
were critical reflections on his own life and achievements, poems,
which were very influential due to their simple and powerful language, he openly and explicitly condemned not only rational philosophy but also all other sciences as mere waste of time, distractions from
coming to know God, and obstacles in the way of gnostic experiences.
In his *Nan and Halwa* (Bread and Sweet) he says (and I quote just a
few lines):

> Formal science is nothing but altercation;
> It results in neither intoxication nor contemplation
>
> …
>
> There is no science but the Quranic Commentary and hadith
> The rest is the deception of the perverse Satan.
> The mysteries will never become known to thee,
> If thou hast for student a hundred Fakhr-i Razi.
>
> …
>
> How long wilt thou teach the wisdom of the Greeks?
> Learn also the wisdom of those who have faith.
>
> …
>
> How long wilt thou lick the bowl of Avicenna?
> Illuminate thy heart with resplendent lights.[92]

Islamic philosophy in the tradition of combining gnostic, religious
and rational strands, reached its apex in the teachings of Sadruddin
Muhammad Shirazi (1571–1640), better known as Akhund Mulla

---

[90] Devin J. Stewart, 'Notes on the Migration of ʿĀmilī Scholars to
Safavid Iran', *Journal of Near Eastern Studies* **55**(2) (1996), 81–103. For
Sheikh Bahaei' life and works see, Behnaz Hashemipour, "Āmilī: Bahāʾ
al-Dīn Muḥammad ibn Ḥusayn al-ʿĀmilī', in Thomas Hockey (eds). *The
Biographical Encyclopedia of Astronomers, Springer Reference* (New York:
Springer, 2007), 42–43; E. Kohlberg, 'BAHĀʾ-AL-DĪN ʿĀMELĪ',
Encyclopaedia Iranica, availabla at: http://www.iranicaonline.org/arti-
cles/baha-al-din-ameli-shaikh-mohammad-b
[91] S. H. Nasr, 'the School of Ispahan'. op. cit., 910
[92] Quoted in Nasr, ibid., 911–2

Sadra and also as *Sadr Al-Muti'allihin* (the foremost amongst the theosophists).[93] Mulla Sadra was contemporaneous with Descartes and was as influential a philosopher in Islamic culture as was Descartes in the context of European thought. However, the approaches of these two intellectual giants were poles apart. Whereas Descartes was well-versed in philosophy, theology, physics, maths, and had a deep and lasting effect on the development of medicine, despite the fact that he was not a physician[94], Mulla Sadra dedicated his whole intellectual energy to the development of perhaps the finest theosophical system ever introduced within the econiche of Islamic culture. He, like his predecessors in the gnostic tradition, maintained that the only worthwhile knowledge is theosophy. He explicitly criticised Ibn Sina for wasting his time composing works on mathematics and medicine[95].

Mulla Sadra's exquisite system in which rational thinking was combined with esoteric approaches and applied to the teachings of the Quran and the tradition of the Prophet and the Shi'i Imams, came to be known as *Hikmat al-Muta'aliyah* (The Transcendent Theosophy). It seems the use of the term *Hikamt* with its rich connotations in the Quran and the tradition of the Prophet and Imams, was chosen deliberately by the founders of the two Schools of Isfahan and Shiraz to name their respective philosophical systems in a bid to quell the concerns of the orthodox *fuqha* who wield a great deal of power, especially during the Safavid period.

Hikmat al-Muta'aliyah is rich with novel ideas and brimming with interesting arguments and fecund metaphors. It has long been

---

[93]   For Mulla Sadra's life, works and philosophy see, S. H. Nasr, *Sadr al-Din Shirazi and his Transcendent Theosophy: Background, Life and Works* (Tehran: Imperial Iranian Academy of Philosophy, 1978; Fazlur Rahman), *The Philosophy of Mulla Sadra (Sadr al-Din al-Shirazi)*, (Albany: State University of New York Press, 1975); James Winston Morris, *The Wisdom of the Throne: An Introduction to the Philosophy of Mulla Sadra* (Princeton University Press, 1981); Hossein Ziai, 'Mulla Sadra: his life and works', in S. H. Nasr and Oliver Leaman (eds), *A History of Islamic Philosophy*, op. cit., 635–642; Kamal, Muhammad, *Mulla Sadra's Transcendent Philosophy* (Ashgate, 2006); Kalin, Ibrahim, *Knowledge in later Islamic philosophy: Mulla Sadra on existence, intellect, and intuition* (Oxford University Press, 2010); Sayeh Maysami, *Mulla Sadra* (One World, 2013)

[94]   G. A. Lindboom, *Descartes and Medicine* (Amsterdam, Editions Rodopi, 1978), reviewed in *Medical History*, 1980 January; 24(1): 111–112.

[95]   S. H. Nasr, 'Sadr al-Din Shirazi (Mulla Sadra)', in M. M. Sharif (ed.), *A History of Muslim Philosophy*, op. cit., 935

established as the received wisdom and official philosophical doctrine, or to borrow a not very accurate term from Thomas Kuhn,
the dominant theosophical paradigm, in all of those Muslim seminaries in which philosophy is being taught.

Of course the road to success was not as easy for Mulla Sadra as was
with his teacher, Mir Damad, who was a respected figure at the court
of Safavid kings. In fact, under the pressure from the more orthodox
'ulama (clerics) and *fuqha* (jurists), Mulla Sadra was forced to spend
fifteen years in self-exile in a small village, Kahak, near the city of
Qom, before being able to return to Shiraz and establish his School
there at a seminary which is still up and running today.[96] It should
be noted that some decades before Mulla Sadra other philosophers
from Shiraz, such as Sadr al-Din Muhammad Dashtaki
(1425–1564) and his son Ghyiath al-Din Mansur Shirazi (d. 1542)
had established a school of philosophy, also known as the School of
Shiraz. Mulla Sadra has discussed their views in some of his works.[97]

Like Suhrawadri and Mir Damad before him, Mulla Sadra presented a complete metaphysical system which provides explanation
for every aspect of reality, whether God, angels, man, afterlife, the
day of judgement, and so on. His system however, in contradistinc-
tion to the systems developed by his two eminent predecessors was
based on the notion of existential primacy (*Taqaddum Rutbi*) of
being (*wujud*) over quiddity (*mahiyyat*) or the principality (i.e.
reality) of being and accidentally (non-reality) of quiddity.[98]

In constructing his own system, he tried to combine the best
aspects of the views introduced by previous sages, whether the
Presocratic or neo-Platonic or Peripatetic or *Ishraqi* philosophers,
with the wisdom of Sufis and mystics like Ibn Arabi, and the arguments of the theologians, and the teachings of the Quran and the tradition of the Prophet and the Imams, in order to create a coherent
theosophical system, while exposing, a rational manner, the shortcomings of the views of his eminent predecessors.[99]

---

[96] S. H. Nasr, *Sadr al-Din Shirazi and his Transcendent Theosophy*, op.
cit., 35–38

[97] H. Corbin, *History of Islamic Philosophy*, op. cit., 335–337

[98] Muhammad Kamal, *Mulla Sadra Transcendent Philosophy* (Ashgate
Publishing Limited, 2006); David Burrell, 'Aquinas and Mulla Sadra on the
Primacy of Existing', in Ali Paya (ed.), *The Misty Land of Ideas and the Light
of Dialogue: An Anthology of Comparative Philosophy* (London: ICAS Press,
2013), 31–48

[99] Mulla Sadra has presented his metaphysical system in its developed
form in his *magnum opus*, *al-Asfar al-Araba'a* (The Four Journeys)
(Tehran: Entesharat-e Bonyad Hikmat Islami Sadra, 9 vols). Partial

In the realistic outlook of Mulla Sadra the whole realm of being consists of just one reality, namely God. All the rest are His manifestations and therefore have no genuine reality on their own. God is the only necessary being, all the rest are contingent entities. For this particular type of contingency Mulla Sadra has coined a new term, *imakan-e Faqri* (contingency due to existential dependence) which was different from the common notion of contingency, namely, *imkan-e mahuwi*, contingency related to the quiddity or essence, which was used by previous philosophers.[100]

The general picture of Mulla Sadra's worldview was somewhat like the model presented by the neo-Platonic, though with many more added details and extra layers and structures plus a much more pronounced emphasis on the dual principle of unity in diversity and diversity in unity and primacy of being over quiddity.

God, as the only genuine, self-subsistent, being is the cause of all causes. But causes and effects are not different in essence: an effect is just an aspect of its cause. Moreover, since from unity only unity can issue forth, God's first emanation or manifestation, can only be a simple and unified being. This being is referred to by various names, including, the 'supreme intellect', 'the first emanation, and also *haghighat-e Muhammadiyah* (the reality of Muhammad). While the first two terms were common among philosophers of neo-Platonic tendency, this last description was an invention of Muslim mystics.[101]

Mulla Sadra introduced many novel themes and theories into Islamic philosophy and provided convincing solutions for many outstanding problems in not only the field of philosophy but also theology and mysticism. Apart from his doctrine of the unity and existential primacy of existence (*isalat al-wujud*), other doctrines such as the theory of substantial motion (*al-harakat al-jawhariyyah*); God' knowledge (including His knowledge of particulars); a general theory of knowledge; a novel theory concerning human soul; a theory

---

translations of this work are available. For example, Latima-Parvin Peerwani has translated the fourth intellectual journey; *Spiritual Psychology* (London: ICAS Press, 2008)

[100] Mulla Sdara, *Asfar*, the first Journey, op. cit.; Morteza Motahari, *Sharh-e Mabsut Manzumeh* (The Longer Commentary on Manzumeh), 3 Vols. (Tehran: Hikmat Publications, Tehran: 1366/1987); Morteza Motahari, *Dars hay-e Asfar* (The Teachings of Asfar) (Tehran: Sadra Publications, 1382/2003); Morteza Motahari, *Maqalat Falsafi* (Philosophical Papers) (Tehran: Sadra Publications, 2002)

[101] Mulla Sdara, *Asfar*, the first and the fourth journeys, op. cit.

concerning time as the fourth dimension in material beings (though of course not in the sense discussed by Einstein); the theory of bodily resurrection; and rejection of the theory of reincarnation should be included in the long list of his achievements. Close harmony amongst various aspects of Mulla Sadra's philosophical system which has made his system a powerful intellectual tool stems from the unity of its author's thought.[102]

I will not be able to do justice to Mulla Sadra's numerous and rich achievements. Perhaps few words concerning his theory of Substantial Motion could provide a flavour of his approach. For Mulla Sadra, the primacy and principality of existence, means, among other things, that each entity has a personal or individual identity. Existence ought to be contrasted with non-existence. The more perfect an entity the richer its existence, in the sense that it is less contaminated with non-existence, is less dependent upon other beings, has less potentiality and possess more actuality. For non-material entities, their imperfection manifests itself in their absolute dependence upon God for their existence. But in the sub-lunar realm which is the abode of material entities, imperfection obtains an added feature. Here, the degrees of actuality and potentiality determine the degree of perfection of a particular entity with regard to its particular identity.

In this context, change means turning potentiality into actuality. Mulla Sadra argues that individual beings in the sub-lunar realm have their own distinct identities, are experiencing, on a continuous basis the process of actualisation of their potentialities. This process, first and foremost, happens in individual's existential substance and as a result changes in other categories such as quantity (*kamm*), quality (*kaif*), and place (*makan*) will be effected. Time is also a dimension which displays the above sequence of continuous and seamless turning of potentiality into actuality. Human soul is at the beginning just a mere potentiality, under favourable circumstances, it gradually emerges as a result of the interaction of the body of the newly conceived embryo with the environment. The process of actualisation of the potentials embedded in soul continues until the last moment the individual is alive and active. Since both the

---

[102] Mulla Sadra, *Asfar, the first journey,* op. cit.; Morteza Motahari, *Sharh-e Mabsut-e Manzumeh,* op. cit.; Abdolkarm Soroush, *Nahad Na-Aram Jahan* (The Never-at-Rest Essence of the Universe) (Tehran: Mu'assese Farhangi Sirat, 1378/1999); Mehdi Dehbashi, *Trans-substantial Motion and the Natural World* (ICAS Press, 2010)

body and the soul have many different potentials, actualising particular aspects of such potentials becomes a matter of interaction between the individual and its environment. At the end of one's life in this world, one's soul leaves one's body and, depending on the degree of perfection it could have achieved while still in this world, it enters the realm of purgatory or higher up in the chain of being.[103]

In the period after the death of Mulla Sadra until the twentieth century, Islamic philosophy has mostly been a footnote to the Sadraeian system. Grand masters like Mulla Muhsin Faid Kashani, 'Abd al Razzaq Lahiji, Qadi Said Qomi, Mulla Ali Mudarris Zunuzi, Mulla Ali Nuri, Jahangir Khan Qashqaei and many more have, by and large, been busy explicating the intricacies of *Hikmat al-Muti'alliyah* and further developing its latent capacities and potentials. Apart from small steps from within the Sadraeian paradigm to better clarify this or that point or re-present or re-formulate this or that argument by improved versions, the only noteworthy development, which was only significant due to its pedagogical novelty, was the efforts of Mulla Haji Sabzevari (1797–1873), a nineteenth century philosopher to represent the whole of Sadra's system in term of easy to remember poems. His *Manzumeh* (or collections of poems) became the standard textbook in all Persian speaking seminaries for teaching Sadra's philosophy.[104]

It is worth emphasising that parallel with the development of Sadraeian system which was the representative of rational approach among Muslim scholars, anti-rational movements and schools were also on the rise. Ironically the founder of one such movement, Sheikh Ahmad Ahsaei (the founder of Sheikhi movement) had produced an authoritative commentary on Mulla Sadra's *Asfar*.[105] Another influential figure was Muhammad Amin Astarabadi, the founder of Akhbari School in fiqh which advocates a literalist approach to fiqh and Islamic teachings. Mulla Sadra's

---

[103]   Mulla Sadra, *Asfar*, op. cit., First, Third and Fourth Journey. Mulla Sadra's theory of human soul allows him to offer a novel solution for the vexed issue of mind-body problem. Since soul emerges from body and remains in touch with body until the end of life of the individual, the usual difficulties which beset a Cartesian model do not affect his model.

[104]   Seyyed Hossein Nasr, *Islamic philosophy from its origin to the present: philosophy in the land of prophecy* (State University of New York Press, 2006); Morteza Motahari, *Sharh-e Mabsut Manzumeh*, op. cit.

[105]   S. H. Nasr, op. cit. 'Sadr al-Din Shirazi (Mulla Sadra)' 960

son-in-law, Muhsin Fayd was among the main promoters of this school.[106]

Another interesting, though aborted development, was the efforts of an enlightened Qajar prince, Badi' al-Mulk Mirza, to introduce the views of Immanuel Kant to two grand masters of Islamic philosophy, Mulla Ali Mudarris Zunuzi and Mirza 'Ali Akbar Mudarris Yazdi and encourage them to respond to the challenges of the German philosopher by using the machinery of Islamic (mostly Sadraeian) philosophy. 'There is however, little evidence to show that any real dialogue and meeting of minds took place on this occasion. What caused the discussion on Kant's view to come close to some sort of 'dialogue of the deaf' was that, on the one hand, the prince was not competently familiar with Kant's views. And on the other, the masters, perhaps understandably, had stuck to their traditional canons and were not prepared to venture out of their intimate paradigm.'[107]

3. Islamic Philosophy in Iran in the 20th Century

In the early decades of the twentieth century, Iranian left-wing intellectuals, like their counterparts in other parts of the world who have been inspired by the Bolshevik revolution in Russia, embarked on an ideological crusade to promote various aspects of Marxism-Leninism and in particular Dialectical Materialism in Iran. These efforts received a great boost in 1941 with the formation of Soviet backed Tudeh party.

In reply to this ideological onslaught, one of the greatest masters of Islamic philosophy in modern times, Allameh Seyyed Muhammad Hussein Tabatabee (1904–1981), decided to expose the shortcomings of the Marxist ideology by critically assessing its philosophical doctrines. In early 1950s, Allameh began teaching a course of philosophy to a selected group of clerics chosen from among his best students. This course, based on twice-weekly sessions, lasted for about three years. During this period many philosophical aspects of Marxism and Dialectical Materialism were discussed. Allameh's lecture notes were edited and heavily annotated by his best disciple, Ayatollah Morteza Motahari (1920–1979), himself a renowned philosopher in

---

[106]   Robert Gleave, *Scripturalist Islam: The History and Doctrines of the Akhbari Shi'i School* (Brill, 2007)

[107]   Ali Paya & Malakeh Shahi, 'The Reception of Kant and his Philosophy in Iran', *Journal of Shi'a Islamic Studies* **3**(1) (2010), 25

Ali Paya

the tradition of Islamic Philosophy, and was published in five volumes, under the general title of *The Principles and Method of the Philosophy of Realism.*[108]

This book marked a watershed, though unfortunately not a turning point, in the long-standing tradition of Islamic philosophy. It was a watershed in the sense that after centuries of inward-looking, Muslim philosophers applied their talents and also the machinery of Islamic philosophy to an issue outside the usual set of theosophical problems. It did not however develop into a turning-point, in that it remained as, more or less, a one-off project. It did not give rise to systematic application of Islamic philosophy to other newly emerged issues in the Islamic communities. One notable exception was Ayatollah Motahari's subsequent efforts to replicate the model of his teacher, this time with a group of university Professors and students. During my last years of undergraduate studies as an electronic engineer at Sharif University of Technology and postgraduate years at the Department of Philosophy at the University of Tehran, I had the good fortune of attending these classes which continued until few months before the revolution of 1979. Below, I'll come back to the efforts of Ayatollah Motahari and few other philosophers to develop Islamic philosophy along a new and novel path.

The Principles and Method of the Philosophy of Realism consists of fourteen 'articles' each dealing with one important philosophical topic. The two Ayatollahs, Tabatabaee and Motahari did a thorough job in exposing epistemological shortcomings of Marxism and dialectical materialism. For example, they argued that Marxists' theory of knowledge leads to relativism and therefore fails to provide universal knowledge of reality. Dialectical materialism is also problematic in that accepting only one contradiction leads to an untenable epistemic position in which all sorts of bizarre claims can be made and there will be no way to examine them.

The book also for the first time in the history of Muslim philosophy, and almost two decades before David Lewis' *Convention: A Philosophical Study* (1969)[109], and four decades before John Searle's *Construction of Social Reality* (1995)[110] discussed the idea of knowledge about *etebariyat*, i.e. conventions and those socially

---

[108] Seyyed Mohammad Hossein Tababatabee & Morteza Motahari, *Usul-e Falsafa va Ravesh-e Realism* (The Principles and Method of the Philosophy of Realism) (Tehran: 1332/1953)

[109] David Lewis, *Convention: A Philosophical Study* (Harvard University Press, 1969)

[110] John Searle's *Construction of Social Reality* (Penguin Books, 1995)

constructed realities whose function is to respond to man's non-cognitive needs, as against his cognitive needs which are taken care of by science/knowledge. Allameh introduced a highly original and detailed account of the structure of knowledge of conventions of all sorts. He divided the *etebariyat* into pre-social and post-social conventions/social constructions. The first group were, in Searle's parlance, products of individual volitive intentionalities, whereas the second group were products of collective volitive intentionalities. Under the first group Allameh introduced notions such as *wubjub* (necessity), *hosn va qobh* (goodness and badness), *intikhab-e akhaf va ashahl* (the principle of the least effort), *asl-e istikhdam va ijtima'* (the principle of exploitation and living in society), *asl-e motabi'at-e 'ilm* (the principle of following the guidance of knowledge). Under the second group Allameh included *asl-e melk* (the principle of ownership), *kalam* (language), *asl-e riyasat* (the principle of headship), *amr va nahy* (commanding and forbidding). Each of the above general categories is divided into a number of sub-categories. Allameh following a detailed explanation of each category discussed the relationship between our knowledge of *etebariyat* and the entities constructed by them[111].

He also discussed the famous argument concerning the impossibility of deriving an 'ought' from an 'is' first introduced by Hume. However, there is no evidence to suggest that Allameh was aware of Hume's argument. In the context of Islamic philosophy he seems to be the first philosopher who has discussed this issue.

The aim of Allameh Tabatabaee was to refute epistemic doctrines of Marxists who would present their views as 'scientific' and objective and did not seem to be aware of the fact that by linking individuals' knowledge of reality to their social classes, their theory of knowledge loses all its objective credibility. He also intended to expose Marxists fallacy of presenting socially constructed entities and the knowledge thereof as absolute and indubitable truth about material reality.

However, Allameh did not limit his criticism only to Marxists' doctrines, he also challenged the approaches of *Fuqha* (Muslim jurists) who, according to Allameh, had not differentiated between

---

[111]   Seyyed Muhammad Hussein Tabatabaee, *Usul Falsafa Realism* (The principles of a Realist Philosophy), (Qom: Markaz Barrasi-ha-yi Islami, 1357 (solar)), chapter six. This single volume only contains Allameh Tabatabee's main essays without Ayatollah Motahari's footnotes and annotations.

the normative status of the views they had discussed in their legal discussions and factual claims about reality.

Allameh Tabatabee and Ayatollah Motahari had developed their arguments from within a somewhat modified and expanded Sadraeian framework. Nevertheless, despite all its innovative and trailblazing aspects, *The Principles and Method of the Philosophy of Realism*, suffered from a number of shortcomings which have been inherent in the traditional Islamic philosophy since its inception. The three principal shortcomings of this system, as a whole, are as follows:

- Adherence to self-evident truths as the justificatory basis of all knowledge claims;
- Strong emphasis on attainment of certainty as the end goal of epistemic pursuits; and
- Insistence on the so-called *'ilm-I huduri'* (knowledge-by-presence) as the ultimate and most valuable type of knowledge.

However, subscription to the above three theses, as I briefly argue here, deprives Islamic philosophy from ridding itself from the shackles of a dogmatic outlook. For example, the insistence of Muslim philosophers to base their philosophies on the foundation of self-evident truth and seek justification for their knowledge-claims by resorting to this notion has made their systems vulnerable to all sorts of criticisms levelled at the validity of self-evident notions and the process of justification.[112]

Moreover, it seems Muslim philosophers, in their pursuit of achieving certainty, have fallen into the trap of a serious category mistake: they have mistakenly upheld the notion of *ilm-i huduri* 'knowledge by presence' as an epistemic notion. This notion is also referred to as the outcome of a process known as *itihad-i 'aqil va ma'qul* (the unity between the intellect and the intelligible) or *itihad-i 'alim va ma'lum* (the unity between the knower and the known). This process and its end result refer to an existential experiences and not an epistemic state in which we use language and concept to reconstruct our lived experiences.

However, of the three theses introduced above, perhaps the second one, i.e., an emphasis on attaining certainty, is the most important one. It seems such an emphasis on the role of certainty and its place in philosophical investigations is not unrelated to religious

---

[112] See David Miller, 'Overcoming the Justificationist Addiction', *Pazhoheshay-e Falsai* (Philosophical Investigations), 1(1) (1387/2008), 1–16.

teachings in which the strength of believers' faith is gauged by their degree of certainty in God and in the truth of Islamic teachings. The notion of certainty, *yaqin*, is also emphasised in many of the Quranic verses. To make things even more complicated, the Quran introduces three different notions of *yaqin*, which imply a hierarchy, or various degrees, of certainty. These are known as *ilm al-yaqin* (lit. the knowledge of certainty = certainty due to acquired knowledge), *'ain al-yaqin* (lit. the eye of certainty = certainty obtained through direct encounter/ direct 'observable' evidence), and *haq al-yaqin* (lit. the truth of certainty = absolute, indubitable certainty).[113]

Now it seems these degrees of certainty are contrasted to epistemic concepts such as *shakk* (doubt), *ẓann* which is translated into 'surmise' and 'conjecture', and *wahm* (phantasm)[114].

Perhaps prior to the introduction of the views of critical rationalists such as Karl Popper and David Miller, almost all Muslim scholars, were, and the majority of them still are, of the view that certainty is not simply an epistemic state, in fact, its highest state; and failing to obtain it implies not only a serious defect in one's epistemological approach but more worryingly weakness in one's faith in God. It seems that the majority of Muslim scholars, including most, if not all, Muslim philosophers, have never considered the case that certainty is not an epistemic state but a psychological one, and that knowledge can be attained by means of constructing conjectures and projecting them to reality. Of few possible exceptions to this rule which I can mention here, one is Adib Pishawari (1882–1971), a student of Hajj Mulla Hadi Sabzavari, who in the following quatrain seems to come close to a critical rationalist position:

> Whatever you have seen in the books,
> Or have heard from knowledgeable people;
> Is nothing but some myths concerning reality; However,
> Reality is infinite and the number of our myths is always limited.

The other is Abu al-'Ala Ma'rri (973–1058) the blind poet-philosopher well known for his scepticism. He is reported to have said: 'Amma al-Yaqin, Fala Yaqin. Innama Aqsi' al-Ijtihadi an Azannu wa Ahdasa' (Concerning certainty, there is none. For my part, my utmost epistemic endeavour is directed towards making conjectures and hunches).

Apart from general understanding of the meaning of the concept of *yaqin* in the context of Islamic culture and its value and worth in the

---

[113] See, The Quran, 102: 5&7, 56:95, 69:51
[114] Tabatabaee, *Usul Falsafeh Realism*, op.cit., 115

eyes of Muslims, it seems Muslim philosophers, who have always been accused by their fellow theologians, jurists and mystics, of introducing ideas and views which are alien to genuine Islamic teachings, have been extra careful to emphasise the importance of *yaqin* and also the fact that their philosophical systems are capable of achieving it.

However, the emphasis of various schools of Islamic philosophy on their ability to attain certainty as the end goal of their epistemic pursuit has not helped the position of these schools in the eyes of their opponents. The opponents, each in their own way, maintain that certainty can be obtained with much more effectiveness and greater ease through their own ways rather than moving along the torturous path of incomprehensible philosophical reasoning.

The literalists, of different types and orientations among both the Sunnis and the Shi'as, represent one such opponent group. They claim that certainty can be attained by closely following the sharia law. The second group, also of large variety, are the Sufis/Mystics who advocate mystical practices, in place of rational arguments, as the best way of acquiring certainty.

The literal and the mystical approaches, despite all their apparent differences, share a common epistemic attitude: they both, each in its own way, belittle rational approaches and maintain that the truth of faith cannot be attained by it. But when reason is pushed out of the scene, the stage is set for all sorts of non-rational, irrational, and anti-rational behaviours. I conjecture that the failure of Muslim philosophers with regard to the above three theses has played a major role in paving the way for the emergence of extremists (like jihadists) in the midst of Muslims.

Going back to our story of the evolution of Islamic philosophy in the twentieth century, some of the few noteworthy developments concerning the application of the machinery of Islamic philosophy to meet modern intellectual challenges and therefore preparing the ground for further progress of Islamic philosophy in new directions which I can report are the efforts of Ayatollah Motahari, Ayatollah Haeri Yazdi, and Ayatollah Misbah Yazdi (all three among Allameh Tabatabee's better known disciples), and Ayatollah Seyyed Muhammad Baqir Sadr in Iraq (who could also be regarded as one of Allameh's (indirect) disciples.[115]

Of the four figures named above, the approaches of Motahari and Sadr to these challenge were very different from those of Haeri and

[115] For bibliographies of these authors see the catalogue of the Iran's National Library at: http://opac.nlai.ir/opac-prod/search/briefListSearch.do

Misbah. Motahari, as a philosopher with strong religious inclinations, did his best, until his assassination in the early days after the victory of the Islamic revolution, to provide a rational response to the challenges posed mostly by new generations of Marxist writers and activists in Iran. He also tried to respond to the challenges posed by the arguments of philosopher such as Sartre or Russell whose views on family life, which were being promoted by secular intellectuals in Iran, were not in line with Islamic morals. During his relatively short life, apart from many specialised works which were concerned with the elucidation of various aspects of traditional (i.e. Sadraeian) philosophy, he produced many books in response to various intellectual challenges introduced through imported ideas. In books such as *The Man and His Destiny, Divine Justice, Women's Rights in Islam, Reasons and Causes of Inclination towards Materialism and Atheism, A Critique of Marxism* and many others he tried to respond, in a rational fashion, to challenges introduced by modern ideas. His rational approach was informed by a philosophical-cum-theological reasoning. In the last years of his life he came to the conclusion that for Islamic philosophy to undergo a genuine revival it was of utmost importance that epistemological issues, which had always remained under the shadow of theosophical topics, to be taken seriously. He embarked on a project of producing an epistemological system based on the insights of Islamic philosophy.

However, despite dedicating a great deal of time and energy to this project, he was reluctant to publish anything on this subject. He did not feel that he knew enough about modern epistemological developments to be able to critically assess them. His unfamiliarity with Western languages, which would limit his sources to only Persian and Arabic translations of the Western philosophy, added to his frustration. Moreover, at the time, modern epistemological developments, especially in the Anglo-Saxon (Analytic) tradition, were absent from the curricula of the country's universities and there were not competent philosophers who could provide him with an in-depth understanding of these developments in his own language.

In the autumn of 1978 Ayatollah Motahari accompanied Allameh Tabatabee in the latter's trip to the UK for medical treatment. Apparently during his short stay and in discussion with some Iranian PhD students he had got a chance to get a general idea of some of the latest philosophical developments in the West. Almost immediately after his return to Tehran he asked me to visit him at his home where I used to go each weekend along with few others to receive private lessons in Islamic philosophy. I vividly remember the meeting because it coincided with the very day the Shah left Iran for the last time. In that meeting he strongly urged me to travel to the UK to do a PhD in the philosophy of science! It seems he had come to the conclusion that to develop a sound approach towards modern epistemologies, one needed to have first-hand knowledge of philosophy of science and its related fields.

In contrast to Ayatollah Motahari, Ayatollah Misbah, who is at present the Director of an influential right-wing conservative academic institute in Qom, took a more openly apologetic approach towards foreign isms. In his various works he, in the good old tradition of apologists, tried to show that traditional Islamic views, including the Sadraeian system are, by far, superior to all imported isms.

Ayatollah Haeri Yazdi, who, in those days, was the only Ayatollah with two doctorate degrees in philosophy from universities of Tehran and Toronto, was trying to combine his *usli* approaches[116] with his Sadraeian upbringing in dealing with the challenges posed to the traditional doctrines of Islamic philosophy due to the modern epistemic developments since Kant's Copernican Revolution. His arguments however, remained firmly within the framework of traditional Islamic philosophy and despite the novelty of his approach, failed to address modern challenges in a fruitful manner.

Ayatollah Sadr, who was executed along with his sister by the Baath regime in Baghdad, reportedly by Saddam Hussein's direct order, in April 1980, was, like Ayatollah Mutahari, concerned about developing proper philosophical response to the challenges presented by Marxism and other foreign ideologies or philosophical systems. Like Ayatollah Motahari, he also maintained that the intellectual facilities available in Islamic culture could help researchers to develop systems of thought which are free from the defects of Western philosophical schools.

In 1977, and in a trailblazing and influential book, *al-Ussus al-Mantaqiyah li'l Istiqra'* (The Logical Foundations of Induction) he took upon himself to develop an epistemological system based on the resources available in the Islamic intellectual milieu in order to

---

[116] *Usul* is a semantic machinery which assists *fuqha* (jurists) in their dealings with semantic entailments of the verses of the Quran and the traditions of the Prophet and Imams. Its relation to *fiqh* (Islamic jurisprudence) is more or less like the relation of logic to philosophy. It resembles the tools linguists and hermeneutists have developed to discuss meanings of the texts and/or speakers' meanings.

suggest a solution to the vexed problem of induction.[117] The title of the book was however, a misnomer, since the author had no intention of providing logical foundations for induction and maintained that no such foundation can be found.[118]

For developing his novel and critical assessment of the problem of induction, Ayatollah Sadr, on the one hand, relied on the Arabic translation of Bertrand Russell's *Human Knowledge,* and on the other, made use of his detailed knowledge of *usul al-fiqh* and of Islamic philosophy.[119] He criticised Aristotle's and also mashsha'i (peripatetic) philosophers' proposed solution for the problem of induction, arguing that the principle of uniformity of nature, or its variances used by Aristotelians to justify induction, is not self-evident. It relies on induction.

Ayatollah Sadr then criticised Hume's and Mill's arguments. He rejected Hume's claim that causality cannot be established by empirical evidence and also rejected his pessimism concerning the impossibility of finding a solution for the problem of induction. As for Mill's view, he noted that while Mill was right in thinking that causality can be established by inductive means, he was wrong in linking the validity of inductive generalisation to causality.[120]

Having explained the failure of some of the well-known approaches to the problem of induction, Ayatollah Sadr introduced his own epistemological approach which he maintained could solve the problem once and for all. Ayatollah had dubbed his novel theory *Al-Naẓariyah al-Tawalud al-Dhati fi al-Ma'refat al-Bashariyah* (The Theory of Inherent Proliferation in Human Knowledge).[121]

---

[117]   S. M. B. Sadr, *al-Ussus al-Mantaqiyah li'l Istiqra*, (Beirut: Dar al-Ta'aruf li'l Matbu'at, fourth imprint, 1977/1982)

[118]   Prior to this book he had published another major work, *Falsafatuna* (Our Philosophy) to rebut the epistemological doctrines of Marxism. That book however, was mostly relying on arguments developed by Allameh Tabatabee and Ayatollah Motahari in *The Principles and Method of a Realist Philosophy.*

[119]   The first Muslim philosopher who critically and thoroughly discussed Ayatollah Sadr's theory of induction was Abulkarim Soroush: 'Mabni Mantiqi Istiqra' az Naẓr-e Ayatollah Sadr' (The Logical Foundations of Induction from Ayatollah Sadr's Point of View), *Nashr-i Danish*, **15** (1362/1983), 22–43, I have heavily relied on his article in developing this part of the present paper.

[120]   Sadr, *al-Ussus*, op. cit. pp. 69–81. Soroush, op. cit., 24–5

[121]   Sadr, *al-Ussus*, op. cit., 123–131

Ali Paya

This novel theory is based on two pillars, namely, particular notions of certainty and a particular interpretation of probability developed in the light of an *usuli* concept. According to Ayatollah Sadr there are three types of certainties, namely: logical certainty; inherent (subject-based) certainty (*al-yaqin al-dhati*), and objective certainty (*al-yaqin al-mawdu'i*). Logical certainty pertains to the necessary relations between the conclusion of a valid syllogism and its premises and also necessary relations between subjects and predicates of tautologies. Inherent certainty refers to a subjective, psychological type of certainty. But the last type of certainty is achieved on the basis of accumulation of external evidence and the strength of this evidence.[122]

As for his particular interpretation of the probability he introduced a model in which a well-known notion from *usul al-fiqh*, namely, *al-'ilm al-ijmali*, which literally means un-detailed knowledge, was carefully crafted with some aspects of the classic (Laplacian) and the Frequency (von Mises) theories of probability without (so the Ayatollah argued) incorporating their weaknesses. The Ayatollah defined *al-'ilm al-ijmali* in the context of his own theory of probability as 'certain knowledge about an unidentified member of a certain set'.[123]

The Theory of Inherent Proliferation in Human Knowledge which is in itself extremely interesting since it shows how a traditional *mujtahid* and philosopher is grappling with an immensely important philosophical issue, boils down to the following claims for each of which the author provides detailed arguments[124]:

1. One begins one's knowledge pursuit about a particular subject-matter on the basis of a degree of *al-'ilm al-ijmali* about it. This is our opening hunch or conjecture. Some sort of relation of entailment exists among various parts of one's subjective knowledge which is the realm of subjective certainty. This knowledge can be expanded in a piecemeal manner by gradual increase in one's degree of rational belief;

2. One's degree of rational belief concerning a particular subject-matter, based on *al-'ilm al-ijmali* about that subject-matter, can be increased by the application of induction. In this stage due to accumulation of relevant evidence, one's objective certainty concerning the subject-matter under study also

---

122 Sadr, *al-Ussus*, op. cit., 321–334. Soroush, op. cit., 25–6
123 Sadr, *al-Ussus*, op. cit., 271–292
124 Ibid., 381–433

increases. This stage is called the stage of objective proliferation of knowledge (*al-tawalud al-mawduʻi*)

3. In the last stage which is called the stage of inherent proliferation of knowledge (*al-tawalud al- dhati*) increase in the degree of probability and in the objective certainty combined with certain rules of entailment (which are not logical) described by Ayatollah Sadr in details leads to transformation of our initial conjecture into inherent (subject-based) certainty (*al-yqain al-dhati*) concerning the subject-matter of our research.

Ayatollah's Sadr's new subjective theory of induction of course, as some Muslim philosophers have argued, like all other suggested solutions for this problem, fails to achieve its goal.[125] Nevertheless, his bold efforts in developing, perhaps for the first time in the modern history of Islamic philosophy, a novel approach which radically enlarges the horizon of traditional thinking is worthy of praise.

Apart from the projects cited above which had taken, to varying degrees a problem-oriented approach in response to the newly-emerged challenges, the majority of activities in the field of Islamic philosophy whether in seminaries or universities were directed towards transmission and exposition of the views of the past masters. Among the better known expositors of Islamic philosophy in the second half of the twentieth century and the first decade of twenty-first century one should name the late Seyyed Jalal ad-Din Ashtiyani of whom I say few words later, Ayatollah Javadi Amoli in Qom who is the best student of Allameh Tabatabaee and has trained many seminary students in the Sadrraean tradition, and Professor Ibahim Dinani at the University of Tehran who has published, among many other titles, a three-volume cataloguing

---

[125] See Soroush, op. cit., 'Mabni Mantiqi ...', pages 31–42; Some other writers have tried to either critically asses Ayatollah's Sadr's approach to induction or defend his approach against Soroush's criticisms. While both groups have relied on Soroush's arguments, the latter have failed to develop cogent defence of the Ayatollah's views. See A. Khosrow-Panah, 'mantiq-e Istiqra az Didgah Shahid Sadr' (The Logic of Induction from Martyr Sadr's Point of View), *Zehn*, **18** (1383/2004) 29–58; M. M. Hadavi-Tehrani, 'Moʻzal-e Istiqra az Negah-e Shahid Sadr' (The problem of Induction from Martyr Sadr's Point of View), *Keyhan-e Andishe*, **36**(130–147); M. M. Hadavi-Tehrani, 'Naqqadi Mabani Manteqi Istiqra' (Critique of the Logical Foundation of Induction), *Keyhan-e Andishe* **37**, 60–70

and explicating philosophical principles used by all Muslim philosophers.[126]

In contrast to the rarity of the initiatives in making use of the resources of Islamic philosophy in a problem-oriented way to develop novel solutions for modern issues, efforts concerning introducing the heritage of Muslim philosophers, including publication of the works of the past masters, whether in original or in translations (including English translations) and explicatory books/papers on the views of the past masters, have thrived in the past fifty years. In such efforts scholars and academic centres outside of the Islamic lands have played a significant role. The following examples are just few cases in point. During the 1970s, Henri Corbin, with the support of L'Iran et la France Institut, and in collaboration with Seyyed Jalal ad-Din Ashtiyani, and some of other Iranian philosophers, foremost amongst them, Seyyed Hossein Nasr, launched a project whose aim was to introduce later philosophical developments in Iran, especially the achievements of the two schools of Isfahan and Shiraz, to the world outside of Iran. Corbin and his colleagues published a series of books entitled *Selections of the Works of Iranian Divine Philosophers, from the time of Mir Damad and Mir Findereski until Present.*[127] A similar project was pursued by Mehdi Mohahqiq at the Institute of Islamic Studies which was jointly run by Tehran University and the University of McGill in Canada. Among the publications of this Institute Toshihiko Izutsu's translation of Haji Sabzaevari's *Manzumeh* is worth mentioning. Sabzaevari's *Manzume* is unique in the sense that it is the only complete exposition of Mulla Sadra's philosophy which is compiled in shape of memorable poems rather than the usual prose form. For this reason it has been the main textbook of teaching Sadraeian philosophy in Seminaries since the later nineteenth century.

With regard to promotion of Islamic philosophy Seyyed Hossein Nasr should get a particular mention as not only one of the best expositors of this philosophy, especially its *al-Hikmat al-Mashirqiyah* strand, but also perhaps as one its most dedicated promoter in a global, and not only Islam-wide, arena. He has published individually and in collaboration with other Iranian and non-Iranian scholars,

---

[126] I. Dinani, *Qava'id Kolli Falsafi dar Falsafa Eslami* (General Philosophical Principles in Islamic Philosophy) (Tehran: Mu'asses Entesharat Elmi va Farhangi, 3 vols 1365/1386)

[127] S. J. Ashtiyani, et al, *Montakhabati az Asar-e Hokamay-e Elahi Iran az Mir damad va Fenderski ta Asr-e Hazer* (Tehran: L'Iran et la France Institut, 4 vols. 1350/1371)

many papers, books and anthologies on Islamic philosophy and Muslim philosophers in Persian, English, French and Arabic. He has also translated many of the works of Muslim philosophers into, mostly English.

I do not venture to name other scholars (especially the Western scholars) who have been instrumental in developing studies about Islamic philosophy and translating many of the works of Muslim philosophers into European languages. Even citing the names of these scholars with a short introduction of their works exceeds the limits of a lengthy paper; it requires a tome which runs into hundreds of pages. Instead, I shall say few words about the development of Islamic philosophy in the Arab world.

Despite the fact that philosophy has not been a favourite subject in the larger Muslim world, books of Muslim philosophers, especially of the classic period, have always been in print in countries such as Egypt and Lebanon. Efforts for producing edited versions of the works of Muslim philosophers have also been going on in Arab countries on an almost continuous basis. Ibrahim Madkour and more than him Abd al-Rahman Badawi in Egypt ought to be mentioned as two representatives of the generations of editors of classical philosophical texts. In the west side of the Islamic world much attention has been paid to Ibn Rushd and his views in recent decades. Some Arab intellectuals maintain that Ibn Rushd's ideas could be used as a tool for reviving the rational tradition among the Sunni Muslims. Muhammed Abid al-Jabri is a better-known representative of this trend.[128]

4. The Future of Islamic Philosophy

Talking about future trends is always a risky business. Prediction of the future, as we all know, is not possible. I am not, therefore, going to attempt the impossible here. The best I can do is to suggest one or two plausible scenarios for the future development of Islamic philosophy.

But before sharing with you my own conclusion of gazing into my imaginary crystal ball, I should like to recount the account of another writer concerning the future of Islamic philosophy, namely, Muhammad Mian Sharif the editor of a two-volume *A History of Muslim Philosophy* first published in 1966. In the concluding part

---

[128] Muḥammad 'Abid Jabri, *Arab-Islamic Philosophy* (University of Texas Press, 1999)

of his hefty tome which runs into almost 1800 pages, Sharif writes (and I am afraid it is a rather long quote):

> It is hazardous to foretell the future of peoples, nations, and cultures. This is particularly true in a world torn asunder by ideological conflicts and constantly under the shadow of total war. As it is, the fate of the whole human race is hanging in the balance and one spark of folly may set the whole world ablaze, thus falsifying all normal conjectures.
>
> However, unless such an all-pervading calamity befall mankind, one could make a guess about the future of Muslim culture and philosophical thought. The trends we have traced in the life of different Muslim countries ... should give us a fair idea as to what the future may have in store for Muslim thought and culture.
>
> Owing to the developed means of communication, ideas travel easily now-a-days from one place to another, but they always require time to take root in a new soil. The two recent Western philosophies, Existentialism and Logical Positivism, have come to the East, but it will be some time before they penetrate deeply into the Muslim mind. But when they do penetrate the Muslim mind, they are likely to take, to a certain extent, a different shade. ...
>
> It is very doubtful whether the ideas of a social history prevailing in the West will ever be accepted in the East, especially in the Muslim East. In the concluding remarks of part "E" of the Introduction we delineated the philosophy of history to which our study lends support. There we said that it has a negative as well as a positive aspect. Negatively, it is non-organismic, non-cyclic, and non-linear; and positively, it involves belief in social dynamics, in progress in human society though the ages by rises and falls, in the importance of the role of ethical values in social advances, in the possibility of cultural regeneration, in the environmental obstacles as stimuli to human action, in freedom and purpose as the ultimate sources of change, and in the mechanical determinism as an instrument in divine and human hands. This philosophy is as distinct from the philosophy of history advanced in Europe and the United States as from that which is accepted in the Soviet Union. We consider this philosophy in consonance with the teachings of Islam. We believe, it is this ideology in which lies the salvation of the world and not in the ideologies hotly defended and followed in the Western world.

Islamic Philosophy: Past, Present and Future

For my part, I must say, and no doubt I am benefiting from the wisdom of the experiences of the past few decades since Sharif's book, that I do not subscribe to either a historicist view of history, or a deterministic worldview, or an ideological, as against philosophical, outlook concerning the future of Islamic philosophy.

In my view, for Islamic philosophy to be able to play an efficient role in tackling real-life issues, it needs to reconnect with science and technology. It should regard science as a genuine companion in its knowledge pursuit, and not a mere means for justificatory purposes. It also needs to realise that 'certainty' does not belong to the realm of knowledge investigation. The spirit of critical and rational thinking, openness to ideas and views developed in other cultures and civilisation, and tolerance which was once strong among Muslim thinkers must be encouraged and enhanced once gain. Its choice of problems should also be considerably augmented and enriched by an attitude for combining abstract thinking with applied reasoning.

As far as the philosophical and cultural milieu in Iran is concerned, I can say, with some degree of optimism, that in recent decades and especially since the Islamic revolution in 1979, foundation for a radical change in intellectual and philosophical outlooks has gradually been laid in the country. While in the past, the majority of those young souls who would study philosophy, whether at seminaries or at universities, were, by and large, not academically well-equipped and not particularly apt for this field, but had opted for it out of necessity and not choice, in the years leading to the revolution and afterwards many talented students with good backgrounds in science, maths and engineering enrolled in philosophy courses. The introduction of modern trends of philosophical thought, beyond Existentialism and Logical Positivism, has also opened up new opportunities for philosophy students whether in seminaries or in universities to move out of the sphere of traditional teachings and experience new horizons.

Younger generations of philosophers are gaining confidence to challenge the entrenched norms of 'scholarly behaviour' which would discourage criticisms of one's teachers and professors' philosophical views.

Iranian students of philosophy are becoming more and more aware of the importance of relatively newly emerged philosophical fields such as applied philosophy. This awareness has helped them to better appreciate the need for adopting problem-oriented approaches in their philosophical endeavours.

Ali Paya

The fact that fuqha (jurists), despite enjoying a privileged status, have come under increasing pressure with regard to their monopoly over 'representing' the official face of Islam, has provided further breathing space for the emergence of new, critical trends of thinking in the country.

Another factor which could help the development of a more rational approach to Islamic philosophy in Iran and perhaps those other Muslim countries in which philosophy is gradually taking root is the activities of scholars (especially the Western scholars) outside Islamic countries.

Papers and books produced by these scholars, in a way, set some standards for Muslim philosophers to compare and contrast their own levels of scholarship with those of their foreign colleagues. It must be emphasised that in recent years and as a result of strong institutional support for scholarly activities in seminaries in Iran and a similar support for promotion of religious sciences, the number and quality of scholarly journals and publications which are dedicated to the elucidation of various aspects of Islamic philosophy has increased considerably.

Given the fact that neither philosophical nor scientific knowledge claims, as against technological techniques and know-how, could be regarded as culture-specific, such a newly developed philosophy, could only be regarded as 'Islamic philosophy' in the sense I explicated at the outset of this paper, namely, the outcome of intellectual endeavours of individuals who happen to be Muslim or live in Muslim lands or both and make use of, among many other resources, the intellectual machinery developed in Islamic civilisation. This philosophy, provided it upholds its critical and rational approach, could join force with other schools developed elsewhere in tackling problems which are regarded as challenges for modern men wherever they happen to be and to whatever sources of inspiration they happen to be attached.

Of course the above optimistic trends should not be over-emphasised. There are, as there have always been, anti-rational and anti-philosophical tendencies in Islamic societies in general and in their centres of learning in particular. A case in point, is a relatively new anti-philosophical school, known as *makatb-i tafkik* (lit. the Separationist School) based on the views of Sayyid Musa Zarabadi (d. 1353/1934), Mirza Mahdi Gharavi Isfahani (d. 1365/1946), and Shaykh Mujtaba Qazvini Khurāsānī (d. 1386/1966). This trend has powerful bases in many traditional seminaries inside and outside Iran and especially in Mashhad. *Tafkikis* strongly oppose philosophy in all its shapes and forms, even in the sanitised form of

Mulla Sadra's *Hikmat al-Muta'aliah*. In their view even the Quran should be understood by the teachings of the Shi'a Imams.

Nevertheless, it seems to me that new trends, within the general framework of 'Islamic philosophy', are, slowly, but surely moving towards acquiring the critical mass required for making their presence felt. As for an approximate time-scale for reaching such a threshold, I better not hazard making any guess and end my future gazing here.

University of Westminster
a.paya@westminster.ac.uk

Index of Names

Index of Names

Index of Names

Index of Names